Fear of Persecution

Fear of Persecution

Global Human Rights, International Law, and Human Well-Being

Edited by James D. White and
Anthony J. Marsella

LEXINGTON BOOKS

A division of
ROWMAN & LITTLEFIELD PUBLISHERS, INC.
Lanham • Boulder • New York • Toronto • Plymouth, UK

 # 71329859

LEXINGTON BOOKS

A division of Rowman & Littlefield Publishers, Inc.
A wholly owned subsidiary of The Rowman & Littlefield Publishing Group, Inc.
4501 Forbes Boulevard, Suite 200
Lanham, MD 20706

Estover Road
Plymouth PL6 7PY
United Kingdom

British Library Cataloguing in Publication Information Available

Library of Congress Cataloging-in-Publication Data

Fear of persecution : global human rights, international law, and human well-being /
edited by James D. White and Anthony J. Marsella.
    p. cm.
 Includes bibliographical references and index.
 ISBN-13: 978-0-7391-1565-7 (cloth : alk. paper)
 ISBN-10: 0-7391-1565-0 (cloth : alk. paper)
 ISBN-13: 978-0-7391-1566-4 (pbk. : alk. paper)
 ISBN-10: 0-7391-1566-9 (pbk. : alk. paper)
 1. Refugees—International cooperation. 2. Human rights—International cooperation. 3.
Humanitarian assistance. 4. Humanitarian intervention. I. White, James D. (James
Daniel) II. Marsella, Anthony J.
 HV640.F42 2007
 362.87—dc22   2006029785

Printed in the United States of America

♾™ The paper used in this publication meets the minimum requirements of American
National Standard for Information Sciences—Permanence of Paper for Printed Library
Materials, ANSI/NISO Z39.48–1992.

Contents

Acknowledgements

The editors would like to acknowledge the support given by three institutions that made possible the Conference on International Law, Human Rights, and Refugee Health and Wellbeing: Legal, Humanitarian and Health Issues and Directions, held in Honolulu, Hawaii in November, 1999, and from which this book sprung. They were the Center of Excellence in Disaster Management and Humanitarian Assistance, Tripler Army Medical Center, under the direction of Lt. Col. Patricia Hastings; the Toda Institute for Global Peace and Policy, under the direction of Professor Majid Tehranian; and the College of Social Sciences, University of Hawaii. In addition we would like to recognize the work of Ms. Joyce Liu in helping edit the first draft of the conference manuscript.

Introduction

Fear of Persecution

James D. White

In the early 1950s the after effects of World War II were still being felt. The privation and want that had been the norm during the war in Europe continued, with most European countries operating a food rationing scheme: in Britain ration books did not disappear until 1954. Another reminder of the war was the hundreds of thousands of refugees who wandered from country to country or sat hopelessly in vast camps. They were helped by various refugee organizations, many of them ad hoc, but they had no proper legal status, which made questions of rights and settlement problematic at best.

In 1951, six years after the war in Europe had ended, delegates from 26 countries agreed to a "Convention Relating to the Status of Refugees." The agreement was seen as a short-term solution to an immediate problem. It referred only to "events occurring before 1 January 1951," had a primary focus on refugees in Europe, and mandated the newly-created United Nations High Commission for Refugees to solve the problem in three years. Nevertheless, the opening definition of the term "refugee" became an internationally recognized standard: a person who "owing to well-founded fear of being persecuted for reasons of race, religion, nationality, membership of a particular social group or political opinion, is outside the country of his nationality and is unable to, or, owing to such fear, is unwilling to avail himself of the protection of that country, or who, not having a nationality and being outside the country of his former habitual residence . . . is unable or, owing to such fear, is unwilling to return to it." This definition, and the principle of non-forcible return of people to territories where they could face persecution (known as non-refoulement) have become fundamental international law.

But the UNHCR did not fade away. In fact its sad work grew to become a permanent part of the global landscape. According to the UNHCR, at the end of 2004 there was a total global population of 19.2 million people 'of concern'— including refugees, asylum seekers, refugees returning home and people uprooted within their own countries—so-called internally displaced persons (IDPs) (UNHCR, 2005). This figure is controversial, as it may well be too low. The Global IDP Project claimed there were 25 million IDPs alone at the end of 2004, people uprooted within their own country by conflicts and human rights violations, describing internal displacement as "one of the great human tragedies of our time" (Global IDP). The U.S. Committee for Refugees and Immigrants (USCRI) World Refugee Survey 2005 calculated the number of refugees and asylum seekers worldwide to be 11.5 million, while IDPs were counted at 21.3 million, for a total of 33.8 million (USCRI, 2005).

In short: the exact numbers of refugees vary year by year, and the methods of counting them must inevitably be approximate. While the numbers ebb and surge year to year, in recent times even the basic principle of offering the world's most vulnerable people the modest degree of protection promised by the Geneva Convention is questioned. On the occasion of the fiftieth anniversary of the UN High Commission for Refugees, the outgoing High Commissioner, Sadako Ogata, said, "As we enter the new millennium, the fact that the world still finds a need for UNHCR should serve as a sobering reminder of the international community's continuing failure to prevent prejudice, persecution, poverty and other root causes of conflict and displacement" (2000, WWW document).

Today many nations are preoccupied with security issues at the expense of humanitarian concerns, or see the principle of asylum as being abused by those who seek only a new life or better opportunity. In 1951, persecution was usually a question of actions taken by a government: hence the constant use of the words 'nationality' and 'country'. Now, as often as not, people flee from areas where effectively there is no government, no 'country', leading some to question whether such situations meet the criterion of 'persecution' as originally defined by the Convention.

Invisible People

The reasons for their becoming refugees in the first place have changed, and the protections offered them are increasingly eroded. But the underlying reality remains the same: every year there are tens of millions of people around the world who have fled or are in flight from danger, and who are invisible. As long as the flight takes place in a distant land, and the media coverage is minimal, those who are forced to flee rarely impinge on the world's consciousness.

As revealed through official asylum figures, the 'target' countries for refuge are predictable. According to UNHCR, during the period 2000-2004, the United States received the largest number of asylum-seekers (411,700), followed by the United Kingdom (393,800) and Germany (324,200), and then France, Canada, Austria, Sweden, Belgium, the Netherlands and Switzerland (UNHCR, 2005).

But figures for such regulated migration are dwarfed by the floods of refugees, who seek asylum where and how they may. Refugees have the biggest impact on those nations that are ill-prepared to receive them. A 2004 UNHCR report on refugee trends showed that the top countries of refuge in January-September that year were Pakistan (1,124,298), Iran (984,896), Tanzania (649,770), China (299,354) and Serbia and Montenegro (292,415), followed by Saudi Arabia, Armenia, Republic of Congo, Zambia and Guinea (UNHCR, 2004).

The same UNHCR report has a page devoted to "durable solutions" to the problem, which turn out to be voluntary repatriation and resettlement. What is not addressed is the process by which asylum seekers are created, whether repatriation is a realistic solution, what it is that makes a refugee flee or a person to be displaced. In the great majority of cases the cause is as simple as the Convention's definition: fear of persecution. What is also missing in the recitation of statistics is the personal report, the description of what it is like to run away in fear. The following is the account of one boy from Sudan, Chol Paul Guet, whose epic journey across Africa took him from his native land to Ethiopia and then on to a refugee camp in Kenya, where he told his story.

Something Like an Accident

"It was something like an accident when I ran away from my village. We were playing at about 5 o'clock when these people, the soldiers, came. We just ran. We didn't know where we were going to, we just ran. . . . I didn't see the soldiers, I just heard the shooting, the screaming and the bombing that went DUM, DUM, DUM, DUM like this and killed many people. It all just happened, like an accident, and we ran without anything—nothing—no food, no clothes, nothing.

"In the day the sun is hot and your feet burn. So we walked at night when it is cold, because then you don't say all the time, "I want water, I want water." To rest we stood under a tree, but you can die of hunger if you give up and just lie under a tree. . . . We never felt well. We just walked. People died of hunger. I saw many dying. Even my friend died. There was no water, no food. When I saw my friend dying, I carried on walking. You see sometimes you can help, and then sometimes you can't. You are talking about your life. . . .

"Then the United Nations, he came, he saw the people, he went to Geneva to find food, and he came back. I spent three years in Ethiopia and felt well. I went to school and lived with five other boys. Then the United Nations left and we had to run. . . . I say, let us stay here (in the UNHCR refugee camp in Kakume, in Kenya) where it is safe. In England you are safe, now let us stay here safely. Now we want to learn. One day I will be an engineer to build Sudan like the other countries in Africa. I don't know whether my mother and father are dead or alive. I was 9 when I left Sudan. I am 14 now. I am an oldie man now. My mother will not know me." (Wilkes, 1994).

Choi Paul's story is one of moving from one poor place to another, in what Thomas Barnett has characterized as the "non-integrating gap," the areas in the world where roughly two billion of its population live disconnected from the globalization process. Using USRC data Barnett calculates that countries in the 'gap' account for 96 percent of all refugees and 93 percent of internally displaced people. For Barnett, this translates into a global security concern (Barnett, 2004).

Globalization is the right context in which to locate Choi Paul, as he lives in an age of extraordinary global movement. According to the UN Population Division, in 2002 around 175 million persons resided outside the country of their birth, or about three per cent of world population. The number of migrants had more than doubled in the quarter century since 1975. Sixty percent of the world's migrants resided in the more developed regions and 40 percent in the less developed regions. Most of the world's migrants lived in Europe (56 million), Asia (50 million) and Northern America (41 million). Almost one of every 10 persons living in the more developed regions was a migrant. In contrast, nearly one of every 70 persons in developing countries was a migrant. The aspiration to escape the 'gap', and become connected, is strong (UN, 2002).

The imperative to migrate exceeds the capability or the willingness of the globalization core states to accept or assimilate. One consequence is the boom industry in smuggling migrants. They are largely ignored, as when they make it to the developed world they remain invisible, unless they die from asphyxiation in the back of a locked truck on a ship to England, or burn to death in a Paris hotel. There is a scene in Stephen Frears' 2003 film *Dirty Pretty Things* where a trio of illegal immigrants in London are asked who they are. "We are the people you do not see," comes the answer. "We are the ones who drive your cars, and clean your rooms, and suck your cocks." As Audrey Tatou, the actress who plays a Turkish refugee seeking asylum in *Dirty Pretty Things*, says: "When you don't have any identity, any money, any passport, any work, you are nothing."

The Stranger at the Door

Plainly the movement of populations, forced or unforced, is a part of our world. The question becomes one of how do we react to the stranger at the door. This is at once a political and a personal question, and even in a carefully structured situation of controlled and limited migration is controversial. When with much fanfare the European Union was expanded from 15 to 25 members in May 2004, the great majority of the original members chose to continue to enforce tough limits on migration from the ten new members. The migration that does take place is almost all one way: the estimates are that about 220,000 European workers will travel from east to west in search of employment every year by the end of the decade (European Foundation, 2004). Migration has consequently become a major electoral issue in the European 'core'. The climate of insecurity which has been created by 9/11 and subsequent events has also transformed the way migrants are processed or even treated. As the twenty-first century progresses, security concerns are making more and more remote the possibility of onward international travel to a desirable destination for those in fear of persecution. In March, 2003 the US government announced "Operation Liberty Shield", imposing blanket detention on asylum seekers arriving without proper documents from more than 30 unnamed countries. In Chapter 2 of this volume Bill Frelick points out that the primary purpose of the "shield" was to deter those fleeing Muslim countries from seeking asylum in the United States, ironically or purposefully introduced at exactly the same time as the Bush administration was issuing ultimatums to Saddam Hussein, as a prelude to an invasion justified at least in part as action to liberate the Iraqi peoples.

Against this background the refugee is once again marginalized, located at the wrong end of a continuum of problems. If indeed we look at the refugee's story as yet another example of movements of people, then the question of status may become a simple one of classification. If we define classification as the act of distributing people or things into classes or categories of the same type, then what becomes important is how these classes are defined. For example, the biggest single category of movement of people is world tourism: according to the World Tourism Organization, international tourist arrivals reached an all-time record of 760 million in 2004. So how is a tourist different from a refugee? Immediate criteria that spring to mind revolve around economic and social status, closely intermingled with elements of race, ethnicity, religion, gender and so on. But perhaps the biggest divider between the tourist and the refugee is more simple: the tourist—who may indeed be seen as crass, exploitative, insensitive, culturally or personally unattractive—will at some point go home, taking his 'issues' with him. The refugee wants to stay, if he may.

This takes us back to the UNHCR's "durable solutions," all of which have the idea of 'return' as a foundation. What if the wanderer who comes knocking at the door has nowhere that she can call home? In many cultures the person from outside the society is seen metaphorically and sometimes literally as the stranger, and therefore to be regarded as different, not to be trusted and not to be made welcome. The image of the outsider can easily transmute into a picture of something threatening. The refugee, the person without a place, is especially alarming. It can be all too easy to embrace the non-threatening solution of "out of sight, out of mind."

A Semi-Permanent Solution?

Perhaps the most disquieting aspect of the refugee story is the degree to which the status of the refugee has become one of semi-permanence, epitomized by the 'warehousing' of refugees. More than seven million have languished in refugee camps or segregated settlements for ten years or more, some for generations. UNHCR and other advocates conceive of three enduring solutions to refugee outflows: voluntary repatriation, permanent local integration in the country of first asylum, or resettlement to another country. Refugee warehousing, however, has emerged as a de facto fourth and all-too-durable solution.

As the casually brutal phrase implies, warehousing means storing people away like animals in a shelter, with heavily restricted mobility, enforced idleness, and dependency. This denial of the freedom to pursue normal lives is an open violation of their basic rights under the 1951 UN Refugee Convention. The fact of its existence raises troubling questions about how many eyes are averted from the situation, about the fundamental bureaucratic regimes and processes, the political decisions, the media silence, the public indifference which makes it possible to accept archipelagoes of hopelessness dotted around the globe. According to the USCRI, the number of refugees warehoused for five years or more stood at almost 8 million at the end of 2004.

The permanent presence of stateless, unprotected refugee populations forced to live in a constant limbo has resulted in the emergence of two distinct conditions which challenge international social justice and current policies and views regarding refugees. First, the provision of bread or rice, some protection against the elements, and a modicum of personal safety and security cannot alter or erase the tragic memories that are part of the refugee's sense of being and identity. The despair, frustration and anger that inform the lives of the inhabitants of many such camps form the perfect breeding ground for more desperate acts of violence and revenge. In addition, many refugee settlements have reproduced the conditions of authoritarian control and abuse from which the refugees may have sought escape. In many cases, the hopes for asylum, safety and restored personal control have yielded to new levels of vulnerability, dependency and helplessness.

Rational policies regarding intervention, aid and support should be based on a deeper understanding of the strengths as well as the weaknesses of the refugee. Leopold and Harrel-Bond remind us that by definition forced migrants are people who escaped from intolerable situations in which others were trapped, and, like Chol Paul Guet, had the physical strength and mental toughness to survive long and dangerous journeys. We should see them

. . . as more resourceful and enterprising than other people, rather than pitiable cases. In most of the poorer parts of the world, there are desperate skills' shortages, and the potential role of refugees in overcoming them has been largely overlooked, as have the macro-economic benefits of the presence of large potential refugee markets for basic goods (provided they are allowed to earn the money to pay for them) (Leopold & Harrell-Bond, 1994).

The Debate Has Shifted

Unfortunately refugees and the displaced have few advocates and no representation, so possess little potential to have their worth as people acknowleged, let alone impact international policy. This situation of powerlessness has worsened in the twenty-first century. Since this volume was originally conceived the whole climate surrounding the issue of refugees has changed, as the debate about fundamental human rights has shifted. When it was first presented to the editors, Sister Ortiz's searing account of her torture (Chapter 10) might have been seen as an aberration. Now not only are accusations about the use of torture by US and UK military forces widespread and well-documented, but the whole human rights debate has sideslipped into a conversation from the darkest of medieval times. The legitimacy of state torture is a subject for newspaper editorial discussion, lawyers representing the US government dismiss or define away international conventions against torture and other kinds of mistreatment, and US defense and intelligence officials approve torture techniques that the United States condemns in other countries.

There are repeated calls nowadays to revisit and revise the 1951 Refugee Convention, partly in response to the exponential rise in criminal trafficking of people across borders, and partly in an attempt to better balance the refugee's "well-founded fear" of persecution with the demands for increased security in the aftermath of 9/11. What one author in this book (Frelick, Chapter 2) characterizes as "the security model" has taken center stage, with national security concerns taking precedence over human rights, backed by a concerted effort to ignore or marginalize international humanitarian law. This refusal to recognize the plight of refugees extends to situations where the responsibility is plain: many of the Iraqis who have worked for the Americans in Iraq have fled the country, and plead for help or asylum daily. The Bush administration suspended resettlement of Iraqi refugees after 9/11, and did not resume the program until April 2005. A total of 198 were resettled in the United States with refugee status in 2005, and 202 in 2006, a tiny fraction of the tens of thousands reported to be fleeing their country every month (Tavernise and Worth, 2007).

There is a reference point for global human rights: the Universal Declaration of Human Rights, adopted by the General Assembly of the United Nations on December 10, 1948. The Declaration is clear and unequivocal, starting with Article 1: "All human beings are born free and equal in dignity and rights. They are endowed with reason and conscience and should act towards one another in a spirit of brotherhood." We stand to lose something invaluable and irreplaceable if indeed those words are pushed aside. We all suffer if we lose sight of Chol Paul Guet, whose nine-year-old life was turned upside down by something like an accident, and who now, as a teenager, dreams of rebuilding his life and his native land. Those dreams are our best hope for a possible future where human diginity is respected and human wellbeing is valued. But prospects are grim: as this is written the chaos in Darfur in the Sudan, Chol Paul Guet's homeland, continues, with 200,000 civilians killed and refugees flooding into the neighboring country of Chad (Polgreen, 2006). After almost 60 years of persecution, torture, violence and every kind of human rights abuse, the need to protect those who have nowhere to turn for protection from mindless persecution, and to help them heal and grow, is even more essential than it was in those grey postwar years when human rights were declared "as a common standard of achievement for all peoples and all nations."

Background to This Volume

This book arose from the Conference on International Law, Human Rights, and Refugee Health and Wellbeing: Legal, Humanitarian and Health Issues and Directions, held in Honolulu, Hawaii, from November 14th to 18th, 1999. The conference was the brainchild of Dr. Anthony Marsella, conceived of as a benchmark event to launch a new Program in Disaster Management and Humanitarian Assistance (DMHA), which he developed and directed at the University of Hawai'i. Dr. James White acted as coordinator for the conference, which was made possible by financial support from the Center of Excellence in DMHA and supported by a grant from the Toda Institute for Peace.

The announced purpose of the conference was to identify and discuss legal, humanitarian and health consequences issues emerging from the current relationship of international law, human rights and refugee health and wellbeing. Some 30 subject matter experts from around the globe participated, with each person submitting their paper in advance, so that the work of the conference was analysis and discussion, rather than presentation of papers. The conference was also unusual in its interdisciplinary approach to a complex subject, mixing the views of leading academics, policy analysts, senior officials from NGOs and lawyers. The participants were encouraged to revisit their papers in the light of comments and criticisms received, with a view to publishing a volume of edited papers.

Subsequent events, most notably the attacks on the Twin Towers and the Pentagon on September 11, 2001, delayed publication, as most of the papers have had to be substantially revised and the whole book completely re-edited to take account of the changes following 9/11. In the present volume many authors remark on the chill that has been cast from the reaction by the U.S. and other governments to the events of 9/11, in particular the subsequent "war" against terrorism. The original conference was conceived in an atmosphere of guarded optimism encouraging the belief that recognizing and achieving global human rights was a Herculean task, but not an impossible one. The book now in front of the reader reflects a darker vision, of a grim fight ahead simply to hold onto the principle that we are indeed all born equal in dignity and rights.

Structure of the Book

The book is divided into four sections. The first section provides an overview of the plight of internally displaced people (IDPs) and refugees.

Roberta Cohen reminds us that the world has become so interconnected as to make it difficult to ignore the plight of millions of persons uprooted within their own countries, who hitherto have been among the most marginalized. Trapped in the midst of conflict, or forcibly removed from their homes on political or ethnic grounds, they are often deprived of minimum shelter, food and health services, and vulnerable to all manner of human rights abuse. The highest mortality rates ever recorded during humanitarian emergencies have involved internally displaced persons. The major cause of the steep increase in the numbers of IDPs is the parallel rise in internal conflicts emerging from or following the Cold War, and the growing acceptance that the international community should become involved in events taking place inside another country.

Bill Frelick tracks how international responses to refugees have evolved through three stages or paradigms in modern times. During the Cold War refugees were mostly displaced from Communist or communist-dominated countries or from the Middle East and were not considered to have any realistic hope of repatriating to their home countries in any foreseeable future. In the early 1990s, the international refugee regime turned to a source-country model to address the causes of refugee flows, either seeking to prevent the causes of refugee flight or intervening to reverse the causes of refugee flows, thus enabling the quickest return possible of refugees and IDPs. The terrorist attacks of September 11, 2001 marked a third paradigm shift in the international community's response to refugees and complex humanitarian emergencies—the security model. In the early twenty-first century, refugees often came to be regarded with deep suspicion, sometimes seen as being terrorists themselves or as being the sea in which the terrorist fish could hide and swim. The international community, dominated more than ever by the United States, is motivated overwhelmingly by national security concerns, and the consequences for refugees, positive or negative, is a distant afterthought.

The second section looks at a variety of human rights issues. George Kent focuses on the nutrition rights of refugees, calling for a clear statement of principles or guidelines regarding refugees' human right to adequate food, the obligations of host states and the international community, and the mechanisms of accountability.

Richard J. Brennan and Gerald Martone discuss the evolving roles of relief NGO's, which have found themselves increasingly forced to respond to the consequences of war crimes, atrocities, and blatant abuses of human rights. They suggest these agencies should consider reviewing their roles and responsibilities in the areas of human rights and protection, pointing out that there are many practical, effective measures that relief NGO's can incorporate into their field programs that will protect the rights of the populations that they serve.

Harry Minas puts human rights in a cultural context. While the human rights regime has been challenged from a number of quarters, especially by allusion to issues of national sovereignty, culture has also become a reference point. One argument is that human rights as conceived in the UN documents are a Western product which does not sit well in non-Western contexts. Another is that the insistence by Western governments on human rights is being used as a cloak for the promotion of Western commercial, political, and cultural interests.

Weiming Tu argues for going beyond such a presentation, where for example "traditional" Confucian values are seen as opposed to "modern" Western values, though plainly the West continues to exhibit ignorance of the cultures of the rest of the world and insouciance about the peoples who do not speak their languages. He speculates on how a Confucian take on human rights might open up an inquiry on global ethics, bringing about a fundamental reconceptualization of concepts such as "obligation," "responsibility," and "leadership," and locating the justification for rights in the dignity and worth of the self as a center of relationships.

Finally Jeffrey Addicott presents a detailed case history of the reformation of formerly totalitarian military forces such that human rights are fully institutionalized and appropriately reflected in their performance of military duties, which he sees as an essential step in encouraging the spread of new democracies, in turn the key to world peace and stability.

The third section presents three very different approaches to issues of international law. Ved Nanda describes the history and foundations of modern-day refugee law in the inter-state warfare which caused refugee flows in the 1940s. This is no longer the primary source of large-scale movements of people: rather, such movements are a reaction to the repression by governments of their own people. Yet little has changed legally to obligate states to be more open to assisting refugees, and the author seems pessimistic that a basic change in the current refugee regime is possible, no matter how urgently it is needed.

A gloomy note is also struck by Sister Dianna Ortiz, herself a victim of torture, who gives a shockingly vivid description of government-sanctioned torture and international law as seen through the eyes of survivors. She attacks U.S. and Guatemalan government officials for hypocrisy and duplicity when they denounce torture and terrorism and demand obedience to international law, accusing them of a mockery of the words 'human rights' and 'justice.'

Jon Van Dyke makes a painstaking case that the right to obtain financial compensation for human rights abuse such as torture and to have the perpetrator of such an abuse prosecuted and punished is itself a fundamental human right that cannot be taken from a victim or waived by a government. He argues that the only way to bring true healing to a divided society is to face up to the wrongs that were committed, to prosecute those who violated the fundamental human rights of others, and provide compensation to the victims.

The final section turns to ways to build understanding, promote healing and keep the peace. Michael Hoffman calls for identifying strategies that will improve voluntary compliance with international humanitarian law. Before that, there is a need for better understanding of the factors that contribute to poor compliance or breakdowns in the law in the first place; specifically a need for a better understanding of the strategies and tactics behind the commission of war crimes. Without better "diagnostics" of war crimes we will have little success in identifying the methods—the therapeutics—that will curb and prevent them.

Rebecca Knuth echoes this analysis, with her call for genocide to be recognized as a universal problem—that is, a phenomenon with recognizable patterns and forms—and for truly comparative study that probes beyond a specific case. She notes the most encouraging aspect of efforts to respond to genocide is the potential, through modern communication systems, for developing global intolerance of genocidal situations. Her hope is for a global consensus to reject genocide, arising out of a consciousness—similar to the awareness which finally made slavery unthinkable—that is powerful enough to create the will to enforce that rejection.

Michael Wessells' examination of post-conflict healing argues for community-based approaches to the tasks of sustainable healing on a wide scale and of building peace. It illustrates the potential power of healing based on social mobilization that builds local capacities, uses local resources, and activates communities for economic development and social action on behalf of peace and the well-being of future generations.

In an afterword, Brien Hallett reflects on the meaning of forgiveness in a situation of conflict, seeing it as a personal rather than a social virtue. To achieve reconciliation, and thus step outside the kind of bitter circle that ultimately generates the disposed and the refugee, requires the kind of leadership that can imagine a new future of living together, while at the same time encouraging an official, public coming to terms with the past.

References

Barnett, Thomas (2004). *The Pentagon's New Map.* New York: G.P. Putnam's Sons.
European Foundation for the Improvement of Living and Working Conditions (2004). Migration likely to be about 1 percent, survey says. February 26, 2004. www.eurofound.eu.int/newsroom/archive_pressrelease/pressrel_040226.htm.
Global IDP (accessed November 1, 2005). www.idpproject.org/global_overview.htm.

Leopold, M., & Harrell-Bond, B. (1994). An overview of the world refugee crisis. In A.
J. Marsella, T. Bornemann, & S. Ekblad, & J. Orley (Eds.) *Amidst Peril and Pain: The Mental Health and Well-Being of the World's Refugees.* Washington, D.C.: American Psychological Association Press. p.60.

Polgreen, Lydia (2006). Refugee Crisis Grows as Darfur War Crosses a Border. *New York Times*, February 28, 2006.

Tavernise, Sabrina & Worth, Robert (2007). Few Iraqis Are Gaining U.S. Sanctuary. *New York Times*, January 2, 2007.

UNHCR (2004). *Refugee Trends 1 January-30 September, 2004.*

UNHCR (2005). *Asylum Levels and Trends in Industrialized Countries, 2004.*

United Nations Population Division (2002). Number of World's Migrants Reaches 175 million mark. October 28, 2002. www.un.org/esa/population/publications/ ittmig2002/press-release-eng.htm.

USCRI (2005). *World Refugee Survey 2005.*

Wilkes, Sybella (1994). *One day we had to run!* Brookfield, Conn: The Millbrook Press.

Section I: Refugees and Internally Displaced People

Chapter 1. The Global Crisis of Internal Displacement
Roberta Cohen

Chapter 2. Paradigm Shifts in the International Response to Refugees
Bill Frelick

CHAPTER 1

The Global Crisis of Internal Displacement

Roberta Cohen

In 1988, international and non-governmental organizations watched while a quarter of a million people died in the Sudan for lack of food and emergency supplies (Bonner, 1989). They weren't able to help because the international system set up after the second world war to protect people uprooted from their homes extended only to those who fled across borders, not to those at risk inside. As United Nations Secretary-General Kofi Annan aptly described it, "internal displacement [is] one of the great human tragedies of our time" (Annan, 1998, p. xix).

In the world today there are an estimated 25 million persons forcibly displaced within the borders of their own countries by conflict, internal strife and systematic human rights violations. More than 13 million can be found in Africa, 5 to 6 million in Asia, 3 million in Europe, and 3 to 4 million in the Americas (Norwegian Refugee Council, 2005). Of the world's populations at risk, they tend to be among the most marginalized. Trapped in the midst of conflict, or forcibly removed from their homes on political or ethnic grounds, they are often deprived of minimum shelter, food and health services, and vulnerable to all manner of human rights abuse. The highest mortality rates ever recorded during humanitarian emergencies have involved internally displaced persons (Cohen & Deng, 1998). Were they able to cross a border into a neighboring state, they would become refugees and in accordance with the 1951 Refugee Convention receive protection from the United Nations High Commissioner for Refugees

(UNCHR). But internally displaced persons are often blocked from crossing borders because of mountains or other geographic barriers, because the fighting is too fierce, or they may be too old, young or infirm to try. Some may be barred entry by neighboring countries. Being displaced inside their own countries, the international system of protection set up for refugees does not apply to them.

In keeping with traditional notions of sovereignty, persons persecuted, but remaining within their own countries, were excluded from any organized system of international protection. The assumption was that their governments would provide for their well-being and security. When their governments failed to do so, or deliberately subjected their populations to forced displacement, starvation, mass killings and other serious abuses, the international community often stood by passively.

Recognition of the Problem

It was only in the last ten years of the twentieth century that the international community began to acknowledge the gap in the international protection system. A major reason for the acknowledgment was the growing numbers of internally displaced persons. When first counted in 1982, an estimated 1.2 million were displaced in 11 countries. Four years later, the total had grown to 14 million, and by 1997, there were more than 20 million in 35 to 40 countries (Cohen & Deng, 1998). Indeed, in most emergencies, internally displaced persons began to out- number refugees by a two to one ratio. The major cause was the increase in the number of internal conflicts emerging from or following the Cold War. These wars grew from less than ten in 1960 to almost fifty in 1992 (Walker, 1995).

The Cold War's end also helped bring the issue to the fore. When the super- powers were engaged in proxy conflicts, as in Angola, Mozambique and El Sal- vador, no attention was paid to the internally displaced. It was only when these geopolitical struggles began to wane that the plight of the displaced came into view, and was recognized as requiring international humanitarian action. The end of the Cold War also facilitated access to beleaguered populations. Without fears of superpower retaliation, possibilities opened up for crossing borders and responding to the needs of internally displaced persons.

There was also growing acceptance of the idea that events taking place *within* a country should be a legitimate concern of the international community. The human rights movement had long championed this view. President Jimmy Carter, in fact, electrified the world when he declared in 1977 that "no member of the United Nations can claim that mistreatment of its citizens is solely its own business" (Carter, 1977, p. A10). By the late 1980s, humanitarian organizations also began to insist that the international community should find ways to be- come involved when governments denied access to populations at risk.

Thus, in the Sudan in 1989 and 1990, the United Nations used hard diplomatic bargaining to persuade the Sudanese government and the rebel forces to accept *Operation Lifeline Sudan*, which brought food and supplies to internally displaced populations throughout the country (Deng & Minear, 1992). Further, in the cases of Somalia and Rwanda, the Security Council authorized the use of force to facilitate the delivery of relief to displaced persons and other affected populations (Deng, 1995, pp.96-98). Worldwide television coverage (i.e., the "CNN factor") bolstered this trend. Watching starving Sudanese or beleaguered Iraqi Kurds on TV screens increased demands for international intervention and outpourings of aid to persons displaced within their own countries.

To be sure, some of the interest in the internally displaced arose out of a desire to curb refugee flows. The political advantage that had motivated many nations to accept refugees during the Cold War gave way—in the early 1990s—to a desire to limit their entry (Cohen & Deng, 1998). Western governments, and governments in other parts of the world, began to demonstrate less willingness to accept large numbers of refugees, and instead, focused their energies on the need to promote protection and assistance for those displaced within their own countries.

The issue of internal displacement further gained prominence because of the realization that peace and reconstruction in war-torn societies could not take place without the effective reintegration of displaced persons. Many of the countries devastated by civil war—such as Mozambique, Angola, Liberia and Guatemala—had anywhere from one third to three quarters of their population forcibly uprooted. It thus became impossible to talk about reconstruction and development without taking into account the return and reintegration of both refugees and internally displaced persons.

The Challenge of Internal Displacement

Increased attention to the problem, however, has not made it more tractable. Unlike wars between nations, civil wars often divide countries along racial, ethnic, linguistic, or religious lines that do not resolve themselves easily or neatly. When states become monopolized by or identified with one ethnic group to the exclusion or marginalization of others, those displaced groups easily fall into a vacuum of responsibility within the state. Governments often do not see displaced groups as 'their people' or even as citizens that they have to protect. Indeed, they are often seen as 'inferior beings' or even 'the enemy' (Cohen & Deng, 1998). The process of dehumanization that often ensues creates a climate in which the neglect of such persons, and even atrocities against them, are accepted as legitimate.

This is not a new phenomenon. Prior to and during World War II, both Hitler and Stalin forcibly displaced, persecuted, and murdered large numbers of their own citizens on the grounds that they were from different ethnic groups, or because they were members of a social and economic class considered to be 'the enemy,' political opponents, or simply, 'others.' Similarly, in South Africa under apartheid, the white minority government adopted a dehumanizing position towards its black population that enabled the state to forcibly uproot millions of the black population, and to deprive them of all basic human rights.

This alienation between an affected population and its government is at the root of much of today's internal displacement. In the Sudan, which has the largest internally displaced population in the world—5 million—an Arabized government tried for decades to impose an Islamic state on Black Africans in the south of the country, who are primarily Christian and animist. More than 1 million people died over the past decade because of deliberate government campaigns to obstruct international food deliveries to the Dinka and other tribes because of their opposition to government policies (UNHCR, 1994b; U.S. Committee for Refugees, 1998b).

In Kosovo, prolonged Serbian persecution of ethnic Albanians was at the root of the violence and war that took place in 1999. In Turkey and Sri Lanka as well, governments were long at war with their own citizens. In both countries, decades of discrimination, against the Kurds in the case of Turkey, and the Tamils in the case of Sri Lanka, produced violent separatist movements. The governments then used the existence of these movements to justify campaigns of utter destruction against parts of their own population. Of course, by repressing minorities, by refusing to see them as legitimate members of the nation, and by preventing the development of multiethnic societies, governments strengthen the very separatist and terrorist movements they fear.

Internal conflicts in countries *without* governments can be even more devastating. In the failed states, fighting takes place over land, resources, and territorial control, and the belligerents are known to accept almost no ground rules of battle. Civilians become the main targets because they are connected to or perceived to be connected with rival factions or simply because they occupy land and property that are coveted. Stories of child soldiers, of amputations and mass rapes, of plunder of humanitarian assistance and the kidnapping or killing of humanitarian workers frequently emanate from wars in dysfunctional states. Somalia and Sierra Leone easily come to mind, but in Colombia too, whose government controls less than half of the country, fighting over land among paramilitaries, rebel groups and government forces has forced millions from their homes and resulted in substantial deaths (Deng, 1999b; Prendergast, 1997; U.S.C.R., 1998a).

In all civil wars, reaching the displaced can be fraught with danger, largely because each side fears humanitarian assistance will fortify the other. Rival factions not only use aid as a weapon in their struggle but also seek to obstruct assistance to the other side. Governments in particular fear that aid will strengthen or legitimize rebel movements, prolong the war, and undermine their authority.

Access may be further complicated by the different manifestations of displacement. In some countries, internally displaced persons do not congregate in accessible camps or settlements but disperse so as to avoid identification. In Burundi, for example, internally displaced Hutus hid in forests in fear of the Tutsi military, making it difficult to reach them (Deng, 1994). In other countries, such as Colombia, many displaced merge into local communities, where gaining access requires programs that extend to the entire community. In Liberia, as many as three-quarters of a million displaced persons fled to Monrovia, the capital, blending in with the rest of the city, whose population nearly tripled in size during the civil war (Cohen & Deng, 1998).

Although often thought of as a temporary phenomenon, internal displacement is frequently long-term. Civil wars can go on for decades, disrupting not only the lives of the individuals concerned but whole communities and societies. In such cases, both the areas left behind and the areas to which the displaced flee suffer extensive damage. In the areas that have been vacated, property and land are neglected, and community structures collapse as the population thins. In the areas to which people flee, the displaced quickly strip forests and grasslands for housing and fuel, with long-term economic and ecological effects. In Rwanda, the damage done to Akagera National Park will take years to repair (Holtzman, 1997). When flight is to urban areas, social services, water supplies, and sanitation facilities become overburdened, especially when the population doubles or triples in size. Since most conflict and displacement occur in the world's poorest countries, the already weak infrastructure rapidly deteriorates sometimes to the point of collapse.

Conflict and displacement can not only undermine national stability but also spill over borders into neighboring countries. The Great Lakes region of Africa is a good example of how conflict and displacement in one country can inflame the situation in others and lead to massive refugee flows and even military interventions in the region. Similarly in the Balkans, conflict and internal displacement in Kosovo quickly spilled over borders and began to destabilize neighboring states. Internal displacement should therefore be seen not only as a human rights and humanitarian issue but as a political, economic and strategic problem affecting broad geographic areas and requiring regional and international attention.

Addressing Internal Displacement

In the absence of an international system for dealing with the problem of internal displacement, it became necessary to create a conceptual framework, legal standards and institutional arrangements to guide the actions of governments, insurgent groups and international agencies in dealing with the problem.

In 1992, UN Secretary-General, Boutros Boutros-Ghali, appointed a Representative on Internally Displaced Persons, Dr. Francis M. Deng, to study the issue and promote a more effective international response. A former Sudanese diplomat from the south with direct experience of war and displacement, Deng introduced the concept of sovereignty as responsibility as the most suitable conceptual framework for dealing with the problem. Basically, this concept stipulates that states have the primary responsibility to provide for the security and well-being of their uprooted populations. But if they are unable to do so, they are expected to request and accept outside offers of aid. Should they refuse or deliberately obstruct access to their displaced or other affected populations, putting large numbers at risk, the international community has the right and responsibility to assert its concern (Cohen & Deng, 1998).

International involvement in such cases can range from diplomatic dialogue, to negotiation of access, to political pressure, to sanctions, or in exceptional cases to military intervention to ensure the delivery of food and supplies and to provide protection for displaced populations. In his dialogues with governments over a ten-year period, Deng repeatedly made the point that no state claiming legitimacy can quarrel with its commitment to protect *all* of its citizens. Sovereignty must mean accountability to one's population and to the international community in the form of compliance with international human rights and humanitarian agreements. It is noteworthy that no government ever explicitly challenged the concept of sovereignty as responsibility, no doubt because in doing so it would have had to argue that sovereignty allows a state to deny life-sustaining support to its citizens.

Legal Framework

To provide the international community with a basis for action, a legal framework was developed for the internally displaced. At the request of the UN Commission on Human Rights and General Assembly, Deng undertook in 1994 to examine the extent to which existing international law provides adequate protection for internally displaced persons. Working with a team of international legal experts, they made a survey of international human rights law, humanitarian law and refugee law by analogy (Deng 1995, 1998a). It found that while existing law provides substantial coverage for the displaced, it also contains many grey areas and gaps and is scattered through a diverse number of legal instruments. The need to bring together into one document the varied provisions of the law and address the gaps resulted in the development of the Guiding Principles on Internal Displacement, which Deng introduced into the United Nations in 1998 (Deng, 1998b).

The 30 Guiding Principles set forth the rights of internally displaced persons and the obligations of governments, insurgent groups and other relevant actors toward these populations. They are the first international standards specifically tailored to the needs of the internally displaced, and are applicable to all phases of displacement. They offer protection prior to displacement, during displacement and in the return and reintegration phase. In particular, they affirm the right of persons not to be arbitrarily displaced, specify a broad range of rights to be observed when persons are displaced, and articulate the obligation of governments and insurgent groups to facilitate access to the displaced and treat them in accordance with international human rights and humanitarian standards.

One of the most important features of the Principles is that they make explicit for internally displaced persons what had heretofore been implicit in the law. For example, there is a general legal principle that provides all people with recognition before the law, but the Principles go a step further to specify that internally displaced persons shall be issued the documents they need to enjoy their legal rights. In the same vein, the Principles spell out special protection measures for women and children; assert that internally displaced persons may not be forcibly returned to conditions of danger; and provide that the displaced are entitled to compensation or reparation for lost property and possessions.

If there can be said to be a philosophical foundation behind the Principles, it is the concept of sovereignty as responsibility. While positing primary responsibility for the welfare and safety of internally displaced persons with their governments, the Principles provide a role for the international community to provide humanitarian assistance and protection when the governments concerned are unable to fulfill their responsibilities.

Although not a binding legal document like a treaty, the Principles, in a relatively short period of time, have gained considerable recognition and standing. Initially, the Commission on Human Rights and General Assembly acknowledged them, recognized the Representative's intention to use them in his work and encouraged their wide dissemination. By 2003, both bodies expressed "appreciation" of the Guiding Principles, called them "a standard" and an "important tool" and welcomed the fact that "an increasing number of States, United Nations agencies and regional and non-governmental organizations are applying them" (United Nations, 2003). The Security Council also began to cite the Principles in its resolutions and Presidential statements, and in his report to the Council on "The Protection of Civilians in Armed Conflict," the Secretary-General (Annan, 1999a) called upon states to observe the Principles in situations of massive displacement.

The heads of the major international human rights, humanitarian and development organizations, comprising the UN's Inter-Agency Standing Committee (IASC), have endorsed the Principles and requested their staffs to apply them in the field. Regional organizations have followed suit, acknowledging the Principles and disseminating them (Deng, 1999a, 2004a), in particular the African Union (AU), the Economic Community of West African States (ECOWAS), the Inter-Governmental Authority on Development (IGAD), the Council of Europe, the Organization for Security and Cooperation in Europe (OSCE) and the Inter-American Commission on Human Rights of the Organization of American States (OAS). Some like the Inter-American Commission use the Principles as a benchmark to evaluate conditions on the ground, such as in Colombia and Guatemala, while other regional bodies have used the Principles as a framework for facilitating the returns of the displaced.

Most importantly, a small but growing number of governments have begun to develop national policies on internal displacement based on the Guiding Principles, whether Burundi, Colombia, the Philippines, Nigeria, Sri Lanka or Uganda, while other governments have incorporated their provisions into national law, for example Angola, Colombia, Georgia, Peru and Liberia. Non-state actors as well, like the SPLM/A in the Sudan, have also made the Principles a basis for policy toward the internally displaced (Brookings-SAIS Project et al, 2003).

In the forefront of efforts to promote the Guiding Principles have been international and local non-governmental organizations (NGOs), which regularly use the Principles as an advocacy tool with governments and insurgent groups. Displaced communities too have begun to hold discussions with local authorities on the basis of the Principles. Clearly, the document has become a standard to turn to in situations of internal displacement.

As they become more widely known, a global effort has begun to monitor and promote compliance with the Principles' provisions, since they come with no enforcement machinery. Indeed, UN agencies, regional bodies, international and local NGOs and the displaced themselves have all begun to undertake initiatives to make the Principles more widely observed.

At the same time, the argument has been made that the time might be ripe to promote a legally binding treaty, which could have more authority to hold states accountable. But at an international meeting in Vienna in 2002, a group of about 40 experts from UN agencies, regional bodies, NGOs and IDP associations reached a broad consensus in favor of the more evolutionary approach of the Guiding Principles (Brookings-SAIS Project, 2002; Kalin, 2002). Despite their non-binding character, most felt that their continued usage over time would have international impact and change the way internally displaced persons are perceived and treated. This approach was borne out by the World Summit document, adopted by heads of government in 2005, when it recognized the Guiding Principles as "an important international framework for the protection of internally displaced persons" (United Nations, 2005).

At the regional level, the African Union has begun the process of drafting a binding instrument on internal displacement based on the Guiding Principles. If it provides the same level of protection as the Principles, it could expand their standing and usage and bolster their legal basis.

Institutional Reform

At the institutional level, an array of international humanitarian, human rights and development organizations have come forward to offer protection, assistance, and reintegration and development aid to internally displaced persons. These include the UN High Commissioner for Refugees (UNHCR), the International Committee of the Red Cross (ICRC), UNICEF, the World Food Program (WFP), the World Health Organization (WHO), the UN Development Program (UNDP), the Office of the High Commissioner for Human Rights (OHCHR), the International Organization for Migration (IOM), and a host of NGOs.

But the international response system remains largely ad hoc, with the different organizations basically picking and choosing the situations in which they will become involved on the basis of their mandates, resources or other considerations. UNHCR, for example, deems only 5.6 million internally displaced persons out of a total of 25 million to be of concern to the organization (UNHCR, 2005). UNICEF does not engage with all internally displaced children, preferring to focus more on development programs than emergency assistance needs (Cohen & Deng, 1998). The International Committee of the Red Cross (ICRC) becomes involved only when the Geneva Conventions apply and where it is allowed entry (Lavoyer, 1995). The result is that large numbers of internally displaced persons go without protection and assistance.

Although the creation of a new agency to address the needs of the internally displaced could make the response more predictable, neither the political will nor the resources exist to create a new agency. Governments are fearful that such an entity would "interfere" in their internal affairs. Donors oppose duplicating the work of existing agencies at a time when the UN system is under considerable pressure to cut back.

A more persuasive option is designating an existing agency, like UNHCR, to assume the responsibility. UNHCR's experience with protecting uprooted populations makes it the most obvious choice. And every few years, governments, NGOs or experts put forward the idea that UNHCR should take on the responsibility. For example, in January 2000, the United States Ambassador to the United Nations, Richard Holbrooke, proposed that UNHCR assume the internally displaced persons mantle (Crossette, 2000). But other agencies fear that UNHCR will become too powerful and monopolize international resources. In fact, a turf war breaks out every time UNHCR is proposed. UNHCR itself is divided with at least half the staff expressing the fear that taking on the entire burden would change the character of the organization, overwhelm its resources and interfere with its primary purpose of protecting refugees.

Therefore by default the preferred option has been strengthened collaboration among the different agencies already involved, as set forth in the UN Secretary-General's 1997 reform program. But strengthened collaboration will only work well if there is an effective central point that can assign responsibilities to different agencies when protection or assistance gaps arise. As it stands now, the UN Emergency Relief Coordinator (ERC) does not have the authority to make the system work effectively.

Jan Egeland, who is both the ERC and the head of the Office for the Coordination of Humanitarian Affairs (OCHA), takes the problem of internal displacement seriously and has been making a concerted effort to strengthen coordination among the different actors to promote a more predictable response. In 2002 OCHA set up an Internal Displacement Unit, which now has become a Division and constitutes the UN's first office with a group of dedicated staff on internally displaced persons. But while the different agencies participate in the Division and pay lip service to coordination by the ERC, agencies with $1billion budgets and staff in the thousands are not easily coordinated.

Indeed, it remains to be seen how successfully this system will work without greater authority for the ERC and a stronger locus of responsibility in the field for the internally displaced. On the ground, the Resident and Humanitarian Co-ordinators, in charge of coordinating assistance to the displaced, have often been found ineffective in setting up workable divisions of labor to address the needs of the displaced (Bagshaw & Paul, 2004; Deng 2004a). In an effort to improve collaboration, the ERC in 2005 came up with a "sectoral approach," under which the different agencies would be expected to carve out areas of responsibility based on their expertise and carry them out on a *regular* basis in emergencies (Egeland, 2005; McNamara, 2005). UNHCR, it was agreed, would assume the sectoral lead for protection, management of camps and emergency shelter while other agencies would assume responsibility for nutrition, water and sanitation, and early recovery.

It is hoped that the new approach, which has been approved by all the agencies, will begin to reduce the disparity in the way refugees and internally displaced persons are treated by the international community. Too often the lion's share of funding and attention goes to refugees whereas only a fraction is devoted to meeting the needs of the internally displaced. Such was the case in Rwanda, Kosovo, Afghanistan and many other countries (Minear & Kent, 1998; Cohen & Korn, 1999; Cohen, 2002). The imbalance of course spawns conflict —just the opposite of what international assistance is intended to accomplish. In Burundi, for example, in 1993, the conditions in UNHCR camps for refugees were so much better than the conditions for internally displaced persons in camps just up the road that violence and looting resulted (Deng, 1994). A basis for conflict is also created when returning refugees receive seeds, tools and other service packages to help them reintegrate in their villages but internally displaced persons returning to the same villages do not.

While at this point in time, the UN is trying to make the collaborative system work, and donor governments are lending support to this endeavor, the international humanitarian, human rights and development community must be ready to acknowledge if the collaborative approach fails. In such case, radically different institutional arrangements will need to be considered, including the assignment of responsibility for internally displaced persons to one designated agency. In a new study, migration expert Susan Martin proposes that a high commissioner for forced migrants be appointed for both refugees and internally displaced persons (Martin et al., 2005).

Enhanced Protection

Greater attention also needs to be paid to the physical safety and human rights of the internally displaced. Providing security for internally displaced persons is often as important a priority as food, yet most attention in emergencies focuses on providing food, medicine and shelter. When Muslims were threatened with "ethnic cleansing" in Bosnia in the early 1990s, they told UNHCR: "We do not need food, we are not starving to death. We are being persecuted" (UNHCR, 1994a, p. ii). And in Rwanda in 1995, even after the genocide the previous year, one of the largest massacres of internally displaced persons took place in a camp in Kibeho while UN agencies provided relief but paid little or no attention to protection (United Nations, 1995). Nine years later in Darfur, the Sudan, international agencies stepped in readily to provide food but devoted few staff and resources to promote protection (Deng, 2004b). Yet offerings of relief to uprooted persons while ignoring the fact they are being beaten, raped or killed regularly leads to tragic descriptions of the victims as the 'well-fed dead.'

Providing protection for the displaced requires special skills. Access may need to be negotiated, relocations and evacuations undertaken, protected areas created, and intercessions made to ensure that the displaced are not forcibly returned to conditions of danger or subjected to other serious human rights abuse. Even in less threatening situations, there is a need to monitor the treatment of displaced populations and intercede to promote protective action.

Not many international humanitarian and development organizations have these skills or experience. To be sure, the ICRC does, and increasingly UNHCR and a variety of NGOs, such as Medecins Sans Frontieres and the International Rescue Committee, have begun to focus attention on ways to provide protection to internally displaced populations. But many international field staff consider such initiatives beyond their mandates or experience and fear that advocacy on behalf of the displaced will compromise their neutrality or result in their being expelled from the country concerned.

At the same time, agencies have increasingly been experimenting with ways to enhance protection for internally displaced persons. Some have found that increasing their presence in places where there are protection problems can enhance security. Others have found joint stands by groups of agencies to prove effective while also protecting the agencies from being singled out for retribution. Designing assistance programs to enhance protection has proven to be another important means of addressing protection concerns. For example, ensuring that women do not have to go far for firewood, or that latrines are well lit, can reduce the likelihood that women and girls will be raped in a camp. The creation of protection working groups, in which UN agencies, NGOs and local government officials work together to increase protection, is a method increasingly being tried while a standby corps of protection specialists for emergency deployment has been proposed (Cohen & Kunder, 2001; Bagshaw & Paul, 2004). Prompt and efficient reporting of protection problems to those who can act upon them is also critical. In Bosnia, in the early 1990s, military staff and some relief workers were initially silent when they became aware of concentration camps and other gross abuses (Cohen, 1993). Now, it is more likely that information on serious violations will be forwarded by relief organizations to human rights groups and others who can take measures to expose violations and try to stop them.

Although human rights field staff continue to be absent from most emergency situations, human rights organizations have begun to examine whether they should have a more active presence in the field. Indeed, debates have begun over whether the traditional human rights roles of monitoring and reporting should be expanded to include more active protection strategies such as accompanying returns, advocating with the authorities on behalf of the displaced, and helping to strengthen and build local capacities to deal with displacement (Paul, 1999; Neier & Leaning, 1999). A new evaluation of the UN's role in providing protection to the internally displaced specifically calls upon the Office of the UN High Commissioner for Human Rights to play a greater role in protecting displaced populations (Bagshaw & Paul, 2004). Although safety problems for humanitarian staff have markedly increased in recent years, growing recognition of the need to pay attention to the broader political and human rights framework in which aid is provided is slowly beginning to change the way human rights, humanitarian and development field workers approach protection and assistance (Frohardt, Paul, & Minear, 1999). UNHCR's new leadership role in protecting internally displaced persons can also be expected to encourage the greater involvement of human rights bodies in the field (Cohen, 2005).

Military Action

In some situations the only way protection is possible is through military and police action. In these cases, the Security Council may decide that the humanitarian situation is a threat to international peace and security and authorize military force to get supplies in and protect displaced persons and other civilians at risk. Or as in the military intervention in Kosovo, a regional grouping may take it upon itself to become involved.

Military action to protect displaced populations, however, has not always been successful. Indeed, the record to date has been mixed. In Iraq, Western forces under the UN umbrella in 1991 did succeed in creating a safe haven for displaced Kurds in the north of the country in the wake of the Gulf War. But in Somalia in 1992, military forces, while successfully preventing mass starvation, did not disarm the local factions and became embroiled in the conflict (African Rights, 1993). They ultimately failed to provide protection either for themselves or for Somali civilians. In Rwanda in 1995, the record was also mixed. French forces under the UN umbrella did protect internally displaced Hutus in the southwest, but in Kibeho, UN forces stood by while several thousand displaced persons were attacked and killed by the Rwandan army. Although UN forces in this case were specifically authorized to protect the displaced, UNAMIR's numbers were small and it interpreted its mandate as not having to defend the displaced from actions by their own government (Minear & Kent, 1998).

In Bosnia as well, UN forces, while authorized to provide protection to displaced persons in safe areas, stepped aside when the Serbs overran Srebrenica in 1995. This remains one of the more ignominious examples of the international failure to provide protection to internally displaced persons. More than 5,000 Muslim men and boys were separated from their families and marched off to be killed (Human Rights Watch, 1996). As in Rwanda, UN forces were not given the requisite number of troops to provide protection, and their mandate was ambiguous: they were instructed on the one hand to defend the safe areas but on the other to use force only in self-defense—a caveat used to excuse themselves from defending anyone but themselves (Cohen & Deng, 1998).

The lesson to be learned, however, is not that international intervention should be avoided at all cost but rather that international forces charged with protection should be given the numbers, equipment, resources, training and mandates to do the job (O'Neill, 2004). Too often the political will has been absent on the part of the states in the Security Council, and the UN itself has had little experience in deploying troops in internal conflict situations. UN peacekeeping forces, after all, have traditionally been deployed to monitor ceasefires and separate warring armies, not to protect populations in the midst of civil war.

It was NATO—not the UN—that took the decisive action to stop the Serbs after the fall of Srebrenica and Zepa in 1995. But even the robust action of NATO proved problematic. In Kosovo in 1999, the military strategy it chose failed to protect most Kosovar Albanians from attacks and expulsions on the ground. NATO's strategy was a long-term one that focused on hitting military and industrial targets in the Federal Republic of Yugoslavia in an effort to cripple its overall capacity to wage war in the Balkans. The strategy provided little or no protection for the 400,000 or so internally displaced persons trapped inside the province. Even when NATO finally began to concentrate some of its firepower against Serb forces in Kosovo, fear of casualties kept its air strikes at 15,000 feet or more when lower bombing runs would have proved more effective (Cohen & Korn, 1999). Fear of casualties also prevented it from setting up humanitarian supply corridors into Kosovo, or creating safe areas; even airdrops of food and medicines were rejected as too risky. In NATO countries, it was feared that popular support for continuing the war would be eroded if there were troop casualties.

Prevention as Protection

The handling of the Kosovo crisis brings home yet again that by far the most effective protection is not military intervention but preventive measures. Forced displacement, after all, is but a symptom of a far deeper problem within a society. Neither military action nor humanitarian assistance can substitute for the political settlements needed to resolve the disputes and inequities at the heart of conflicts.

To date, the international community has not been prepared to expend the resources and energy needed to prevent or contain crises. Whether in Rwanda, Kosovo, East Timor or more recently Darfur, the warning signs clearly failed to generate the attention and strong political action needed. Although the overriding purpose of the United Nations is to prevent war, its main areas of activity— humanitarian assistance and peacekeeping—focus on the consequences of conflict rather than on its causes. Clearly needed are international and regional organizations that insist on the mediation and management of disputes, bring pressure to bear on potential warring parties, limit the supply of arms, and offer development aid, investment and debt relief to those who will work to bring conflicts under control. Macedonia is a case in point. Both the European Union and NATO have played important roles in staving off conflict and displacement in that country by bringing pressure to bear on the Slav government to include Albanians more fully in the political and economic life of the country and by insisting that the Albanian separatists renounce violence.

International development and financial institutions like the World Bank also need to become involved earlier on to help stabilize situations, prevent conflict and displacement, and contribute to return and reintegration. By getting involved earlier on, these organizations stand a better chance of influencing the outcome and laying a foundation for peace.

Conclusion

Clearly, the international system set up after the second world war to protect only refugees is incomplete and inadequate to the challenge of today's human rights and humanitarian emergencies. The internal conflicts that rage in Africa, Asia, Europe and the Americas produce far larger numbers of internally displaced persons than refugees. It is the totality of the problem that needs to be addressed.

Over the past ten years, there has been some movement toward providing protection and assistance to those who are internally displaced. Conceptual, normative and institutional frameworks have been developed and international organizations are increasingly on the ground offering assistance when governments are unable or unwilling to help their displaced populations. International involvement has even become predictable in staving off cases of mass starvation.

But in cases of genocide, massacres or 'ethnic cleansing,' international action is still determined case by case, largely because states have not defined it to be in their interest to take the risks required. Although the UN Secretary-General has begun to speak of a "developing international norm in favour of intervention to protect civilians from wholesale slaughter" (Annan, 1999b, p. 4), the establishment of what might be called a right to humanitarian protection or an international responsibility to protect (United Nations, 2005) has not yet emerged to justify international action in all situations. No country was prepared to send forces to Rwanda at the height of the genocide in 1994. Nor were troops forthcoming in the case of Burundi when the Secretary-General in 1996 proposed an international force to forestall predicted massacres (Cohen & Deng, 1998). In Kosovo and East Timor, the international intervention that did take place provided protection to the displaced but only *after* most of the damage was done, while in Darfur, in 2004, international findings of crimes against humanity did not result in the African Union's receiving from the world community the support it needed to deploy troops rapidly, in sufficient numbers or with a mandate to directly protect displaced persons (O'Neill, 2005).

"Traditional notions of sovereignty" are nonetheless being challenged and redefined (Annan, 1999b, pp. 1-2). The world has become sufficiently interconnected so as to make it difficult to ignore the plight of millions of persons uprooted within their own countries. People at risk are no longer viewed as solely a national problem. The UN Secretary-General and world leaders have begun speaking out in support of uprooted populations. Donor governments have been earmarking more funds for the displaced while governments with displaced populations find that there are political and economic costs to pay when they use their sovereignty as a barricade behind which to mistreat and abuse their citizens. Regional organizations in Europe and Africa have begun to train special military and police forces to protect civilians, and civil society in many countries has become vocal in defense of the displaced. This provides some hope that the twenty-first century may see the beginnings of an international system that undertakes comprehensively to protect persons uprooted and at risk within their own countries.

References

African Rights (1993). *Somalia, Operation Restore Hope: A Preliminary Assessment.* London: African Rights.

Annan, K. (1998). Preface. In R. Cohen and F. M. Deng, *Masses in Flight: The Global Crisis of Internal Displacement* (pp. xix). New York, NY: Brookings Institution.

Annan, K. (1999a). Report of the Secretary-General to the Security Council on Protection of Civilians in Armed Conflict. S/1999/957, 8 September 1999. New York, NY: United Nations.

Annan, K. (1999b). Secretary-General Presents His Annual Report to General Assembly, Press Release SG/SM/7136, GA/9596, 20 September 1999.

Bagshaw, S. & Paul, D. (2004). *Protect or Neglect? Toward a More Effective United Nations Approach to the Protection of Internally Displaced Persons.* Brookings-SAIS Project on Internal Displacement and UN Office for the Coordination of Humanitarian Affairs' Inter-Agency Internal Displacement Division. November.

Bonner, R. (1989). Famine. *New Yorker,* March 13, pp. 85-101.

Brookings-SAIS Project on Internal Displacement (2002). *International Symposium on the Mandate of the Representative of the UN Secretary-General on Internally Displaced Persons: Taking Stock and Charting the Future.* Vienna, December 12-13, p.9.

Brookings-SAIS Project on Internal Displacement, the Representative of the Secretary-General on Internally Displaced Persons and UNICEF (2003). Seminar on Internal Displacement in Southern Sudan, Rumbek, February.

Carter, J. (1977). Transcript of President Carter's Address at the United Nations. *New York Times,* March 18, p. A10.

Cohen, R. (1993). Human Rights and Humanitarian Action Go Hand-in-Hand. *Refugees,* No. 92, pp.4-7.

Cohen, R. (2002). Afghanistan and the challenges of humanitarian action in time of war. *Forced Migration Review,* June, pp.23-27.

Cohen, R. (2005). UNHCR: expanding its role with IDPs. *Forced Migration Review,* Supplement, October, pp.9-11.

Cohen, R. & Deng, F. M. (1998). *Masses in flight: The global crisis of internal displacement.* Washington DC: Brookings Institution.

Cohen, R., & Korn, D. A. (1999). Failing the internally displaced. *Forced Migration Review*, August, pp.11-13.

Cohen, R. & Kunder, J. (2001). Policy Brief: Humanitarian and Human Rights Emergencies. Washington DC: Brookings Institution, June, p.7.

Crossette, B. (2000). U.N. studies how refugees qualify to get assistance. *New York Times*, January 14, p.A7.

Deng, F. M (1994). Profiles in displacement: Burundi, *E/CN.4/1995/50/Add.2*, United Nations Commission on Human Rights, November 28, 1994. New York, NY: United Nations.

Deng, F. M. (1995). Compilation and analysis of legal norms, Report of the representative of the secretary-general on internally displaced persons to the commission on human rights, *E/CN.4/1996/52/Add.2, December*. New York, NY: United Nations.

Deng, F. M. (1998a). Compilation and analysis of legal norms, part II: Legal aspects relating to the protection against arbitrary displacement, Report of the representative of the secretary-general on internally displaced persons to the commission on human rights, *E/CN.4/1998/53/Add.1*, February 11. New York, NY: United Nations.

Deng, F. M. (1998b). The guiding principles on internal displacement, Report of the representative of the secretary-general on internally displaced persons to the commission on human rights, *E/CN.4/1998/53/Add.2*, February 11. New York, NY: United Nations.

Deng, F.M. (1999a). Report on internally displaced persons, prepared by the Representative of the Secretary-General, General Assembly, A/54/409, 29 September 1999. New York, NY: United Nations.

Deng, F. M. (1999b). Don't overlook Colombia's humanitarian crisis. *Christian Science Monitor*, October 6, p. 9.

Deng, F.M. (2004a). Report on mass exoduses and displaced persons, prepared by the representative of the secretary-general on internally displaced persons to the commission on human rights, E/CN/4/2004/77, 4 March 2004. Geneva: United Nations, pp. 10-13.

Deng, F.M. (2004b). Report on Mission to the Sudan—The Darfur crisis, prepared by the representative of the secretary-general on internally displaced persons, E/CN4/2005/8, 27 September 2004. Geneva: United Nations, pp.11,16.

Deng, F. M., & Minear, L. (1992). *The challenges of famine relief: Emergency operations in the Sudan.* Washington, DC: Brookings Institution.

Egeland, J. (2005). Towards a stronger humanitarian response system, *Forced Migration Review*, Supplement, October, pp. 4-5.

Frohardt, M., Paul, P., & Minear, L. (1999). *Protecting human rights: The challenge to humanitarian organizations, Occasional Paper #35.* Thomas J. Watson Jr. Institute for International Studies, Brown University.

Holtzman, S. (1997). Conflict-induced displacement through a development lens. Paper prepared for Brookings Institution.

Human Rights Watch (1996). *World Report.* New York: Human Rights Watch.

Kalin, W. (2002), "How Hard is Soft Law?" *Recent Commentaries about the Nature and Application of the Guiding Principles on Internal Displacement.* Washington DC: Brookings-CUNY Project on Internal Displacement, April.

Lavoyer, J-P. (1995). Protection under international humanitarian law. In *Internally Displaced Persons*. Symposium, 23-25 October. Geneva: International Committee of the Red Cross, pp.26-36.

Martin, S. et al (2005). *The Uprooted: Improving Humanitarian Responses to Forced Migration.* New York: Lexington Books.

McNamara, D. (2005). Who does what? *Forced Migration Review*, Supplement, October, pp. 6-7.

Minear, L., & Kent, R. C. (1998). Rwanda's internally displaced: A conundrum within a conundrum. In R. Cohen and F. M. Deng (Eds.), *The forsaken people* (p. 92). Washington, DC: Brookings Institution.

Neier, A., & Leaning, J. (1999). Human rights challenges. In, J. Leaning, S. M. Briggs, and L. C. Chen (Eds.), *Humanitarian Crises,* pp.195-209. Cambridge, Mass.: Harvard University Press.

Norwegian Refugee Council (2005). Global IDP Project Map, "Internally Displaced People Worldwide," March.

O'Neill, W.G. (2004). *A New Challenge for Peacekeepers: The Internally Displaced.* Washington, DC: Brookings-SAIS Project on Internal Displacement, April.

O'Neill, W.G. & Cassis, V. (2005). *Protecting Two Million Internally Displaced: The Successes and Shortcomings of the African Union in Darfur.* Washington DC: Brookings-Bern Project on Internal Displacement, November.

Paul, D. (1999). Protection in practice: Field-level strategies for protecting civilians from deliberate harm. *Relief and Rehabilitation Network,* Paper #30, July. London, England.

Prendergast, J. (1997). *Crisis response: Humanitarian band-aids in Sudan and Somalia.* London: Pluto Press.

UNHCR(1994a). *Information notes on former Yugoslavia,* January. Geneva, Switzerland: UNHCR.

UNHCR Division of International Protection (1994b). *UNHCR's operational experience with internally displaced persons.* Geneva, Switzerland: UNHCR.

UNHCR (2005). Fact File on People of Concern to UNHCR, March, available at http://www.accord.org.za/ct/2005-3/ct3_2005_pp28-29.pdf.

United Nations (1995). Internal review of the case of the Kibeho Incident: Lessons for the Future, Report of the Inter-Agency Task Force on Internally Displaced Persons, November. Geneva, Switzerland: United Nations.

United Nations (2003). Commission on Human Rights, Resolution 2003/51, 23 April.

United Nations (2005). General Assembly, World Summit Outcome Resolution A/RES/60/1, 15 September, para. 132, available at *http://www.un.org/Depts/dhl/resguide/r60.htm*

U.S. Committee for Refugees (1998a). *Colombia's silent crisis: One million displaced by violence.* Washington, DC: U.S. Committee for Refugees.

U.S. Committee for Refugees (1998b). News: 1.9 million dead from Sudan's civil war. December 10. Washington, DC: U.S. Committee for Refugees.

Walker, P. (1995). Working for internally displaced persons: Prospectsfor the future. In *Internally Displaced Persons, Symposium,* October 23-25, p.75. Geneva, Switzerland: International Committee of the Red Cross.

CHAPTER 2

Paradigm Shifts in the International Responses to Refugees

Bill Frelick

What is known as the international refugee regime, the organized international community's collective response to refugees, has seen three major paradigms since the drafting of the 1951 Refugee Convention and the creation of the UN High Commissioner for Refugees (UNHCR) in the aftermath of World War II.

First, from roughly 1948 until 1991, the international refugee regime operated according to the exilic model—refugees for the duration of the Cold War were mostly displaced from Communist or communist-dominated countries or from the Middle East and were not considered to have any realistic hope of repatriating to their home countries in any foreseeable future. The international refugee regime was largely preoccupied with establishing their rights in exile and, where possible, in finding durable solutions outside the country of origin, and, where not possible, with warehousing refugees in camps, often for decades.

The close of the Cold War ended a period of static political blocs and unchanging borders. It also meant that the international community, led by one super power, the United States, was more likely to intervene to change situations on the ground that caused refugee flows, thus enabling the return of the displaced. Consequently in the early 1990s, the international refugee regime shifted to a second fundamental paradigm. It turned away from the exilic model of response to refugee crises, and sought a source-country model to address the causes of refugee flows. The international community would either seek to prevent the causes of refugee flight or intervene to reverse the causes of refugee flows, thus enabling the quickest return possible of refugees and internally dis-placed persons. Under the source-country paradigm, refugees were less likely to be offered permanent asylum outside their home countries. Instead, they were provided temporary protection close to the border or a "safe area" was carved out on their behalf inside the country of origin, with the intention of protecting them pending an international intervention that would enable their return.

A decade later, the terrorist attacks of September 11, 2001 appeared to mark the beginning of a third paradigm in the international community's response to refugees and complex humanitarian emergencies—the security model. Whereas refugees during the Cold War were looked upon in near heroic terms as free-dom-lovers escaping tyranny (the reigning image being the Berlin Wall), and refugees in the 1990s were arguably the "tail wagging the dog" that inspired military interventions in such diverse places as Haiti and Kosovo, in the early twenty-first century, refugees often came to be regarded with deep suspicion, sometimes seen as being terrorists themselves or as being the sea in which the terrorist fish could hide and swim. Fear of terrorism often exacerbated pre-existing xenophobic and racist tendencies. Closing borders and denying asy-lum—the security model—became part of counter-terrorist strategies to the detriment of fundamental principles of refugee protection that had been in place, however weakly, under both the exilic and source-country solutions models.

Paradigm 1: The Cold War and the Exile

The traditional international refugee regime was not oriented to tackling the root causes of refugees in their countries of origin. It was based on the notion of asy-lum, or providing refuge first, and worrying about durable solutions later, often much later. The refugee regime, forged as it was during the Cold War, had, therefore, an exilic bias, the assumption that refugeehood, with some exceptions, meant permanent exile (Coles, 1989).

During the Cold War, the possibility of repatriation often seemed unrealistic, even illusory. Although refugee policy makers during the Cold War routinely articulated three solutions for refugees—voluntary repatriation, local integration, or third-country resettlement—refugees had little objective reason to hope for the fundamental changes in their home countries that would allow their safe repatriation and also had no meaningful chance of being integrated locally in overburdened and unwilling countries of first asylum (Robinson, 1989). In most cases the only durable, practical solution was third-country resettlement.

In reality, only a tiny fraction of the world's refugees, estimated at less than one percent of the total, were ever removed from their misery and allowed to resettle in prosperous countries far away from the zones of conflict. The vast majority of refugees were condemned to protracted stays in often fetid and over-crowded refugee camps. By the time of the shift to the third paradigm (Septem-ber 2001), there were still millions of refugees warehoused for protracted periods of time, caught between seemingly intractable situations in their countries of origin and the unwillingness of the international community to find alternative solutions. These included 4.5 million Afghan refugees, mostly in Pakistan and Iran, (many having been refugees for more than two decades), more than four million Palestinians (refugees for more than 50 years), as well as hundreds of thousands of Sudanese, Angolans, Iraqis, Ethiopians, Eritreans, Burmese, Somalis, Liberians, refugees from western Sahara, Angolans, Vietnamese (mostly in China), Rwandese, Nepalese, and Tibetans, many of whom had been living in camps or under other restrictions for a decade or longer (USCR 2002).

In the few instances in which it was successful, the exilic refugee regime was based on a carefully wrought system of burden sharing intended to relieve pressures on countries of first asylum—those states that, through an accident of geography, were subjected to influxes of refugees from neighboring countries. In order to permit refugees to seek asylum from persecution outside their own country—a principle enshrined in Article 14 of the Universal Declaration of Human Rights—keeping the doors open to first asylum countries was long regarded as the *sine qua non* of international refugee protection (United Nations, 1948). Distant countries, frequently more stable politically and with greater resources than first asylum countries, lent support to countries of first asylum not only through financial and material assistance, but also by sharing the human burden through resettlement. Third-country resettlement served a direct protection function for refugees still endangered in countries of first asylum; it was also used to convince first asylum countries to maintain open borders for new refugee arrivals. Finally, third-country resettlement served as a durable solution for refugees with no prospect for repatriation or local integration. It not only gave refugees a chance to start a new life, but also served to relieve first-asylum states of the long-term burden of integrating large refugee populations.

Vietnam: First Asylum and Resettlement

The exilic model took its essential form in the mid-1970s in response to the Vietnamese exodus. Following the triumph of communist forces in 1975, the international community recognized that Vietnamese refugees had no prospects for return and virtually no hope of permanently remaining in neighboring Southeast Asian states. Led by the United States, distant countries struck a bargain with the first asylum states, to keep their doors open and provide at least temporary asylum. In return, the distant states would bear the lion's share of the financial costs of maintaining the refugees in first asylum, and would share the human burden as well by agreeing to resettle refugees outside the region. During the next 20 years, more than 1.3 million Vietnamese were admitted to the United States (USCR, 1996).

The United States and allied governments applied the resettlement model to other refugee emergencies as well. At least some among the millions of Cambodians and Laotians, Afghans and Iranians, Ethiopians and Somalis found durable solutions to their plight as the United States and its partner resettlement states admitted them from countries of first asylum.

Refugee screening was a key component of such resettlement. Although a refugee's initial escape across a border was usually sudden, chaotic, and uncontrolled, permanent resettlement to a distant third country was usually highly organized, selective, and prolonged. However committed third countries might have been to the principle of international burden sharing, refugee resettlement remained discretionary. Resettlement governments regularly exercised their discretion to screen out persons not meeting the refugee standard, as well as undesirables: those who might fear persecution if returned, including criminals; suspected persecutors of others; and others whose faults might be less egregious. The United States wrote this discretion into the Refugee Act of 1980, which provided the statutory framework for the resettlement procedure. The Refugee Act reserved resettlement to refugees "of special humanitarian concern" (United States Government. Immigration and Nationality Act § 207. 8U.S.C. § 1157) to the United States, often based, in practice, on specific ties to the United States, such as family ties or for having been persecuted or threatened with persecution for having overtly sided with the U.S. government.

The resulting system, while undoubtedly saving far more lives than just those actually resettled, was nevertheless far from perfect. Countries of first asylum could legitimately protest that resettlement states were 'creaming off' the best and the brightest, and leaving them with the 'residuals'—the unskilled, the unhealthy, the uneducated—who were the most threatening or burdensome to local communities. As the years dragged on, first asylum countries also complained that the character of refugee flows changed, and that these migrants began to appear less interested in seeking asylum than in looking for resettlement (Robinson, 1988). The first asylum states complained of a "magnet effect" that they said would continue to attract refugee claimants motivated by the lure of immigration to far-off lands, leaving themselves with larger and larger pools of screened-out residuals with no place to go (McCalmon, 1994). These perceptions and realities led to attempts to 'fix' the existing system.

In an effort to deter hazardous boat departures and to exercise greater control over who might enter and leave, the international community created an alternative way for would-be refugees to exit their country through orderly, legal departures directly from their country of origin (and feared persecution). In 1979, Vietnam signed a memorandum of understanding with UNHCR agreeing to allow Vietnamese with close family links abroad to depart legally. The resulting "Orderly Departure Program" brought 387,763 Vietnamese to the United States between 1980 and 1994, as well as 136,511 to third countries (USCR, 1994).

This solution, in turn, became a model for other large U.S.-engineered refugee admission programs. One program targeted refugees from Cuba, which also involved deterring dangerous boat departures. A second program focused on Soviet (and ex-Soviet) Jews and Evangelical Christians, and was the largest in-country refugee-processing program thus far, through which the United States admitted more than 400,000 people between 1988 and 1998 (USCR, 1999).

Paradigm 2: The 1990s, Source-Countries and Safe Areas

The 1990s has been characterized as a "decade of experimentation" in refugee protection and humanitarian response (Newland, 1999). The ad hoc experiments included temporary protection regimes (as opposed to permanent asylum arising out of refugee status determinations), cross-border humanitarian assistance, including "humanitarian corridors" in conflict zones, and "safe areas" within refugee-producing countries, as well as outright military interventions for purportedly humanitarian reasons. These approaches emphasized not just quick repatriation but prevention of refugee flows in the first place. While preventing the human rights abuses that cause refugee flows or quickly resolving them is obviously the best outcome for the refugee, it became clear in the 1990s that many refugee-producing situations were not readily preventable or soluble. In such cases, the international community seemed to grow increasingly impatient with the refugees themselves, and its commitment to the traditional principle of asylum itself came into question.

Four complex humanitarian emergencies of the 1990s particularly characterized the shift to a model of solutions-oriented humanitarian intervention within the source country, accompanied by creating safe areas inside the country or offering temporary protection outside the country followed by rapid repatriation: northern Iraq (1991), Haiti (1992-1994), Bosnia (1992-1995), and Rwanda (1994-1996). In most of these humanitarian emergencies, the international community—comprised of governments, usually led by the United States, humanitarian institutions, such as the UN High Commissioner for Refugees (UNHCR) and nongovernmental organizations (NGOs)—took measures to contain or reverse refugee flows, using humanitarian relief as one of the means to contain the refugee flow. Military protection of relief, establishment of no-fly zones, and safe area declarations often bolstered such efforts.

While the rhetoric—and undoubtedly the motivation—of many actors in the international community was humanitarian and predicated on the idea of attenuating the causes of refugee flows, in reality it was often powerful governments, the protagonists with a vested interest in avoiding refugee flows, who became the major sponsors of "protection" or "prevention" schemes inside countries that generated refugee flows or potential refugee flows. The UN agencies involved in peacekeeping and humanitarian response, and their NGO partners often found themselves trying not only to protect internally displaced persons (IDPs) within their countries of origin, but also working to prevent their escape.

Although the exilic refugee regime upheld the principle that people have a right to seek and enjoy asylum from persecution outside their country, the international community had never agreed to bind itself to that principle. The 1951

Refugee Convention (United Nations) does not include a positive requirement to provide asylum, although this would appear to be a corollary of fulfilling the *nonrefoulement* (Article 33 of the Refugee Convention and Protocol; United Nations, 1951), which prohibits the return of a refugee to a place where his life or freedom would be threatened. The idea of protection without asylum—that uprooted people could be protected inside their home country before they became refugees—was a guiding principles of the source-country paradigm.

Addressing refugee flows at the point of origin, while providing humanitarian benefits, nevertheless politicized the international response to refugees as never before. As the United States experienced first hand during the 1980 Mariel Boat exodus, refugee flows can serve to relieve internal political pressures on refugee-producing countries while destabilizing refugee-hosting ones. A decade later, with the Cold War behind it, the international community was no longer willing to accept this dynamic. The focus shifted away from providing asylum outside the country of origin. The international community committed itself to protecting first-asylum states and to keeping the pressure on refugee-producing states. The outstanding question was that of the safety of the refugees themselves. Would they become pawns in a test of wills between their home government and its adversaries?

A focus on preventing flows and keeping potential refugees in the source country shifted the focus away from the relatively straightforward humanitarian task of caring for refugees after they crossed a border. The new model was one of creating short-term protection in pockets within the country of origin, or in some other extraterritorial site, while seeking fundamental changes that would enable the displaced to go home as soon as possible.

Northern Iraq (1991): Safe Haven

In the aftermath of the Persian Gulf War, the anti-Iraq alliance devised a way to avoid *refoulement* and yet not provide asylum outside the potential refugees' country of origin.

As an exodus of Iraqi Kurds massed on the Turkish border, the United States, Great Britain, and France declared a "safe haven zone" in northern Iraq. Unlike the Vietnamese refugee experience, in which the United States had cajoled and coerced Thailand, Malaysia, and other neighbors of Vietnam to provide temporary asylum, this time, the United States agreed to help keep the refugees out and deny them asylum in Turkey rather than persuade or pressure Turkey to provide first asylum.

Pushing refugees back at their border normally constitutes *refoulement*. Here, however, the Western Alliance declared that it was providing a protective shield inside Iraq, thus avoiding returning refugees to persecution, even while returning them, or compelling them to stay, within the territory of the persecuting state.

The authorization for the creation of the northern Iraq safe area, known as Operation Provide Comfort, was based on a tenuous reading of UN Security Council Resolution 688. This resolution framed the threat to international peace and security not as the human rights abuses perpetrated by the Iraqi government on its citizens, but rather as "the massive flow of refugees toward and across international frontiers." The refugees themselves were seen as the threat to international order and stability. Resolution 688, in fact, affirmed the sovereignty, territorial integrity, and political independence of Iraq, while also insisting that the Iraqi government "allow immediate access by international humanitarian organizations to all those in need of assistance in all parts of Iraq." There was no explicit authorization for U.S., British, and French military forces to enter northern Iraq to establish Operation Provide Comfort, and it would be a stretch, indeed, to regard such forces as "international humanitarian organizations."

While history is likely to judge Operation Provide Comfort as a success, and certainly the northern Iraqi Kurds regard it as having strengthened their hand in creating an autonomous political zone within Iraq, it nevertheless subverted both the idea from the Geneva Conventions of neutralized zones established with the consent of all parties to a conflict to shelter civilians from the dangers of war (Fourth Geneva Convention, 15), as well as the right to seek asylum outside one's country (Universal Declaration of Human Rights, Article 14).

Haiti (1992-1994): Interdiction, Intervention, and Off-shore Safe Havens

The Haitian refugee crisis from 1992 to 1994 directly confronted the United States with defining the responsibilities of a first asylum country—in this case, itself. Rather than allowing a mass refugee influx as it had so often called upon poor third world countries to do during the Cold War (and as it had done itself with respect to refugees fleeing from Cuba), the United States contrived various means to avoid opening its territory to Haitian asylum seekers. Most egregiously, for a time it interdicted and summarily returned Haitians with no screening. Although, on its face this was *refoulement*, the U.S. Supreme Court gave this practice its blessing in *Sale v. Haitian Centers Council*, through a convoluted opinion holding that the Refugee Convention and Protocol are not self-executing and that U.S. law, the Immigration and Nationality Act (INA), which implements the prohibition on *refoulement*, only applies within U.S. territory.

Although the U.S. Supreme Court essentially gave the Clinton Administration *carte blanche* to *refoule* refugees interdicted outside U.S. territory, Clinton appeared uncomfortable with such arbitrary power. After several false starts, he established a "safe haven" outside both Haiti and the United States—the U.S. naval base at Guantánamo Bay, Cuba. The INA did not apply at Guantánamo. Refugees could be held there indefinitely without screening, without due process rights. Interestingly, Guantánamo bore one particular similarity to northern Iraq:

as in northern Iraq, although ultimate sovereignty rested with an enemy state, in this case, Cuba, actual control was in the hands of the United States.

The prompt return of the Haitians to Haiti was assumed from the very beginning of the Guantánamo operation. In June 1994 this author spoke to the U.S. military commander at Guantánamo, who said that the camp would be closed in six months. He also said that the refugees would not be allowed to proceed to the United States. One can only speculate about the extent to which the refugee issue drove foreign policy. In any event, the United States and its partners intervened in Haiti, sending in international troops and restoring President Bertrand Aristide to power in October 1994. Six months after Guantánamo was established as a temporary safe haven camp, it was closed. The U.S. authorities declared a fundamental change in the status of Haiti so that the refugees could safely return. Those who refused to return voluntarily were forced back.

Would the United States have intervened to restore President Aristide to power if not for the fear of a continuing exodus of boat people and a desire not to establish a permanent refugee camp at Guantánamo? It appeared that the United States' willingness to embark on a major military intervention in Haiti was not for the usual foreign policy objectives, but rather primarily to effect the return of refugees and to change the conditions that would cause more to flee.

Bosnia (1992-1995): Temporary Protection and Safe Havens

The Western Europeans' reaction to the influx of Bosnians was not unlike that of the United States towards the Haitians. Although the Europeans did not have the options of high seas interdictions and detentions of refugees on island compounds they were equally intent on preventing Bosnian access to asylum procedures and due process rights, and fashioned a "temporary protection" regime that was predicated on the return of the Bosnians to their homeland. Hand in hand with the temporary protection regime came a visa regime that restricted Bosnian access to most West European territories.

The international community was slow to create safe areas inside Bosnia a lá Operation Provide Comfort, in large part because, unlike Iraq in 1991, there was insufficient political will to devote the forces necessary to ensure protection. The international community tried to establish airlifts or "safe corridors" for delivery of food to unsafe areas, such as Sarajevo and Gorazde, and in February 1993 resorted to food air drops to enclaves, such as Srebrenica, that couldn't be reached safely. The UN Security Council in 1992 passed Resolution 770 calling on states to take "all necessary measures" to facilitate the delivery of relief supplies. The then U.S. Secretary of State made an explicit connection between providing humanitarian assistance to areas that were unsafe and discouraging refugee flows:

We must also funnel humanitarian assistance to hundreds of thousands more who are besieged inside Bosnia, so that they do not become the next wave of refugees. It will require the opening of safe corridors to accomplish this goal. (Eagleburger, 1992)

Finally, on April 16, 1993, the UN Security Council declared Srebrenica a "safe area," supposedly obviating the need to escape (or for its desperate residents to be evacuated). But the safe area rhetoric never became a reality. Although the UN Security Council declared other besieged areas in Bosnia as "safe areas" as well (Resolution 824 of May 6, 1993), safety did not follow from UN Security Council guarantees; in fact, the safe areas became among the least safe places in the world.

The Bosnian safe areas were not neutral, demilitarized zones established with the consent of all parties to the conflict, but, instead, were central to the demographic map-drawing battle that was at the heart of ethnic cleansing — and resistance to it. The Muslim (Bosniac) political leaders were adamantly opposed to any evacuations of their own civilians from safe areas, even when evacuation was demonstrably the desire of many of those trapped in the enclaves. Bosniac forces also waged hit and run operations from within the eastern enclaves, compromising their humanitarian character and provoking the Serbs. After Serb forces overran Srebrenica on July 11, 1995, revealing the utter impotence of the Dutch blue helmeted troops assigned to protect it, the name Srebrenica came to symbolize the failure of the safe area concept. With echoes of the Nazi Holocaust, Serb forces separated males and females who had taken shelter at the Dutch UN compound, and led the men and boys off to be executed. Many other Bosniac men and boys were killed as they desperately sought to escape to the Bosnian army lines.

Although the international community did not want to concede or tolerate ethnic cleansing by providing for orderly evacuation of refugees, it was not willing to muster the military resources necessary to protect them in place. Its position also came to appear less than principled insofar as Western Europeans appeared resistant to providing asylum (the temporary protection regimes established by most West European governments were followed, almost immediately in almost every case with the imposition of visa requirements for Bosnians). Therefore, for the most part, permanent (and often even temporary) asylum was not available in Western Europe, and Bosnians either were forced to remain in unsafe safe areas or within temporary protection bubbles designed to prevent the acquisition of legal immigration rights and to discourage local integration. After the fall of Srebrenica and as Serb forces closed in on another safe area, Gorazde, the international community finally responded with more robust force, bombing Serb positions. This action, together with a Croatian military offensive, forced the signing of a peace accord negotiated in Dayton, Ohio and signed in December 1995, which redrew the map of Bosnia and called for the return of refugees and IDPs.

With a redrawn Bosnia divided along ethnic lines, many refugees and IDPs originating from areas where they were in the ethnic minority no longer had viable prospects of return to their places of origin. In Germany and elsewhere, however, courts decided that Bosnians could be returned to parts of Bosnia where they were in the ethnic majority, even if it meant not returning to their original homes—in effect, creating internally displaced persons.

Rwanda (1994-1996): Operation Turquoise and Coerced Repatriation

After the genocidal wave of killings erupted in Rwanda in 1994, followed by the advance of the Rwanda Patriotic Front against the Hutu perpetrators of the genocide, the safe haven concept was formally broached by the French for the first time in Africa. Operation Turquoise, a "safe humanitarian zone" created by the French in southwest Rwanda in 1994, showed the extent to which humanitarian rhetoric could be bent to political purposes. Operation Turquoise was a unilateral French initiative, endorsed by the UN Security Council, purportedly to create a safe haven for both Tutsis and Hutus in a corner of southwest Rwanda. It was reminiscent of the Operation Provide Comfort safe haven in northern Iraq, which the United States, Great Britain, and France established with ambiguous UN Security Council blessing, and which was not limited to providing humanitarian aid, but also discouraged cross-border refugee movements. It had the additional geopolitical purpose of stopping the advance of one side in an internal conflict with the effect (intentional or not) of propping up the other.

Although the region where Operation Turquoise was established had been the scene of Hutu genocidal massacres directed against the Tutsi minority, France, as a backer of the previous Hutu Power government, appeared to be providing protection and support to members of the deposed government, the pro-French perpetrators of the genocide, although French troops did also protect some Tutsis from being massacred.

While the displaced Hutus in the humanitarian zone of southwestern Rwanda could be fed and sheltered, and did, indeed, avoid much of the misery experienced by their compatriots in the Zairian refugee camps in Goma, their situation was not safe. Although the perpetrators were never identified, violence continued in the Operation Turquoise zone, particularly at night; the Rwandan authorities attributed the attacks to camp residents attacking people outside the camps. Citing security concerns, and insisting that it was safe for displaced civilians to return, the new Rwandan authorities demanded that the camps in the southwest be closed, including Kibeho, the largest camp, which held up to 120,000 people.

In April 1995, after France had turned over the operation to UNAMIR, the Rwandan Patriotic Army (RPA) moved to force the displaced out of Kibeho. What happened next is a matter of dispute. At night, dozens of people were killed outside the camps by machete attacks. During the day, provocations appeared to escalate between camp residents and RPA troops, as the RPA tightened the cordon around the camp, making it impossible for camp residents to cook meals, use the latrine, or even to lie down to sleep. At a certain point the tense stand-off erupted into a full-fledged massacre as RPA troops, in full view of UN peacekeepers and international humanitarian relief organizations, killed at least hundreds and probably thousands of people. The Kibeho massacre demonstrates the failure of "humanitarian intervention" in the country of origin in lieu of asylum beyond the country's borders, particularly when "safe areas" were not established as genuine oases of neutrality, but rather served political objectives of both the quasi-imperial powers and local players.

In the Great Lakes, however, safety was not assured for about two million Rwandese refugees who crossed the borders of Rwanda into Zaire, Tanzania, Burundi, and Uganda. Former soldiers and militiamen who had been responsible for the genocide in Rwanda controlled the refugee camps in eastern Zaire, where about 1.4 million refugees initially congregated, and they showed every sign of intending to regroup and counterattack the RPA. Tens of thousands died at the outset from dysentery, cholera, and other diseases. The situation in the summer and fall of 1994, particularly in Goma, was extremely dangerous and chaotic. From the outset of the crisis, UNHCR pushed for repatriation of the refugees. This reflected both a sense that asylum in Zaire, in particular, and the other neighboring countries was not a viable option, and that the new government established in Kigali in July 1994 would ensure the safe return of refugees.

That was not to be the case, however. UNHCR sponsored an investigation by a highly respected American refugee expert, Robert Gersony, to assess conditions for repatriation in Rwanda in the summer of 1994. Gersony and his team interviewed returnees throughout Rwanda, as well as refugees in Zaire, Burundi, and Tanzania. Gersony found evidence of large-scale indiscriminate killings in the spring and summer both during and after the expulsion of the former government and militias. UNHCR offices also reported a systematic pattern of arrests and disappearances of refugees and returnees (Ogata, 2005).

Despite a suspension of returns after the release of the Gersony report in September 1994, UNHCR remained committed to repatriation as the solution to the crisis. The High Commissioner at the time, Sadako Ogata, wrote in her memoir:

> My position from the very beginning was to favor an early return of the refugees. Given the massiveness of the outflow, the camps could not be viable for long, and I was in search of early solutions. The fact that I supported the Gersony mission attests to my readiness for early preparation. The suspension [of returns in late September 1994] resulting from Gersony's report was clearly a setback for the return of refugees. I opted to continue the search for solutions. In December, as we noted the signs of improvement of security in Rwanda, we lifted the suspension and entered a phase of facilitation of those who volunteered to return. (Ogata, 2005)

The fixation on a quick-repatriation approach, even in the face of credible and compelling evidence of serious human rights abuses directed at returnees, indicates not only the desperate sense of danger in Zaire and the incapacity of the international community to protect and assist refugees there, but also an almost ideological commitment on the part of the High Commissioner to the source-country solution.

The situation in Zaire became increasingly dangerous. Former soldiers and militiamen threatened and intimidated refugees and international humanitarian workers. Médecins sans Frontières-France, CARE International, and others pulled out, saying that the humanitarian character of the refugee camps had been compromised by armed elements. As the new Rwandan government called for the return of refugees, the neighboring states were also preoccupied with the burgeoning instability and violence. UNHCR, faced with an international community unwilling to provide international forces to provide security in the camps, offered to pay for Zairean troops sent by strongman Mobutu Sese Seko to police them. Backed by the new Tutsi-dominated government in Rwanda, and assisted by toops from Rwanda and its ally Uganda, Zairean rebels, the Alliance of Democratic Forces for the Liberation of Congo (AFDL), swept through Zaire in November 1996, forcing many refugees back into Rwanda, smashing camps in Zaire's Kivu region, massacring thousands, and scattering refugees, armed Rwandan Hutus, and the Zairean police forces deeper into Zaire (Rieff, 2002; Ogata, 2005).

As a consequence of perceptions that Rwandan refugees in neighboring countries would be the cause of instability and that Rwanda itself was relatively quiet, UNHCR and other key actors in the international community acquiesced when the governments of Zaire, Burundi, and Tanzania forcibly repatriated hundreds of thousands of Rwandese refugees in August 1995 (from Zaire), July and August 1996 (about 75,000 refuges from Burundi), November 1996 (more than 500,000 from Zaire), and December 1996 (about 500,000 refugees from Tanzania) (Amnesty International, 2004).

Rwanda deserves its place among the international community's ad hoc experiments with quick solutions to refugee problems both because of Operation Turquoise, as well as the international humanitarian community's willingness to countenance coerced repatriation relatively shortly after one of the history's most intense genocides (an estimated 800,000 people killed in a span of nine weeks). The acquiescence of UNHCR and others was based, at least in part, on an assessment that conditions inside Rwanda were safer than they were in countries of asylum, particularly eastern Zaire, and that refugees were not able to make informed choices regarding repatriation because of the control, intimidation, and disinformation to which they were subjected by the militant groups that controlled the camps.

The international response to the Rwandan refugee emergency shows an international community unable or unwilling to provide the resources (including international military forces) to maintain safe asylum outside the source country, but willing to give the benefit of the doubt to the government of the home country, despite it clearly being a party to the conflict and having a questionable record with respect to the treatment of returnees.

Paradigm 3: Security and the Twenty-First Century

The "War on Terrorism" that has dominated international relations in the first decade of the twenty-first century represents the third major paradigm since the establishment of the modern international refugee regime in the aftermath of World War Two. It represents a significant erosion in the principles of refugee protection, particularly the right to seek and enjoy asylum from persecution, and a diminished interest in finding solutions to refugee plight.

The security model that came to the fore in the 2000s was foreshadowed in the 1990s. In the United States, two major pieces of legislation that were adopted in 1996, the Anti-Terrorism and Effective Death Penalty Act (AEDPA) and the Illegal Immigration and Immigrant Responsibility Act (IIRIRA), significantly restricted access to the asylum system in the name of bolstering security, and were prompted in significant measure by the first terror attack on the World Trade Center in 1993 (Schrag, 1999).

Writing in 1995, T. Alexander Aleinikoff noted the paradigm shift then occurring, but predicted that what he called the "source control" might be more about containment than about truly altering the human rights conditions in source countries at the root of refugee flows. Without predicting the coming counter-terrorism-fueled backlash, he nevertheless saw the restrictionist tendencies that would come to characterize the security paradigm:

> Rather than a paradigm shift, then, we may well be witnessing the troubling use of a humanitarian discourse to mask a reaffirmation of state-centeredness. That is, the emphasis on repatriation and root causes will help developed states justify the new strategies adopted to "solve" their asylum "crises," yet deeply entrenched practices of nonintervention will prevent serious measures to improve human rights situations in countries of origin. If this analysis is correct, then the story of change is not about the melding of refugee law into human rights law; rather, it is the exchange of an exilic bias for policies of containment—detention of asylum seekers, visa requirements, closing opportunities for resettlement, push-backs, and return. These policies are grounded less in a desire to breach the walls of state sovereignty than in an attempt to keep third world refugee problems from inconveniencing the developed states. (Aleinikoff, 1995)

If UN Security Council resolution 688 in 1991 characterized the prospect of a "massive flow of refugees toward and across international frontiers" from Iraq as a threat to international peace and security, then the characterization of refugees as possible security threats accelerated with the terrorism preoccupation.

Refugees were to be feared not simply because their numbers and needs might be overwhelming, but also because terrorists, criminals, or other malevolent actors might be hiding among them. Another often articulated view was that people purporting to be refugees might actually be making fraudulent claims in order to evade immigration controls, or, at the least, that they were "jumping the queue" of an orderly system that, in fact, did not really exist for admitting the overwhelming majority of refugees. As barriers to irregular international migration became ever more formidable, refugees and asylum seekers turned increasingly to smugglers and traffickers to evade migration controls. Consequently, refugees and asylum seekers were sometimes conflated in the popular imagination with the smugglers and traffickers as cohorts in criminal enterprises. In addition, popular sentiment in many host countries often came to regard the refugees living among them as culturally or politically incompatible with the host society. These factors have resulted in a xenophobic backlash in which sympathy for the plight of refugees has often been superseded by mistrust and prejudice.

The most obvious sign of this paradigm shift has been the waning of the granting of asylum in Western industrialized countries. UNHCR reports that the number of asylum requests in 50 industrialized countries fell by 22 percent, from 508,100 in 2003 to 396,400 in 2004, and that asylum applications have dropped by 40 percent since 1991 (UNHCR, 2005). In Germany, once the leading asylum receiving state in Europe, the number of asylum applications filed in 2004 was the lowest since 1984. The drop was particularly marked for the industrialized states outside Europe. Canada and the United States received 48 percent fewer asylum requests in 2004 than in 2001, and asylum requests fell by 74 percent in Australia and New Zealand (UNHCR, 2005).

The terrorist threat has lead to a major devaluing of refugees. During the Cold War-reign of the exilic paradigm, refugees were valued as people who "voted with their feet," as proof of the bankruptcy of communism and of the tenacious will for freedom. During the 1990s source-country paradigm, refugees were generally seem sympathetically as victims of war and human rights abuse, and, more strategically, were valued as providing a rationale for the international community to challenge the sovereignty of despots, and, in some cases, to depose them.

The War on Terror, however, paints a more ambiguous military and political picture. Terrorist cells, while they may enjoy the support of certain rogue states, are hidden and secretive, their organizational structure varied and ad hoc. Unlike the ethnic cleansers of the Balkans or the Great Lakes, terrorists are not seen as being particularly interested in displacing civilian populations, largely because they have no territorial objectives. On the other hand refugee camps are perceived as breeding grounds for terrorists, as well as the locations where they can hide and hatch their plots. In reality, if al-Qaeda can be used as an example, terrorists generally do not come from destitute backgrounds and have not personally lived lives of misery (9/11 Report, 2004).

Under the security paradigm, refugees are devalued to the point where providing asylum or intervening to provide source-country solutions are trumped by the desire to keep terrorists out. As with the previous paradigms, these are not formalized international-community positions, but rather represent general trends, for which there will certainly be exceptions. That being said, the author suggests four examples, in addition to the asylum systems of Western industrialized countries, where the new paradigm seemed to be operating in the first half of the 2000s: Chechnya, Afghanistan, Iraq, Colombia and Haiti.

Chechnya (1999-2004): Displaced and Off-limits

Neither the outbreak of war in Chechnya in 1999 (for the second time in the decade), nor the hundreds of thousands of uprooted people it created, registered more than a blip international community's humanitarian response radar screen. The factors that have conspired for such silence included five main elements: (1) the widely held view that this was an essentially age-old ethnic conflict between Russians and a wild, uncontrollable tribal people; (2) deference accorded Russia, the erstwhile superpower, for its activities in an area considered within its hegemony, particularly when Russia bristled at perceived interference with its internal affairs; (3) a perception by the international humanitarian community of a lack of leverage; (4) concern for the safety of international humanitarian workers in Chechnya and surrounding areas, and (5) the stigma attaching to the Chechens themselves as terrorists or terrorist supporters.

The international humanitarian presence on the ground in Chechnya has been almost non-existent since the execution-style murders of six International Committee of the Red Cross delegates in 1996. When the few other international humanitarian organizations, such as UNHCR and Médecins sans Frontières ventured into Chechnya and nearby areas, their aid workers were kidnapped, causing these, and other organizations, such as Organization of Security and Cooperation in Europe (OSCE) monitors, to pull out.

Russia has also kept international humanitarian organizations at arms length by closing down missions, obstructing visas, and using its power as a permanent member of the UN Security Council to render UN agencies, in particular, ineffective. Without actually having to exercise its veto power, the threat of a veto alone has been sufficient to silent the Security Council as a forum for addressing human rights in Chechnya, and to stymie Security Council authorization of efforts to provide humanitarian aid to its victims. In the aftermath of 9/11, human rights organizations observed that the Bush Administration tempered its prior modest criticisms of Russian human rights violations in Chechnya. This was interpreted as U.S. deference to the Russians as newfound allies in the War on Terror, and a new American evaluation of the Chechens less as victims worthy of sympathy and more as perpetrators of terrorism or harborers of terrorists (HRW, 2002).

At the 58th session of the UN Human Rights Commission, in March-April 2002, the first meeting after 9/11, a resolution that called on Russia to invite UN monitors to investigate human rights violations in Russia was narrowly defeated, an indication that pressure on Russia by the international community regarding human rights violations had eased.

Displaced Chechens were poorly assisted, and even more poorly protected. Those displaced within Chechnya itself, particularly the residents of Grozny, were reduced to living in rubble with no prospects for income generation and little available humanitarian assistance. The more than 100,000 who fled into neighboring Ingushetia were under almost constant pressure by the Russians to return to Chechnya. Displaced persons living in tent camps were harassed, food and utilities cut off, and the camps closed. The international community remained largely silent. No one from the international community attempted any kind of intervention in the region of origin to address the causes of the forced displacement; asylum for Chechens was not forthcoming (there were no resettlement programs for Chechen refugees), and the forced return of Chechens from Ingushetia happened in the absence of effective international monitoring.

Afghanistan (2001-2004): Stigmatized Refugees

At the time of the 9/11 attacks, more than four million Afghan refugees were estimated to be living in Pakistan and Iran and another million as being displaced inside Afghanistan (USCR 2002). Many had been stuck in exile since the Soviet intervention in 1979. Through two decades of misery they had been prevented from return by a succession of wars, droughts, tribal infighting, and communist, warlord, or Taliban-inspired persecution and intolerance.

During the Cold War, the West valued the refugees in Pakistan as "warrior-refugees" who would wage a proxy war against the Soviet Union. At the time, refugees were often regarded as chips to be played by the superpowers and their proxies as part of strategies to destabilize the enemy, and humanitarian principles of neutrality were often ignored in the process (Loescher, 1993).

During the experimental period of the 1990s, Afghanistan remained off the international radar screen, as an essentially static backwater of little interest or concern. But its very obscurity pushed it to center stage following the 9/11 attacks. Many of the al-Qaeda terrorists, including Osama Bin Laden, tracked their political origins to participation with the Afghan Mujahideen waging guerrilla war-jihad against Soviet forces and their Afghan allies in the 1980s. During the 1990s, al-Qaeda built its bases in Afghanistan with the support of the Taliban rulers, and recruited terrorist candidates from among the Afghan refugees in Pakistan whose only opportunity for education was in the madrassas, privately funded Islamic schools that included a heavy dose of anti-Western indoctrination (9/11 Report, 2004).

After the 9/11 attacks, about 100,000 residents of Kabul fled the capital, fearing a U.S. attack. When the bombs actually started falling in October 2001, the movement of panicked civilians towards the borders accelerated. The expected new mass influx of refugees into Pakistan and Iran never materialized, however. Many Afghans, particularly among the internally displaced, simply lacked the means to leave; others having lived through decades of war and deprivation calculated that their chances were no worse staying put. But another factor was the increased resistance of neighboring Pakistan and Iran to a new influx of refugees. Pakistan and Iran, which had kept their borders open to refugees through two decades of war, famine, and persecution, closed their borders to would-be refugees (although in Pakistan's case the official, but not particularly effective, closing of the border occurred earlier in the year).

Unlike 1991, the United States did not work with its allies to create a "safe zone" along either border or in any enclave where international military forces would feed and protect civilians. On the contrary, military meals-ready-to-eat (MREs) were dropped out of planes just as other planes were dropping bombs (and, in an ironic twist, were sometimes indistinguishable to the people on the ground, since the yellow plastic MREs looked very much like cluster bombs).

Those resourceful refugees who were able to pay smugglers to evade border controls were treated as non-people by the authorities of the respective countries. Local authorities interfered with UNHCR attempts to register or assist them, and resisted constructing new refugee camps or admitting new arrivals into the old camps. Most of the refugees who did manage to cross a border remained with family or friends, or rented space from strangers, but in any case were hidden. The relatively few who managed to enter camps, such as Jalozai in Pakistan, were left to fend for themselves, building their own makeshift shelters with sticks and scraps. Iran set up two camps, Makaki and Mile 46, on the Afghan side of its border, where some assistance was provided, but where safety was not at all assured. In fact, armed Afghan elements were present in and around the camps, and fighting at one point broke out between pro- and anti-Taliban factions within the Makaki camp. Iran not only pushed back would-be refugees at the border, but used the cover of war to forcibly repatriate tens of thousands of Afghans who had been living in Iran from before the U.S. military campaign.

While the U.S. government crafted a "humanitarian" strategy inside Afghanistan hand-in-hand with its military strategy, it remained essentially silent on the refugee issue and the closing of borders to Afghans seeking to escape (Rieff, 2002). Its main preoccupation was to catch Osama Bin Laden and his cohorts and to prevent their escape across Afghanistan's borders. The sealing of the borders by Afghanistan's neighbors, therefore, was consistent with U.S. military objectives, notwithstanding long enshrined refugee principles that bar the repulsing of refugees to a place where their lives or freedom would be threatened (UNHCR Convention, 1951).

The low regard for refugees continued in the years following the 2001 military intervention. Although UNHCR reported in early 2005 that more than three million Afghan refugees had repatriated, it also reported that more than two million remained in Pakistan and Iran (UNHCR, 2005). Tolerance for Afghan refugees in Iran and Pakistan had long since abated, and many returnees reported having been harassed and coerced to leave (AI, 2003). Despite ongoing security problems in many areas of Afghanistan, continuing human rights abuses, discrimination against women and minorities, and localized factional fighting, Afghan asylum seekers in the West were fewer in number (an 83 percent decrease in asylum applications filed from 2001 to 2004—UNHCR, 2005) and found decreasing receptivity to their claims (AI, 2003).

While Afghanistan in the early 2000s arguably continued the 1990s paradigm of a source-country solution, the difference was that refugees were hardly a factor in the international community's calculations other than as possible cover for al-Qaeda members to escape the country. There was virtually no support from any of the involved governments, local or Western, to promote the right of refugees to cross borders to seek asylum or to provide real protection for them inside Afghanistan. A significant humanitarian assistance operation did develop in the country hand in hand with militarized pacification operations, but the primary motivation for the intervention was security, even if it did have positive humanitarian consequences and ultimately led to millions of Afghans being able to return home during the next several years.

Iraq 2003-2004: Mistrusted Refugees

While Iraq in 1991 epitomized the source-country solution paradigm, the international community's engagement in Iraq in 2003-2004 showed security concerns trumping humanitarian considerations, and refugees and internally displaced persons being ignored at best, and rejected at worst as possible security threats.

Unlike the aftermath of the 1991 Persian Gulf War when Saddam Hussein crushed the Kurdish and Shi'a uprisings and caused a massive refugee flow, the initial phase of the U.S.-led invasion and occupation in spring 2003 produced hardly any refugees, and was generally seen by Iraqis who had suffered decades of internal and external displacement as an opportunity to go home. Initially, the U.S.-led Coalition Provisional Authority (CPA) negotiated with the International Organization for Migration (IOM) to work on plans for the IDP returns. But almost immediately, both the civilian leaders of the CPA and their military counterparts actively discouraged both IDP and refugee returns as potentially destabilizing factors.

Instability in Iraq would go well beyond migratory pressures, however, and by late 2003 IOM had to shelve its plans and the NGOs had to leave for their own safety. Despite Iraq being on the news every night, and the presence of possibly hundreds of thousands of repatriating refugees from Iran and of hundreds of thousands of internally displaced persons (including people freshly displaced as a result of military operations), UNHCR's repeated requests to international donors to fund its humanitarian operations in Iraq were almost completely ignored (UNHCR, 2004).

The most significant refugee out-migration was surreptitious, and almost by mutual consent of the refugees themselves and the parties to the conflict, was ignored. Some 250,000 Iraqis fled to Jordan where they remained under more or less benign neglect as an undocumented and ignored population until the November 2005 hotel bombings, at which point Jordanian authorities began cracking down on Iraqis without documents and the situation for Iraqis attempting to flee the war became increasingly precarious. More than 500,000 also Iraqis fled into Syria from the time of the U.S.-led invasion through the end of 2005 (Refugees International, 2005). They were not registered by the Syrian government, not assisted by UNHCR, and not acknowledged by the United States or other governments. They did not live in collective centers; their existence was almost entirely ignored. At various times, U.S.-led forces tried to block the border with Syria, and to pressure the Syrians to tighten their own border, both to block the escape of Ba'athist leaders as well as to prevent the infiltration of insurgents (Wilson, 2005). But the international community studiously ignored the humanitarian dimension of the problem in either Jordan or Syria.

Prior to 9/11, the United States had engaged in several Iraqi refugee resettlement initiatives, including the evacuation of Iraqis from northern Iraq following the incursion into the autonomous region by government forces in September 1996, the resettlement of predominantly Shi'a Iraqis from the Rafha camp in Saudi Arabia during the 1990s, as well as resettlement of Iraqi refugees in Turkey and elsewhere in the region.

That ended abruptly on September 11, 2001, however. Refugees who had been accepted for U.S. resettlement were literally stopped on the tarmac, and a moratorium on all refugee admissions worldwide was imposed. Although refugee resettlement eventually resumed for other nationalities, albeit with fewer numbers admitted and under much greater scrutiny than before, the moratorium remained in place for Iraqi refugees without regard to their individual circumstances. By the end of 2004, Iraqi refugee resettlement to the United States had not resumed, the refugees accepted for admission before September 11, 2001 remained in limbo, and no new interviews were scheduled.

At the same time, as the insurgency grew in strength and as the sectarian divisions within Iraq deepened, increasing members of Iraqi religious minorities and people accused of collaborating with the U.S.-led occupation began fleeing, or attempting to flee, Iraq (UNHCR, 2004). The United States, and the rest of the West, ignored this. Likely factors included an unwillingness on the part of the United States and other members of the coalition to provide refuge for people fleeing Iraq at the same time that they were sending their own soldiers there to fight and die, and a basic distrust of the refugees as being security threats at a time of war with their home country.

On March 17, 2003, the same evening that President George W. Bush delivered his 48-hour ultimatum to Saddam Hussein and his sons to leave Iraq, Secretary of Homeland Security Tom Ridge announced Operation Liberty Shield, under which asylum seekers from Iraq and 32 other unnamed countries "where al Qaeda, al-Qaeda sympathizers, and other terrorist groups are known to have operated" were to be subjected to mandatory detention for the duration of their asylum procedures. The Department of Homeland Security said that about 60 percent of the people from the designated Operation Liberty Shield countries were Iraqis. The obvious irony was that a war that was purportedly being fought, at least in part, to secure the liberty of Iraqis, would result in the first instance in the deprivation of liberty for those fleeing Iraq to seek asylum, and that the implicit purpose of the "shield" was to deter Iraqis (and others fleeing predominantly Muslim countries) from seeking asylum in the United States.

Enhanced security measures made it far more difficult to travel internationally to seek asylum after 9/11, particularly from the Middle East and predominantly Muslim countries. The number of Iraqi asylum seekers in the West decreased by 80 percent from 2001 to 2004 (UNHCR, 2005). Given the levels of fear, violence, and uncertainty within Iraq, it is certainly reasonable to speculate that the war in Iraq would have produced significantly more refugees if they had had a way of escaping the country, but, in fact, enhanced security measures precluded the option of seeking asylum both because of the difficulty of crossing Iraq's borders and because of security-imposed obstacles on onward international travel.

Colombia: War on Terror Undercuts Asylum Claims

Asylum seekers and refugees from Colombia, a predominantly Christian country in South America, might not at first glance appear to have been touched by the War on Terror. But, several of the armed groups operating there, including the United Self-Defense Forces of Colombia (AUC), the Revolutionary Armed Forces of Colombia (FARC), and the National Liberation Army (ELN), were designated by the U.S. State Department as "foreign terrorist organizations."

The AUC, FARC, and ELN pervaded nearly all aspects of Colombian life, and were a major reason why at the time of the 9/11 attacks Colombia had the second largest number of internally displaced persons in the world, about two million. However refugees attempting to flee the country and seek asylum in the United States found themselves being denied asylum precisely because a designated terrorist group had persecuted them.

The Anti-Terrorism and Effective Death Penalty Act (AEDPA) of 1996, sections 302 and 303, codified at 18 USC § 2339B and 8 U.S.C. § 1189, made it a crime punishable for up to life imprisonment for a person to provide "material support" to a designated terrorist organization. The Immigration and Nationality Act was amended to include as a ground for exclusion from the United States engagement in "terrorist activity," defined to include "providing any type of material support...to any individual the actor knows or has reason to believe has committed or plans to commit a terrorist activity" (INA § 212(a)(B)(iii)(III)).

UNHCR estimated that at least 70 percent of Colombian refugees referred to the United States for resettlement had been forced by the FARC or other designated foreign terrorist organization to pay "taxes" or other types of coerced payment. But the U.S. law made no explicit allowance for a waiver of the material support provision for people who are forced to give terrorists food, shelter, or money. The reality in Colombia, however, was that the AUC, FARC, and ELN placed civilians under severe duress, which often included threats of harm, torture, or death to oneself or a loved one, to make such payments.

Because they decide refugee status within the context of U.S. law, both immigration judges within the United States and U.S. immigration officials in Latin America considering UNHCR's referral of refugees for U.S. admission began denying or deferring these cases. For many Colombian refugees and asylum seekers, therefore, the basis of their refugee claim—coercion to pay "taxes" to one of these groups on the list of foreign terrorist organizations or else risk possible death—was the very same act that rendered them ineligible for asylum or refugee admission to the United States. Although Colombians were the first nationality group to face the "material support" bar, asylum seekers and refugees from Burma and elsewhere soon began facing the same obstacle (Refugees International, 2005).

Haitian Refugees (2004): Barred on National Security Grounds

Haitian refugees have been discussed earlier as an example of the 1990s source country approach. In one of the many ironies discussed in this chapter, the paradigm shift to the security model revolved in part around the same figure: President Jean Bertrand Aristide, who was restored to power in 1994 through a U.S.-led international intervention and deposed ten years later with U.S. involvement as well.

During the crisis of the mid-1990s, the United States tried several different approaches with respect to Haitian boat people, settling finally on the safe haven at Guantánamo Bay, Cuba. In late February 2004, when political violence and lawlessness were sweeping Haiti in the days leading to Aristide's forced departure, President Bush declared, "I have made it abundantly clear to the Coast Guard that we will turn back any refugee that attempts to reach our shore." He ordered stepped-up Coast Guard patrols off the coast of Haiti and directed the Coast Guard to return fleeing refugees. During the last weekend in February, 905 Haitians took to the sea, were intercepted by U.S. Coast Guard cutters, and every one was summarily returned to Haiti.

The 905 were dumped on the Haitian Coast Guard dock at Port-au-Prince, some in shackles, and had to be escorted at gunpoint through a taunting crowd (Associated Press, 2004). No one knew at the time what governmental (or non-governmental) authority was functioning at that location during the weekend when the Haitian president was forced from office and removed from the country. No one from the US embassy met the Haitians as they were disembarked. No one from UNHCR was present. No one from the Haiti's National Migration Office was present.

President Bush made no pretext of protecting refugees. In fact, his statement flouted the principles that follow from his use of the word "refugee" itself, a term with a precise legal definition that carries with it an obligation on the part of states to offer protection. Bush's unyielding stance undoubtedly deterred many would be refugees from attempting the dangerous boat journey, and, unlike the crisis of the mid-1990s, Haiti produced virtually no refugees in 2004, despite evidence of widespread human rights abuses inside the country.

Even before the events of 2004, the Bush Administration had acted to make sure that any Haitians that evaded interdiction and landed in the United States would be subjected to automatic detention. In October 2002, a wooden boat filled with Haitians had succeeded in evading the normal Coast Guard contingents and landing in Key Biscayne, Florida. An immigration judge ruled that a teenager on the boat, David Joseph, should be released to his uncle, a legal resident living in Brooklyn, N.Y., who was willing to post a $2,500 bond. The judge found that David posed no threat if released. Finding his asylum claim to be credible, the judge said he was unlikely to abscond. The government appealed, but the Board of Immigration Appeals affirmed the judge's ruling to release David. It found that the judge correctly applied the rules regarding release on bond to avoid unnecessary, prolonged detention.

Then, in April 2003, Attorney General John Ashcroft stepped in. Citing his decision regarding David as a precedent ruling, he ruled that all Haitian boat arrivals should be jailed. He invoked "national security" as his rationale, not because David Joseph himself ever harmed or threatened anyone, but in order that a surge of other boat people from Haiti would not "injure national security by diverting valuable Coast Guard and DOD [Department of Defense] resources from [their] counter-terrorism and homeland security responsibilities" (Benesch, 2003). Consequently, even for Haitian refugees, coming from a nationality group that had no involvement with terrorism whatsoever, either as victims or perpetrators, U.S. policy makers invoked national security and counter-terrorism to deter their quest for safety and freedom.

Conclusion

The security paradigm of the 2000s has fortified physical barriers at borders, tightened travel restrictions, and created new legal definitions that preclude refugees and would-be refugees from ever being considered for protection, inside or outside their countries of origin. The international community, dominated more than ever by the United States, may or may not intervene to change the governments of the countries that produce refugees. But its doing so is motivated overwhelmingly by national security concerns, and the consequences for refugees, positive or negative, is a distant afterthought.

References

Aleinikoff, T. Alexander (1995). State-centered Refugee Law: From Resettlement to Containment. In E. Valentine Daniel and John Chr. Knudsen (Eds.), *Mistrusting Refugees* (257-271). Berkeley: University of California Press.

Amnesty International (2003). Afghanistan: Out of Sight, Out of Mind: The Fate of Afghan Returnees. AI Index: ASA 11/014/2003, June 2003.

Amnesty International (2004). Rwanda: Protecting Their Rights: Rwandese Refugees in the Great Lakes Region. AI Index: AFR 47/016/2004, December 15, 2004.

Associated Press (2004). Coast Guard Patrols Increase, March 8, 2004.

Benesch, Susan (2003). Haitians Trapped by 'War on Terrorism,' *Amnesty Now*, Volume 29, Number 3, Fall 2003, p. 13.

Broneé, S.A. (1993). The History of the Comprehensive Plan of Action. *International Journal of Refugee Law, 5(4)*, pp. 534-535, 574-575.

Coles, G. (1989). Approaching the refugee problem today. In G. Loescher and L. Monahan (Eds.), *Refugees and International Relations* (pp. 387-93, 403-4). Oxford, UK: Clarendon.

Eagleburger, Lawrence, S. Intervention, London Conference, Queen Elizabeth II Conference Center, London, August 26, 1992.

Frelick, B. (1992). Preventive Protection and the Right to Seek Asylum: A preliminary look at Bosnia and Croatia. *International Journal of Refugee Law, 4(4)*, pp. 439-454.

Frelick, B. (1993). Preventing Refugee Flows: Protection or Peril? In, V. Hamilton (Ed.), *World Refugee Survey* (pp. 5-13). Washington, DC: USCR.

Frelick, B. (1995). Special Issue: The Death March from Srebrenica. *Refugee Reports*, 16 (7).

Human Rights Watch (2002). Russia: Displaced Chechens in Ingushetia Face Abuses, New York: HRW, September 23, 2003.

Loescher, Gil (1993). Beyond Charity: International Cooperation and the Global Refugee Crisis. Oxford: Oxford University Press, pp. 88-89.

McCalmon, B. (1994). Winding it up in Hong Kong: The Increasing Impatience with Vietnamese Asylum Seekers. *Georgetown Immigration Law Journal, 8*, pp. 333-340.

National Commission on Terrorist Attacks Upon the United States (2004). *The 9/11 Commission Report*. New York: W.W. Norton, pp. 55, 160-161, 231-235.

Newland, K. (1999). The Decade in Review. In V. Hamilton (Ed.), *World Refugee Survey* 1999 (pp. 14-21). Washington, DC: USCR.

Ogata, Sadako (2005). *The Turbulent Decade: Confronting the Refugee Crises of the 1990s.* New York: W.W. Norton.

Refugees International (2005). Iraqi Refugees in Syria: Silent Exodus Leaves 500,000 in Need of Protection and Aid. *Refugees International Bulletin,* November 15, 2005.

Refugees International (2005). Thailand: Complications in the Resettlement of Burmese Refugees. *Refugees International Bulletin,* December 8, 2005.

Rieff, David. (2002). *A Bed for the Night: Humanitarianism in Crisis.* New York: Simon and Schuster, Inc.

Robinson, C. (1989). Sins of Omission: The New Vietnamese Refugee Crisis. In, V. Hamilton (Ed.), *World Refugee Survey* (p. 5). Washington, DC: USCR.

Schrag, Phillip G. (1999). *A Well-Founded Fear: The Congressional Battle to Save Political Asylum in America.* New York: Routledge, 39-44.

United Nations (1948). Universal Declaration of Human Rights. United Nations General Assembly Resolution 217A (III)

United Nations (1951). Convention Relating to the Status of Refugees. 189 U.N.T.S. 150.

United Nations (1967). Protocol Relating to the Status of Refugees. 19 U.S.T. 6223, 606 U.N.T.S. 267.

United Nations High Commissioner for Refugees (2005). Another 1 Million Afghan Refugees Are Likely to Return Home by 2006. Geneva: UNHCR, February 17, 2005.

United Nations High Commissioner for Refugees (2005). Asylum Levels and Trends in Industrialized Countries, 2004. Population and Data Unit/PGDS, Division of Operational Support, Geneva: UNHCR. (Available at: http://www.unhcr.ch/statistics.

United Nations High Commissioner for Refugees (2004). Iraq: Despite Repeated Requests, No Contributions Received This Year. Geneva: UNHCR, June 1, 2004.

United Nations High Commissioner for Refugees (2004). UNHCR Return Advisory Regarding Iraqi Asylum Seekers and Refugees. Geneva: UNHCR, October 22, 2004.

United States Government (1980). Immigration and Nationality Act § 207. 8U.S.C. § 1157).

U.S. Committee for Refugees (1992). *World Refugee Survey 1992.* Washington, DC: USCR.

U.S. Committee for Refugees (1994). The Orderly Departure Program, FY 94. *Refugee Reports, 15 (12),* p. 5.

U.S. Committee for Refugees (1996). Indochinese refugee activity: Cumulative since April 1975. *Refugee Reports, 17 (12),* p. 5.

U.S. Committee for Refugees (1996). Safe haven collapses in northern Iraq: U.S. evacuates 2,000. *Refugee Reports, 17 (9),* p. 11.

U.S. Committee for Refugees (1999). Regional Refugee Ceilings and Admissions to the United States, FY 87-2000. *Refugee Reports, 20 (12),* p. 9.

U.S. Committee for Refugees (2000). *World Refugee Survey 2000.* Washington, DC: USCR.

U.S. Committee for Refugees (2001). *World Refugee Survey 2001.* Washington, DC: USCR.

U.S. Committee for Refugees (2002). *World Refugee Survey 2002.* Washington, DC: USCR.

Wilson, Scott (2005). Iraqi Refugees Overwhelm Syria: Migrants Who Fled Violence Put Stress on Housing Market, Schools, *The Washington Post,* February 3, 2005, p. A18.

Section II: Human Rights Issues and Concerns

Chapter 3. Refugees' Human Right to Adequate Food
George Kent

**Chapter 4. The Role of Relief NGO's in Human Rights
and Protection**
Richard J. Brennan
Gerald Martone

Chapter 5. Culture and Human Rights
Harry Minas

Chapter 6. A Confucian Perspective on Human Rights
Weiming Tu

**Chapter 7. Institutionalizing Human Rights in the Militaries of
the Emerging Democracies: The Case of Peru**
Jeffrey F. Addicott

CHAPTER 3

Refugees' Human Right to
Adequate Food[*]

George Kent

Global Governance

Although there is no global government as such, there is global governance. Global governance is undertaken by the nations of the world through their international activities, often with the support of international agencies that act in their behalf. We can say that global governance is undertaken by and in behalf of the international community, even if that community is not precisely defined.

The guiding principle of this analysis is that the international community is subject to human rights obligations similar to those of states. Thus, if a particular action by a national government would be viewed as a human rights violation, then a similar action by, say, the World Bank, probably should be viewed as a human rights violation as well. International governmental agencies are creations of nation states and act in their behalf. Consequently they are subject to much the same obligations as those states (Kent, 1994).

---

[*] With the permission of the publisher, this chapter draws on material in the author's *Freedom from Want: The Human Right to Adequate Food*, published by Georgetown University Press in 2005.

The idea that the international community has specific obligations is no more ambiguous than the concept that the state has specific obligations. The "international community," like the "the state" is a social construct (Soguk, 1999). National governments represent states and act on their behalf. In much the same way, international governmental organizations represent and act on behalf of the collectivity of states, the international community. The various specialized organizations at the global level can be viewed as analogous to the specialized ministries at the national level. They are answerable not to some high level executive but to the collectivity of states.

The issue of the international community's obligations may be seen with special clarity through examination of its obligations with respect to refugees because, by definition, refugees are not under the protection of their home states. My purpose here is to explore this specifically with reference to refugees' human right to adequate food.

Issues in Refugee Nutrition

The nutrition problems of refugees are well documented by the United Nations System Standing Committee on Nutrition through its Nutrition Information in Crisis Situations publications, formerly known as the Refugee Nutrition Information System.1 While these data clearly show that refugees suffer from serious and sustained nutrition problems, they do not lay out all the dimensions of the problem. In 1999 reporters from the Los Angeles Times compared relief efforts for Africans and for refugees in the Balkans.

> The Office of the U.N. High Commissioner for Refugees is spending about 11 cents a day per refugee in Africa. In the Balkans, the figure is $1.23, more than 11 times greater.
>
> Some refugee camps in Africa have one doctor for every 100,000 refugees. In Macedonia, camps have as many as one doctor per 700 refugees—a ratio far better than that of many communities in Los Angeles.
>
> Refugees at most camps in Albania, across the border from Kosovo, have readily available clean water. In Eritrea, on the Horn of Africa, families as large as 10 are given about 3 gallons of water to last three days, according to Mary Anne Fitzgerald, a Nairobi, Kenya-based spokeswoman for Refugees International.
>
> The camps in Africa hold as many as 500,000 people. Up to 6,000 refugees there die each day from cholera and other public health diseases. In Macedonia, the largest camp holds 33,000 people. So far, there have been no deaths from public health emergencies such as an epidemic or starvation. . . .
>
> World Food Program officials say both European and African refugees are getting about 2,100 calories a day of food rations. But for the Kosovo Albanians, those calories come in the form of tins of chicken pate, foil-wrapped cheeses, fresh oranges and milk. In some ready-made meals, there is even coffee and fruit tarts. . . .

That contrasts with Africa, where refugees are far less likely to get ready-made meals and have to make most of their food from scratch—a practice reflecting the simpler lifestyles of the area, say U.N. officials. Instead of meals, the refugees are given basic grains such as sorghum or wheat (Miller & Simmons, 1999).

The major issues, then, are the many instances of inadequacy of nutrition services for refugees, and beyond that, the question of whether these services are provided in ways that are fair and just. Miller and Simmons acknowledge that the enormous difference between the treatment of refugees in Europe and Africa may be a matter of racial discrimination. They report that wealthy donors in the developed world and the aid agencies they support feel more sympathy—and reach deeper into their pockets—for those with similar skin tones and back-grounds. They quote the opinion of a refugee worker who worked in both Africa and the Balkans that race plays a big role, and that it is easier for Europeans and Americans to identify with the Kosovo refugees they see on television than with those in remote parts of Africa.

According to Miller and Simmons some suggest that the differences in treatment are both explained and justified by the differences in the refugees' prior living standards:

> The primary explanation for the stark contrasts, according to U.N. and aid groups, is the difference between the backgrounds of the refugees on the two con-tinents.
>
> In Africa, where many refugees eke out an existence in seminomadic tribes, the bare provisions of shelter and health care offered by the refugee camps are a step up in life for many.
>
> But in Europe, where many of the refugees from Kosovo, a southern province of Serbia, the main Yugoslav republic, had two cars, a city apartment and their own business, a night in a canvas tent with cold food is misery.
>
> "You've got to maintain people's dignity," said Bob Allen, a camp manager who has worked in both Africa and Europe for the relief agency CARE.
>
> "The life in Africa is far more simple. To maintain the dignity and lifestyle of Europeans is far more difficult" (Miller & Simmons, 1999).

This reference to dignity resonates with human rights thinking. It suggests that in assuring the right to an adequate livelihood, "adequate" may have to be understood differently in different circumstances.

Should those who are used to having more get more in emergency situa-tions? Before answering too quickly, we should recall that in many assistance programs in developed countries, emergency assistance is explicitly designed to allow people to maintain the lifestyle to which they had been accustomed.

Also, it might be argued that richer people should get more generous assis-tance because their countries probably have contributed more to the supply of resources used for assistance. A contrary argument would be that richer people in trouble should get less from the global agencies because they have better prospects for getting help from other sources.

Maybe it does cost less to save poor people. Does this mean we should spend less on them, or does it perhaps means that we should save more of them?

How should donated food be distributed? In the abstract we might imagine a large-scale funneling operation in which there is first an allocation to continents, then to host countries, then to camps, and then to individual persons within camps. At each stage there would be a question of what allocation mechanisms and principles are in fact in place, and what mechanisms and principles should be in place. The first-order guideline might be that all individuals should get equal rations. However, it would quickly be seen that other considerations must be taken into account as well. Some people have greater needs than others. Some resourceful individuals are able to provide for themselves, at least in part. Some camps or some individuals may not be accessible. Corrections may have to be made for unauthorized redistribution that occurs within camps.

However, this funneling-down image is not appropriate because there is not one central pool of resources to be allocated. Most donor contributions are tied contributions, in the sense that they are designated for particular situations. Donors might not be willing to contribute as much if they did not get to decide where their contributions would be used.

Donor bias may be an accurate explanation of the skewed distribution of assistance, but it need not be accepted as a justification for those facts.

Even where good clear standards are set regarding appropriate food supplies and nutrition-related services, these standards frequently remain unmet. The reasons for gaps in supply and shortfalls in rations received are manifold and often context-specific. However, Mears (1998) groups the more important causes as follows:

o   Restricted access to the affected population for reasons of remote locations, insufficient infrastructure (roads, transport networks, etc.), seasonal closures, and possible insecurity
o   Lack of resources and variable donor commitment
o   Disagreement over accuracy of beneficiary numbers linked with registration
o   Erratic distribution system
o   Erratic monitoring of distribution and complaints

Donor countries provide much of the food supplied to refugees, either through direct commodity supplies or through the provision of funds to purchase foods on local markets. In addition, there is considerable self-provisioning by resourceful individual refugees. Self-provisioning may be based on gardening, raising small animals, or purchasing food in local markets. Trading outside of refugee camps can increase or decrease the total food supply within them.

The Human Right to Adequate Food

In this volume Nanda points out the absence of clear obligations of states with regard to refugees, but at the same time he observes, "Refugees and displaced persons are technically entitled to the protection of their basic human rights by the international community . . ." (See Nanda, Chapter 8). The international community is obligated to act to assure the realization of the human rights of refugees in much the same way as states are obligated to act to assure the realization of the human rights of all people living under their jurisdiction.

The human right to adequate food of refugees derives from the general human right to adequate food that applies to every individual (Kent, 2005). These rights must be understood, and then they must be interpreted in accordance with the particular circumstances of refugees.

The articulation of the human right to adequate food rights in modern international human rights law begins with the Universal Declaration of Human Rights of 1948. The declaration asserts in article 25(1) that "everyone has the right to a standard of living adequate for the health and well-being of himself and his family, including food . . ." (United Nations, 1948).

The right was reaffirmed in two major binding international agreements. In the International Covenant on Economic, Social and Cultural Rights (which came into force in 1976), article 11 says that "The States Parties to the present Covenant recognize the right of everyone to an adequate standard of living for himself and his family, including adequate food, clothing, and housing . . ." and also recognizes "the fundamental right of everyone to be free from hunger . . ." (United Nations, 1976).

In the Convention on the Rights of the Child (which came into force in 1990), two articles address the issues of food and nutrition. Article 24 says that "States Parties recognize the right of the child to the enjoyment of the highest attainable standard of health . . ." (United Nations, 1990, paragraph 1) and shall take appropriate measures "to combat disease and malnutrition . . . through the provision of adequate nutritious foods, clean drinking water, and health care" (paragraph 2c). Article 24 also says that States Parties shall take appropriate measures . . . " To ensure that all segments of society, in particular parents and children, are informed, have access to education and are supported in the use of basic knowledge of child health and nutrition [and] the advantages of breast-feeding. . ." Article 27 says in paragraph 3 that States Parties "shall in case of need provide material assistance and support programmes, particularly with regard to nutrition, clothing, and housing" (United Nations, 1990).

In human rights law, the call is not simply for adequate food but more broadly for an adequate standard of living. Article 25, paragraph 1 of the Universal Declaration of Human Rights (United Nations, 1948) says:

Everyone has the right to a standard of living adequate for the health and well-being of himself and of his family, including food, clothing, housing and medical care and necessary social services, and the right to security in the event of unemployment, sickness, disability, widowhood, old age or other lack of livelihood in circumstances beyond his control.

Thus, food is just one of several elements contributing to an adequate standard of living.

In November 1996, the World Food Summit concluded with agreement on the Rome Declaration on World Food Security and World Food Summit Plan of Action. The plan called for clarification of the meaning of the right to food. As part of that process, in April 1999 the United Nations' Sub-Committee on Nutrition held a major conference on "Adequate Food: A Human Right" (United Nations Administrative Committee on Coordination, Subcommittee on Nutrition, 1999). On May 12, 1999 the United Nations' Committee on Economic, Social and Cultural Rights released its General Comment 12 on The Right to Adequate Food (United Nations Committee on Economic, Social, and Cultural Rights, 1999). In paragraph 6 (United Nations Committee on Economic, Social, and Cultural Rights, 1999) the committee defined the right as follows:

The right to adequate food is realized when every man, woman and child, alone or in community with others, has physical and economic access at all times to adequate food or means for its procurement.

General Comment 12 provides an authoritative analysis of the meaning of the right to food. Further elaboration was provided by the release in June 1999 of Eide's *Updated Study on the Right to Food* (Eide, 1999).

Like all other human rights, the human right to adequate food should be recognized and realized because it is the right thing to do. However, taking the human rights approach can also provide other sorts of "value added," which have been articulated by the Office of the High Commissioner for Refugees (Jessen-Petersen, 1999, p. 32):

HCR fully favors the adoption of a rights-based approach in the refugee protection and assistance context. Its added value lies in the fact that a rights-based approach:

  o   Ensures that humanitarian action is based on the rights of the beneficiaries and is not simply a gratuitous act of charity
  o   Calls for treating the refugee as an "active claimant" and not merely a "passive recipient," hereby giving the refugee a voice and power with which to participate to seek to meet their own basic needs
  o   Underlines the legal obligations of States to meet the basic needs of the most vulnerable individuals (including refugees), and ensures that the work of humanitarian agencies such as UNHCR provides support to

States in fulfilling their responsibilities, rather than being a substitute for State action (or inaction)

o   Helps provide a principled, predictable and structured framework within which humanitarian work can be undertaken and this, in turn, will help to define both the objective and content of humanitarian aid more clearly—particularly in the development and implementation of policy and programs

o   Places humanitarian action within a rights-based framework that serves to define more clearly the respective areas of expertise and the responsibilities of the many different humanitarian actors (e.g., UNHCR and WFP have signed a Memorandum of Understanding which covers co-operation in the provision of food aid to refugees, returnees and, in specific situations, internally-displaced persons.)

o   Provides a stronger incentive for donor support for humanitarian efforts as traditional donor States (and their constituencies) often have a well-developed awareness of human rights as a basis for government action and by moving the debate away from charity (where the usual arguments of compassion fatigue and prioritization are invoked) to the language of rights and duties, the imperative for donor support can be made more forcefully.

Rights-based nutrition programs for refugees may be more efficient and effective than many of the current programs. However, even if that were not so, as a matter of principle it is important that rights of refugees in regard to nutrition and other matters are clarified and honored.

The Adequacy Question

Basic standards for nutrition have been worked out in several different contexts. Some focus on food requirements, while others consider food as only one part of a broader set of services. Food-based standards take forms such as recommended daily allowances. In contrast, a broader, service-based set of standards is illustrated by the "nutrition minimum package" for children designed by the program called BASICS—Basic Support for Institutionalized Child Survival (Sanghvi, 1997). The Sphere Project has formulated detailed minimum standards for nutrition and food aid in humanitarian assistance (Sphere Project, 2000). For refugees in particular, the World Food Programme and the United Nations High Commissioner for Refugees have established Guidelines for Calculating Food Rations for Refugees (World Food Programme and High Commissioner for Refugees, 1997).

Biologically, the basic nutrient requirements are roughly the same for all human beings of about the same size. Thus, it might seem that what constitutes "adequate food" could be addressed as a purely technical question, with answers differentiated only on the basis of data on the individual's age, gender, and body weight. Standards for refugees might reasonably be adapted from other sectors, such as the military (Committee on Military Nutrition Research, 1999). The concern with establishing basic minimum standards on the basis of technical considerations alone leads naturally to the design of some sort of standardized meal that could be packaged in a factory and distributed in mass quantities. Thus we now have the standard Humanitarian Daily Ration, comparable to the U.S. military's MREs—Meals Ready to Eat.

This purely technical perspective is much too narrow. Human rights advocates recognize that the feedlot approach to nutrition violates human dignity. It fails to recognize that food is only one element in the broader context of a right to adequate livelihood, and that in turn is embedded in the entire human rights framework. The human right to adequate food must be realized in a way that does not violate the individual's other human rights. General Comment 12's (United Nations Committee on Economic, Social, and Cultural Rights, 1999) paragraph 7 acknowledges that "The precise meaning of 'adequacy' is to a large extent determined by prevailing social, economic, cultural, climatic, ecological and other conditions . . ." Paragraph 8 explains that the core content of the right to adequate food implies:

> The availability of food in a quantity and quality sufficient to satisfy the dietary needs of individuals, free from adverse substances, and acceptable within a given culture;
>   The accessibility of such food in ways that are sustainable and that do not interfere with the enjoyment of other human rights.

These elements are then explained further in the subsequent paragraphs. Paragraph 11, for example, explains that "Cultural or consumer acceptability implies the need also to take into account, as far as possible, perceived nonnutrient-based values attached to food and food consumption . . ." Thus, there is no suggestion that all individuals—or all refugees—must be treated identically.

There is a difference between treating people equitably (fairly) and treating them equally (identically). Hardly anyone would argue that everyone should be paid the same regardless of what work they do, but we should all insist that people are treated equitably, with, for example, equal pay for equal work. Making everyone eat the same thing (as in a prison) might be equal treatment, but it would be far more equitable and dignified to recognize that there are differences among people, and give them all some appropriate choices.

There is a serious practical problem that would arise if all refugees were treated identically. If refugees everywhere were to be provided with the same standard of service—somewhere between that provided to the Europeans and that provided to the Africans—there would be enormous management problems. Europeans would be dissatisfied. In Africa, people might rush to be identified as refugees and try to get into refugee camps because that would make them materially better off than they had been. Since people and their circumstances differ, there is no reason to believe that treating everyone identically, regardless of their circumstances, would contribute to maintaining reasonable standards of human dignity. The answer must lie somewhere between the highly skewed system now in place and the mechanistic ideal of treating everyone the same, without consideration of their particular circumstances.

In designing a rights approach to the nutrition of refugees generally, it might be sensible to begin with a focus on the most vulnerable among them. Guidance might be drawn from the guidelines for infant feeding in emergencies proposed by the Emergency Nutrition Network (Ad Hoc Group on Infant Feeding in Emergencies, 1998). Or one could begin with clear rights particularly for those who are severely malnourished. The World Health Organization's manual on Management of Severe Malnutrition is generally useful, and Chapter 8 provides suggestions specifically for "Management of Malnutrition in Disaster Situations and Refugee Camps" (World Health Organization, 1999).

In setting standards of adequacy, it may be useful to focus more on the results obtained than on the specific character of the "inputs." That is, instead of focusing narrowly on nutrition, it might be more useful to focus on objectives relating to the broader concept of adequate livelihood. A basic measure here would be survival. We might say that the core objective of nutrition programs for refugees should be to minimize morbidity and mortality associated with malnutrition. The level of nutrition-related services required to achieve this should be viewed as the minimum requirement.

From this perspective, any enhancement of nutrition-related services beyond the level that would reduce morbidity and mortality could be viewed as a luxury. If European refugees would not die if they were not given raspberry tarts, maybe they should not be given tarts. Of course, if they found a way to make or buy tarts with the basic resources provided to them, that would be their choice to make.

The concern here is with the minimum obligations of the international community and its representatives such as the World Food Program, the United Nations High Commissioner for Refugees, and the International Federation of Red Cross and Red Crescent Societies. Other parties might want to provide extra rations for particular refugees because of cultural affinities, shared religions, kinship, or other reasons. They should be free to do so. For example, in the humanitarian assistance it provides, Saudi Arabia should be free to favor other Muslim countries. But that assistance should be provided directly, and not through the WFP, UNHCR, and IFRC. The international governmental agencies should be obligated to provide assistance without discrimination based on the recipients' religious, cultural or other characteristics.

People Must Be Respected

Suppose that the cheapest way to provide the basic nutrients that would keep people alive is through mass-produced pellets, optimized in the way a feedlot manager would calculate the most cost-effective mix of feed components. Deviating from this standardized pellet to accommodate special needs would be costly. If the money available for food is limited, we face a dilemma: should we distribute the pellets to as many needy people as possible, thus maximizing the number of lives saved? Or should we accommodate special needs, allowing people to live with at least some measure of human dignity, even if that means that fewer lives are saved?

My answer is to refuse to accept this formulation of the problem. With appropriate enabling conditions, people are producers of food, and not just consumers. People are smarter and more industrious than cattle. People must be respected and treated as capable human beings. Instead of investing effort into designing the best possible pellet, we should be finding ways to enable people to move progressively toward providing for themselves as they would in a normal, healthy society. Moving toward feedlot types of operations moves us toward the wrong kind of governance, whether in refugee camps or in other social situations. While highly standardized rations might be sensible for a short period in acute crisis situations, creating sustained dependency on feed pellets or prepackaged rations would disempower people. In all circumstances, people must be treated in ways that empower then.

While there are serious problems of obtaining and allocating scarce resources, some of what is required is not so scarce. Nutrition status depends not only on food supplies but also on health services and on care, especially for children. For small children, who are most vulnerable to malnutrition, the critical issue may not be food supply as such but the supply of appropriate health and care services. For example, conditions supportive of proper breastfeeding can make a very big difference. Refugees themselves can participate in the production, preparation, and distribution of food, and they can participate in the delivery of health and care services. In other words, refugees themselves can to some extent be viewed as assets, as resources for addressing the issues of concern to them.

Rights Systems

Useful guidance for the management of humanitarian assistance is already provided in various forms. For example, the Fundamental Principles of the International Red Cross and Red Crescent Movement speaks (International Federation of the Red Cross, 1996) of the principles of humanity, impartiality, neutrality, independence, voluntary service, unity, and universality. There is a Code of Conduct for the International Red Cross and Red Crescent Movements and

NGOs in Disaster Relief (International Red Cross and Red Crescent Society, 1995). As noted earlier, in the section on adequacy, a great deal of work has already been done to specify appropriate nutrition standards in assistance programs. Specifying what foods and nutrition-related services refugees ought to get is useful, but more than that is required to assure the realization of their human right to food and nutrition. These different pieces might be brought together systematically through more explicit use of the rights framework.

A rights system can be understood as a kind of cybernetic self-regulating arrangement designed to assure that rights are realized. In any cybernetic system, a goal is decided upon, and means are established for reaching that goal. In addition, there are specific means for making corrections in case there are deviations from the path toward the goal. This is the self-regulating aspect of the system. Rights systems function in this way. Any government may have policies saying, for example, that there is to be freedom of speech, and social security, and many other good things. They may even be promised in the nation's constitution. But we know that there are many cases in which governments go off course and fail to deliver on their promises. In nations where there is an effective rights system, however, there are specific mechanisms for calling the government to account, that is, for making course corrections. The most fundamental of these mechanisms of accountability is for rights holders themselves to have effective remedies through which they can complain and have the government's behavior corrected. Human rights rest on the legal principle *ubi jus ibi remedium*—where there is a right there must be a remedy.

On the basis of this understanding, we can say that any rights system has three distinct parties: those who are the rights holders, those who are the duty bearers, and those who are the agents of accountability. The task of the agents of accountability is to make sure that those who have the duty carry out their obligations to those who have the rights.

To describe a rights system, we need to know the identities and functions of these three parties, and we would also want to know the mechanisms or structures through which these functions are to be carried out. Thus, we would want to know:

o   The nature of the rights holders and their rights
o   The nature of the duty-bearers and their obligations corresponding to the rights of the rights holders
o   The nature of the agents of accountability, and the procedures through which they assure that the duty bearers meet their obligations to the rights holders. The accountability mechanisms include, in particular, the remedies available to the rights holders themselves

While there are many different kinds of rights systems, the global human rights system is distinctive in that it deals only with rights that are universal, enjoyed by all individuals simply by virtue of their being human.

This three-part framework can be used by any national government or other sort of administrative unit concerned with drafting law or policy designed to assure the realization of rights. This framework can also be used for adapting specific programs such as national welfare programs or nutrition programs to conform to the human rights approach. The program's policies may be reformulated so that its clients have clear entitlements to its services, and so that the program makes explicit commitments to honor those entitlements. That commitment can be made concrete by establishing a complaint procedure through which those who feel they have not obtained their entitlements can get a fair hearing and, if necessary, have the situation corrected.

Specifying the Obligations

Having rights means having clear entitlements to particular services, and this requires more than establishing aspirational standards. It is also necessary to establish institutional arrangements that will assure that the standards will be met. Where refugees have specific rights, the obligations of others to assure their realization should be specified. Careful distinctions must be made between the obligations of host states and the obligations of the international community. In general, the obligation of host states is to assure that the rights of refugees are recognized as equivalent to the rights of others under their jurisdiction. Since many host states have limited capacity to provide the resources needed for refugees or for their own people, the international community must be viewed as the backup, the provider of last resort.

A human-rights based approach would begin with the concept that refugees, as individuals, have specific rights, and included among these are specific entitlements in relation to food and nutrition. However, specifying what the refugees ought to get, framed perhaps as minimum standards, is not enough. If refugees have rights to these services, there must be institutional arrangements in place to assure that these standards are met. Thus, the specific corresponding obligations of the host state and of the international community must be spelled out, and suitable accountability mechanisms must be put in place.

The rights and the corresponding obligations need to be concretized. For example, the position taken might be that "Every refugee has a right to consume at least 1900 calories per day" or "Every refugee under five years of age has a right to be at least 80 percent of his/her standard weight." If the international community accepts this, it is then obligated to do whatever needs to be done to realize that right. The international community has the same four levels of obligation identified for the host state in General Comment 12 (United Nations Committee on Economic, Social, and Cultural Rights, 1999), namely

   o   to respect existing access to adequate food

- o to protect (in order to) ensure that enterprises or individuals do not deprive individuals of their access to adequate food
- o to fulfil (facilitate) (in order to) strengthen people's access to and utilization of resources and means to ensure their livelihood, including food security.
- o to fulfil (provide) the right to adequate food.

Limiting the Obligations

The international governmental agencies that assist refugees such as UNHCR, WFP, and IFRC are constrained because they only pass through resources provided by donors. They are agents of the international community, not the international community itself. The obligations fall ultimately on the nations of the world, not on the agents that administer the resources. In time it may be feasible to create a form of international taxation so that all members of the international community contribute their fair share. However, so long as taxation is not feasible, the question is whether donors would be willing to make concrete long-term commitments, accepting them as obligations. Are the donor nations of the world willing to commit themselves to, say, assuring that all refugees will have at least some specified quantity and quality of food and some basic package of services?

It is possible for international commitments to be open-ended. In regard to security issues, for example, the UN Security Council frequently authorizes members to "take all necessary measures" to achieve a given objective. With regard to issues of humanitarian assistance, however, the international community tends to be more cautious. Those who are obligated to assure the realization of rights will resist if there is no clear limit to those obligations. For example, if a commitment was made to provide 1900 calories a day to all refugees, and there was no fixed limit to the number of refugees, that would be an open-ended commitment. Entitlements must somehow be capped. Rights to food or nutrition must be stated in terms of concrete rules specifying what categories of people are entitled to what sort of goods and services under what conditions. There must be clarity not only with regard to their entitlements but also with regard to their limits.

Whether or not the donors are able to make firm commitments, the agencies could adopt principles based on the human right to adequate food to guide the allocation of whatever resources are available to them. For example, it could be said that no matter what total amount of food is provided to a particular camp, each individual in the camp is entitled to an equal share of it, or that children must have their needs fulfilled before others.

The objective of a rights-based approach to assistance is not necessarily to demand that more resources should be provided; it is also important to assure that the resources that are available are used effectively for meeting needs. The argument to the donors is that under this approach they would not necessarily be spending more; they would be spending better. Clear recognition of the human right to adequate food can provide a means for introducing effective performance accountability, and thus increase the efficiency and effectiveness of refugee nutrition programs.

The Work Ahead

It would be useful to have a clear statement of principles or guidelines regarding refugees' human right to adequate food, the obligations of host states and the international community, and the mechanisms of accountability. This should be worked out with participation from representatives of the refugees themselves, the assistance agencies (both governmental and nongovernmental), the donor agencies, and human rights agencies. To launch the effort, guidance should be drawn not only from international human rights law but also from the several different statements of principle that have been formulated to guide humanitarian assistance activities.

In a very preliminary way, we can suggest some of the basic principles to be considered. For example, there should be a principle of non-discrimination. This does not mean that everyone should be treated identically. Rather, it means that no groups should be singled out to be treated in ways that are harmful to them or that put them at a disadvantage. To the extent feasible, assistance should be provided through means that are empowering and that respect the dignity of those who receive that assistance. Nutrition-related services, and not just the food, should be provided in culturally appropriate ways.

The helplessness that appears to overwhelm many refugees comes in part from the ways in which they are treated (Soguk, 1999). As in any normal society, refugees themselves should have ample and steadily increasing opportunities to participate in providing for their own nutrition and other needs. Means must be found to increasingly involve refugees themselves in making the decisions and taking the actions that affect their situations.

Human rights work means much more than setting standards. There is a need to acknowledge that refugees have specific human rights in relation to food and nutrition. The corresponding obligations must be plainly identified, and there must be a system for holding those who carry the obligations accountable. Most importantly, refugees themselves must know to what services they are entitled, and they and their representatives must have some effective means for holding those responsible to account. Where there are no effective remedies, there are no effective rights.

Refugees' human right to adequate food, or indeed all the human rights of refugees, are not special. Refugees are not a distinct species with distinct incapacities. Their circumstances of the moment may be special, but their rights as human beings are not. They are entitled to the same things as everyone else who is human, and this means they have a right to live a life that is as normal as possible. They must be enabled to grasp increasing control over the shape of their own lives. They must be increasingly enabled to provide for themselves. This means that their human rights must be recognized and realized.

The primary obligation for assuring the realization of human rights rests with the state. Where that obligation is not or cannot be carried out, for whatever reason, specific obligations then fall on the international community. Those obligations of the international community with regard to human rights need to be acknowledged, clarified, and carried out.

Notes

1.   These publications can be accessed through http://www.unsystem.org/scn/ Publications/html/rnis.html. Overviews of refugee nutrition also are provided in the periodic reports on *The World Nutrition Situation* from the United Nations System's Standing Committee on Nutrition.

References

Ad Hoc Group on Infant Feeding in Emergencies (1998). *Infant feeding in emergencies: Policy, strategy and practice.* Dublin, UK: Emergency Nutrition Network, Department of Community Health and General Practice.

Committee on Military Nutrition Research, Institute of Medicine (1999). *Military strategies for sustainment of nutrition and immune function in the field.* Washington, DC: National Academy Press.

Eide, A. (1999). *The right to adequate food and to be free from hunger: Updated study on the right to food.* E/CN/4/Sub.2/199/12, 28 June. Geneva, Switzerland: United Nations Economic and Social Council. Commission on Human Rights. Sub-Commission on Prevention of Discrimination and Protection of Minorities.

International Federation of Red Cross and Red Crescent Societies (1996). *The fundamental principles of the International Red Cross and Red Crescent Movement.*

International Red Cross and Red Crescent Society (ICRC) (1995). Code of conduct for the International Red Cross and Red Crescent Movement and NGOs in disaster relief. *International Review of the Red Cross, 310,* p. 119.

Jessen-Petersen, S. (1999). Food as an integral part of international protection. *SCN News, 18* (July), pp. 32-33.

Kent, G. (1994). The roles of international organizations in advancing nutrition rights. *Food Policy, 19(4),* pp. 357-366.

Kent, G. (2005). *Freedom from Want: The Human Right to Adequate Food.* Washington, D.C.: Georgetown University Press, 2005.

Mears, C and Young, H. (1998). *Acceptability and use of cereal-based foods in refugee camps: Case studies from Nepal, Ethiopia, and Tanzania.* Oxford, UK: Oxfam Working Paper.

Miller, T. C and Simmons, A. (1999). Relief camps for Africans, Kosovars worlds apart. *Los Angeles Times,* May 21, 1999.

Nanda, V. P. (2006). History and foundations for refugee security, health and well-being under international law. See Chapter 8.

Sanghvi, T and Murray, J. (1997). *Improving child health through nutrition: The nutrition minimum package.* Arlington, VA: Basic Support for Institutionalizing Child Survival (BASICS) Project, for the U.S. Agency for International Development.

Save the Children Fund UK (1997). *Household food economy analysis: Kakuma Refugee Camp, Kenya.* Nairobi, Kenya: SCF-UK Food Economy Assessment Team.

Soguk, N. (1999). *States and strangers: Refugees and displacements of statecraft.* Minneapolis, MN: University of Minnesota Press.

Sphere Project (2000). *The Sphere Project: Humanitarian charter and minimum standards in disaster response.* Geneva, Switzerland: The Sphere Project.

United Nations (1948). *Universal Declaration of Human Rights.* United Nations General Assembly Resolution 217A (III).

United Nations (1976). *International Covenant on Economic, Social and Cultural Rights.* http://www.unhcr.ch/html/menu3/b/a_cescr.htm

United Nations (1990). *Convention on the Rights of the Child.* http://www.unhchr.ch/html/menu3/b/k2crc.htm

United Nations Administrative Committee on Coordination, Sub-Committee on Nutrition (1999). Special issue, *Adequate Food: A Human Right. SCN News,* 18(July). www.unsystem.org/asccsn.

United Nations Administrative Committee on Coordination, Subcommittee on Nutrition (1999). *Adequate food: A human right.* New York, NY: United Nations.

United Nations Economic and Social Council, Committee on Economic, Social and Cultural Rights (1999). *Substantive issues arising in the implementation of the International Covenant on economic, Social and Cultural Rights: General Comment 12 (Twentieth Session, 1999), The Right to Adequate Food (art. 11), ECOSOC E/C.12/1999/5.* Geneva, Switzerland: United Nations.

World Food Programme and United Nations High Commissioner for Refugees (1997). *Guidelines for Calculating Food Rations for Refugees.* New York, NY: United Nations.

World Food Summit (1996). *Rome declaration on the world food security and world food summit plan of action.* New York, NY: United Nations.

World Health Organization (1999). *Management of severe malnutrition: A manual for physicians and other senior health workers.* Geneva, Switzerland: WHO.

CHAPTER 4

The Evolving Role of Relief Organizations in Human Rights and Protection

Richard J. Brennan
Gerald Martone

The primary mission of non-governmental organizations (NGOs) involved in humanitarian assistance is to provide emergency relief to those affected by disasters. This assistance usually involves the provision of food, shelter, water, medical services, vaccinations, and other essential items and services. The relief NGOs have traditionally had a limited role in addressing issues such as human rights violations and refugee protection, as these areas have generally been considered the responsibility of governments, United Nation (UN) agencies, and human rights groups. Over the past 15 years, however, relief NGOs have found themselves increasingly in environments where they are forced to respond to the consequences of war crimes, atrocities, and blatant abuses of human rights (Waldman and Martone, 1999). Crises in Afghanistan, Somalia, Rwanda, Bosnia, Liberia, East Timor, Sudan, Northern Uganda, the Democratic Republic of Congo and many other countries have forced NGOs to reconsider their missions, their responsibilities, and the moral and ethical principles that guide their activities.

According to the World Health Organization's Report on Violence and Health, the twentieth century was perhaps the most violent period in human history (World Health Organization, 2002). Relentless open warfare, ethnic violence, and political oppression ravaged over thirty countries around the world. Contemporary warfare, especially since the end of the Cold War, has been a particularly brutal conflagration of terror tactics in which non-professional armies and insurgents—ignorant of or unconcerned with the Geneva conventions and the rules of war—routinely denied the basic rights of civilians and defy their dignity (Burkle, 1999). Fighting armies and rebel groups use forced movements and violent deportations of people as a deliberate military strategy.

Thus humanitarian agencies are finding themselves in situations where they must be more circumspect and re-evaluate their approach to these brutal and unspeakable situations. Rather than responding to acts of nature, humanitarian aid workers are directly confronting the consequences of unconscionable abuses of the most basic of human rights and the perverse humiliation of life in exile.

In order to better envision the role of relief NGOs in the area of human rights, it is necessary to review several bodies of international law, the principles underlying those laws, and the mandates of organizations responsible for implementing and enforcing them. From there it will be possible to outline the dilemmas that relief NGOs must address in responding to human rights and protection issues, and their ultimate roles and responsibilities in these areas.

Human Rights: History and Definition

The term "human rights" is relatively new, only coming into common usage since the end of World War II and the establishment of the United Nations. But the modern concept of human rights has its historical origins in ancient Greece and Rome where the doctrines of natural law initially developed. The evolution of the concept of natural law, which emphasized the duties of man, to the set of values and principles that we acknowledge today as human rights has therefore taken close to 2,000 years. The specifics of those rights have been codified and developed in a series of documents that has included the Magna Carta (1215), the English Bill of Rights (1689), the American Declaration of Independence (1776), the American Bill of Rights (1791), and the Universal Declaration of Human Rights (1948) (Robertson, 1999).

It is probably fair to assert that there is today widespread acceptance of the principle of human rights throughout the world. There is, however, no universal agreement on the definition, nature or scope of these rights. Indeed, the spectrum of rights claimed by groups and individuals continues to grow. To better understand the development and the content of modern human rights, it is useful to consider the "three generations of human rights" (Weston, 1991).

The first generation of civil and political rights stressed the concept of liberty. They are outlined in Articles 2 to 21 of the Universal Declaration of Human Rights. Included among them are freedom from all forms of racial discrimination; the right to life, liberty and security of person; freedom from torture; freedom from arbitrary arrest; the right to a fair and public trial; the right to seek asylum from persecution (but not the right to be granted asylum); freedom of religion; freedom of speech; freedom of association; and the right to private property. The main emphasis is on freedom from externally applied limitations, rather than on rights to certain entitlements. These rights have their roots in the reformist movements of the seventeenth and eighteenth centuries, and are closely associated with the English, American, and French revolutions. They stress liberal individualism and the limited role of government, thereby safeguarding society against the abuse and misuse of political power.

The second generation of social, economic, and cultural rights emphasizes egalitarianism. These rights have their origins in the socialist traditions of the nineteenth century and represent a reaction to the abuses of capitalist development. In particular, second generation rights developed out of a response to the exploitation of the working class and of the colonial peoples by industrialists and other business leaders. They are outlined in Articles 22 to 27 of the Universal Declaration of Human Rights. They include the right to social security; the right to work; the right to equal pay for equal work; the right to rest and leisure; the right to a standard of living adequate for the health and well-being of self and family; and the right to education. This set of values stress rights to entitlements, rather than freedom from limitations, and therefore imply a greater involvement of the state in the life of the community.

The third generation of solidarity rights stresses the concept of fraternity, or brotherhood. It has its origin in the twentieth century and reflects, in part, the emergence of the Developing World. These rights are less clearly defined than the first two generations of rights, but are implied in Article 28 of the Universal Declaration of Human Rights. They include the right to self-determination; the right to development; the right to peace; the right to a healthy environment; and the right to disaster relief. Solidarity rights are more collective in nature than other human rights, which place greater emphasis on the individual. They are also more difficult to legislate and to enforce.

The relative importance, priority, and acceptability of each generation of rights varies among societies. The Western democratic tradition places greater emphasis on civil and political rights, while other states such as China give greater priority to social and economic rights. The United Nations has adopted a holistic approach to its definition of human rights and has affirmed the interdependence of all three generations of rights.

In addition to the Universal Declaration of Human Rights of 1948, several key documents have elaborated and further defined the scope of human rights. These human rights "instruments" include a number of United Nations treaties, conventions, declarations, and principles. Together, they constitute the core of what is known as international human rights law. Key among them are the Covenant on Economic, Social and Cultural Rights (1966); the Covenant on Civil and Political Rights (1966); the Convention on Elimination of Racial Discrimination (1965); the Convention on Elimination of All Forms of Discrimination Against Women (1979); the Convention Against Torture (1984); and the Convention on the Rights of the Child (1989).

In most of the conflicts and complex humanitarian emergencies of the past two decades, all of these human rights are regularly violated. Of particular concern is the fact that many belligerents continually ignore the most basic of rights afforded to civilians: the right to life, liberty, and security. Summary executions, mass killings, rape, abductions, torture, and ethnic cleansing represent the most extreme forms of human rights violations (Robertson, 1999). These abuses pose great challenges to relief NGOs, whose primary mission is to provide humanitarian assistance to the victims of disasters. The scale of brutality and inhumanity witnessed by these organizations in recent years demands a response. The question of roles and responsibilities of relief NGOs in the promotion, protection, and monitoring of human rights presents several dilemmas.

International Humanitarian Law and Human Rights

Complex humanitarian emergencies (CHEs) usually occur in the context of military conflict, exposing civilians to the violence of war. The obligations of warring parties during military conflict are outlined in a series of documents that together constitute international humanitarian law (IHL). Chief among these documents are the four Geneva Conventions, the two Additional Protocols, and the Hague Convention. IHL is the dominant body of international law that applies during times of warfare. Although international human rights law is also applicable during conflict, IHL takes precedence at these times. The complex emergencies of the past two decades have been characterized by gross violations of both bodies of law.

The history, principles, and assumptions behind IHL and international human rights law demonstrate some significant differences (Bruderlein, 1999). IHL had its origins in 19th century Europe as a reaction to the horrors and carnage of war. The subsequent development of the Geneva Conventions aimed to protect non-combatants, by placing constraints on the conduct of war. The four Geneva Conventions outline the obligations of the warring parties in the care of wounded soldiers, in the treatment of shipwrecked sailors, in the conduct towards prisoners of war, and in the protection of civilians (Perrin, 1996). IHL does not aim to prevent war, to end war, or even to promote justice. Rather, it accepts conflict as a normal part of the human condition and therefore outlines the rules by which war should be conducted.

While the foundation of IHL has always been on humanitarian principles, the signatories of the Geneva Conventions were motivated in large part by self-interest and pragmatism. The signatories to the First Geneva Convention in 1864 agreed to protect the enemy's wounded, as they believed that their own wounded would also require protection. The Second (1906) and Third (1929) Geneva Conventions aimed to provide safeguards for shipwrecked sailors and prisoners of war respectively, as these young men would be needed to contribute to the development of growing industries back in their own countries at the end of the conflict. This appeal to self-interest and pragmatism stands in contrast to the principles of international human rights law, which invokes universal and inalienable rights rooted in natural law as a means of justification.

In addition to the two underlying principles of self-interest and pragmatism, the Geneva Conventions were initially drafted on two main assumptions. The first of these was that there was little military advantage in the deliberate targeting of civilians. In fact this tactic had been considered a potential disadvantage by military strategists, as the main purpose of battle was to defeat the opposing military force. Targeting civilians would result in the diversion of war-fighting resources, the consumption of ammunition, and moral outrage among civilized populations. Protection of civilians during times of war was codified in the Fourth Geneva Convention of 1949. The second assumption was that the conduct of combatants was already subject to a code of what has been termed the "warrior's honor" (Ignatieff, 1997). This code provides the soldier with a moral and ethical construct to guide his/her conduct on the field of battle. It serves to restrain the soldier from committing the worst of abuses and violations. The concept of a warrior's honor has long existed in history and appears to be present in most cultures. In fact, there is evidence to suggest that soldiers comply more vigorously with their own code of honor than to a civilian rule of law. Legal consequences are poor deterrents for adherence to the rules of engagement during war in the lawless environments of contemporary conflicts.

The two assumptions of non-targeting of civilians and of the recognition of a warrior's code break down during many of today's complex humanitarian emergencies. The observance of IHL in these conflicts has therefore been poor and its enforcement problematic. To understand the reasons for these difficulties, it is important to consider the settings in which IHL was initially conceived and how the nature of today's wars has changed. IHL has its roots in a period when wars were fought between professional armies, usually from different nations within Europe. It has been cynically described as representing the "European rules of war" and as codifying the "European warriors' honor." But many of today's wars are fought by untrained, undisciplined, and non-professional soldiers in Africa, Asia and Eastern Europe, who have never heard of the Geneva Conventions (Burkle, 1999). The irregular forces, private armies, rebel militias, and mercenaries involved in today's conflicts frequently follow no clear chain of command. In many recent wars, the deliberate targeting of civilians is a major military tactic, the goals of which are to intimidate, to terrorize, and to ethnically cleanse. The warrior's honor is frequently an unfamiliar concept, especially where soldiers are encouraged to commit atrocities such as rape, summary executions, and mass killings. It has been difficult to convince child soldiers in Sierra Leone, militant Islamic fighters in Afghanistan, or irregular Serbian forces in Kosovo of the need to observe the laws of war. The example of Serbia is particularly illustrative of this point, as it is known that soldiers of the Yugoslav People's Army had been well-trained in the Geneva Conventions.

In spite of widespread disregard and violations, IHL remains highly relevant in today's conflicts. Protection of non-combatants, especially civilians, is still considered a major priority by the United Nations agencies, humanitarian organizations, and international governments that respond to CHEs (Paul, 1995). Because abuses of both IHL and international human rights law occur during CHEs, and that there are overlaps between these bodies of law, there has been an increased interest and involvement of human rights organizations in the response to conflict. But IHL remains the dominant body of law that applies to situations of war, as it clearly sets out the responsibilities of the warring parties. In addition, authorities can never derogate or repeal IHL but they may derogate their

responsibilities under international human rights law in exceptional circumstances.

The increasing convergence and overlap of activities by organizations committed to the promotion of both IHL and human rights has been reflected in the
development of a number of recent documents. The most important among
these are the Ottawa Landmines Treaty, the UN's Guiding Principles for the
Protection of Internally Displaced Persons, and the Optional Protocol to the
Convention of the Rights of the Child, which sets a minimum age of 18 years for
enrollment in military duty.

Refugee Rights

Refugees are entitled to the basic rights outlined in the Universal Declaration of
Human Rights and the Geneva Conventions. However, because their rights
have been violated in their own states, and they have been forced to seek asylum
in other countries, refugees have a special status under international law (United
Nations High Commission for Refugees, 1999). The special rights of refugees
have been outlined in the 1951 Convention Relating to the Status of Refugees.
Some of these rights may be restricted during emergencies, as may the rights of
any citizen.

The key rights guaranteed under the Convention include freedom from discrimination; freedom of religion; free access to the courts of law of all signatory
states of the Convention; the right to housing; the right to education; the right to
emergency relief and assistance; freedom of movement within the territory; and
the right not to be expelled from the country of asylum, unless the refugee poses
a threat to national security or public order.

The most important right guaranteed to refugees under the Convention is the
right to be protected against forcible return ("refoulement") to the territory from
which they have fled. The principle of non-refoulement is well established in
international law, as it is addressed in a number of other international conventions and declarations. Therefore, all states are obliged to respect this principle,
whether or not they are signatories to the Refugee Convention.

The status of internally displaced persons (IDPs) under international law is
less well established than that of refugees. While the Universal Declaration of
Human Rights does apply to IDPs, they are not strictly guaranteed the same
rights to protection under the Refugee Convention. The difference between a
refugee and an IDP is therefore both technical (refugees have crossed an international border; IDPs remain within the borders of their own country) and legal.
The United Nations High Commissioner for Refugees (UNHCR), whose mandate is to protect refugees, has been granted the authority to also address the
needs of IDPs, only on an ad hoc basis, by the United Nations (United Nations
High Commission for Refugees, 1999).

The term "protection" refers to the spectrum of activities that are designed
and undertaken to ensure the rights of refugees and other vulnerable groups.
Protection has faced greater challenges in recent years, as the rights of war-

affected populations are regularly violated (Leaning, 1999). The issue of enforcing protection has presented the international community with a number of legal, ethical, and practical dilemmas.

In the one unifying covenant governing humanitarian conduct, the Code of Conduct for the International Red Cross and Red Crescent Movement and NGOs in Disaster Relief, none of the ten principles delineates a commitment to the protection of vulnerable civilian populations. The practical dimensions of political advocacy, community mobilization and public protest are conspicuously absent. This critical gap in an otherwise practical code demonstrates how reluctant aid agencies have been in dealing with the intransigent root causes of abuse.

Enforcement of International Human Rights Law, IHL, and Refugee Law

Responsibilities and mandates for ensuring compliance with IHL, international human rights law, and refugee law are shared among a number of governmental, United Nations, intergovernmental, and non-governmental agencies and bodies. But the mechanisms developed to ensure that these bodies of law are observed have failed to meet their stated objectives in many recent CHEs. The result has been a failure to ensure protection of, and assistance to, war-affected populations. To better understand these problems, it is useful to discuss the responsibilities and limitations of governments and other agencies in the implementation of IHL and human rights.

States have the primary responsibility for compliance with all forms of international law. The main obligation for the implementation of IHL lies with the governments and combatants involved in the conflict. Ironically it is these very actors that are usually responsible for the greatest violations of IHL today. This issue presents several problems as the Geneva Conventions do not outline any penalties for non-compliance, nor do they specify any external mechanism of enforcement, should the involved parties fail to meet their obligations.

In response to the failure of governments to address severe abuses of IHL and human rights, the United Nations and the international community may mobilize international peacekeeping forces. Too often, however, there has been a lack of political will to ensure that the mandates of these forces include protection of civilians and other vulnerable groups. This has resulted in ongoing abuses of IHL and human rights despite the presence of international peacekeepers. The mandate of UNPROFOR (United Nations Protection Force in former Yugoslavia), for example, was to ensure the protection of the humanitarian aid effort, but it did not extend to the protection of civilians. Major atrocities, such as the massacre of over 6,000 men from the Bosnian town of Srebrenica in 1995, demonstrated that the mere presence of international peacekeepers could not guarantee the protection of civilians. A similar situation occurred when the

UNAMIR (United Nations Mission in Rwanda) forces failed to intervene in the genocide of over 500,000 Rwandan Tutsis and moderate Hutus in 1994.

Under the Geneva Conventions, the International Committee of the Red Cross (ICRC) has a special role in implementing IHL. It is officially the promoter and custodian of IHL, and is therefore involved in both protection and assistance activities. Its roles include informing warring parties of their obligations under IHL; visiting prisoners of war; monitoring compliance with IHL; informing combatants of their observations and making recommendations; tracing missing persons; and the provision of humanitarian aid. But ICRC is not always present in all zones of conflict and does not always have the resources to adequately respond to the protection needs of war-affected populations. In addition, ICRC has been criticized for its refusal to publicize flagrant abuses of IHL and human rights because of its policies of neutrality and impartiality.

The mandate of the United Nations High Commissioner for Refugees is to provide international protection to refugees, consistent with the rights outlined in the Refugee Convention. One of its main roles is to coordinate the activities of non-governmental organizations concerned with the welfare of refugees, including protection. But UNHCR does not always have the field presence nor the resources to adequately protect refugees. It has therefore been criticized for failing to provide adequate protection to civilians in a number of recent conflicts, including Afghanistan, Somalia, Bosnia, and Chechnya. And although its statute allows UNHCR to have operational involvement with non-refugees, the responsibilities of UNHCR for IDPs are less well defined and predetermined than its responsibilities for refugees.

In light of the increased brutality and impunity of recent CHEs, many non-governmental organizations are also reviewing their roles in the promotion, implementation, and protection of IHL and human rights. The primary mission of most relief NGOs is the provision of assistance to refugees and other disaster-affected populations. They are not specifically mandated by international conventions to provide protection and few of these organizations have claimed a specific role in protection. In fact, a recent review of the mission statements of 16 relief NGOs demonstrated that only two specifically include protection as an organizational objective (International Rescue Committee; Relief International). But relief NGOs frequently have the most field presence of all international organizations during CHEs (Hoy, 1998) and have the greatest access to individuals in need of protection. Many of these organizations are now exploring practical methods by which they may increase their capacity to protect refugees and other vulnerable populations.

Non-governmental organizations from the human rights movement have developed an increased interest and field presence in response to CHEs over the past several years. Their involvement in CHEs represents a significant shift in mission for these organizations. Traditionally human rights NGOs have concentrated their activities on investigating and publicizing the human rights abuses of individuals rather than those of populations. Their activities have previously aimed to support individual victims of torture, arbitrary imprisonment, disappearances, and summary executions. But they are now also involved in the collection and documentation of population-based information about human rights abuses (Physicians for Human Rights, 1999). Their objectives are to disseminate and publicize this information in an effort to embarrass and stigmatize violators of human rights, i.e. "the mobilization of shame." It is hoped that in doing so they will force a cessation of these violations and/or motivate the international community to respond. Unfortunately, many of the groups guilty of flagrant abuses of human rights are hardly chastened by this type of adverse publicity, and the international community has often been too slow to respond appropriately to atrocities and widespread violations of human rights.

Dilemmas in Ensuring Human Rights and Protection

In order to successfully protect the rights of the victims of CHEs, an integrated, field-based response is required. The protection and rights of vulnerable populations should be the responsibility of all agencies responding to humanitarian crises: governments, UN agencies, international donors, ICRC, peacekeeping forces, relief NGOs, and human rights organizations. The most appropriate means by which relief NGOs should respond to violations of the rights of individuals in the setting of CHEs have been, however, associated with controversy (Neier, 1999).

The main principles by which most relief agencies provide assistance are humanity, neutrality, impartiality, and independence. These principles have been key factors in ensuring that warring parties grant humanitarian agencies access to populations in need. Neutrality implies a non-political stance of not supporting or criticizing a particular political or military group, even when one may be guilty of abuses against non-combatants. One of the major concerns of involvement in human rights and protection activities for relief agencies is that it may threaten their neutrality and, therefore, their access to populations. Agencies that do investigate or publicize abuses of IHL or human rights are more likely to be ejected by local authorities and would therefore not be in a position to provide assistance to those in need.

The organization that is best known for its adherence to the principle of neutrality is the ICRC. In response to violations of IHL, the ICRC informs only parties involved in the conflict, reminds them of their obligations, and makes recommendations about appropriate courses of actions. It usually does not publicize these violations to the outside world nor draw attention to them. In this way it ensures that it is able to continue to monitor and promote compliance with IHL.

The doctrine of neutrality has become increasingly controversial in light of worsening abuses of human rights in today's conflicts. The modern human rights movement refuses to remain neutral and silent in the face of obvious abuses. The views of ICRC and the human rights movement represent, in effect, two different moral philosophies. Both are motivated by humanitarian principles. But the ICRC accepts war as a fact of life and attempts to ensure compliance with the laws of war. In so doing, it is able to maintain access, provide assistance, and promote and monitor the rights of non-combatants as outlined in IHL. The human rights movement, however, views war as a moral violation and aims to draw attention to abuses of IHL and international human rights law. It believes that coordinated moral, political, and military pressure from the international community represents the most realistic means of bringing an end to widespread abuses of human rights.

Unlike the ICRC and relief NGOs, human rights groups are not in the business of providing humanitarian assistance. Human rights groups have, in fact, been critical of relief and UN agencies for continuing to provide assistance when it was obvious that much of the aid was being diverted to support the perpetrators of human rights abuses. In addition, they have criticized these agencies and peacekeeping forces for accommodating violators of human rights, in order to continue the delivery of aid. Recent examples include Somalia, Bosnia, Afghanistan, and Rwanda.

For relief NGOs, the issue of neutrality poses a potential dilemma. By remaining neutral they may be granted access to those in need by the warring parties and provide much-needed humanitarian assistance. This aid may, however, be manipulated by perpetrators of atrocities and human rights abuses to support their own activities (Anderson, 1999). If relief agencies choose not to be neutral and to publicize violations of international law, the warring parties may restrict their access to populations in need. They are therefore in a position in which they are unable to fulfill their primary mission, i.e. the provision of assistance.

Some observers are of the opinion that while neutrality is a laudable goal, humanitarian assistance can never be truly neutral when dealing with the perpetrators of flagrant abuses of human rights. It was, in fact, this very point of divergence from the rigid neutrality of the ICRC that inspired the formation of Medecins Sans Frontieres (MSF) during the Biafran war in 1967 (Medecins Sans Frontieres, 1997). At the time, the Nigerian army was preventing relief commodities from reaching its citizens in the secessionist areas. Opposed to the silent diplomacy of ICRC, the founders of MSF spoke out about the atrocities that they had witnessed. MSF chose a path of moral activism and "temoignage," i.e. witnessing.

In places such as Bosnia, Rwanda, Angola, and Sierra Leone, violations have occurred on such a scale that they have demanded a response by relief agencies. In the refugee camps in Goma, Zaire, for example, MSF and the International Rescue Committee (IRC) withdrew their teams as a protest against the manipulation of aid by militant Hutus, who were responsible for the genocide in Rwanda. Even the ICRC has become more vocal in denouncing violations of IHL in recent years and it has also participated in the campaign to ban landmines.

Many relief agencies have been forced to review their commitment to the concept of neutrality. Some observers regard neutrality as a utopian ideal that may no longer be achievable or appropriate in many settings. Impartiality and solidarity, rather than neutrality, may prove to be the more enduring and relevant guiding principles of humanitarian action. As one observer noted, "Neutrality cannot be maintained when responding to complex emergencies: it is irresponsible to pretend otherwise. In some situations it would be morally repugnant to remain neutral" (Seybolt, 1996).

The Role of Relief NGOs in Human Rights and Protection

Given the scale of atrocities and abuses in today's CHEs, it is not a question of whether relief agencies should address the issues of human rights and protection, but to what degree and by which methods. Each agency should be in a position to determine its involvement in these activities based on its organizational mandate and its assessment of the needs on the ground. A spectrum of options is open to relief NGOs whose response to violations usually lies somewhere on the continuum between the ICRC (neutrality, discretion, non-disclosure) and human rights organizations (public denouncements, vocal political advocacy) (ICRC, 2001).

The attention paid by relief agencies to human rights and protection issues has increased significantly in recent years. UNHCR has published a field guide on the protection of refugees for NGOs to assist them to incorporate protection issues into their field programs ((United Nations High Commissioner for Refugees, 1999). The Sphere project, which has established minimum standards for relief agencies, promotes a rights-based approach in its opening Humanitarian Charter to the provision of humanitarian assistance (Sphere Project, 2004). The Sphere standards, in fact, have been reviewed to ensure that they address protection issues in each field sector. In addition, several prominent relief NGOs have established organizational departments to address issues of protection, advocacy, and policy.

Interventions responding to perpetrations of human rights violations can be categorized into three types: persuasion in an attempt to convince and compel authorities; denunciation in order to pressure and shame authorities; and substitution to replace authorities that have failed to meet their responsibilities (Paul, 1999).

The challenge for relief agencies is to address the needs of war-affected populations in a principled manner that upholds humanitarian principles and human rights simultaneously. The rights-based approach to aid, as touched on in Sphere Humanitarian Charter, assumes that the rights to material and non-material assistance are inseparable. This approach therefore encompasses all human rights, i.e. civil, political, economic, cultural, social, and solidarity. From this view, access to assistance is not about charity or largesse towards beneficiaries, but rather it is about legal obligation towards rights holders.

Given their strong field presence and local knowledge, relief agencies are particularly well placed to promote and protect the rights of refugees and other vulnerable populations. Humanitarian workers often directly witness abuses of human rights and they should therefore be prepared to respond to the protection needs of the populations that they serve. As previously noted, agencies that have protection as a specific component of their mandate, including UNHCR and ICRC, may not have the field presence nor the resources to address protection issues in all settings. And peacekeeping forces often do not have the mandate to provide protection to civilian populations.

Relief agencies should therefore develop organizational policies and strategies to tackle the issues of human rights and protection. Many practical measures can be taken to secure the rights of refugees and other vulnerable populations. Included among these are:

Field Presence

The presence of relief workers in the field, thereby acting as witnesses, has been acknowledged as a means of deterring human rights abuses. Presence by itself may not be sufficient to confer protection, however. It must be associated with an active programmatic agenda if it is to be effective. NGO staff must be engaged in the community and actively participating in the relief effort if they are to truly offer protection to the surrounding population. Field presence and positive engagement have the added advantage of contributing to the sense of solidarity with the community being served.

The concept of "preventive protection" was called into question following the crises in Bosnia and in the Rwandan refugee camps in Goma, Zaire. In these settings, gross violations of human rights continued in spite of the presence of humanitarian workers and peacekeeping forces. Despite these criticisms, it is almost certain that there would have been more massacres, more ethnic cleansing, and more atrocities if the humanitarian community were not present at these times. The key point about presence is that for it to be truly effective, it must include a field-based strategy that includes humanitarian assistance, programmatic interventions for protection, and monitoring and reporting of human rights violations.

The legitimacy of this preventive protection intervention is demonstrated by the singular mandate of several non-governmental organizations that employ a deliberate tactic of providing international volunteers to live within at-risk communities or along side targeted human rights activists as a "Protective Accompaniment" strategy to deter attacks or aggression.

Dr. Francis Deng, the former Representative to the UN Secretary-General on Internally Displaced Persons, has acknowledged that the active presence of international organizations had acting as a deterrent to abuses of human rights during the on-going humanitarian crisis in Colombia. He has stated that "The presence of international personnel . . . has served to provide protection to civilians at risk in outlying areas . . . both international and non-governmental organizations could expand their presence and programs. . . . International support is imperative" (Deng, 1999).

In addition to the indirect deterrent effect of international attention and the witnessing role, this secondary prevention may also come in other forms. Humanitarian agencies demonstrably model an ethos of distinction between combatants and non-combatants and implied an ethical message of the sanctity of civilians. As Madame Ogata stated in her statement in 1997 to the UN Security Council, " . . . Humanitarian action is not just about relief . . . but also ensuring physical protection. . . . The challenge must be to bring safety to the people rather than people to safety."

Assistance as Protection

The very fact that war-affected populations have been forced from their homes with reduced access to the necessities that sustain life is a gross violation of their basic rights. The major objective of humanitarian relief is to reduce the rates of death and illness that are associated with these violations. The life-saving interventions of the provision of food, clean water, sanitation services, shelter, and basic medical care may therefore themselves be considered key protection activities.

While public health interventions may reduce the rates of mortality due to epidemics of measles or cholera, they do not of themselves guarantee the physical security of the populations at risk. Thus, humanitarian assistance may reduce the consequences of human rights violations, but it does not prevent those violations from occurring. This distinction is exemplified when the humanitarian objective, "stop the dying" is nuanced to "stop the killing."

The withdrawal of humanitarian assistance has also been used as a means of protesting human rights violations. Several NGOs have ceased the delivery of aid in order to protest that the scale of human rights abuses is excessive and would no longer be tolerated. As noted previously, both MSF and IRC withdrew their teams from the refugee camps in Goma in 1995 when it became clear that Hutu extremists were manipulating the international aid for their own purposes and preparing to initiate further attacks on ethnic Tutsis. In addition, the IRC ceased assistance to one Bosnian town when it became clear that ethnic cleansing was continuing despite its protestations. The decision to withdraw aid is never taken lightly as it may worsen conditions for those most in need. Sometimes aid groups are forced to choose between the lesser of two evils: continuing aid at the expense of strengthening the perpetrators of human rights abuses; or ceasing aid to weaken the perpetrators, but at the same time potentially placing those in need at greater peril.

Assessment and Analysis

An assessment by a qualified protection officer will help to determine major protection issues and to identify vulnerable groups. The goal of assessments should be to provide practical recommendations that may then be incorporated into the design of field programs in various sectors. Local community members should participate in the assessment and help to identify the availability of local resources.

The assessment should attempt to identify potential threats (e.g. abductions, rape, forced conscription, trafficking, domestic violence, militias, landmines) and associated vulnerabilities (e.g. unaccompanied children, unaccompanied elderly, women collecting firewood, ignorance of mine fields) (United Nations High Commissioner for Refugees, 1999). Many relief NGOs do not have staff that are appropriately trained to conduct such assessments and these NGOs should collaborate with other organizations that do have the necessary expertise, including UNHCR and ICRC. Participation in Protection Working Groups and the deployment of Protection Technical Advisors will help NGOs to identify threats and vulnerabilities in their own areas of operation, leading to the development of appropriate interventions.

Program Planning

Practical recommendations from the assessment should then be incorporated into the design of field programs. Opportunities to address protection issues should be sought in all sectors, including health, food aid, water and sanitation, shelter, and education. In particular, interventions that address the special needs of vulnerable groups, including women and children, should be considered. Strategic placement of activities and staff may significantly reduce the incidence of violations. Simple steps such as the appropriate positioning of latrines for security and privacy may reduce the risk of sexual violence. In displaced persons camps, women who are forced to collect firewood in the surrounding areas have frequently been the victims of rape, as has occurred recently in Darfur, Sudan. The introduction of other options for cooking, including solar cookers, fuel-efficient stoves, and alternative fuel sources, such as kerosene, may significantly reduce the exposure of women to sexual violence (Women's Commission, 2006). The provision of identity documents for refugee and local staff, such as identification cards, may also be beneficial to prevent harassment and abuse. Bosnian staff of international NGOs found that they were usually able to pass through checkpoints and avoid forcible conscription into military service if they possessed such documentation.

Many other simple interventions may significantly contribute to the protection of vulnerable groups. Two examples drawn from the recent experience of the IRC help to demonstrate how opportunities to implement practical protection measures may arise. During an IRC assessment in Guinea, it was determined that children who were not enrolled in school were at greater risk of being forced into military service. An active campaign to increase school enrollment ensued reducing the conscription of child soldiers. In Albania following the Kosovo crisis, IRC medical staff were instructed to inquire whether all babies born to Kosovar mothers in Albania were given birth certificates. If they had not, IRC personnel informed the parents of the local procedure to obtain one. This ensured that these children would not have the problems of subsequently being declared "stateless" which would result in them having further rights denied in the future.

In order to ensure that the objectives of a specific protection intervention are being met, quantitative and qualitative indicators can be designed that allow field teams to assess the impact of the intervention. Examples may include the number of reported attacks against women in a refugee camp or the proportion of eligible children enrolled and attending school.

Staff Training

Training of NGO staff and community members on key rights and protection issues is an important component of any protection strategy. Too often staff receive an inadequate orientation prior to their field assignment. They are therefore unfamiliar with the policies of their own organization in the areas of human rights and protection. As a result staff may be uncertain about how to respond when they have witnessed or been informed of major rights violations (Paul, 1995).

All personnel should be provided with basic information on IHL, international human rights law, and refugee law. Additionally, they must be oriented to the threats and vulnerabilities of the region in which they are being deployed. This will be important not only in helping them to address the issue of their own personal security, but also in understanding the broader risks faced by the community.

Staff should be guided on how to incorporate protection issues into the development of their own programs. In addition, they must be provided with specific information on how to respond when they have witnessed or been notified about a particular violation. Knowing what information to report and to whom it must be reported are important core issues. For example, staff from several relief NGOs in Albania during the Kosovo crises were successfully trained on how to report cases of suspected sexual assault and forced prostitution to the local authorities.

Monitoring and Reporting

There is a compelling argument that all NGOs should contribute to the careful documentation and reporting of human rights abuses. In many circumstances, these agencies may be the only external witness to significant violations. Their subsequent silence would ensure that no response by appropriate authorities would then be possible.

Documentation and reporting of abuses does not imply that all agencies need to publicize their observations. Some NGOs may be concerned that if they publicly protest they will place their own staff at risk or lose access to the populations that they serve. At the very least, NGOs that have witnessed or been informed of violations should pass their findings on to the bodies responsible for addressing these issues, such as UN agencies, local authorities, or peacekeeping forces. Alternatively they may facilitate reporting of abuses by journalists or human rights organizations.

Some NGO staff do not consider that human rights monitoring should be a component of their mission. Others expressed the concern that they had neither the training nor the capacity to engage in such activities. These findings demonstrate the need for relief agencies to develop an organizational policy that will assist staff in the appropriate documentation and reporting of suspected human rights violations.

Advocacy

Public advocacy is an effective tool that has been used by a number of NGOs to draw attention to the protection needs of refugees and other vulnerable populations. Organizations such as MSF, International Rescue Committee, CARE, and Save the Children have used several methods to motivate the international community to respond to those needs. Direct lobbying of governments and United Nations agencies, skillful use of media, and rallying of public support have raised the profile of humanitarian crises and of the associated violations of human rights.

Relief agencies can become effective advocates because of their strong field presence and their credibility. Through their activism, they have often been able to mobilize greater international resources to ensure the health and security of those in need. They are also in a position to call governments to account when they do not fulfill their commitments or when they rescind their promises. Through their advocacy, NGOs must continue to remind the international community of its obligations to assist and protect civilian populations during times of conflict and deprivation. For example, a series of mortality survey in the Democratic Republic of Congo between 2000 and 2004 have demonstrated the strong link between insecurity and high rates of mortality due to infectious diseases and malnutrition (Coghlan, 2006). Data from the surveys have been used effectively to advocate for increases in both humanitarian aid and the numbers of peacekeeping troops (OCHA, 2006).

Conclusion

The complex humanitarian emergencies of the past two decades have been characterized by gross violations of human rights, including summary executions, mass killings, forced displacement, systematic rape, torture, and ethnic cleansing. Although the rights of individuals affected by conflict are outlined in a series of international treaties and conventions, mechanisms to enforce these rights frequently fail. Governments, who have the main responsibility for pro-

tecting the rights of individuals, are often the perpetrators of human rights violations, or lack the will to enforce the rights guaranteed under international law.
In addition United Nations agencies, the International Committee of the Red
Cross, and peacekeeping troops frequently lack the resources, field presence, or
mandate to protect the rights of war-affected civilian populations.

Relief NGOs, whose traditional mission is to provide humanitarian assistance, frequently work in settings where the scope and scale of human rights
violations demand a response. These agencies must therefore review their roles
and evolve their responsibilities in the areas of human rights and protection.
Several relief agencies have established organizational departments, strategies,
and policies to address protection and advocacy issues. There are many practical, effective measures that relief NGOs can incorporate into their field programs that will protect the rights of the populations that they serve. The monitoring of human rights violations, alerting the public and the media, training
public officials in human rights principles, and educating war-affected people
about their rights must become a central element of relief assistance interventions.

Bibliography

Anderson, M. (1999). *Do No Harm: How aid can support peace—or war*. Boulder,
    Colodado: Lynne Rienner.
Bruderlein, C. & Leaning, J. (1999) The new challenges of humanitarian protection.
    BMJ. 319, pp. 430-435.
Burkle, F.M. (1999). Lessons learnt and future expectations of complex emergencies.
    BMJ. 319, pp. 422-426.
Coghlan, B., Brennan, R.J., Ngoy, P., et al (2006), Mortality in the Democratic Republic
    of Congo: a nationwide survey. *Lancet,* 367, pp. 44-51.
Deng, F.M. (1999). Don't overlook Colombia's humanitarian Crisis. Christian Science
    Monitor, October 6, 1999, p. 75.
Hoy, Paula (1998). *Players and Issues in International Aid*. West Hartford, Conn:
    Kumarian Press, 1998.
ICRC (2001). Strengthening protection in war—a search for professional standards.
    Geneva: ICRC.
Ignatieff, M. (1997). *The Warrior's Honor*. New York: Henry Holt and Co.
Leaning, J. (1999). Medicine and international humanitarian law. BMJ. 319, pp. 393-
    394.
Medecins Sans Frontieres (1997). *World in Crisis*. London: Routledge.
Neier, A. & Leaning, J. (1999). Human rights challenges. In Leaning, J., Briggs S.M.,
    Chen, L.C. (Eds), Humanitarian Crises. Cambridge: Harvard University Press.
OCHA (2006). *Action Plan 2006: Democratic Republic of Congo*. Brussells: OCHA.
Paul, Diane (1995). The Role of Non-governmental Organizations in the Protection of
    Civilians Under Threat: Practical Considerations. Jacob Blaustein Institute for the
    Advancement of Human Rights/Center for the Study of Societies in Crisis.

———— (1999). Protection in practice: Field-based strategies for protecting civilians from deliberate harm. Relief and Rehabilitation Network: Network Paper 30. London: Overseas Development Institute, 1999.

Perrin, Pierre (1996). *War and Public Health.* Geneva: ICRC.

Physicians for Human Rights (1999). *War Crimes in Kosovo: a population-based assessment of human-rights violations against Kosovar Albanians.* Boston, Maryland:PHR.

Robertson, G. (1999). *Crimes Against Humanity.* London: Penguin Press.

Seybolt, T.B. (1996). The Myth of Neutrality. *Peace Review,* Vol. 8, 4, pp. 521-527.

Sphere Project (2004). *Humanitarian Charter and Minimum Standards in Humanitarian Assistance.* Geneva: International Federation of the Red Cross.

United Nations High Commissioner for Refugees (1999). *Protecting refugees: A field guide for NGO's.* Geneva: Atar S.

Waldman R. & Martone G. (1999).   Public Health and Complex Emergencies: NewIssues, New Conditions. *American Journal of Public Health,* Vol. 89 Issue 10, pp.1483-1485.

Weston, B.H. (1991).   Human Rights, in Goetz P.W. (ed) *Encyclopaedia Brittanica* Edition 15, Vol 20. Chicago: Encyclopaedia Britannica, pp. 656-664.

World Health Organization (2002). *World Report on Violence and Health.* Geneva: World Health Organization.

Women's Commission for Refugee Women and Children (2006). *Beyond* Firewood:Fuel Alternatives and Protection Strategies for Displaced Women New York: Women's Commission and Girls.

CHAPTER 5

Culture and Human Rights

Harry Minas

Britannus (shocked):
Caesar, this is not proper.
Theodotus (outraged):
How?
Caesar (recovering his self-possession):
Pardon him Theodotus: he is a barbarian, and thinks that
The customs of his tribe and island are the laws of nature.

George Bernard Shaw
Caesar and Cleopatra, Act II

The international human rights regime, codified in the United Nations Charter, the Universal Declaration of Human Rights, the Covenants, and a range of other instruments, is now more than 50 years old. Successive decades since 1948 have seen the further elaboration of human rights, both in treaty and customary law, and the ever-increasing enumeration of rights. The Universal Declaration of Human Rights (1948) is an aspirational document, making recommendations and exhorting states to behave in certain ways. The Declaration's provisions are transformed into legally binding obligations on states parties through the two Covenants (ICCPR, 1966; ICESCR, 1966). These represent the two dominant sets of human rights embodied in the Declaration—civil and political rights, and economic, social and cultural rights.

The covenant that has received most attention in the West, and has been the subject of controversy and disagreement, is the International Covenant on Civil and Political Rights (ICCPR, 1966). The rights declared in the ICCPR may be broadly classified into five groups:

o   Protection of the individual's physical integrity (torture, arbitrary arrest, arbitrary deprivation of life)
o   Procedural fairness when a government deprives an individual of his liberty (arrest, trial procedures, conditions of imprisonment)
o   Equal protection (race, gender, religion)
o   Freedom of belief, speech, association
o   Right to political participation.

These groups of rights lie on a continuum from those over which there is broad formal/verbal consensus among states (regardless of degree of observance) to those whose purposes, basic meanings and validity are formally disputed (Steiner & Alston, 1996).

The International Covenant on Economic, Social and Cultural Rights (ICESCR, 1966) has received relatively little attention in the West but has been a focus of attention particularly in Asia. The substantive rights asserted in the ICESCR include the right to:

o   self-determination
o   work, and just and favorable conditions of work
o   rest and leisure
o   form and join trade unions and to strike
o   social security
o   special protection for the family, mothers and children
o   an adequate standard of living, including food, clothing and housing-physical and mental health
o   education
o   participation in cultural life

Although the interdependence of civil and political rights and economic, social and cultural rights is widely acknowledged, the two sets of rights may sometimes appear to be in conflict and states frequently attach greater importance to one set or the other.

The human rights regime has been challenged from a number of quarters. The first of these challenges (and probably the most important) is based on defence of national sovereignty. Many countries have responded to criticism by asserting national sovereignty and by claiming that criticisms of human rights constitute interference in the internal affairs of the nation.

Such a response does not only come from states that are regarded as having a poor human rights record. In early 2000, the Australian government was criticized by the UN Committee monitoring compliance with the International Convention on the Elimination of All Forms of Racial Discrimination (ICERD,

1965) on the grounds that the mandatory sentencing laws of the Northern Territory and Western Australia were discriminatory in that their impact fell disproportionately on Aboriginal communities in those two jurisdictions (Committee on the Elimination of Racial Discrimination, 2000). The response of the Australian Government was to say in effect that these laws had been enacted by democratically elected state and territory governments and that UN criticism of these laws was an unwarranted intrusion into Australia's domestic affairs. The government went further and announced that it was reviewing its commitment to the UN committee system that oversees compliance with treaty obligations in the context of an Australian Government review of the effectiveness of the UN Committee system (Minister for Foreign Affairs, 2000).

An important challenge on cultural and development grounds concerns the discussion of so-called 'Asian' values. The argument has essentially been that human rights as conceived in the UN documents are a Western product which does not sit well in non-Western contexts. This view is clearly articulated by Kausikan (Steiner & Alston, 1996, p. 227): "The diversity of cultural traditions, political structures, and levels of development will make it difficult, if not impossible, to define a single distinctive and coherent human rights regime that can encompass the vast region from Japan to Burma, with its Confucian, Buddhist, Islamic, and Hindu traditions. . . . What is clear is that there is a general discontent throughout the region with a purely Western interpretation of human rights. . . . [H]uman rights touch upon extraordinarily delicate matters of culture and values."

A more pointed objection is that the insistence by Western governments on human rights as they are framed in the UN instruments is being used as a cloak for the promotion of Western commercial, political, and cultural interests, what Geertz (1998) refers to as "colonialism by other means." Such resentments may account for the fact that more than forty Asian states, of varying political and cultural complexions, signed the Bangkok Declaration criticizing the prevailing human rights regime in 1993 (Engle, p.311). However, appeals to 'culture' have also served to dignify economic imperatives, as when the Bangkok Declaration objected to the practice of using human rights standards as a precondition for financial aid (Tay, p.755). It appears necessary to accept that states will continue to accord precedence to their own self-interest while ascribing their actions to higher motives such as 'human rights' or 'cultural preservation'.

What Are Rights?

In approaching this question it is useful to make a distinction between legal and moral rights (Hartney, 1995).

Legal and Moral Rights

Laws differ from moral discourse in that the truth of any legal statement depends ultimately on the utterances and acts of competent legal authorities. Whatever is legal or illegal is so because it was made so by the appropriate authorities. Whether this agrees with moral judgments is not relevant. This is true of legal rights. The utterance of a competent legal authority that a right has been conferred is conclusive evidence that a legal right has been conferred. According to Hohfeld, legal rights refer to four different properties or statuses: (1) a claim—imposes a legal duty on someone else; (2) privilege or liberty—the absence of a legal duty: (3) power—the capacity to change legal relations: (4) immunity—protection against a change in one's legal position. Legal rights do not create insurmountable difficulties nationally or internationally, despite frequent differences in interpretation, as long as there are established procedures to judge the merits of competing claims.

The notion of moral rights is used in two ways: one, someone has a right to something (e.g. life, dignity, education, health care, etc.) and two, someone has a right to do something (such as freedom of speech, freedom of movement). In the first case the existence of the right imposes a duty on someone else. In the second, it is the right-holder's behavior that is the focus. To say that he/she is free to act in this way is to say that it is not morally wrong for him/her to act in this way and that he/she is free to do so. These rights correspond to the first two senses of legal rights, that is claim-rights and liberty-rights.

A right consists of the following five elements (Dunne & Wheeler, 1999): a right-holder (the subject of the right), who has a claim to some substance (the object of the right) which he/she might assert, or demand, or enjoy, or enforce (exercising the right) against some individual or group (the bearer of the correlative duty), while citing in support of her/his claim some particular ground (the justification of the right).

The core of rights language is the principle that the good or interest (of the right holder) is protected by a duty imposed on the duty bearer, for our purposes the state. Not all goods or interests generate rights. It is only when there is a centrally important, moral reason to protect a good or interest that we conceive of a right as having been generated. Individual rights have been described as "political trumps held by individuals" in that they will over-ride a collective goal. Rights are powerful instruments or, as some have expressed it, packages of normative advantages. They brook no discussion or negotiation.

Problems immediately appear in a number of ways. There are different conceptions of the "good," of what is morally wrong or right, in different societies. Different political philosophies will differ in their judgments concerning the importance of certain individual and group goods and interests. The order of priority of conflicting rights will differ. An important issue here is the relative priority given by different societies to conflicting individual and group (including state) rights.

Foundations for Human Rights

Vitally important for our discussion are the dominant conceptions about the origins or sources of a right, that is the ground or justification of a right. Dunne & Wheeler (1999) have set out a framework for illustrating the various background social theories of human rights.

Table 1. Background Social Theories of Human Rights

	A. Universalism	B. Cultural Relativism
1. Foundationalism	1A. Liberal natural rights	1B. Traditional communitarianism
2. Anti-foundationalism	2A. Cosmopolitan pragmatism	2B. Communitarian pragmatism

Modified from Dunne & Wheeler (1999)

1A. Liberal natural rights. The UN instruments are firmly grounded in traditional (western) natural law thinking and liberal philosophy. Thomas Jefferson asserted that his countrymen were a "free people claiming their rights as derived from the laws of nature and not as a gift of their Chief Magistrate" (Steiner & Alston, p. 168). The UN Charter seeks to reaffirm faith in fundamental human rights. The Preamble to the 1948 Universal Declaration states that "recognition of the inherent dignity and of the equal and inalienable rights of all members of the human family is the foundation of freedom, justice and peace in the world" (UDHR, 1948, Preamble, para 1). These rights, then, are universal and inalienable (absolute) and need not depend on the legal and ethical foundations of different communities for their existence. Such rights take precedence over the laws or customs of a particular state. This view of human rights arises out of a natural law tradition, which maintains that there is a unity of humankind regardless of cultural difference. The question of how the contents of these rights are to be discerned is answered by asserting that the faculty of reason, which is a constant across cultures, enables all to discern what is the correct moral code whereby life should be lived. An important implied belief is that of an essential, knowable, and immutable human nature. This approach fails to address, let alone answer, a number of questions. For example: Why is the balance in favor of rights rather than duties? If human nature is essential, knowable and immutable, how is it that moral practices vary between and within cultures, and how is it that moral commitments and practices have changed so dramatically within any one culture over time?

1B: Traditional communitarianism. The argument here is that rights exist by virtue of the community of which we are part, and that because communities differ in their conceptions of the good, so also will rights differ. The argument is that morality is culturally contingent and that values can only be grounded in tradition. Where the individual is firmly embedded in a complex social and ethical communal matrix it is difficult to conceive of the possibility that individuals can possess universal rights that they can assert against the community or the state. This is the cultural relativist argument. The foundation here is cultural tradition linked to the view that essential, particularly moral, elements of culture endure.

2A: Cosmopolitan pragmatism. According to Dunne & Wheeler (1999) this is exemplified by the views of Parekh (1999), who rejects both moral foundationalism (that there is one human nature and therefore one true expression of fundamental rights) and moral relativism, while maintaining a commitment to universalism in human rights. He argues that the only basis for such universalism is a dialogue between equals from which is generated agreement about a minimal set of universally acceptable human rights. "Our concern is not to discover values, for they have no objective basis, but to agree on them. . . . Values are a matter of collective decision, and like any other decision are based on reasons. Since moral values cannot be rationally demonstrated, our concern should be to build a consensus around those that can be shown to be rationally most defensible" (Parekh, p. 140).

2B: Communitarian pragmatism. This argument rejects objective or timeless foundations for human rights and regards them as contingent and negotiated preferences that make sense in dealing with practical and moral problems. "[W]hen rights are properly understood, they entail a communitarian conception of human relations, relations of mutual assistance, social solidarity, and important kinds of equality. . . . [E]ach human being is both the subject or right-holder and the respondent or duty-bearer. . . . By the effective recognition of the mutuality entailed by human rights, the society becomes a community" (Gewirth, 1996, p. 6).

Culture

Culture is the means whereby the infinite complexity of the world is reduced to a manageable simplicity. It provides a map that guides us in how to see, what to believe, what to value, how to behave, how to interpret the world of others and the environment, and how to think about ourselves. One's culture provides off-the-shelf answers to some of life's most complex problems and dilemmas, particularly when ethically difficult decisions have to be made in difficult circumstances.

It is important to keep in mind that, as well as serving the many enabling functions referred to above, culture also constrains the possibilities that are available to members of the culture—from the universe of possibilities for belief, values, and behavior—in that culture prescribes and proscribes. To varying extents, depending on the range of acceptable beliefs, values and practices, a culture limits the freedom of individuals and groups, and limits the range of possible solutions to problems. The human rights regime both prescribes the minimum that states must do for their citizens and proscribes the freedom of states in dealing with their citizens. As noted by Engle (2000), references to 'culture' in opposition to external demands for human rights standards are often synonymous with appeals to the principle of national sovereignty, but on occasion state actors genuinely see their national culture as being incompatible with certain 'universal' tenets.

Culturally Derived Values

Culturally derived values are particularly important when considering the relevance of culture to human rights. Hofstede (1980) studied culturally derived values in samples of people from more than 50 countries. From these studies four bipolar factors emerged: Individualism-Collectivism, Power Distance, Uncertainty Avoidance, and Masculinity-Femininity. Particular individuals may score high or low on each of these factors, and groups may have high or low mean scores. The pattern of scores on these factors constitutes the individual's or the group's value orientations. The Individualism-Collectivism and Power Distance dimensions are of particular interest to us here.

Individualism-Collectivism
Individualist societies are those in which the interests of the individual are paramount, and where great value is accorded to full autonomy, responsibility, self-reliance, and self-expression. Collectivist societies are those in which people from birth onwards are integrated into strong, cohesive groups which, throughout peoples' lifetime, continue to protect them in exchange for loyalty. The interests of the group generally take precedence over the interests of individuals.

Power Distance
The concept of power distance refers to the extent to which the less powerful members of institutions and organizations (such as the family, school, work or-

ganizations, and the community at large) within a society expect and accept that power is distributed unequally. In such a culture the individual "knows his place." Social mobility is discouraged and difficult to achieve. Social structures are hierarchically organized, as are interpersonal relationships within the family and within broader society.

Figure 1: Power Distance by Individualism-Collectivism

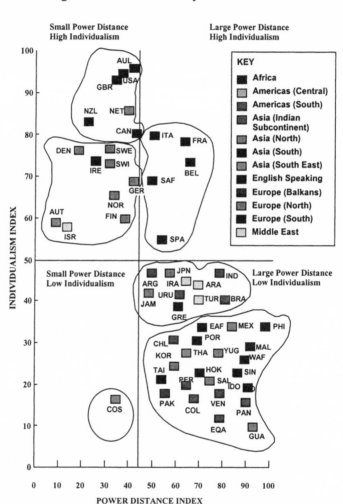

Adapted from Hofstede (1980)

Mean scores on the Individualism-Collectivism and the Power Distance dimensions are shown in Figure 1 (Hofstede, 1980). It can be seen from this chart that Anglo-origin countries and the countries of north-western Europe are separated from most other countries by a substantial cultural gulf.

Countries with the cultural values of high individualism and low power distance will be more likely to conceive of rights that are individual in focus, and that emphasize equality. They are more likely to emphasize the ICCPR. More collectivist countries will be more likely to focus on collective rights and individual duties, and will be more likely to accord differential rights to members of various sections of the society. They are more likely to emphasize the ECSR. Singapore's Lee Kuan Yew, for example, argued that '[t]he expansion of the right of the individual to behave or misbehave as he pleases has come at the expense of orderly society' (Engle, p.319).

An awareness of such differences in values and ethical commitments is essential if there is to be a basis for informed discussion between culturally different groups that is intended to build consensus on the nature and scope of human rights. The necessity of a respectful approach to local cultures has become steadily more apparent to human rights advocates. For example, Bell suggests that 'it is more likely that the struggle to promote human rights can be won if it is fought in ways that build on, rather than challenge, local cultural traditions' (Engle, p.323).

Are Rights Absolute (Inalienable)?

Let us now turn to the question of whether rights are absolute or inalienable.

Article 29(3) of Universal Declaration of Human Rights (United Nations, 1948) is revealing. It states that, "These rights and freedoms may in no case be exercised contrary to the purposes and principles of the United Nations." However, two types of provisions in the ICCPR limit states' obligations and individual rights: (1) provision for temporary derogation, and (2) limitation clauses within articles.

Of the first type of provision, Article 4, dealing with a public emergency, permits a temporary derogation from many of the rights declared by the Covenant, for example in relation to rights relating to free speech, arrest and detention. "In time of public emergency which threatens the life of the nation and the existence of which is officially proclaimed, the States parties to the present Covenant may take measures derogating from their obligations under the present Covenant to the extent strictly required by the exigencies of the situation, provided that such measures are not inconsistent with their other obligations under international law and do not involve discrimination solely on the ground of race, color, sex, language, religion or social origin" (ICCPR, 1966, Article 4). Note that political views are not mentioned in this list of unacceptable grounds for discrimination. Interestingly, paragraph 8 of the Bangkok Declaration, which put the case for a more context-based humans rights regime, also declined to mention political views, arguing that 'international norm-setting' should be influenced by 'national and regional particularities and various historical, cultural and religious backgrounds'. (Engle, p.320)

The second type of provision includes a number of articles from limitation clauses. For example, there is the Article 18 limitation which states: "Freedom to manifest one's religion or beliefs may be subject only to such limitations as are prescribed by law and are necessary to protect public safety, order, health, or morals or the fundamental rights and freedoms of others" (ICCPR, 1966, Article 18). Note the inclusion of morals in this list. Or consider the Article 19 limitation: The right to freedom of expression "carries with it special duties and responsibilities. It may therefore be subject to certain restrictions . . . .for the protection of national security or of public order, or of public health or morals" (ICCPR, 1966, Article 19). In Articles 21 [right to peaceful assembly] and 22 [freedom of association] the restrictions that are permissible are those that are "necessary in a democratic society in the interests of national security or public safety, public order, the protection of public health or morals or the protection of the rights and freedoms of others" (ICCPR, 1966, Articles 21, 22).

These restrictions and limitations demonstrate that while the declared individual rights are presented in the instruments as universal, fundamental and inalienable they are not absolute in that the interests of States and the communal welfare take precedence over the rights of individuals, as do the interests of the United Nations itself.

Rorty (1999) argues that the notion of 'inalienable human rights' is not dissimilar to other slogans such 'obedience to the will of God.' Both are simply ways of saying that argumentative resources have been exhausted. "Talk of the will of God or of the rights of man, like talk of 'the honor of the family' or of 'the fatherland in danger' are not suitable targets for philosophical analysis and criticism. None of these notions should be analyzed, for they are all ways of saying, 'Here I stand: I can do no other' " (Rorty, 1999, p. 83).

Are Rights Universal?

There are many challenges to the assertion of the inherent universality of human rights. I will mention only two. The first centers on assertions of the right to development over individual rights where these are perceived to be in conflict. The second is a consideration of human rights in the context of religious law.

A continuing tension is the apparent conflict between individual human rights and the view that social and economic rights must be upheld and strengthened by a right to development. This is sometimes linked to the argument that the West is using apparent concerns for human rights as a cover for economic protectionism, for example by developing new norms for workers' rights, the impact of which is to reduce Asian competitive advantage in manufacturing. The West, on the other hand, asserts that the right to development is used as a means of justifying repression (Hurrell, 1999). In a government paper entitled "Human Rights In China" the argument was put that in China, a developing country with limited resources, social turmoil could threaten the most basic right, that to subsistence, and that, in the interests of the rights of the community, the state is entitled to restrict individual freedoms such as freedom of speech (Dunne & Wheeler, 1999). This was linked to a strict claim of national sovereignty and rejection of interference in China's internal affairs. Despite these views, China signed the 1993 Vienna Declaration on Human Rights which commits China to the view that "all human rights are universal, indivisible and inter-related." As Kausikan has noted, '[i]nternational law has evolved to the point that how a country treats its citizens is no longer a matter for its exclusive determination' (Engle, p.326).

However, the head of the Chinese delegation to the Vienna Conference asserted that "one should not and cannot think of the human rights standard and model of certain countries as the only proper one, and demand all other countries to comply with them" (Dunne & Wheeler, p.15). The official PRC view was reiterated by President Jiang Zemin during his visit to the United States in 1997. "Concepts on democracy, on human rights, and on freedom are relative and specific, and they are to be determined by the specific national situation of different countries" (Van Ness, 1999, p. 8). In relation to such arguments Sen (2000) has put the persuasive case that conflicts between the right to development and individual rights are more apparent than real, and that freedom is essential for economic development. It is also worth noting that nations such as Singapore, which some contend is the 'ideological champion' of 'Asian values' (Mortimer, in Tay, p.746), have become sufficiently economically successful that 'recognition of a right to development seems less pressing' (Engle, p.328).

The Sudanese human rights scholar Abdullah Ahmed An-Na'im (1990, 1992) has written about human rights in the Muslim world. Some interpretations of Shari'a conflict with international human rights standards in a number of ways. An example is the Shari'a law of apostasy. Apostasy is punishable by death, in conflict with freedom of religion and conscience. The law of apostasy also limits the right of free speech in relation to the tenets of Islam. It should be remembered in relation to religious freedom that the Catholic Church punished heresy and tried to stamp out what it perceived as heresy by persecution and religious wars. It was not until 1965 that the Vatican Council published the Declaration of Religious Freedom—Dignitatis Humanae (Rawls, 1999). An-Na'im (1992) considers the issue of the Koranic punishment of amputation of the right hand for theft as a lenient and merciful punishment compared with what the offender would suffer in the next life if the religious punishment were not enforced in this life. He argues that there is no interpretation of Islam that would prohibit such punishment, and that Muslim governments would see no conflict between this culturally sanctioned practice and their acceptance of the requirement (in the Declaration and the Covenants) that no-one shall be subjected to torture or to cruel, inhuman or degrading treatment.

Beliefs, values and all other aspects of culture and politics are hotly contested intra-culturally as well as across different cultures. The arguments of An-Na'im for a re-interpretation of the Qur'an is an excellent example of this intra-cultural pluralism (Rawls, 1999, p. 151). It is such interpretation and re-interpretation of cultures by the members of those cultures that ensures that they remain vibrant, relevant and adaptive to changing circumstances.

The above snapshots do not, of course, convey anything of the richness, plurality and complexity of Chinese or Islamic views on matters of importance. They indicate simply this: that legitimate views that are held on culturally defensible grounds can be in direct conflict with UN accounts of human rights. These examples illustrate that, even if there is agreement on the principle of human rights, there are fundamentally different conceptions of human rights. There is a lack of agreement about the nature of such rights or their substantive scope, which is to say, their definition. "Some of the most basic questions have yet to receive conclusive answers. Whether human rights are to be viewed as divine, moral, or legal entitlements; whether they are to be validated by intuition, custom, social contract theory, principles of distributive justice, or as prerequisites for happiness; whether they are to be understood as irrevocable or as partially revocable; whether they are to be broad or limited in number and content - these and kindred issues are matters of ongoing debate and will remain so as long as there exist contending approaches to order and scarcities among resources" (Steiner & Alston, p. 170).

Conclusions

Conceptions of human rights are the product of cultural evolution and have occurred in a manner somewhat analogous to the evolution of language. The capacity for and the use of language are universal. However, the specifics of language vary from place to place and over time. All cultures have conceptions of the good but the details of these conceptions also vary over time within any one culture and from place to place. These elaborations of conceptions of the good (religious, humanist, pragmatist) inform how cultures deal with the problem of injuries and humiliations inflicted on the weak by the strong, particularly by the state and its institutions.

Human rights are not fundamental in the sense conveyed by the UN instruments, that is as rooted in natural law. Rights are historically and culturally contingent. They are neither universal nor inalienable. This should not be surprising since human beings and social systems are not everywhere the same and both people and social systems are far from immutable. The very universalism that is such a central feature of human rights discourse, and that liberalism promotes, has come into sharp "conflict both with other universalisms with similar intent . . . and with a large number of alternative versions of the good, the right, and the indubitable, Japanese, Indian, African, Singaporean, to which it looks like just one more attempt to impose Western values on the rest of the world—the continuation of colonialism by other means" (Geertz, 1998).

The most prominent and widely known feature of the UN instruments is the broad aspirational declarations that are derived from a particular philosophical tradition, Western liberalism. This may contribute to suspicion concerning motives and a less than full commitment from those with very different political and ethical traditions. International human rights standards that are perceived to be alien to or at variance with the values and institutions of a people are unlikely to elicit commitment or compliance.

All of this does not preclude the development of a culture of human rights, and it is this that we should be working towards. This can only happen if we have an agreed framework for working together on such a project. The minimum requirements for such a framework are mutual respect and genuinely negotiable positions. An-Naim makes the important point that "Most African and Asian countries did not participate in the formulation of the Universal Declaration of Human Rights because, as victims of colonization, they were not members of the United Nations. When they did participate in the formulation of subsequent instruments, they did so on the basis of an established framework and philosophical assumptions adopted in their absence" (Steiner & Alston, pp. 210-211).

Kausikan (Steiner & Alston, p. 229) suggests, I think correctly, that it is imperative to find a balance between "a pretentious and unrealistic universalism and a paralyzing cultural relativism." From the liberal philosophical tradition, the political theory of John Rawls, as articulated in Theory of Justice (Rawls, 1971), in Political Liberalism (Rawls, 1993) and, most recently, in The Law of Peoples (1999), can make a significant contribution to thinking about how to achieve such a balance. The central conception is that of an overlapping consensus between irreconcilable comprehensive doctrines, whether they are religious, philosophical or moral. Rawls (1999, p. 151) describes as a "perfect example" of overlapping consensus the approach taken by An-Na'im (1990) who has argued that the earlier Mecca teachings of Muhammad should inform the interpretation of the Qur'an rather than the later teachings of the Medina period. "The Qur'an does not mention constitutionalism, but human rational thinking and experience have shown that constitutionalism is necessary for realizing the just and good society prescribed by the Qur'an. An Islamic justification and support for constitutionalism is important and relevant for Muslims. Non-Muslims may have their own secular or other justifications. As long as all are agreed on the principle and specific rules of constitutionalism, including complete equality and non-discrimination on grounds of gender or religion, each may have his or her own reasons for coming to that agreement" (An-Na'im, 1990, p. 100).

In the process of building an international culture of universal respect for, and protection of, human rights there can be no consensus on the source of authority concerning the nature and scope of rights, whether it be from natural law or religious belief. Universal rights must therefore be created through the free agreement of equal participants in a continuing discussion. In such a discussion it will be essential that all relevant perspectives and intellectual and ethical traditions play an equal part.

The useful question is not what is right, or legitimate or authoritative, but on which important matters can we reach agreement? A central purpose of human rights discourse and of the international human rights regime is to prevent the manifold evils visited by states on their citizens. The only source of authority for this endeavor is the free agreement of people with diverse beliefs and commitments. An agreed set of human rights would have enormous international moral authority, and might find its way easily into relatively uncontested international law.

> "Rights is a child of the law; from real law come real rights; but from imaginary laws, from 'law of nature', come imaginary rights...Natural rights is simple nonsense; natural and imprescriptible rights (an American phrase), rhetorical nonsense, nonsense upon stilts" (Bentham, 2002).

References

An-Na'im, A. A. (1990). *Toward an Islamic reformation: Civil liberties, human rights, and international law.* Syracuse, NY: Syracuse University Press.

An-Na'im, A. A. (1992). Toward a cross-cultural approach to defining international standards of human rights: The meaning of cruel, inhuman, or degrading treatment or punishment. In A.A. An-Na'im (Ed.), *Human Rights in Cross-Cultural Perspectives: A Quest for Consensus.* Philadelphia: University of Pennsylvania Press.

Bentham, Jeremy (2002). Nonsense Upon Stilts. In Philip Schofield, Catherine Pease-Watkin & Cyprian Blamires, *Rights, Representation and Reform: Nonsense Upon Stilts and Other Writings on the French Revolution.* Oxford: Oxford University Press.

Committee on the Elimination of Racial Discrimination (2000). Concluding observations by the Committee on the Elimination of Racial Discrimination: Australia. 19/4/2000. CERD/C/304/Add.101.[http://www.unhchr.ch/html/menu2/6/cerd/cerds56.htm#56th]

Dunne, T. & Wheeler, N. J. (1999). Introduction: Human rights and the fifty years' crisis. In, T. Dunne & N. J. Wheeler (eds.), *Human Rights in Global Politics.* Cambridge, Cambridge University Press, pp. 1-28.

Engle, K. Culture and Human Rights: The Asian Values Debate I Context. International Law and Politics, Vol. 32 (2000), pp. 291-333.

Geertz, C. (1998). *The World in Pieces: Culture and politics at the end of the century.* Focaal: Tigdschrift voor Antropologie, 32, pp. 91-117.

Gewirth, A. (1996) The community of rights. Chicago, The University of Chicago Press, p.6.

Hartney, M. (1995). Some confusions concerning collective rights. In W. Kymlicka (Ed.), *The rights of minority cultures*. Oxford, UK: Oxford University Press, pp. 202-227.

Hofstede G. (1980). *Culture's consequences: International differences in work-related values*. London, UK: Sage Publications.

Hurrell, A. (1999). Power, principles and prudence: Protecting human rights in a deeply divided world. In, T. Dunne & N. J. Wheeler (Eds.), *Human Rights in Global Poltics*.Cambridge, UK: Cambridge University Press, pp. 277-302.

International Convention for the Elimination of All Forms of Racial Discrimination, adopted 21 Dec.1965, entered into force 4 Jan. 1069, 660 United Nations Treaty Series 195. [http://www.unhchr.ch/html/menu3/b/d_icerd.htm] Accessed 26 September 2004.

International Covenant on Civil and Political Rights, adopted 16 Dec. 1966, entered into

force 23 March 1976, G.A. Res. 2200A (XXI), UN Doc. A/6316 (1966), 999 United Nations Treaty Series 171. [http://www.unhchr.ch/html/menu3/b/a_ccpr.htm] Accessed 26 September 2004.

International Covenant on Economic, Social and Cultural Rights, adopted 16 Dec. 1966, entered into force 3 Jan 1976, G.A. Res. 2200A (XXI), UN Doc. A/6316 (1966), 993 United Nations Treaty Series 3. [http://www.unhchr.ch/html/menu3/b/a_cescr.htm] Accessed 26 September 2004.

Minister for Foreign Affairs (2000) Improving the effectiveness of United Nations Committees. Press release 29.9.2000.[http://www.dfat.gov.au/media/releases/foreign/2000/fa097_2000.html] Accessed 26 September 2004.

Parekh, B. (1999). Non-ethnocentric universalism. In, T. Dunne & N. J. Wheeler (Eds.), *Human Rights in Global Politics*. Cambridge, UK: Cambridge University Press, pp. 128-159.

Rawls, J. (1971). *A Theory of Justice*. Cambridge, MA: Harvard University Press.

Rawls, J. (1993). *Political Liberalism*. New York: Columbia University Press.

Rawls, J. (1999). *The Law of Peoples*. Cambridge, MA: Harvard University Press.

Rorty, R. (1999). *Philosophy and Social Hope*. London: Penguin Books.

Sen, A. (2000). *Development as Freedom*. New York: Alfred A. Knopf.

Steiner, H. J. & Alston, P. (1996). *International Human Rights in Context: Law, Politics, Morals*. Oxford, UK: Clarendon Press, p. 227

Tay, S.S.C. (1996). *Human Rights, Culture, and the Singapore Example*. McGill Law Journal, Vol. 41 (1996): pp. 743-780.

United Nations (1948). Universal Declaration of Human Rights adopted 10 Dec. 1948, G.A. Res. 217A (III), UN Doc. A/180, at 71. [http://www.unhchr.ch/udhr/index.htm] Accessed 26 September 2004.

Van Ness, P. (1999). *Debating Human Rights: Critical essays from the United States and Asia*. London, UK: Routledge.

CHAPTER 6

A Confucian Perspective on Human Rights

Weiming Tu

The original conception of human rights in the Universal Declaration of 1948 includes economic, social and cultural rights as well as political rights. This is compatible with group rights as well as individual rights. Human rights are inseparable from human responsibilities (United Nations, 1948). Although in the Confucian tradition, duty-consciousness is more pronounced than rights-consciousness—to the extent that the Confucian tradition underscores self-cultivation, family cohesiveness, economic well-being, social order, political justice and cultural flourishing—it is a valuable spring of wisdom for an understanding of human rights broadly conceived. The argument that Confucian humanism is incompatible with human rights needs to be carefully examined. Human rights as "the common language of humanity," to borrow from former United Nations Secretary-General Boutros Boutros-Ghali, is a defining characteristic of the spirit of our time (Boutros-Ghali, 1993). The foundation of the Universal Declaration has been broadened and strengthened by governments, non-governmental organizations and conscientious citizens throughout the world for almost half a century when an unprecedented international effort was made to inscribe not only on paper but on human conscience the bold vision of a new world order rooted in respect for human dignity as the central value for political action.

The Enlightenment Roots of Human Rights

In an historical and comparative cultural perspective, this vision emerged through a long and arduous process beginning with the Enlightenment movement in the modern West in the eighteenth century. The Enlightenment mentality is the most dynamic and transformative ideology in human history. Major spheres of interests characteristic of the modern age are indebted to this mentality: science and technology, industrial capitalism, market economy, democratic polity, mass communication, research universities and professional organizations. So are the values that underlie the rise of the modern West: liberty, equality, progress, the dignity of the individual, respect for privacy, government for by and of the people, and due process of law. We have been so seasoned in the Enlightenment mentality that we assume the reasonableness of its general spiritual thrust. We find the values it embodies self-evident. The Enlightenment's faith in progress, reason, and individualism may have lost some of its persuasive power in New York, London, and Paris but it remains a standard of inspiration for intellectual leaders throughout the world. Beijing, Hong Kong, Taipei, and Singapore are no exception.

However, we are acutely aware of the destructive power of the Enlightenment mentality as well. The runaway technology of development may have been a spectacular achievement of human ingenuity in the early phases of the Industrial Revolution, but the Faustian drive to explore, to know, to conquer, and to subdue has been the most destabilizing ideology the world has ever witnessed. As the Western nations assumed the role of innovators, executors, and judges of the international rules of the game defined in terms of competition for wealth and power, the stage was set for growth, development and, unfortunately, exploitation. The unleashed juggernaut blatantly exhibited unbridled aggressiveness toward humanity, nature, and itself. This unprecedented destructive engine has for the first time in human history made the viability of the human species problematic. Mainly because of our own *avidya* (the Buddhist concept of ignorance), we have joined the list of endangered species.

Human rights discourse may be conceived as the contemporary embodiment of the Enlightenment spirit. While it does not directly address the question of human survival, it specifies the minimum requirements and basic conditions for human flourishing. It is a powerful, if not the most persuasive, universal moral discourse in the international arena. It may very well be the most effective, if not the only, "instrument" by which the states' ordinary standards of behavior can be judged by outsiders without infringing the prerogatives of sovereignty.

Human Rights as an Evolving Discourse

With this background in mind, we should heed the advice of Boutros-Ghali (1993) that our human rights discourse should avert a dual danger:

The danger of a cynical approach, according to which the international dimension of human rights is nothing more than an ideological cover for the *realpolitik* of States; and the danger of a naïve approach, according to which human rights would be the expression of universally-shared values toward which all the members of the international community would naturally aspire.

The universality of human rights broadly conceived in the 1948 declaration is a source of inspiration for the human community. The moral and legal imperative that any civilized state treat its citizens in accordance with the political rights guaranteed by its own constitution is still a compelling argument. The desirability of democracy as providing to this day the most effective framework in which human rights are safeguarded seems self-evident. However, human rights movement as a dynamic process rather than a static structure requires that the human rights discourse be dialogical, communicative, and—hopefully— mutually beneficial.

The Evolution of the Human Rights Agenda

The gradual evolution of the human rights agenda in the United States, a country blessed with a very strong tradition of civil society which immensely impressed the sage French aristocrat Alexis de Tocqueville in the middle of the 19th century illustrates the dynamism of the process. While the framers of the American Constitution were profoundly serious about political rights, they were not particularly concerned about either civil or economic rights. It was not until the late 19th century that Socialists, indeed Communist thinkers, addressed the maldistribution of wealth and income, the concentration of capital, and the exploitation of labor as central political issues. The perception of justice as fairness is as much a socialist as a liberal contribution. It was in the late 1960s that the Civil Rights Movement made substantial progress in solving the American dilemma of racism, which to this day remains a serious threat to the vitality of the American body politic. We should also remind ourselves, especially those in the United States, that the whole issue of immigration rights, particularly in reference to the Jewish population in the former Soviet Union, was an important aspect of U.S. official human rights agenda in the 1970s. This clearly indicates that a sophisticated understanding of human rights as evolving enterprise in the West itself requires historical consciousness, geopolitical analysis and, most of all, self-reflexivity.

Seen from comparative cultural and trans-generational perspectives, the inclusive agenda of the United Nations Declaration of Human Rights reflects both the pragmatic idealism and optimistic aspirations of the post-War World mentality at its most generous and future-oriented moment. It may not be far-fetched to characterize it as a manifestation of the American spirit in its most broad-minded internationalist incarnation. All three generations of human rights as an evolving moral discourse are accounted for: (1) political rights, (2) economic, social, and cultural rights, and (3) group rights. The comprehensiveness of the agenda, which may have resulted from negotiation and compromise, suggests that, under American leadership, the international community was willing to subscribe to a moral vision not only for human survival but also for human flourishing.

Implicit in such a document is the idea of a good society, the value of a humane form of life for all members of the human community, and the ethic of responsibility of all "civilized" governments to work toward a common goal of universal peace. With this background understanding in mind, although the situation in the 1990s presents new challenges unanticipated and perhaps unimaginable more than forty years ago, it also affirms the prescient goodwill of the original drafters of this unprecedented historical document.

The Vienna Declaration and Programme of Action resulting from the World Conference on Human Rights in June 1993 (Vienna Declaration, 1993) directs our attention to women, children, minorities, disabled persons and indigenous peoples, groups not included in the original conceptions of human rights. The three key regional meetings in Tunis, San Jose, and Bangkok were an integral part of the preparatory process for the Vienna Conference on which several human rights declarations outlining particular concerns and perspectives of the African, Latin American and the Caribbean, and Asia-Pacific regions were produced (Boutros-Ghali, 1993). The recognition of inter-dependence between democracy, development and human rights led to the cooperation of international organizations and national agencies in broadening the concept of human rights to include the right to development (United Nations, 1995). While this confluence of social and economic concerns may have undermined the effectiveness of some national and international instruments focusing on well-defined political rights, it has engendered new mechanisms for the promotion of human rights.

The Social Summit convened in Copenhagen in January 1995 which focused on the critical issues confronting the global community (poverty, unemployment, and social disintegration) is indicative of a new awareness that human rights ought to be broadly defined to include economic, social, and cultural dimensions of the human experience (United Nations, 1995). The idea of human dignity features prominently in the documents in preparation for the Summit. Indeed, the participants of the Seminar on the Ethical and Spiritual Dimensions of Social Development organized by the preparatory committee strongly endorsed the view that human rights which have more to do with ethics, law and politics and whose respect can be verified and measured constitute preferred means of putting into practice the concept of human dignity. They also underscored the inseparability of human rights as a political agenda and human dignity as an ethico-religious concern (United Nations, 1995).

The Confucian Challenge

This renewed awareness of ecumenical character of the original U.N. Declaration serves as a critique of the claim that since human rights are understood variously according to culture, history, stage of economic development, and concrete political situation, they cannot be universally appreciated as values and aspirations for the global community. However, this does not call into question the underlying assumptions of Confucian "core values": the perception of the person as a center of relationships rather than simply as an isolated individual; the idea of society as a community of trust rather than merely a system of adversarial relationships; and the belief that human beings are duty-bound to respect their family, society, and nation. Indeed, these values are not only compatible with the implementation of human rights. They can, in a sophisticated way, enhance the universal appeal of human rights. The possible contribution of in-depth discussion on Asian values to a sophisticated cultural appreciation of the human rights discourse must be fully explored.

Actually, there is virtual consensus that since respect for rights and exercise of responsibility are evidence of human dignity, individual rights and responsibility are inseparable in all domains of human flourishing: self-cultivation, regulation of family, order in society, governance of state, peace throughout the world, and harmony with nature. In any concrete experience of human encounter, rights, and responsibility form an interactive mutual relationship signifying a necessary continuum for human well-being (Gardner, 1986). The Asian, specifically Confucian, values discussion which emerged in the regional meeting in Bangkok in 1993 provide us with an opportunity to develop a truly ecumenical agenda allowing the human rights discourse to become a continuously evolving and edifying conversation (Ghai, 1994; Muzaffar, 1993). The danger of using Confucian values as a cover for authoritarian practices notwithstanding, the authentic possibility of dialogue, communication, and mutually beneficial exchange must be fully explored. The perceived Confucian preference for duty, harmony, consensus, network, ritual, trust, and sympathy need not be a threat to rights-consciousness at all.

The critique of acquisitive individualism, vicious competitiveness, pernicious relativism and excessive litigiousness help us to understand that Enlightenment values do not necessarily cohere into an integrated guide for action. The conflict between liberty and equality and the lack of concern for community have significantly undermined the persuasive power of human rights based exclusively on the self-interests of isolated individuals. Confucian values as richly textured ideas of human flourishing can serve as a source of inspiration for representing human rights as the common language of humanity. The challenge is how we can fruitfully introduce a Confucian perspective on the evolving human rights discourse without diffusing the focused energy of the national and international instruments that have been promoting political rights with telling effectiveness in some selected areas of the world. The difficulty, however, is that the concretely demonstrable successes of the narrowly focused political rights persuasion are not easily sustainable. The confrontational, if not politically arrogant and culturally insensitive, strategy is predicated on an outmoded faith in instrumental rationality. It is doubtful that it can continue to work well as a liberalizing and democratizing force in the global community.

In the long-term, a better strategy is to cultivate a communal critical self-awareness that instruments for promoting human rights, while universally connected, are firmly grounded in indigenous Asian conditions as well. Through intercultural dialogue, face-to-face communication and mutually beneficial exchange, a truly ecumenical conceptualization of human rights can overcome the narrowly defined instrumental rationality, intellectual naiveté, and self-imposed parochialism characteristic of the current state of affairs in North America. The time is ripe for a comparative civilizational discourse on human rights not only a moral basis for the new discourse on world order but a spiritual joint venture for human co-existence and mutual flourishing.

The Relevance of Community and Family

A key to the success of this spiritual joint venture is to recognize the apparent absence of the idea of community, let alone the global community, in the Enlightenment project. "Fraternity"—the functional equivalent of community (remember in the French revolution the three cardinal virtues of liberty, equality, and fraternity)—has received scanty attention in modern Western economic, political, and social thought. Surely, "community" features prominently in "Kant's (and Adam Smith's) strong commitment to a cosmopolitan political ideal" (Cohen, 1996). This may have been the continuation of the Greek idea of polis and more specifically the Stoic tradition, "a tradition in which we also find an image of concentric circles of human attachments, extending outward to the community of humankind" (Cohen, 1996). Yet it is undeniable that in modern Western political philosophy the tension is so exclusively focused on the relationship between the individual and the state that all forms of human-relatedness, including the basic dyadic relationships of the family, are relegated to the background. It seems that contemporary political theoreticians in the West, either by choice or by default, have abdicated their responsibility to consider family as a critical issue in adjudicating the relationship between the individual and the state, allowing the sociologists and anthropologists to worry about the political implications of the family. The situation in the United States begins to change mainly as a result of the recent attention on "family virtues" in national political debates.

Family, which plays so crucial a role in political order, is not absent in the major classics in Western political thought. Aristotle's *Politics*, Locke's *Second*

Treatise, Rousseau's *Social Contract*, Kant's *Rechtslehre*, and Hegel's *Philosophy of Right* all provide thought-provoking accounts of the family. Furthermore, "the leading contemporary philosopher, John Rawls, explores the role of the family as a fundamental unit of moral education" (Cohen, 1996). Yet, as Professor Joshua Cohen of the Massachusetts Institute of Technology notes, that from Aristotle to Hegel the main thrust of the political theories is make a clear distinction between the affective and ethical bonds operative in the family on the one hand and politics on the other(Cohen, 1996). By sharply contrasting political obligations from filial piety, they perceive a major rupture between familial and political relation. Understandably, they do not see the relevance of ethical behavior in the privacy of the family to the moral obligations of the public domain. It seems curious that the family is absent in the definition that man is a political animal.

The unintended negative consequences of this inattention to the relevance of family to politics are grave. The incongruence between what we do as a responsible and responsive member of the family and as a rights-bearing and self-interested political animal is a case in point. This incongruence may have contributed to the development of a public persona informed by values that are clearly antithetical to moral self-cultivation. As a result, our willingness to tolerate preposterous inequality, faith in the salvific power of greedy self-interest, and the unbridled affirmation of aggressive egoism have greatly poisoned the good well of progress, reason, and individualism.

The need to express a universal ethic for the formation of a global village and to articulate a possible link between the fragmented world we experience in our ordinary daily existence and the imagined community for the human species as a whole is deeply felt by an increasing number of concerned intellectuals. This requires at the minimum the replacement of the principle of self-interest no matter how broadly defined, with the Confucian golden rule: "Do not do to others what we would not want others to do to us" (Analects, V: 11). Since the new golden rule is stated in the negative, it will have to be augmented by a positive principle:

> In order to establish ourselves, we must help others to establish themselves; In order to enlarge ourselves, we must help others to enlarge themselves (Analects, VI: 28).

An inclusive sense of community based on the communal critical self-consciousness of the reflective minds is an ethico-religious goal as well as a philosophical ideal. The centrality of the family as politically significant and self-cultivation as a public good rather than a private concern must be recognized.

Spiritual Resources

The mobilization of three kinds of spiritual resources is necessary to ensure that this simple vision be grounded in the historicity of the cultural complexes informing our way of life today.

Western Spiritual Resources

The first kind involves the ethico-religious traditions of the modern West, notably Greek philosophy, Judaism, and Christianity. The very fact that they have been instrumental in giving birth to the Enlightenment mentality makes a compelling case that they reexamine their relationships to the rise of the modern West in order to create the new public sphere for the transvaluation of typical Western values. The exclusive dichotomy of matter/spirit, body/mind, sacred/profane, man/nature, or even creator/creature, must be transcended to allow supreme values such as the sanctity of the earth, the continuity of being, the beneficiary interaction between the human community and nature, and the mutuality between humankind and heaven to receive the saliency they deserve in both philosophy and ideology. The Greek philosophical emphasis on rationality, the biblical image of man "having dominion over the fish of the sea, and over the fowl of the air, and over the cattle, and over all the earth, and over every creeping thing that creepeth upon the earth" (Genesis, 1:26), and the so-called Protestant work ethic provide necessary if not sufficient sources for the Enlightenment mentality. However, the unintended negative consequences of the rise of the modern West have so undermined the sense of community implicit in the Hellenistic, the Greek idea of the citizen, the Judaic idea of covenant, and the Christian idea of fellowship or universal love. It is morally imperative for these great traditions, which have maintained highly complex and tension-ridden relationships with the Enlightenment mentality, to formulate their critique of the blatant anthropocentrism inherent in the Enlightenment project.

Especially noteworthy, is the rich reservoir of symbolic resources for self-cultivation in the spiritual traditions of the West. The Greek idea of philosophy as "love of wisdom" clearly indicates that thinking, as the contemplative mode of life, is essentially a spiritual exercise for the sake of communal as well as personal self-transformation. The three Western traditions are all dedicated to the spiritual transformation of the person as an ultimate concern. The Biblical question, "What is man, that thou art mindful of him?" (Psalm, 8:4), is profoundly ethical as well as religious. The human responsibility for taking care of the community (family, clan, neighborhood, village, society, or nation) as the proper home for human flourishing is a moral imperative in Greek, Judaic, and Christian traditions.

Non-Western Spiritual Resources

The second kind of spiritual resources are derived from non-Western historical civilizations which include: Hinduism, Jainism, Sikhism, and Buddhism in South and Southeast Asia; Confucianism and Taoism in East Asia; and Islam. It is both intriguing and significant to note that Islam ought to have been considered an integral part of Western civilization, because Islam in fact contributed to the emergence of the Renaissance and therefore, by implication, the advent of the Enlightenment mentality. Yet in North American and Western European societies, Islam has in recent years often been stigmatized by the academic community, the mass media, and the government as radical otherness. These ethico-religious traditions provide very sophisticated and practicable resources in world views, rituals, institutions, styles of education, and patterns of human relatedness. Moreover, they can help to develop new ways of understanding the world and styles of life both as continuation of and as alternative to the Western European and North American exemplification of the Enlightenment mentality.

Industrial East Asia, under the influence of Confucian culture among other indigenous traditions, has already developed a less adversarial, less individualistic, and less self-interested modern civilization. The co-existence of market economy with government leadership, democratic polity with meritocracy, and individual initiatives with group orientation has made this region economically and politically the most dynamic area of the world since the Second World War. The Westernization of Confucian Asia including Japan, the two Koreas, Mainland China, Hong Kong, Taiwan, Singapore, and Vietnam may have forever altered the spiritual landscape, but its indigenous resources, including Mahayana Buddhism, Taoism, Shamanism, Shintoism, and other folk traditions, have the resiliency to resurface and make their presence known in the new synthesis. The cultural implications of the contribution of Confucian ethics to the rise of industrial East Asia for the possible emergence of Hindu, Jain, Buddhist, and Islamic forms of modernity are far-reaching.

If an ethic, significantly different from the Protestant ethic, can provide impetus for the spirit of capitalism, the Weberian thesis will have to be broadened to incorporate non-Western modernizing experiences. It is certainly too facile to generalize, at this juncture, that Islamic, Buddhist, Jain, and Hindu ethic can all become contributory factors in the development of the spirit of capitalism. The Confucian example suggests that, given the right combination of economic, political, social, and cultural forces, intertwined with, if not generated by, the ethico-religious traditions of a specific area, all of these non-Western axial-age can become congenial to modernization (market economy, democratic polity, and individualism). Strictly speaking, these traditions will persist in the modernizing process and shape modernity in a variety of forms.

The caveat, of course, is that having been humiliated and frustrated by the imperialist and colonial domination of the modern West for more than a century, the rise of industrial East Asia symbolizes the instrumental rationality of the Enlightenment heritage with a vengeance. Indeed, the mentality of Japan and the Four Mini-Dragons is today characterized by mercantilism, commercialism and international competitiveness. Surely the possibility of their developing a more humane and sustainable community should not be exaggerated. Nor should we undermine the promise of an alternative and yet more appealing form of modern civilization. The Islamic-Confucian dialogue in Malaysia, as ways of exploring practicable measures as well as theoretical guidance for the realization of such a promise, is worth noting.

Indigenous Spiritual Resources

The third kind of spiritual resources involve the "primal" or the indigenous traditions such as native American, Hawaiian, Maori, Malaysian, Taiwanese, and numerous other nativistic tribal traditions. They have demonstrated with physical strength and aesthetic elegance that a sustainable human form of life has been possible since the Neolithic age. The ecological implications for our practical living are far-reaching. Their style of human flourishing is not a figment of the mind but an experienced reality in our modern age.

A distinctive feature of primal traditions is a profound sense and experience of rootedness. Each indigenous religious tradition is embedded in a concrete place symbolizing a way of perceiving, a mode of thinking, a form of living, an attitude, and a world view. A natural outcome of primal peoples' embeddedness in concrete locality is their intimate and detailed knowledge of their environment; indeed demarcations between their human habitat and nature are often muted. Implicit in this model of existence is the realization that mutuality and reciprocity between the anthropological world and the cosmos at large are both necessary and desirable. A critique of the Enlightenment mentality and its derivative modern mindset from primal consciousness as interpreted by the concerned and reflective citizens of the world could be thought-provoking.

An equally significant aspect of the primal way of living is the ritual of bonding in ordinary daily human interaction. The density of kinship relations, the rich texture of interpersonal communication, the detailed and nuanced appreciation of the surrounding natural and cultural world, and the experienced connectedness with ancestors point to communities grounded in ethnicity, gender, language, land, and faith. The primordial ties are constitutive parts of their being and activity. In Huston Smith's characterization, what they exemplify is participation rather than control in motivation, empathic understanding rather than empiricist apprehension in epistemology, respect for the transcendent rather than domination over nature in worldview, and fulfillment rather than alienation in human experience (Smith, 1991). As we begin to question the soundness or even sanity of some of our most cherished ways of thinking such as regarding knowledge rather than wisdom as power, asserting the desirability of material progress despite its corrosive influence on our soul and justifying the anthropocentric manipulation of nature even at the cost of destroying the life-support system, primal consciousness emerges as a source of inspiration.

A scholar of world spirituality, Ewert Cousins, in response to the ecological crisis, poignantly remarks that, as we look toward the twenty-first century with all the ambiguities and perplexities we experience, earth is our prophet and the indigenous peoples are our teachers (Cousins, 1991; Cousins, 1992). Realistically, however, those of us who are seasoned in the Enlightenment mentality cannot abdicate the hermeneutic responsibility to interpret the meaning of the earth's prophecy and to bring understanding to the primal peoples' message. The challenge is immense. For the prophecy and the message to be truly heard in the modern West, we may have to voice them through active and transformative dialogue with non-Western Axial-age civilizations. Such a collaborative effort across cultural and other boundaries is necessary to enable primal consciousness to be fully present in our self-reflexivity as we address issues of globalization.

A critique of the Enlightenment mentality and its derivative modern mindset from primal consciousness as interpreted by the concerned and reflective citizens of the world is already underway. It may not be immodest to say that we are beginning to develop a fourth kind of spiritual resource from the core of the Enlightenment project itself: our disciplined reflection, a communal rather than an isolated individual act, is a first step towards a new kind of thinking envisioned by religious leaders and ethical teachers. The feminist critique of tradition (especially the broadly conceived and yet, at the same time, historically and culturally grounded humanistic feminism), the environmental concerns (notably the spiritually informed project of deep ecology), the persuasion of religious pluralism, and the various forms of communitarian ethics (Aristotelian, Thomist, Hasidic, or republican) are obvious examples of this new awareness. The need to go beyond the Enlightenment mentality without either deconstructing or abandoning its commitment to rationality, liberty, equality, human rights, and distributive justice requires a thorough reexamination of modernity as a layered concept and modernization as a complex process.

The Confucian Way

Asian intellectuals have been devoted students of Western learning for more than a century. They have been students of Dutch learning (*Rangaku*, to use the Japanese expression), British learning, French learning, German learning, and more recently, American learning for industrial East Asia, and Westernized Soviet learning for socialist East Asia. Now that Asian intellectuals are well informed by the Enlightenment project of the West without losing sight of their own indigenous resources, the time seems ripe for European and American intellectuals in academia, government, business, and the mass media to appreciate what Confucian humanism, among other rich spiritual resources in Asia, has to offer toward the cultivation of a global ethic. On this view, the human rights advocacy need not be a thinly disguised modern Western hegemonic discourse.

Central Premises in the Confucian Discourse

The central *Problematik* in the Confucian discourse consists of four issues as exemplified in the *Book of Mencius*. The first one is *renqinzhibian*—the essential difference between man (humanity) and beast (other members of the animal kingdom). The second one is *yixiazhibian*—the essential difference between civilization and barbarism. The third one is *yilizhibian*—the essential difference between rightness and profit. The fourth one is *wangbazhibian*—the essential difference between kingship (benevolent government) and hegemony (politically powerful and economically efficient but morally inadequate polity; Tu, 1993; Tu, 1995).

In the Confucian perspective, human beings are not merely rational beings, political animals, tool-users, or language-manipulators. The Confucians seem to have deliberately rejected simplistic reductionist models. They define human beings in terms of five integrated visions.

o   Human beings are sentient, capable of internal resonance not only between and among themselves but also with other animals, plants, trees, mountains, and rivers, indeed nature as a whole.
o   Human beings are social. As isolated individuals, human beings are weak by comparison with other members of the animal kingdom but if they are organized to form a society, they have inner strength not only for survival but also for flourishing. Human-relatedness as exemplified in a variety of networks of interaction is necessary for human survival and human flourishing. Our sociality defines who we are.
o   Human beings are political, in the sense that human-relatedness is, by biological nature and social necessity, differentiated in terms of hierarchy, status, and authority. While Confucians insist upon the fluidity of these artificially constructed boundaries, they recognize the significance of "difference" in an "organic" as opposed to "mechanic" solidarity. Hence the centrality of the principle of fairness and the primacy of the practice of distributive justice in a humane society.
o   Human beings are also historical beings sharing collective memories, cultural traditions, ritual praxis, and "habits of the heart."
o   Human beings are metaphysical beings with the highest aspirations not simply defined in terms of anthropocentric ideas but characterized by the ultimate concern to be constantly inspired by and continuously re-

sponsive to the Mandate of Heaven.

The Confucian way is a way of learning, learning to be human. Learning to be human in the Confucian spirit is to engage oneself in a ceaseless, unending process of creative self-transformation, both as a communal act and as a dialogical response to Heaven. This involves four inseparable dimensions—self, community, nature, and the transcendent. The purpose of learning is always understood as for the sake of the self, but the self is never an isolated individual (an island) but a center of relationships (a flowing stream). The self as a center of relationships is a dynamic, open system rather than a closed, static structure. Therefore mutuality between self and community, harmony between human species and nature, and continuous communication with Heaven are defining characteristics and supreme values in the human project (Tu, 1993).

Since the Confucians take the concrete living human being, here and now, as their point of departure in the development of their philosophical anthropology, they recognize the embeddedness and rootedness of the human condition. Therefore, the profound significance of what we call primordial ties—ethnicity, gender, language, land, class, and basic spiritual orientation—intrinsic in the Confucian project is a celebration of cultural diversity (this is not to be confused with any form of pernicious relativism). Often, the Confucians understand their own path as learning of the body and mind (*shenxinzhixue*) or learning of nature and destiny (*xingmingzhixue*). There is a recognition that each one of us is fated to be a unique person embedded in a particular condition. By definition, we are unique particular human beings, but at the same time each and every one of us has the intrinsic possibility for self-cultivation, self-development, and self-realization. Despite fatedness and embeddedness as necessary structural limitations in our conditionality, we are endowed with infinite possibilities for self-transformation in our process of learning to be human. We are, therefore, intrinsically free. Our freedom, embodied in our responsibility for ourselves as center of relationships, creates our worth. That alone deserves and demands respect.

Learning to be Human

The Confucian way for human survival and human flourishing, then, is predicated on the two basic ethical principles already mentioned: "Do not do unto others what we would not want others to do unto us." This is a principle of considerateness, a principle of reciprocity. The reason that it is stated in the negative is based on the belief that what is best for me may not be best for my neighbor. This, on the surface, seems to violate the basic requirement of universality in ethical thinking. Yet, the need for one's critical self-awareness is not only the recognition of the integrity of the other but also the practical value of "analogical imagination"(Tracy, 1981). The practice of sympathetic understanding (a form of "embodied knowing") enhances one's self-knowledge, as Confucius notes (Analects, VI: 28), "the ability to take that which is near at hand as an analogy is indeed the method of humanity!"

The second principle is duty-consciousness; it is a manifestation of the ethic of responsibility: "In order to establish ourselves, we must help others to establish themselves; in order to enlarge ourselves, we must help others to enlarge themselves." This is not simply altruism; it is not that because I have a great deal of surplus energy or extra resources available, I might as well, for goodness sake, share with others. Rather, as I am a center of relationships, my own human flourishing necessitates that I involve myself, in the spirit of empathy to be sure, in the affairs of others. The word "help," added in the English translation, directs toward not only the others but ourselves as well for, in the literal sense, the Chinese text simply notes "desiring to establish ourselves (myself), we (I) establish others."

In this process of learning to be human, five basic virtues are to be embodied: *humanity, rightness, civility, wisdom,* and *trust.* Humanity, or perhaps more appropriately rendered as co-humanity, entails a feeling of sympathy. Rightness is often understood in a nuanced way. For example, when a student presented the Taoist argument: "how nice would it be if we can repay malice with kindness," Confucius retorted, "how are you going to repay kindness?" His recommendation was then (Analects, XIV:34): "repay malice with rightness (uprightness); repay kindness with kindness." Aside from humanity (co-humanity) and rightness, there are also the virtues of civility, wisdom, and trust. Civility, an idea that the recently deceased American sociologist, Edward Shils (1910/1995), considered essential for the development of any "civil society." The Confucian notion of ritual (*li*), as a civilized mode of conduct, has much richer and more complex connotation than civility entails, but, in the present context, it can serve as a functional equivalent of civility. Impressed by the sophisticated discourse on civility in the *Analects,* Shils, partly in jest, honored Confucius as a forefather of 'civil society' (Shils, 1996). Wisdom, then, is not insights derived from contemplation as the Greeks would have it. Rather, it is closely associated with knowing persons and doing things. Confucian wisdom is the cumulative result of 'embodied thinking' (Tu, 1985; Tu, 1987; Tu, 1992) on daily practical living. Wisdom grows out of conscientious engagement in social praxis instead of speculative meditation on abstract ideas. Trust, then, evokes the "gravity of spirit" such as fidelity, community, cooperation, and commitment.

Whether politics should be understood as moral leadership, or politics is just the distribution or the arrangement of power; whether economics is simply enhancement of profit, or embedded in economics is the management of wealth and resources implicit in the idea of justice and fairness; whether we cherish religious pluralism or we submit ourselves to religious exclusivism; whether we consider multiculturalism as a value or we simply accept our own language and our own way of life as the most and even the only authentic expression of modernity. These are not simply Confucian issues; these are issues we need to address as reflective modern persons, if we are serious in transforming "human rights" into a universal language of humanity.

We can actually envision the Confucian perception of human self-development, based upon the dignity of the person, in terms of a series of concentric circles: self, family, community, society, nation, world, and cosmos (refer to Figure 1). We begin with a quest for true personal identity, an open and creatively transforming selfhood which, paradoxically, must be predicated on our ability to overcome selfishness and egoism. We cherish family cohesiveness. In order to do that, we have to go beyond nepotism. We embrace communal solidarity, but we have to go beyond parochialism to fully realize its true value.

Figure 1. Confucian Perception of Human Development

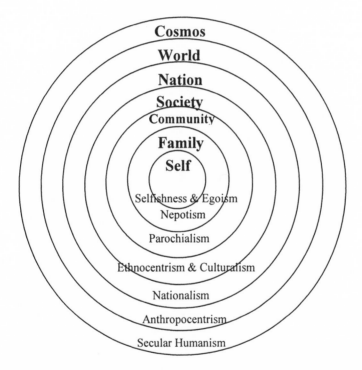

We can be enriched by social integration, provided that we overcome ethnocentrism and chauvinistic culturalism. We are committed to national unity, but we ought to transcend aggressive nationalism so that we can be genuinely patriotic. We are inspired by human flourishing but we must endeavor not to be confined by anthropocentrism, the full meaning of humanity is anthropocosmic rather than anthropocentric. On the occasion of the international symposium on Islamic-Confucian dialogue organized by the University of Malaya (March, 1995), the Deputy Prime Minister of Malaysia, Anwar Ibrahim, quoted a statement from Huston Smith's *The World's Religions*. It very much captures the Confucian spirit of self-transcendence:

> In shifting the center of one's empathic concern from oneself to one's family one transcends selfishness. The move from family to community transcends nepotism. The move from community to nation transcends parochialism and the move to all humanity counters chauvinistic nationalism (Ibrahim, 1997).

We can even add: the move towards the unity of Heaven and humanity (*tianrenheyi*) transcends secular humanism, a blatant form of anthropocentrism characteristic of the intellectual ethos of the modern West. Indeed, it is in the anthropocosmic spirit that we find communication between self and community, harmony between human species and nature, and mutuality between humanity and Heaven. This integrated comprehensive vision of learning to be human is the core of Confucian humanist concerns.

Implications for Human Rights Discourse

Confucians do not opt for an ideal speech situation. Nor are they ready to defend a new 'communicative rationality' (Habermas, 1984) based upon abstract principles. They do, however, ask fundamental questions. Should we understand the self as an isolated individual or as a center of relationships? Should we approach our society as a community based upon trust or simply the result of contractual arrangements of conflicting forces? As we begin to appreciate that we are so much embedded in our linguistic universe, not to mention our historicity, that we cannot escape a de facto parochialism, no matter how open-minded we intend to be and how liberated we think we are, we must respect alternative intelligence and radical otherness.

East Asian intellectuals are earnestly engaged in probing the Confucian traditions as spiritual resources for economic development, nation building, social stability, and cultural identity. While they cherish the hope that their appreciation of their own cultural values will provide ethical moorings as they try to locate their niche in the turbulent currents of the modern world, they remain active participants in the Enlightenment project. The revived Confucian values are no longer fundamentalist representation of nativistic ideas; they are, by and large, transvaluated traditional values compatible with and commensurate to the main thrust of modern ideology defined in term of Enlightenment ideas. Actually, since East Asian intellectuals have been devoted students of the modern West for several generations, the Enlightenment values, including human rights, have become an integral part of their own cultural heritage.

The critical issue, then, is not traditional Confucian values versus modern Western values, but how East Asian intellectuals can be enriched and empowered by their own cultural roots in their critical response to already partially domesticated Enlightenment heritage. The full development of human rights requires their ability to creatively transform the Enlightenment mentality of the modern West into a thoroughly digested cultural tradition of their own; this, in turn, is predicated on their capacity to creatively mobilize indigenous social capital and cultural asset for the task. They must be willing to confront difficult and threatening challenges, identify complex real options, and make painful practicable decisions.

The conflicts between liberty and equality, economic efficiency and social justice, development and stability, individual interests and the public good, not to mention rights and duty, are harsh realities in practical living. The enhancement of liberty, economic efficiency, development, individual interests, and rights are highly desirable, but to pursue these values exclusively at the expense of equality, social justice, stability, the public good, and duty is ill-advised. As the supposedly exemplification of modernity—North America and Western Europe—continue to show ignorance of the cultures of the rest of the world and insouciance about the peoples who do not speak their languages, East Asia cannot but choose its own way. It is in this sense that a Confucian perspective on human rights is worth exploring.

Confucian humanism offers "an account of the reasons for supporting basic human rights that does not depend on a liberal conception of persons, and that operates from within an ethical outlook dominated by notions of persons as embedded in social relations and subject to the obligations associated with those relationships: therefore an account that responds to the concern about sectarianism" (Cohen, 1996). The liberal ideas of the persons as fundamentally choosers of their aims and of rights as ways to acknowledge the human capacity to formulate and revise their aims affirm individuals to have worth or dignity in abstraction from social setting. Thus John Rawls defines individuals as "self-authenticating sources of valid claims." (Cohen, 1996) These individualistic claims are "regarded as having weight of their own apart from being derived from duties and obligations owed to society" (Cohen, 1996). On the contrary, the Confucian position asserts:

> The notions of persons standing in social relationships and of duties associated with positions in those relationships remain fundamental in that rights are presented as flowing from the demands of these duties and an account of the worth of human beings that is tied to their fulfill social responsibilities (Cohen, 1996).

While the Confucian position seems to subscribe to a view that Rawls rejects in his political doctrine, it gets to the basic rights incorporated into the Universal Declaration without presupposing the ideas of the person commonly associated with liberalism.

Furthermore, as bearers of obligations, we can demand proper treatment as conditions for fulfilling the obligations we are assumed to have. Similarly, our human worth is predicated on our ability to fulfill responsibilities, we can demand of others—as a condition of acknowledging that worth—that they assure the conditions required for fulfilling our responsibilities. If we become more powerful and influential, we are more obligated, responsible, and duty-bound to assure the well-being of others.

As a corollary, we can demand that those in power fulfill their responsibility of caring for the good of society. The basic human rights can, therefore, flow from political leadership. Rights understood in this way are not derived from "ascribed roles in a social hierarchy justified by religious or aristocratic values." Nor, strictly speaking, are they derived from "duties and obligations owed to society." It is in the dignity and worth of the self as a center of relationships that the justification for rights is located.

Paradoxically, the Confucian personality ideals—the authentic person (*junzi*), the worthy (*xianren*), or the sage (*shengren*)—can be realized more fully in the liberal-democratic society than either in the traditional imperial dictatorship or a modern authoritarian regime. East Asian Confucian ethics must creatively transform itself in light of Enlightenment values before it can serve as effective critique of the excessive individualism, pernicious competitiveness, and vicious litigiousness of the modern West (Tu, 1994).

Yet those of us, who are blessed with the political rights in the first world, must recognize that, in a comparatively cultural perspective, our style of life, corrupted by excessive individualism, pernicious competitiveness, and vicious litigiousness, is not only endangering the well-being of others but also detrimental to our own wholesomeness. Our willingness to learn from significantly different conceptualizations of the rights discourse and to respond openly and responsibly to criticisms of deficiency in our own human rights records must serve as a precondition for our determination to share our experience with the rest of the world and to make sure that human rights violations are clearly noted and properly corrected by the instruments at our disposal. An inquiry on global ethic, with this attitude in mind, is relevant to and crucial for human rights discourse on the international scene toward the next century.

References

Analects (1999). Translation with modification based on *Sources of Chinese Tradition*. Compiled by Wm. Theodore de Bary and Irene Bloom; with the collaboration of Wing-tsit Chan. New York, NY: Columbia University Press, 1999.

Boutros-Ghali, B. (1993). *Human rights: The common language of humanity*. Statement made at the opening of the World Conference on Human Rights: The Vienna Declaration and Programme of Action, June. New York: United Nation's Department of Public Information, p.5.

Cohen, J. (1996). "Comments on Tu Weiming, 'A Confucian Perspective of Human Rights,'" at the China Forum sponsored by the MIT International Science and Technology Initiative, April 29, 1996, unpublished manuscript.

Cousins, E. (1991). Statement. In S. Friesen (Ed.), *Local Knowledge, Ancient Wisdom.* Honolulu, HI: East West Center.

Cousins, E. (1992). *Christ of the 21st Century.* Rockport, MA: Element.

Gardner, D. K. (1986). *Chu Hsi and the Ta-hsueh: Neo-Confucian reflection on the Confucian cannon.* Cambridge, MA: Council on East Asian Studies, Harvard University.

Ghai, Y. (1994). Human rights and governance: The Asian debate. *Occasional Paper No. 4, The Asia Foundation: Center for Asian Pacific Affairs.*

The Holy Bible (1976). Authorized King James Version. Lynchburg, VA: The Old-Time Gospel Hour.

Habermas, J. (1984). *The Theory of Communicative Action. Volume 1.* Boston: Beacon Press.

Ibrahim, A. (1997). "Islam-Confucianism Dialogue and the Quest for a New Asia," in *Islam and Confucianism: A Civilizational Dialogue*, ed. Osman Bakar, Kuala Lumpur: University of Malaya Press.

International Commission of Jurists (1959). *The rule of law in a free society.* Geneva, Switzerland: International Commission of Jurists.

Muzaffar, C. (1993). *Human rights and the New World Order.* Penang, Malaysia: Just World Trust.

Rawls, J. (1971). *A Theory of Justice.* Cambridge, MA: Belknap Press of Harvard University Press.

Shils, E (1996). Reflection on Civil Society and Civility in the Chinese Intellectual Tradition. *Confucian Traditions in East Asian Modernity.* ed. Tu Wei-ming. Cambridge, MA: Harvard University Press, 1996.

Smith, H. (1991). Unpublished paper presented to the International Conference on "An Exploration of Contemporary Spirituality: Axial-Age Civilizations and Primal Traditions," June 10-14. Honolulu, HI: Institute of Culture and Communication, East-West Center.

Tracy, David (1991). *The Analogical Imagination.* NY: Crossroad.

Tu, W. (1985). "Embodying the Universe: A Note on Confucian Self-Realization," in *Confucian Thought*, Tu Wei-ming, Albany: SUNY.

Tu, W. (1987). "Lun Jujia de 'tizhi'—dexing zhi zhi de hanyi," (On "embodied knowing"—the implications of moral knowledge in the Confucian tradition) in Liu Shu-hsien, ed., *Jujia lunli yentaohui wenji* (Essays from the seminar on Confucian ethics; Singapore: Institute of East Asian Philosophy).

Tu, W. (1992). "A Confucian Perspective on Embodiment" in *The Body in Medical Thought and Practice*, ed. Drew Leder, Boston : Kluwer Academic Publishers.

Tu, W. (1993). *Way, learning, and politics: essays on the Confucian intellectual.* Albany: State University of New York Press,

Tu, W. (1994). Beyond the Enlightenment Mentality. *Worldviews & Ecology*, ed. Mary Evelyn Tucker, Maryknoll, N.Y.: Orbis Books.

Tu, W. (1995). Menzi: Shi de Zijue (Mencius: The Self-consciousness of *Shi*), in *Guoji Ruxue Yanjiu* , vol. 1 (International Confucian Studies), Beijing: Renmin Chubanshe.

United Nations (1948). *Universal Declaration on Human Rights*, G.A. Res. 217A, U.N. Doc. A/810.

United Nations (1995). *Ethical and Spiritual Dimensions of Social Progress*. New York, NY: United Nations.

United Nations (1995). The human rights to development. *United Nations World Summit for Social Development*. New York, NY: American Association for the International Commission of Jurists, Inc.

United Nations (1993, June). *World Conference on Human Rights: the Vienna Declaration and Programme of Action, June 1993, Vienna, Austria)*. New York, NY: United Nations Department of Public Information.

CHAPTER 7

Institutionalizing Human Rights in the Militaries of the Emerging Democracies: The Case of Peru

Jeffrey F. Addicott

In the quest for bettering the quality of human life, human rights have had a major impact in shaping world opinion and events, as well as serving as the basis for a consensus definition regarding the fundamental pillars upon which all just governments should be anchored (Rummel, 1994). As the preamble to the Universal Declaration of Human Rights asserts, human rights serve "as a common standard of achievement for all peoples and all nations."

Although in its most comprehensive meaning, human rights encompasses all those principles and concerns associated with ensuring respect for the inherent dignity of the individual human being, many scholars view human rights as chronologically evolving in generations. The first generation of human rights deals with the individual's fundamental right to be secure in the most sacred asset of all—his or her person. By international treaty obligation and customary international law, only this category of human rights law is binding on all nations. Specifically, a State violates international human rights law if, as a matter of State policy, it practices, encourages, or condones seven types of actions. Set out at Restatement (Third) of the Foreign Relations Law of the United States (1987) §702; Customary International Law of Human Rights, those actions consist of:

1) genocide
2) slavery or slave trade
3) the murder or causing the disappearance of individuals
4) torture or other cruel, inhuman, or degrading treatment or punishment
5) prolonged arbitrary detention
6) systematic racial discrimination (United Nations Centre for Human Rights, 1992)
7) a consistent pattern of gross violations of internationally recognized human rights

University of Virginia law professor John Norton Moore argues that the best way to predict whether a given nation will engage in human rights violations is via his "radical regime" syndrome. According to Moore, Tipson, & Turner (2005), the elements of a radical totalitarian regime include:

o a failing centrally-planned economy
o severe limitations on economic freedom
o a one party political system
o the absence of an independent judiciary
o a police state with minimal human rights and political freedoms at home
o a denial of the right to emigrate
o the heavy involvement of the military in political leadershi
o a large percentage of the GNP devoted to the military sector
o a high percentage of the population in the military
o leaders strongly motivated by an ideology of true beliefs including willingness to use force
o aggressively anti-Western and antidemocratic behavior
o selective support for wars of national liberation, terrorism
o disinformation against Western or democratic interests

Clearly, if human rights are to flourish they must be rooted in the soil of a democracy which is protected by a military that has incorporated democratic principles. With the emergence of the nascent democracies in the post-Cold War era, a most urgent problem involves the reformation of former totalitarian militaries such that human rights are fully institutionalized and appropriately reflected in their performance of military duties. This chapter will argue that the United States is uniquely qualified to assist in the implementation of a new paradigm for the prevention of war and the promotion of human rights into the military's training and doctrine. The paradigm is illustrated through a unique U.S. Army legal effort conducted in Peru in the early 1990's that actually assisted a foreign military in the institutionalization of human rights.

Demands of Non-traditional Military Roles

New non-traditional roles for the U.S. military—such as promoting human rights training—have placed fresh demands on the military legal profession represented by the Judge Advocate General's Corps (JAGC). The JAGC consists of Army officers that serve as lawyers, or judge advocates. Judge advocates advise and respond to a variety of legal problems including military justice, military administration, and international law issues. By doctrine, military lawyers oversee all of the regulatory requirements associated with providing law of war, code of conduct, and standards of conduct training to all U.S. soldiers (Burger, 1978; Elliott, 1983; Parks, 1980). In order to deal more effectively with the legal issues related to new military missions, the Army JAGC developed a separate legal discipline in the late 1980s, called "Operational Law" (OPLAW) (Addicott, 1990).

In accordance with the working definition of Operational Law, "that body of law, both domestic and international, impacting specifically upon legal issues associated with the planning for and deployment of U.S. forces overseas in both peacetime and combat environments" (Graham, 1987), judge advocates are concerned with legal issues associated with law of war, security assistance, intelligence law, status of forces agreements, contracting, claims, combined training exercises, humanitarian assistance, civil affairs, peace operations, drug interdiction, training of foreign military legal officers, and other related matters.

The most challenging and novel OPLAW mission for U.S. military judge advocates rests in providing legal reform assistance to the militaries of the new democracies. A successful strategy to achieve these democratization goals must be based on three clearly focused themes directed to the host nation military (and appropriate civilian government officials) (Foreign Assistance Act, 1961; Public Law No. 87-195, 75 Stat. 424) (1) instilling a greater respect for internationally recognized standards for human rights; (2) fostering greater respect for and an understanding of the principle of civilian control of the military; and (3) improving military justice systems and procedures to comport with internationally recognized standards of human rights.

Peru—A Case Study in Conflict

An encouraging example of the spread of democracy can be seen in Latin America. Just 20 years ago some 90 percent of countries in Latin American functioned under some form of non-democratic military rule, today, the vast majority of these countries operate under popularly-elected civilian governments. The Western Hemisphere is now virtually all democratic, but, as one might expect, a number of Latin American countries are having serious troubles in establishing and/or maintaining the institutions necessary for the full blessings of democracy and human rights.

One of the key nations in the so-called drug war in the Andean Region is Peru—a struggling democracy plagued with every ingredient of conflict imaginable. At the same time, however, Peru also stands as a model for the future.

Peru is a land of stark contrasts, both in its social order and in its terrain. Like many developing countries, it is faced with economic hardship and unacceptable levels of social inequality—factors that significantly hinder the development and fostering of democratic institutions. Peru is also beset by the twin-headed serpent of subversion and illegal drug trafficking, factors that further inhibit the promotion of fundamental human rights. Apart from Colombia, there are few places in the world where the forces of organized subversion, staggering economic hardship, and illegal narcotics trafficking have so deeply threatened the basic societal order.

The total strength of the Peruvian armed forces is around 70,000. By law, all men and women who reach military age (18) must register for conscription, but only males are required to serve in the enlisted ranks for a period of 18 months. Like other functional militaries, women are not allowed in combat roles and comprise only a small portion of the total force.

There can be little serious debate about whether human rights abuses have been carried out by the Peruvian military in the ongoing conflict against insurgents, particularly in the late 1980's and early 1990's. Secret military trials, torture, rape, disappearances, and extra-judicial killings are the violations most often cited. In their 1993 Human Rights and U.S. Security Assistance Report (Amnesty International, 1993) Amnesty International listed the following concerns targeted primarily at the military of Peru: (1) killings and disappearances by security forces; (2) killings and torture by opposition groups; (3) judicial proceedings falling short of international fair standards; (4) extrajudicial executions of unarmed demonstrators by security forces; (5) torture and ill-treatment of hundreds of political detainees; and (6) government failure to investigate and prosecute past and present human rights violations.

Disappearances have always been chief among the human rights concerns. Almost all disappearances in Peru are attributed to either the Peruvian military or national police. In contrast to the subversives, who always carry out their executions in public, government forces do not desire such publicity. According to official figures supplied by the Public Ministry's Fiscalia for Human Rights (American Embassy, 1993), there were 279 disappearances in 1991 and 282 in 1992. Over the period between 1982 and 1993, the United Nations estimates the number of unresolved disappearances caused by government forces at 2,640. This figure likely underestimates reality.

In addition, the use of the military to try civilian suspects has resulted in a firestorm of criticism, primarily directed at the manner in which the military performs investigations and trials. When one considers the seriousness of the threat posed by the subversives and narco-traffickers during this period, however, it is clear that any similarly situated government would be required to resort to emergency measures to deal with forces that threatened freedom itself. In the case of Peru, this has sometimes meant expanding the use of the military into areas typically left to the civilian police and judicial systems.

Finally, although the primary concern regarding the Peruvian armed forces during this period rested in the military's poor record of respect for human rights, little attention was paid to the record of their opposition, the *Partido Comunista del Peru en el Sendero Luminoso de Mariategui* (Shining Path). Commonly referred to as the *Sendero*, it was the nation's largest terrorist organization (Strong, 1992). Devoted to overthrowing the Peruvian government, in the early 1990's it was considered the most radical and powerful Marxist revolutionary movement in the Western Hemisphere. The subversives were guilty of violating every category of human rights imaginable—incorporating terrorist tactics into their official doctrine. For instance, when one Sendero was asked why children were killed by the Shining Path, he coldly replied, "In the jungle, we don't consider a 10-year old a child" (Strong, 1992).

Institutionalizing Human Rights in Peru's Armed Forces

The story of how the U.S. Army JAGC was able to test the new paradigm for war prevention by assisting a foreign military to incorporate human rights values took place in the case of Peru from 1992 to 1994. Confronted by organized subversives, drug cartels, economic hardships, and an ineffective State infrastructure, the Peruvian military sought the assistance of the U.S. Army JAGC to institutionalize human rights training into their armed forces. By requesting U.S. assistance to develop a human rights training program for their soldiers, the Peruvian military desired to raise its status as a professional fighting force and improve a clouded human rights record.

The Peruvian request came in the face of an unprecedented wave of devastating terrorist attacks throughout the country. By the spring of 1992, the Shining Path had almost brought the nation to a standstill, and many U.S. analysts predicted the imminent overthrow of the government (Speck, 1992). Sensing that the Peruvian authorities were on the defensive, the terrorists engaged in an all out campaign of mass bombings aimed at populated areas, power plants and public utilities. On any given day, bomb blasts could be heard throughout Lima, the capital city. In addition, citizens in the capital would wake to the bloody Sendero calling card of slaughtered black dogs hanging from lampposts and power wires throughout the city.

While then President Alberto Fujimori launched a series of highly controversial emergency initiatives to better cope with the growing terrorist threat (including dissolving the Congress), he also directed the military to improve its human rights record. The Peruvian military quickly acknowledged that the natural

temptation for soldiers and even commanders to respond in kind to terrorist brutality had to be halted. In addition, in their own right, the military had been
guilty of numerous human rights abuses to include disappearances, torture, and
destruction of civilian property. After more than ten years of fighting the
Sendero, the military leadership of Peru concluded that not only was such behavior by government troops counterproductive in securing the support of the
people, but that the international image of the Peruvian military as a legitimate,
law-based institution had suffered greatly.

In light of the clear resolve of the Peruvian government and military to improve their human rights record, the Commander-in-Chief of the United States
Southern Command (SOUTHCOM) turned to the International and Operational
Law Division, Office of The Judge Advocate General, Department of the Army
(DAJA-IO), to develop and implement a program to assist the Peruvian military
in human rights reform. Apart from this broad mandate, SOUTHCOM provided
no further guidance.

Two U.S. Army judge advocates traveled to Peru in 1992 to assess the problem. Later, they developed and executed the first-ever phased plan to reform the
entire training program in human rights for the Peruvian military. These two
officers were the author, a Lieutenant Colonel from DAJA-IO, and Major An-
drew Warner, a senior instructor at the International and Operational Law Division, the (now) Judge Advocate General's Law Center and School (JAG
School). In what developed into an unprecedented program to institutionalize
human rights training into the Peruvian armed forces, the American effort (JAG
team) lasted for almost 17 months—from August 1992 until January 1994.

After the initial site survey of the Peruvian armed forces, which revealed a
complete lack of emphasis on human rights training in the military, the U.S.
team determined that human rights training had to be institutionalized into the
fabric of the military establishment. The JAG team focused their efforts on three
chronological steps:

First, develop a viable curriculum on human rights in the form of a handbook
that would be used as the standard training text for the Peruvian military.

Second, train a professional cadre of Peruvian instructors to teach the curriculum in the handbook to Peruvian soldiers and, more importantly, to have this
cadre train other officers in how to teach human rights. In this way Peruvian
officers would be capable of teaching classes based on the handbook to all soldiers in the military—a train-the-trainer approach.

Third, obtain a formal commitment from the appropriate Peruvian high
command to make human rights training based on the handbook a mandatory
requirement for all of its forces.

By emphasizing the adoption of a uniform text on human rights, the U.S. legal team sought a coherent, consistent approach to human rights training
throughout the Peruvian military. In a nutshell, the target of the reform program
was the system, not just a select group of people. If human rights training and

the means to provide it were truly institutionalized, inculcation would continue for all Peruvian soldiers long after the U.S. legal team departed.

Phase I: Site Survey to Formulate a Concept Plan

The first phase of the plan was a site survey in Peru to assess requirements, resources, and capabilities. Once this was done, a concept plan for providing assistance could be developed. In August 1992, the JAG team of Addicott and Warner traveled to Lima, Peru, to discuss the overall human rights situation with their Peruvian counterparts and with the U.S. Embassy personnel.

Through a series of wide ranging meetings, the team accessed the character, ethos, and make-up of the Peruvian military. In the past, ideological dispositions varied between the branches of service. Indeed, prior to the collapse of the Soviet Union, Peru functioned as a socialist State and was a major recipient of Soviet aid. Up to 90 percent of Peruvian military equipment came from the Soviet Union and about 70 percent of its army reflected Soviet doctrine, either in military training or equipment. The Air Force retained approximately 45 percent Soviet-made equipment and training. Only the Navy had remained strongly pro-West, sending their officers to the U.S. Naval Academy for training and refusing to engage in Soviet assistance programs. As a result of this ideological schism, the various branches of the military often refused to communicate with one other. Obviously, this historical fragmentation would make reaching a consensus on a standardized human rights initiative extremely difficult.

Nevertheless, meetings with U.S. military officials at the Military Assistance and Advisory Group (MAAG) in Lima revealed that the door was open in Peru for human rights initiatives, especially with the recent capture of Abimael Guzman, the head of the Sendero Luminoso. With direct guidance from the MAAG Commander, then Colonel Alfred E. Valenzuela (Valenzuela retired in 2004 as a Major General), it was clear that any changes in human rights initiatives would have to enlist the close support of the most senior levels of the Peruvian military hierarchy.

As the site survey ended, the JAG team concluded that human rights training in the armed forces of Peru was at best ad hoc and at worst non-existent. While the Peruvians expressed a sincere desire to improve their human rights record and to receive human rights instruction, there was no movement towards creating a standardized methodology to teach human rights to the soldiers, let alone a military legal facility designed and equipped to train Peruvian judge advocates and commanders in these specialized areas. The Peruvian military was suffering from a profound institutional breakdown in the sphere of human rights training. Some of the most salient manifestations of this problem were the following:

First, Peruvian soldiers, particularly those in the field, received little if any meaningful human rights training. The absence of such training contributed to a lack of discipline in the ranks and an inability to cope with the stresses associated with fighting a guerrilla type conflict. Clearly, Peruvian soldiers in the field had to be given adequate and meaningful human rights training if they were to be held accountable and if they were expected to better perform their mission of protecting the people.

Second, while there were some general military regulations calling on soldiers to adhere to human rights, there existed no standard human rights text that was available to all military and police forces. Soldiers did not even know what the most basic human rights were, nor what was required of them in the realm of human rights. The JAG team concluded that human rights training had to be given in a standardized fashion so that all Peruvian soldiers received at least the same basic acceptable international standards. Then, if violations occurred, it would be the fault of the particular individual, not the government. In a system that operates under the rule of law, culpability must always rest with the individual.

Third, there was no military legal facility designed or equipped to train Peruvian judge advocates, or other officers, in how to teach human rights to soldiers. Without a systemic approach to developing a cadre of instructors, any new human rights material that was developed, no matter how good in content, would suffer without a systemic approach to providing proper instruction.

Fourth, despite continuing lip service to improving human rights, no effort by the Peruvian high command had been made to address any of the issues necessary to institutionalize training into the fabric of the military. There simply was no emphasis on creating a methodology to provide for human rights instruction to the soldiers.

It was apparent that the usual "show-case" method of sending a U.S. mobile training team (MTT) to Peru with a mandate to teach a "one shot" course on human rights would be totally inadequate to rectify the systemic problems outlined. The U.S. JAGC team concluded that there must be two foundations for any program. First, there must be a uniform set of human rights rules contained in a standard handbook. Second, there must be a viable mechanism to inculcate those rules into the armed forces so that every member receives the same training on a continuous basis. In short, the rules and a system for their distribution must be institutionalized.

Cultural, language, and social considerations suggested that the solution rested in creating a standard Peruvian flavored human rights handbook and then training Peruvian instructors—"training-the-trainers"—to use the book in classroom instruction for soldiers. This method stood the best chance for success as the U.S role would be as a helper and not as an ethnocentric overseer. If successful, such an approach would provide the Peruvian military with a permanent Peruvian human rights text and a cadre of trainers—a Peruvian message to a Peruvian audience.

Phase II: Formulating the Idea for a Handbook

The development and process of gaining the necessary approval for the plan would require a major investment of time and effort by both the United States and Peru. Since the plan had to be viewed as a Peruvian project, the U.S. JAG team decided to hold an ice breaking week-long human rights course in Lima to bring together the leadership of all the military services, the national police, and the fiscal (civilian lawyers). The concept for the course would cover a variety of topics related to human rights and the law of war. But, more importantly, the U.S. team hoped that the course would serve as a catalyst for developing a standardized handbook.

In October 1992, six Peruvian judge advocates—representing the Peruvian Army, Navy, and Air Force—traveled to The JAG School in Charlottesville, Virginia. The JAG School is the Army's legal training center for all army military legal officers and is located adjacent to the University of Virginia School of Law. The purpose of the two-week trip was to prepare the Peruvians to teach classes for the course in December 1992. This was accomplished through a close working relationship with their American counterparts. With the help of U.S. Air Force reservist Major Enrique Arroyo, an extensive Spanish language deskbook was developed and reproduced for the participants of the Lima course (Office of Judge Advocate General, 1992). The deskbook covered human rights law, law of armed conflict, international law, criminal investigations, rules of engagement and contained key documents in each of these areas.

The second purpose for bringing the Peruvians to the JAG School was to train them in how to teach human rights classes effectively. By doing so, the U.S. team hoped that these officers could help form the nucleus of a permanent pool of Peruvian instructors who could be drawn on to teach human rights to other Peruvian officers who, in turn, would provide instruction to their soldiers in every part of the nation.

The human rights course was held from December 15 to 19, 1992, in Lima, Peru, at the National War College. The instruction covered the rights and responsibilities of individuals in a democratic society; the duties of soldiers, commanders, police, and other government officials in relation to human rights; and the universally recognized basic standards of human rights. Civilian control of the military and the military's role in a democratic society were also stressed.

Approximately 50 participants, consisting of senior field commanders from all services (35 percent of the audience), the national police, judge advocates, fiscals, and civilian human rights groups attended the course. The Peruvian high command had fulfilled their promise to bring together a wide array of the military and civilian officials from the government. It was later discovered, that this was one of the rare occasions that the various military services, the police, the judiciary, and members of the civilian government came together to discuss issues associated with human rights in Peru. Much of the course involved open discussions of how to best instill a greater respect for internationally recognized human rights in the military. The closing ceremony was an extremely formal occasion, complete with pomp and circumstance, roll call presentation of diplomas, and a formal dinner afterwards. In attendance at the ceremonies were the senior officials from the Peruvian Ministry of Defense, the Ministry of the Interior, the Department of Justice, the National Police Department, and the Acting U.S. Ambassador.

Phase III: Institutionalizing the Human Rights Handbook

Prompted by the success of the December 1992 course, the Peruvian Army accepted the U.S. invitation to return to the JAG School to begin work on drafting a standard human rights handbook for the Peruvian Army. This step was viewed as a major accomplishment. In conjunction with the JAG team, JAG School staff (namely computer and audio-visual experts), and several Spanish speaking Air Force and Army Reserve legal specialists, provided a draft Spanish handbook entitled, "Ten Commandments of Human Rights" (Office of Judge Advocate General, 1993). The draft handbook consisted of ten basic rules related to human rights and ten graphics to portray each rule.

Finally, in Lima, Peru, on April 19, 1993, after extensive negotiations between LTC Addicott and Peruvian officials of the Instruction and Doctrine Division regarding the final text, the draft was revised and the final handbook was officially approved as the human rights text for·the entire Peruvian military and national police. Aside from other changes to the original draft, the title of the approved version of the handbook was changed to Decalogo de las Fuerzas del Orden (Ten Commandments for the Forces of Order) (Commando Conjunto De Las Fuerzas Armadas, 1993). The title change reflects the fact that the handbook was intended for training all of the security forces in Peru, not just the Peruvian Army.

With the book officially approved, the JAGC legal team then assisted in training a cadre of officers who would be responsible to teach the materials to the Peruvian forces. The JAG team never pointed out specific Peruvian deficiencies or allegations of human rights abuses, but instead concentrated on relevant human rights and law of war abuses that had occurred in American history and let the Peruvian trainers then draw parallel conclusions about their own situation and the absolute necessity for covering such issues in associated discussions on the handbook. In particular, the JAG team relied heavily on extrapolating U.S. military lessons learned from the My Lai massacre, where American soldiers unlawfully killed over 300 women and children during the Vietnam Nam War. Throughout discussions with the Peruvian instructors, the My Lai incident served as a vehicle to reveal the necessity for viable human rights training for soldiers, the duty to report and investigate human rights abuses, the duty to disobey illegal orders, and the importance of leadership integrity (Addicott & Hudson, 1993).

Because the Peruvians were essentially involved in a "civil war" with the Sendero, the JAG team also drew on illustrations from the American Civil War (1861-1865) to further demonstrate the necessity for abiding by first generation human rights principles. For example, the JAG team contrasted the war crimes committed by Union General William T. Sherman—primarily in his unlawful destruction and larceny of civilian property in the federal movement from Atlanta, Georgia, to North Carolina in 1864—with the humanitarian conduct of the Confederate Army of Northern Virginia under General Robert E. Lee, during his two campaigns into Northern States. The Peruvian officers quickly grasped the distinction between Lee and Sherman and how the lessons applied to them. The Peruvians understood that apart from being morally reprehensible, atrocities committed against civilians supportive of the Sendero did not help resolve the conflict.

In every respect, the "Ten Commandments for the Forces of Order" followed the old military acronym "KISS" ("keep it simple stupid"). In form and function, it was carefully designed to meet the needs of the average Peruvian solider as well as his commander. For the solider, this would be a 19-year old with limited reading capabilities; the average commander was around 26 and literate. The "Ten Commandments for the Forces of Order" was designed to be short yet concise, consisting of 27 pages of action words to detail straightforward concepts.

Except for the last page, which was for note taking, every other page contained a large multi-colored graphic which depicted the particular commandment being emphasized in the text. In this way, the picture strongly reinforced the written commandment. Furthermore, the graphics were carefully designed to communicate the concept in a stand alone fashion, so that the illiterate could understand the basic meaning from the pictures alone. Thus, the soldier who could not read was still able to listen to the instruction and, page by page, follow along in class through the pictures.

Once the handbook was given to the solider during the human rights instruction, the soldier was expected to maintain control of the book for the duration of his military enlistment. Measuring 5.25 by 3.75 inches, the handbook was pocket sized to enable the soldier to carry it with him in his uniform. To resist the rigid environment of the jungles and high mountains of Peru, the handbook was constructed of hard plastic-type paper.

Because the vast majority of the people of Peru are Catholic, the idea for listing "ten commandments" on human rights was an attempt to draw on the Christian tradition to add a moral legitimacy to human rights observance. Thus, Peruvians would automatically associate the need to pay attention to the Ten Commandment for the Forces of Order with the moral requirement to follow the Ten Commandments in the Bible. While this approach was successful in Peru, it may not be relevant to non-Christian cultures, although a similar approach could be used in drawing on the moral or religious tradition of a non-Christian society. The Ten Commandments as listed in the book are:

1. Contribute to social peace by respecting human rights.
2. Respect human life.
3. Respect the integrity of the people and human dignity.
4. Respect the property of others.
5. Understand that orders are issued to protect the public.
6. Do not commit sexual abuse.
7. Do not torture.
8. Every detainee has the right to a judicial trial.
9. Human rights violations do not go unpunished.
10. You are a guardian of democracy and are respectful of human rights.

The ten points that were chosen to comprise the ten commandments were elected not just to set out the prohibitive behavior, but to explain to the soldier the basic rationale and necessity for his behavior. Experience has shown that soldiers must not only know what the rules of conduct are, but they must fully understand the rationale behind the rules. Informing the soldier that he will be punished if he does not comply with the rules is not enough; he must understand why the rules are necessary. Only in this way can the recurring question—"Why should I abide by the rules of conduct, if the subversives do not?"—be answered in a meaningful fashion.

To assist in understanding the necessity for following the rules, the terrorist strategy of the subversives was fully explained in the discussions that accompanied all the commandments. The security forces were briefed on Sendero techniques such as conducting hit and run attacks on carefully selected targets and then intentionally hiding themselves within the civilian population to blur the distinction between combatants and noncombatants. In this way, the soldiers learned that the subversives hope either to hide from military attack or, according to Sendero doctrine, to provoke indiscriminate attacks on the civilian population by government forces (Strong, 1992).

Phase IV: Quantifying the Results

The most common critique concerning human rights reform efforts revolves around the issue of evaluation: how can one tell if real change has occurred? In the case of the Peru initiative, there has been a significant improvement in the Peruvian military human rights record since 1993. It is no coincidence that this marked improvement coincides with the Peru initiative outlined in this chapter. With the implementation of the Peru initiative, the Peruvians have made tremendous strides in not only improving compliance with internationally recognized human rights, but in actually punishing those accused of violations. In fact, within one year of the inauguration of the handbook, every member of the military had received human rights training based on the handbook and a system for teaching incoming personnel was firmly established. Addicott personally accompanied the Peruvian training teams from one end of the nation to the other as an observer in the process (1992-1994).

While Peru still has one of highest number of disappeared persons in the hemisphere, the statistics from 1992 to 1994 presented a dramatic decline in all categories of human rights abuses. For example, the National Coordinator of Human Rights reported just over 70 disappearances for 1993, down from almost 300 in 1992. U.S estimates put the number of disappearances for 1993 at 75 (Brooke, 1994). And, "[a]s of May 1994, the Coordinadora had documented 59 cases of enforced disappearance attributed to the Peruvian security forces—of whom 8 reappeared and 51 remain disappeared—and 35 cases of extrajudicial killings (including ten cases attributed to rondas collaborating with the military)" (Coordinadora, 1993; The Washington Office on Latin America, 1994). Extrajudicial killings by government forces also declined dramatically. In 1991 there were 133 alleged cases, with 114 reported in 1992 and less than 50 reported in 1993. In contrast, the subversives were responsible for 903 assassinations in 1991 and 727 assassinations in 1992 (Coordinadora, 1993; The Washington Office on Latin America, 1994). The figures for 1993 indicate that the number of Sendero assassinations reached over 900 for that year. The majority of Sendero victims in 1993 were civilians who were often tortured to death.

One of the most promising signs of reform, and one that needs continued emphasis even today, is in the area of holding government forces accountable for human right crimes. During the Fujimori era, military trials of soldiers accused of such atrocities began in earnest in 1992, something that had not occurred under previous administrations. For example, Army Lieutenant Javier Bendzu Vargas and two of his subordinates were tried, convicted, and sentenced to prison terms in 1992 for directing the 1991 massacre of 14 peasants in the Huancavelica Emergency Zone. In addition, in the La Cantuta disappearances (the ten suspected Sendero supporters who were later found murdered), the military concluded their investigation, arrested ten military personnel (including several Army officers) and tried them.

Before the trials, Gisela Ortiz, a sister of one of the murdered students, stated: "If justice is done, then maybe we can be sure this kind of thing won't happen again" (Schmidt-Lynch, 1994). In February 1994, the military court acquitted one of the soldiers and convicted the rest. A general officer received four years confinement, two majors each received 20 years confinement, and seven enlisted soldiers were given sentences ranging from five to 20 years. Trials have also been conducted for the National Police. In November 1993, seven out of ten national police officers tried were convicted and sentenced to prison terms for the 1991 murder of three university students in Callao. The two direct perpetrators of the murders each received 18 years confinement; sentences ranging from 15 years to two years were handed out to the less culpable.

With the end of the internal war on the terrorists in Peru and the vast improvement in human rights record of the armed forces, the Peruvian Congress passed a 1995 law granting amnesty to members of the security forces for human rights abuses. In addition, following the departure of President Fujimori in 2000, the new government of Alegandro Toledo has seen the creation of a Truth and Reconciliation Commission to examine the over 6,000 allegations of forced disappearances, assassinations, and other grievous violations of human rights.

What Made the Peru Initiative a Success?

There can be no question that many of the armed forces of the new democracies are serious in their desire to create solid institutional development of human rights training. Nevertheless, factors vary in different countries and the type of assistance needed may not require full structural reform as was the case in Peru. While the Peru initiative saw programmatic change from top to bottom, other countries may only need to strengthen or modify existing human rights training programs. Even so, the lessons learned from the Peru initiative can be extrapolated and applied to any nation serious about human rights training for their armed forces.

First, as demonstrated throughout the Peru initiative, any program to promote human rights values within foreign militaries must be built upon institutionalizing those values into the fabric of that force. Programs designed merely to have U.S. personnel teach human rights on one or more occasions will have limited long-term impact and will fail to instill pride and responsibility into the host military which comes from designing and delivering their own human rights curricula for training.

Second, formal requests for this type of long-term assistance must always originate from the host nation government. Through diplomatic avenues, U.S. representatives' in-country should always approach the issue of developing a human rights training program from a joint perspective: what the two nations, together, are going to do. In this manner, the host nation is engaged in the reform effort at the very beginning of the process. In Peru, the idea of developing some type of viable human rights training had been percolating for several years. Since the U.S. representatives in-country best know the local politics and personalities, their complete support is essential. The lesson to apply in future efforts is fundamental—only a unified U.S. team working together toward the common long-term objective will be able to launch and sustain a successful program.

Third, closely related to developing solid requests for assistance from the host nation, is the task of getting firm commitment for the end result—real programmatic change. Since the task of institutional reform may require a total restructuring of the current system, including the elimination of programs that are counterproductive, the complete cooperation of the senior leadership in the host nation is absolutely essential. This commitment must be obtained as soon after the U.S. site survey assessment as possible.

Fourth, once the host nation has agreed to the concept of long-term reform, it is important that the U.S. working team not get too far out ahead in advocating that each country come up with the same "ten commandments of human rights." Sensitivity is critical. Planners must take into account nationalistic and other characteristics peculiar to each military in developing a human rights curriculum. While international human rights will be the same, they may be expressed and tailored in different manners. In addition, American assistance must be offered at the pace of the host nation; institutionalizing these principles may not come easily to people long ruled by totalitarian systems.

Fifth, one idea that needs further exploration, is the concept of increased regional military cooperation in human rights training. In this manner human rights values are developed within the context of regional cooperation.

Sixth, Army judge advocates designed and implemented the Peru initiative as an additional duty to their normal jobs in order to verify the concept of institutional assistance and to determine the logistical, administrative, and personnel requirements of such a program. The U.S. military now knows that the concept works and works well. The Army JAGC also knows that a full-time effort with several countries exceeds the current personnel and resource allocations. With additional personnel and funding, however, this new long-term assistance strategy shows great promise. In fact, the Peru initiative proved to be an extremely cost effective means of assistance, with total costs to the United States well below $100,000 dollars.

Seventh, as in all relations with foreign nations, one needs to be particularly sensitive to concerns from the opposite end of the domestic political spectrum in the host nation. In this vein, the possibility exists that opposition groups might seize on any American assisted program as the opening wedge to advance their own anti-West agenda. Efforts to include as broad a list of participants and "organizers" as possible are helpful to defuse this potential problem. In Peru, the U.S. team brought in as many civilian human rights groups as possible into the process.

Eighth, a distinctive characteristic of a long-term program is the need to stay engaged. Indeed, quality control mandates that the U.S. military continue to monitor the program once it has been instituted. In this context, measurable standards for positive advancement need to be developed. This can be done by counting the number of soldiers trained and by closely following the reports of human rights violations. As demonstrated by the impressive drop in human rights violations since the implementation of the program, the human rights effort in Peru has already borne fruit (Coordinadora, 1993). Accordingly, it is essential that contacts be continued to allow the institutionalization to grow from the roots. Planners for future efforts must understand that such initiatives are not isolated events; tracking the program is just as critical as establishing the program.

Finally, the apparent success of the American effort to institutionalize human rights training in the Peruvian armed forces must be tempered by the fact that human rights training can only be effective to the degree that it is inculcated into the psyche of the military. With a standardized human rights training handbook that is truly their own, an officer corps that has been trained in how to teach human rights, and an armed force that has received human rights instruction, the Peruvians now have a solid methodology to continue the effort.

Conclusion

In addressing the issue of promoting democratic reform in the militaries of emerging democracies like Iraq and Afghanistan, the United States must focus on the positive aspects of the Peru initiative. In particular, the parallels between the Peru and Iraq are striking. Like Peru in the case study, Iraq is plagued by terrorist elements that have no regard for human life and seek the destruction of democracy. Similarly, the Iraqi military has little frame of reference for how to embrace human rights ideals suitable for a democratically based military. As in the Peruvian study, the Iraqi military needs assistance to understand that the terrorists must be dealt with under the rule of law. Furthermore, the fact that the actions of the democratically based military will always be under close scrutiny (the abuses at Abu Ghraib is an example) is something that the new Iraqi military needs to understand as a fact of life. And the best way to deal with the inevitable abuses by "bad apples" is to self-report, investigate and punish the offenders (as the U.S. military did in the Abu Ghraib cases).

If the United States is going to offer realistic assistance that can make a difference, there is no alternative—U.S. policy makers have to focus on developing an assistance program that can provide the lasting benefits of institutional reform. By any standard of evaluation, the Peruvian initiative stands as a model for a meaningful American strategy. For simplicity, focus, and potential for positive change in the militaries of the new democracies its greatest asset is its target of institutional change. If the United States is serious about promoting peace through the new paradigm of war avoidance, it is time to abandon the "show-case" approach to human rights.

In Iraq, this seems to be already happening. According to the Staff Judge Advocate for the U.S. Army Third Infantry Division, Colonel William Hudson, Jr., the Peru handbook has been adopted with suitable modifications for use in training the new Iraqi military. By February 2006 18,000 copies had been distributed, with an additional 10,000 booklets available. The handbook was part of the curriculum for the Iraqi Army Basic Training Academy. US and Iraqi Judge Advocates were training Iraqi Army recruits in Arabic on three topics: human rights (using the adopted Peru handbook); rules of engagement; and the Iraqi Code of Military Justice. Hudson also reported on the Iraqi JAG training program. Each Iraqi Brigade Judge Advocate was a new "hire" from the Iraqi civilian legal field because this is a completely new job specialty in the Iraqi Army (Hudson, 2006).

If the Peru initiative described above is one way to move forward in the war prevention paradigm, the next step is for the U.S. Congress to create a new single statutory funding authority granting lead agency to the U.S. Army JAGC to execute similar reform missions (GAO/T-NSIAD-93-7, 1993). This new legislation could read:

(1) Goal: To assist in institutionalizing human rights values and the concept of civilian control in the militaries of the emerging democracies.

(2) Achievement: (a) assist in the development of a viable teaching curriculum and standard handbook on human rights for the requesting contact military; (b) assist in training a cadre of host nation military instructors (train the trainers approach) to deliver the curriculum to the host nation soldiers; (c) obtain the necessary formal commitments through written regulation from the highest levels of the host military to implement mandatory human rights training based on the curriculum and handbook for all military personnel; and (d) ensure the institutionalization of the human rights program within the military by maintaining close professional contacts.

The post-Cold War era has witnessed the establishment of dozens of new governments committed to democracy and human rights. In 1972, only 40 nations were democracies. In 2005, 120 nations were deemed democracies (including Iraq and Afghanistan). When one considers the fact that stable democracies do not engage in aggressive war and do a far better job in terms of promoting human rights, promoting the spread of new democracies may be seen as the key to world peace and stability.

References

Addicott, J. F. (2006). *Terrorism Law: Cases and Materials*. Tucson, Arizona: Lawyers and Judges

Addicott, J. F. (1990). Operational Law note: Proceedings of the First Center for Law and Military Operations Symposium. *Army Lawyer*, December, p. 47.

Addicott, J. F., & Hudson, W. A. (1993). 25th Anniversary of My Lai: Time to Inculcate the Lessons. *Military Law Review*, pp. 139, 153.

Addicott, J. F., & Supervielle, M. E. F. (1999). Promoting Human Rights Values in Cuba's Post-Castro Cuba. *Journal of National Security Law Review*, pp. 3, 11.

Amnesty International U.S.A. (1993, May). Human Rights and U.S. Security Assistance.

Brooke, J. (1994). 18 Months later, 10 killings haunt Peru's army. *New York Times, January 12, 1994*, p. A3.

Burger, J. A. (1978). International Law—the Role of the Legal Advisor and Law of War Instruction. *Army Lawyer*, September, p. 22.

Charlton, J. (1990). *Legal Briefs*.

Commando Conjunto De Las Fuerzas Armadas (1993). *Decalogo de las Fuerzas del Orden (Ten Commandments for the Forces of Order).* Lima, Peru.

Coordinadora (1993). Annual Report. Lima, Peru: Human Rights Office.

Department of Defense (1992). *The Defense Institute of Security Assistance Management 3 (12th ed.).* Washington, D.C., Department of Defense.

Dessler, D. E. (1991). Beyond Correlations: Toward a Causal Theory of War. *International Studies Quarterly,* pp. 35, 327-355.

Elliott, H. W. (1983). Theory and Practice: Some Suggestions for the Law of War Trainer. *Army Lawyer,* July, p. 1.

Feeny, T. J., & Murphy, M. L. (1988). The Judge Advocate General's Corps, 1982-1987. *Military Law Review,* pp. 4, 22.

GAO/T-NSIAD-93-7 (1993). *Exchange Programs: Observations on International Educational, Cultural, & Training Exchange Programs, Mar. 23, 1993.* GAO Code 711011.

Graf, F. A. (1988). Knowing the Law, *Proceedings of the US Naval Institute, Vol. 114 June.* Published in Annapolis, MD. pp. 58-61

Graham, D. E. (1987). Operational Law: a Concept Comes of Age. *Army Lawyer,* July, p. 9.

Hudson, William A. (2006). E-mail to the author dated February 27, 2006.

Lake, A. (1993, October 21). *Address from Special Assistant to the President for National Security Affairs, School of Advanced International Studies.* Washington, D.C.

Martin, D. (1988). A Human Rights Agenda: The Routine and the Special. *Virginia Journal of International Law, 885,* p. 28.

Moore, J. N. (1997). *Enhanced Effectiveness in United Nations Peacekeeping, Collective Security, and War Avoidance.* Unpublished manuscript. Charlottesville, VA.

Moore, J. N., Tipson, F. S., & Turner, R. F. (2005). *National Security Law, Second Edition.* Durham, N. Carolina: Carolina Academic Press.

Newman, F. C., & Weissbrodt, D. (1990). *International Human Rights.* Cincinnati, Ohio: Anderson Publishing.

Office of the Judge Advocate General (1992, December). *Human Rights Deskbook.* Charlottesville, VA: The International and Operational Law Division, The Office of the Judge Advocate General, the Pentagon.

Office of the Judge Advocate General (1993, January). *Ten Commandments of Human Rights.* Unpublished manuscript, on file with the International and Operational Law Division, Office of The Judge Advocate General, the Pentagon, Charlottesville, VA.

Parks, W. H. (1980). The Law of War Advisor. *JAG Journal, 1,* p. 31.

Ray, J. L. (1993). Wars Between Democracies: Rare or Nonexistent? *International Transactions, 18(3),* pp. 251-276.

Rostow, E. V. (1993). *Toward Managed Peace: The National Security Interests of the United States, 1759 to the Present.* New Haven, CT: Yale University Press.

Rummel, R. J. (1991). Power Kills; Absolute Power Kills Absolutely. *Journal of Peace Research.* Haiku Institute of Peace Research, Oct. 20, 1991, p. 17.

Rummel, R. J. (1994). *Death by Government: Genocide and Mass Murder in the Twentieth Century.* Somerset, New Jersey: Transaction Publishers.

Russett, B. (1993). *Grasping the Democratic Peace: Principles for a post-Cold War World, 4th edition.* Princeton, New Jersey: Princeton University Press.

Salguero, C. (2000). Tense Times in Peru. *U.S. News & World Report,* October 2, p. 31.

Schindler, D., & Toman, J. (1988*). The Laws of Armed Conflict.* Norwell, MA: Kluwer Academic.

Schmidt-Lynch, C. (1994). Peru Shunts Key Rights Case to Military Courts. *Washington Post,* February 9, A24.

Speck, M. (1992). Caught in Peru's Crossfire. *Miami Herald International Edition*, December 8, p. A1.

Strong, S. (1992). *Shining Path.* New York: Times Books.

The Washington Office on Latin America (1994, July). *After the Autogolpe: Human Rights in Peru and the U.S. Response.* Washington, DC: The Washington Office on Latin America.

Unclassified cable from American Embassy, Moscow to White House, Washington, D.C. (1994, January 14). On file with author. U.S. Embassy, Moscow, Russia.

Unclassified cable from the American Embassy Lima, Peru to Secretary of State, Washington, D.C. (1993, October 19). On file with author. Lima, Peru.

United Nations Centre for Human Rights (1992). *Fact Sheet No. 18, Minority Rights.* U.N. document, GE 91-18616.

United States Government (1993). *The Foreign Assistance Act of 1961.* U.S.C. § 2301.

U.S. Army's Center for Strategy and Force Evaluation (1993, September). *Peacekeeping Operations.* Fort Leavenworth, KS: Department of the Army.

Section III: International Law

Chapter 8. History and Foundations for Refugee Security, Health and Well-Being under International Law
Ved P. Nanda

Chapter 9. Government Sanctioned Torture and International Law
Sister Dianna Ortiz

Chapter 10. The Fundamental Human Right to Prosecution and Compensation
Jon M. Van Dyke

CHAPTER 8

History and Foundations for Refugee Security, Health, and Well-Being under International Law

Ved P. Nanda

The history and foundations of modern-day refugee law began in the refugee crises in Europe following World War II, and many of the provisions of the cornerstone Refugee Convention reflect a world scene that no longer exists. Interstate warfare which caused refugee flows in the 1940s and the consequent development of the current refugee law is no longer the primary source of large-scale movements of people. Instead, the primary source is repression by governments of their own people. The refugee system, under which protection is provided on an individualized basis, is generally unresponsive to the mass flows being witnessed today; and the scene of most refugee crises has shifted from Europe, as was predominantly the case in the 40s and 50s, to the South.

However, little has changed legally to obligate states to be more open to assisting refugees. Although, under tremendous pressure from refugee movements, states are generally willing to accept a more expansive definition of "refugee," the person legally entitled to relief under the Refugee Convention, refugees suffer from assaults on their physical security, instances of refoulement, non-adherence by states to asylum procedures, increasing xenophobia in some countries, and coercion to repatriate (United Nations, July 2004). Consequently, the existing regime for protection of refugees requires reshaping to be appropriately responsive to the needs of the present.

Introduction

The current international refugee law is a product of an earlier time and special circumstances—mass displacement after World War II—and is seemingly unable to meet the needs of the present. Consequently, because of the history of refugee law, combined with the increasingly large number of asylum seekers in the developing countries, the refugee crisis poses a formidable challenge for the world community. Not only is the sheer number of refugees and displaced persons overwhelming, the trend is toward a narrower interpretation of refugee law and more restrictive asylum policies by governments. To illustrate, there is no recognition of victims of persecution by non-state actors. Similarly, those who flee war, famine, economic deprivation, and natural disasters are not recognized as refugees because of a lack of individualized persecution that is direct and targeted, as required under the 1951 U.N. Convention Relating to the Status of Refugees (United Nations, 1951).

Restrictive procedures under the 1990 Schengen[1] and Dublin[2] Conventions result in permissions for asylum-seekers in the European Union to apply for asylum only in the first member state they enter or the state that issued their visas. There are also strict restrictions limiting asylum in the European Union to nationals of other European Union states. In the post-Cold War era, refugees are facing stringent visa requirements, and there are sanctions against air carriers that bring foreigners to the country without visas (Coman, 1998). There exist distant resettlement programs, safe, third-country rules and arrangements, and immigration agreements, with the outcome being that asylum seekers are often denied access to territory or to asylum procedures. Also there are instances of mass refoulement in blatant violation of international refugee law. As the United Nations High Commission for Refugees' mission is to provide legal protection, not just humanitarian assistance, a large number of those seeking protection are deprived of that protection because of substantial gaps in the existing refugee protection regime.

Equally important, there is inconsistent and only partial observance by governments of the rights guaranteed to refugees under international human rights law—internationally recognized under applicable international agreements and generally accepted principles of international law—and international refugee law. Specifically, under the former, "aliens" are guaranteed civil and political as well as economic and social rights; under the latter, "refugees" are to be accorded "the same treatment as is accorded to aliens generally" (U.N. Refugee Convention, 1951, art. 7).

Thus, the challenge the world community faces is primarily to ensure adequate and effective protection to refugees and displaced persons and to provide for their human rights, including political and economic rights, and especially their security, health, and well-being. This necessitates a reform of the existing international refugee regime.

Nature and Extent of the Refugee Crisis

The basis for present refugee law was the system set up to handle those fleeing Nazi persecution and returning after the end of the World War II. However, as the refugee problems in Europe subsided, mass influxes of refugees began in the less developed countries of Asia, Africa, and Latin America (Khan, 1976). Europe and the nations of the West had by and large been insulated from such refugee movements until the Balkan crises in the 1990s.

During the year 1999 several new refugee problems arose because of conflicts in Kosovo, East Timor, and Chechnya. Ethnic cleansing, forced mass expulsions of people, and grievous deprivations of human rights led to displacement of over one million people in Kosovo and several hundred thousand in East Timor and Chechnya. Although many refugees and displaced persons returned to their homes in Kosovo and East Timor, the number of refugees and displaced was higher at the end of 1999 than at its beginning.

As of June 2000, the estimated number of refugees, asylum-seekers, and internally displaced persons worldwide was more than 35 million—an increase of 5 million from the previous year (USCR, 2000). The number of refugees and asylum-seekers was more than 14 million and those internally displaced by persecution or armed conflict numbered over 21 million—25 percent more than the prior year—although the survey noted that the real number of internally displaced may be much higher, as the estimates of such numbers are often fragmentary and unreliable. The vast majority of these uprooted people are in the Southern hemisphere. The Office of the United Nations High Commissioner for Refugees (UNHCR) numbered 22.3 million people "of concern to UNHCR" at the end of 1999, as compared with 21.5 million at the beginning of that year (UNHCR, 2000). Bill Frelick, Refugee Policy Director for Human Rights Watch and former Policy Director for the U.S. Committee for Refugees, said at that time:

> These are grim numbers. It is sobering to realize that millions of people on this earth, particularly refugees and displaced persons in Africa, have begun the new millennium living in conditions that are in some ways similar to those that existed a full millennium earlier: in huts or exposed to the elements, without adequate clothing, sanitation, or health care, preyed upon by their fellow men, and effectively unprotected by rule of law (www.uscr.org/news/press_releases/2000/061300a.htm).

Sadly, the new millennium has not witnessed a significant decline in the number of refugees and asylum seekers or internally displaced persons (IDPs). The United States Committee for Refugees (USCR) estimates the annual numbers of the former to range during the years 2000-2005 from 11.5 million to 14.9 million worldwide (USCR, 2004, 2005), while acknowledging that "[s]tatistics on refugees and other uprooted people are often inexact and controversial" (USCR, 2005). It estimates the number of internally displaced at the end of 2002 at 20.8 million and at the end of 2003 23.6 million (USCR, 2003, 2004). The UNHCR estimates the global number of refugees at the end of 2004 to be 13.2 million, including Palestinian refugees (UNHCR, 2005). In a December 31, 2004, report, the Secretary-General's Representative noted that "in the Darfur region of the Sudan . . . over 1.6 million have been internally displaced and 200,000 displaced across the border Chad" (United Nations, 2004). An earlier report by the Secretary-General's Representative had stated that contrary to the Sudanese government's assertions about the improvement in the security situation in Darfur there was "evidence of persistent insecurity, including ongoing killings, rape and armed robbery, among other abuses" (United Nations, 2004). The UNHCR numbered more than 17 million people as "persons of concern" (including refugees, asylum-seekers, stateless and selected IDPs and returned IDPs) as of 1 January 2004 (UNHCR, 2004), which increased to 19.2 million at the end of 2004 (UNHCR, 2005).

The Applicable International Refugee Regime

As a general rule, refugees and displaced persons are entitled to the enjoyment of their internationally recognized human rights. They are also subject to a special international regime under which they are accorded protection by the competent international organizations and by the states through which they transit or in which they seek temporary refuge or permanent settlement. The classification of persons fleeing—and thus the obligation of receiving states to assist them— depends most significantly on the reason for their flight, a relic of public international law.

Persons Entitled to Protection

A refugee is a person who has lost the protection of the government of the state of his/her nationality or permanent residence and has fled that state seeking refuge and assistance in another country. This concept—loss of protection of one's government—has been at the heart of the refugee definition since its first use in the "Nansen Agreements" in the 1920s, which specifically protected refugees from designated geographical areas of trouble (Khan, 1976).

Persons who have fled their state due to persecution, or a well-founded fear of being persecuted, for reasons of race, religion, nationality, membership of a particular social group, or political opinion, are generally referred to as "Convention refugees," "asylum-seekers," or "asylees." Under the most widely accepted international instrument on refugees, the 1951 Convention Relating to the Status of Refugees, only persons meeting these criteria are officially referred to as "refugees." The system addresses individual claims for protection and is generally not responsive to situations of mass influx. Refugees who have fled or attempted to flee but who have not been allowed to leave or have not yet been able to leave the country are generally referred to as "displaced persons" (if they have left the territory of the country of danger), or "internally displaced persons" (if they have not left the territory) (U.N. Report, 1998), or simply "refugees."

No generally accepted binding international instrument encompasses the situation of those who have fled massive human rights abuses, civil wars, external aggression, occupation, foreign domination, or events seriously disturbing the public order. A few regional arrangements, however, apply to such people. The UNHCR, non-governmental organizations, and ad hoc groups provide relief in these situations as they are able. Because of the growing refugee crisis and perceived inadequacies of the existing international treaty on refugees, the 1951 Refugee Convention (United Nations, 1951) concepts of "temporary refuge" and "temporary asylum" are being applied to transitional arrangements.

Until 1938, the Assembly of the League of Nations approved specific programs for refugees coming from certain countries. Between 1938 and 1950, however, analysis shifted away from geographical areas to the motives for a refugee's flight (Hathaway, 1990). In 1938, faced with refugees fleeing from Nazi Germany, the Intergovernmental Committee on Refugees first referred to criteria for protection based upon the reasons for those persons' flight: that they "must emigrate on account of their political opinions, religious beliefs, or racial origins" (Hathaway, 1990). Then in 1946 the Economic and Social Council of the United Nations, in establishing the International Refugee Organization (IRO), employed the concept of "persecution" or fear of persecution "based on reasonable grounds" (Constitution, IRO, 1946). These twin criteria of a specified reason and a subjective fear have remained in force and have come to require objective proof. At the same time, the focus of consideration shifted from the collective group movement to the individual refugee.

At present the definition of "refugee" set forth in the Refugee Convention (United Nations, 1951) is technically adhered to by most states, even nonparties to that Convention and/or the 1967 Protocol (Refugee Protocol, 1967). There remain, however, serious limitations in the present scheme, which is incapable of effectively addressing mass flows of refugees. Problems which have emerged include, for example, the exclusion of most of the world's actual refugee population from the definition of "refugees" who are entitled to protection (Perluss & Hartman, 1986), and the use by many countries of increasingly restrictive interpretations of the refugee definition to exclude and deter numbers of otherwise eligible refugees. A trend has, however, developed toward a broader concept of "refugee."

In 1991, the United Nations High Commissioner for Refugees commented:

An ongoing practice was the restrictive interpretation in some countries of various elements of the refugee definition contained in the Refugee Convention and its 1967 Protocol, coupled with the requirements that applicants for refugee status satisfy an excessively stringent burden and standard of proof. For example, a handful of countries rejected asylum-seekers on the grounds that, although they demonstrated a well-founded fear of persecution, they could not prove that said fear extended to the whole of the territory of their country of origin (UNHCR, 1991).

These restrictive practices continue, as a 2005 UNHCR report entitled "2004 Global Refugee Trends" notes: "The legal status of more than a quarter (29%) of the refugees is unclear."

Regional Arrangements

A number of regional refugee regimes have been created which demonstrate the expanded concept of "refugees" to include "humanitarian refugees." In 1966 the Asian-African Legal Consultative Committee (AALCC) drafted the Bangkok Principles (AALCC, 1966). Although the principal causes of refugee flows in that region could be ascribed to foreign domination, for example in Palestine, Rhodesia, and South Africa, and to liberation struggles of colonial territories, the AALCC did not broaden the Refugee Convention's (United Nations, 1951) limitation of "refugee" to victims of political persecution.

The first step toward a more inclusive definition was taken in 1969 when the then Organization of African Unity (OAU), now the African Union, adopted the OAU convention Governing the Specific Aspects of Refugee Problems in Africa (OAU, 1969). The members of the OAU had acceded to, or were encouraged to accede to the Refugee Convention (United Nations, 1951), but desired as well to provide for the special problems of the African Continent. Accordingly, the definition of "refugee" used in the OAU Convention consists of two parts: (1) a reiteration of the Refugee Convention definition, and (2) an additional definition under which the term "refugee" also applies to every person who—owing to external aggression, occupation, foreign domination or events seriously disturbing public order in either part or the whole of his country of origin or nationality—is compelled to leave his place of habitual residence in order to seek refuge in another place outside his country of origin or nationality.Under the American Convention on Human Rights, drafted by the Organization of American States (OAS) in 1969, "[e]very person has the right to seek and be granted asylum in a foreign territory, in accordance with the legislation of the state and international conventions, in the event he is being pursued for political offenses or related common causes" (OAS, 1969, art. 22, para. 7).

The 1984 Cartagena Declaration on Refugees (Inter-American Commission on Human Rights, 1984) followed the precedent of the OAU Convention by recommending that the definition of "refugee" to be used in Central America be expanded to cover also "persons who have fled their country because their lives, safety, or freedom have been threatened by generalized violence, foreign aggression, internal conflicts, massive violation of human rights or other circumstances which have seriously disturbed public order." Although the Cartagena Declaration is not binding on states, it expressed the sentiment of 10 Central American official delegations that the classic definition had failed to meet modern refugee needs. It is noteworthy that the Cartagena Declaration has received the full support of the Inter-American Commission on Human Rights, which urged OAS member states to give its conclusions "their most vigorous support" (Inter-American Commission on Human Rights, 1984). And the OAS General Assembly recommended that member states apply the Declaration in dealing with refugees in their territory (OAS, 1985).

State Practice in Recognition of Refugees
Historically individual state practice has also demonstrated support for a broader concept of "refugee." Many states admit refugees fleeing from conditions other than persecution, either by law or simply on an ad hoc basis. This protection takes the form of temporary or, less often, permanent refuge or political asylum. The United States started granting "extended voluntary departure" to selected groups of refugees, under which those persons are allowed to remain temporarily in the United States for foreign policy and humanitarian reasons (Heyman, 1987). However, since the late 1980s, because of the enormity of the problem, 'compassion fatigue' seems to have set in.

From the beginning, the Refugee Convention (United Nations, 1951) was open for extension beyond its strictest terms. Originally, the mandate of UNHCR (U.N. General Assembly, 1950) was limited to protection of refugees as defined under the Refugee Convention (United Nations, 1951). However, by 1957, the concept of the High Commissioner's "good offices" was being employed by the General Assembly to allow UNHCR to provide protection and assistance to the refugees who did not meet the Refugee Convention definition (U.N. General Assembly, 1957). In 1965, the U.N. General Assembly authorized UNHCR to provide protection to non-Convention refugees on the same terms as Convention refugees (U.N. General Assembly, 1965). In 1975, it termed the situations of Convention and non-Convention refugees "analogous" because both were victims of man-made events over which they had no control (U.N. General Assembly, 1975). In 1985, the General Assembly urged all states to "support the High Commissioner in his efforts to achieve durable solutions to the problem of refugees and displaced persons of concern to his office" (U.N. General Assembly, 1985).

Other frequent statements by the General Assembly and UNHCR have evidenced a merging of the two concepts, "refugee" and "displaced person" (Goodwin-Gill, 1986). The approval by the international community of a constant expansion of UNHCR's mandate over many years and through many crises, coupled with its financial support for UNHCR's work and requests for and acceptance of assistance from UNHCR, have indicated a widespread trend toward seeing this larger group as entitled to protection (Hailbronner, 1986). However, for practical reasons, there is no effort to expand the definition of the "Convention refugee." States may be willing to assist but they are unwilling to accept the obligation to do so, for under international law states generally determine their own policies regarding the admission of refugees and displaced persons. Duties of states toward refugees and displaced persons are undertaken through conventions or assumed voluntarily for reasons of politics, humanitarianism, or international cooperation.

There are no international conventions which require the admission of refugees and displaced persons, nor has there arisen any such requirement under customary international law. Consequently, states are free to enact their own laws and regulations governing such admission (Goodwin-Gill, 1983). In doing so, they are often guided by generally accepted humanitarian principles of international law. States have also entered into international and regional treaties that pertain to the admission of refugees and displaced persons. Although no document requires states to admit refugees, article 31 of the Refugee Convention (United Nations, 1951), which forbids states parties from penalizing refugees who have entered the territory illegally, provides at least for temporary admission.

The OAU convention is the one international agreement that goes beyond the usual treaty language by providing that all member states of the OAU shall accept the obligation under the 1951 Refugee Convention (OAU, 1969). However, whether the OAU Convention has the legal capacity to bind member states of the OAU which are not parties to the Refugee Convention has not been tested.

Although international law does not specify any obligations on the part of states toward refugees, states have recognized the principle of non-refoulement, a prohibition on returning refugees to countries where their lives will be in danger, which remains a cardinal principle of refugee protection. I will discuss this principle later in the chapter.

The response of states in admitting refugees depends upon: geographic location; political factors; whether the attempted entry is by individuals, small groups, or large numbers; the cause of the refugees' flight; and whether they are arriving directly from their country of origin or via a third country. It also depends upon whether or not the country where refuge is sought has accepted the 1951 Refugee Convention or the 1967 Protocol as part of its domestic legislation.

A number of states employ screening of refugee claims at the border. Others may reject refugees at the border without any procedural review. Many states continue to detain refugees in contravention of UNHCR guidelines. Such detentions are often lengthy. Also, minimum due process, entitling a refugee to appeal an adverse determination of eligibility for protected status, is unevenly available. As early as 1989 the UNHCR reported on the procedures employed by 51 states parties to the 1951 Refugee Convention or 1967 Protocol, noting that 28 of the 51 states allowed appeals and 17 did not (UNHCR, 1989). The uneven state practice of granting minimum due process protection to those seeking refugee status continues.

Human Rights of Refugees and Displaced Persons

Refugees are among the most vulnerable groups in the world, which explains the development of norms for their protection evolving from humanitarian law, that is, the law of warfare. Refugees and displaced persons are technically entitled to the protection of their basic human rights by the international community and the countries through which they transit or in which they seek temporary or durable refuge. But, while the international community has on the one hand endeavored to protect the basic human rights of refugees, on the other it has been unable to prevent gross violations and deprivations of those rights in many instances.

As a corollary to long-term or permanent refuge, refugees must be allowed rights and privileges conducive to providing the capability to contribute to their host country and to restructure their lives. Under human rights law and humanitarian law, the international community and states of transit and refuge are obligated to protect the basic human rights of refugees and displaced persons to life, personal safety, shelter, food, basic health care, religion, and family.

The state of refuge may confine refugees to camps. Under these circumstances, the country is to ensure that such camps are maintained in a humanitarian manner and away from areas of risk to the refugees.

The reality may be the opposite. For years, UNHCR has reported on situations where refugees and asylum seekers were kept in closed camps as a matter of policy. Surrounded by barbed wire and surveyed by police and armed personnel, they were obliged to remain in such camps until either resettled elsewhere or returned to their respective countries of origin. Such circumstances have led to severe strain among the camp inhabitants and serious outbreaks of violence have occurred, sometimes leading to deaths of inhabitants, as well as serious threats to UNHCR staff .

An early UNHCR report had detailed worrisome situations where refugees in camps fell victim to undisciplined elements of the armed forces of the country of asylum, subversive elements from the country of origin who had infiltrated the camps, and/or third governments attempting to co-opt refugees into their service (UNHCR, 1991). Given the resulting lack of freedom of movement and access to the outside world, camps and detention centers usually make refugees more vulnerable instead of less.

Applicable Human Rights Instruments
Both refugees and displaced persons are entitled to the protection of their human rights in accordance with various international documents. In 1948, the General Assembly of the United Nations declared certain rights to which everyone has an entitlement. This would include, by implication, both refugees and displaced persons: "Everyone is entitled to all rights and freedoms set forth in this Declaration, without distinction of any kind, such as race, color, sex, language, relig-

ion, political or other opinion, national or social origin, property, birth or other status" (United Nations General Assembly, 1948).

Under the International Covenant on civil and Political Rights, states parties have the corresponding obligations:

> Each State Party to the present Covenant undertakes to respect and to ensure to all individuals within its territory and subject to its jurisdiction the rights recognized in the present Covenant, without distinction of any kind, such as race, color, sex, language, religion, political or other opinion, national or social origin, property, birth or other status (ICCPR, 1966).

This provision would likewise relate to both refugees and displaced persons. In 1968, the International Conference on Human Rights at Teheran proclaimed: "The Universal Declaration of Human Rights states a common understanding of the peoples of the world concerning the inalienable and inviolable rights of all members of the human family and constitutes an obligation for the members of the international community" (International Conference on Human Rights, 1968). Refugees and displaced persons would obviously also be included within the scope of this undertaking.

In 1985, the General Assembly, in adopting the Declaration on the Human Rights of Individuals who are not Nationals of the Country in which They Live, recognized that "the protection of human rights and fundamental freedoms provided for in international instruments should also be ensured for individuals who are not nationals of the country in which they live. . . ." (Declaration, 1985). The term "individuals" here would include both refugees and displaced persons.

On a regional level, in 1950, the members of the Council of Europe, in drafting the European Convention for the Protection of Human Rights and Fundamental Freedoms, agreed that: "The High Contracting Parties shall secure to everyone within their jurisdiction the rights and freedoms defined in Section I of this Convention" (Council of Europe, 1950). This provision would include both refugees and displaced persons who come within the jurisdiction of each Convention state party.

The states participating in the Inter-American Specialized Conference on Human Rights, held at San Jose, Costa Rica, in 1969, undertook "to respect the rights and freedoms recognized herein and to ensure to all persons subject to their jurisdiction the free and full exercise of those rights and freedoms, without any discrimination for reasons of race, color, sex, language, religion, political or other opinion, national or social origin, economic status, birth, or any other social condition." (OAS, 1969, art. 1). The same article stipulates that "person" means "every human being," thus including refugees and displaced persons.

Some other human rights instruments provide additional protection to refugees by referring to the aforementioned international instruments. Under the 1951 Convention, refugees—subject to the availability of more favorable provisions in other instruments—are accorded the same treatment as are accorded to other aliens within a state. As aliens are also included within the above-mentioned provisions, the effect of the 1951 Convention is to restate these provisions in favor of those persons coming within the definition of a refugee: "Except where this Convention contains more favorable provisions, a Contracting State shall accord to refugees the same treatment as is accorded to aliens generally" (United Nations, 1951, p. 12, para. 4, line 8).

Many rights are enumerated in the 1951 Convention for persons granted asylum with regard to such matters as employment, property, and naturalization. Any such rights to be granted to other refugees by the country of refuge depend upon the durability of the refugee's settlement and the resources and ability of the country.

Civil and Political Rights
The 1951 Convention guarantees to all refugees a variety of rights which are defined for the most part in relation to the rights of other groups—the nationals and other aliens—of the host country (United Nations, 1951 , arts. 14, 13, 26, 29). It also guarantees the application of the Convention provisions to all refugees without discrimination as to race, religion, or country of origin (art. 3), and it provides for issuance of identity papers and travel documents for refugees in order to facilitate movement (arts. 27, 28). The problems encountered by UNHCR are in enforcement of some of these guarantees rather than the applicability of the provisions themselves. Notably, freedom of movement, ownership of movable and immovable property, employment, identity papers, travel documents, and naturalization are frequently problematic for refugees vis-à-vis their host countries. Some of these problems may often result from factors beyond the control of the host government, but they may also be manipulated by the host country to avoid creating a "pull" on refugees in the nature of too-favorable conditions.

Regarding the right to work, recognition of that right to refugees is becoming the universal rule, but there remains a tendency to give priority to nationals. Freedom of movement is closely linked to access to employment and accompanying restrictions, such as the limitation that refugees necessarily settle where there is available work. Security considerations with regard to the distance of settlements from borders also affect the freedom of movement. A distinction exists between free choice of the place of residence for refugees and freedom of movement itself, as they are not necessarily the same.

Naturalization procedures vary between states. Article 34 of the Refugee Convention (United Nations, 1951) calls on contracting states to "facilitate the assimilation and naturalization of refugees," and to expedite the proceedings in favor of refugees. This remains the "final goal" of the refugee process, but also presents difficulties for the refugee who then becomes unable to repatriate. Because states regard the grant of nationality as a favor rather than a requirement, they employ widely divergent practices and policies. Within a state, too, there may be differences in the treatment of individual refugees, and of refugees from different countries.

Security

Although the international community seeks to protect refugees, the refugees are frequently the victims of brutal attacks from their host country's population and from their countries of origin (UNHCR, 1989). Such attacks are variously motivated, but they are all contrary to basic principles of international law. It should be axiomatic that the requirement for protection of refugees lasts from the time that they leave the country of their nationality until a durable solution for them is found. The vehicle through which this is most often accomplished is the UNHCR.

It should be noted, however, that the authority of the Office of the high Commissioner is not supranational and is limited to moral authority based upon the High Commissioner's function and the supervisory task which s/he is given. His/her only weapon is persuasion, and s/he depends entirely on the spirit and the willingness to cooperate shown by governments. The Office of UNHCR is hindered in its duty by logistical limitations and the impediments placed by states (UNHCR, 1989).

The principle that a state is obligated to protect refugees inside its borders is well established in international law and therefore also binds non-signatories of the 1951 Refugee Convention—it is found in the Universal Declaration of Human Rights' statement (U.N. General Assembly, 1948) of rights pertaining to all, without regard to their nationality or their status vis-à-vis the country of their residence, and it is clearly expressed in general terms in the United Nations Charter. The 1966 International Covenant on Civil and Political Rights protects more specifically the right to life, to be free from torture, cruel, inhuman or degrading treatment, and punishment, to be free from arbitrary detention and, if detained, the right to be treated with humanity (arts. 6, 7, 9, 10); the American Convention on Human Rights (OAS, 1969) codifies the right to humane treatment, and the principle that "[e]very person has the right to have his physical, mental and moral integrity respected" (arts. 4, 5); the Declaration on the Human Rights of Individuals who are not Nationals of the Country in Which they Live declares the right to security of person, and the right not to be subjected to arbitrary arrest or detention or cruel, inhuman or degrading treatment (arts. 5, 6); and common article 3 of the Geneva Conventions and Protocol II to the Geneva Conventions both provide basic norms of humanitarian law applicable to refugees as well as displaced persons (Meron, 1988).

In response to the plight of internally displaced persons, the United Nations has established "relief corridors" in recognition of the right to humanitarian access. In response to the plight of the Kurds and the Shiite Muslims in the aftermath of the Gulf War, the United Nations appointed Sadruddin Aga Khan as the Executive Delegate of the UN Secretary General for the UN Humanitarian Programme for Iraq, Kuwait and the Iraq/Iran and Iraq/Turkey Border Areas

(Memorandum, 1991). The government of Iraq and the UN Executive Delegate entered into the Memoranda of Understanding under which the United Nations established UN Humanitarian Centers in Iraq/Iran and Iraq/Turkey borders. It is also noteworthy that in December 1991, the UN General Assembly adopted a resolution centralizing UN relief efforts and creating a single worldwide humanitarian aid coordinator (Leopold, 1991).

Notwithstanding the enumeration of the refugees' right to be protected, the inconsistent and only partial observance of these guaranteed rights for the benefit of aliens has a direct impact on the lives and well-being of refugees and their families. Regardless, insofar as the state of refuge deals with refugees within its borders in good faith, given the nature and scope of the refugee problem as it exists, the economic and naturalization rights of the refugee must—for all practical purposes—depend upon the durability of the refugee's sojourn or settlement in the state of refuge, and upon the state's resources and the demands upon them.

Asylum

After the adoption of the Universal Declaration of Human Rights (U.N. General Assembly, 1948), which contains a provision for the "right to seek and to enjoy in other countries asylum from persecution" (art. 14), the UN Human Rights Commission recommended that a special convention be entered, with the objective of establishing an individual right to asylum. In 1967, the General Assembly unanimously approved the Declaration on Territorial Asylum (U.N. General Assembly, 1967). However, it subsequently abandoned the Draft International Convention on Territorial Asylum, which would have called on states to give at least temporary asylum (Nanda, 1981). Although at present there does not exist a universal obligation to provide asylum, an individual right to asylum is being recognized in some places on a regional level.

International Instruments on Asylum

Article 14 of the Universal Declaration of Human Rights provides: "(1) Everyone has the right to seek and to enjoy in other countries asylum from persecution. (2) This right may not be invoked in the case of prosecutions genuinely arising from nonpolitical crimes or from acts contrary to the purposes and principles of the United Nations" (U.N. General Assembly, 1948).

Article 22(7) of the American Convention on Human Rights (OAS, 1969) states as follows: "Every person has the right to seek and be granted asylum in a foreign territory, in accordance with the legislation of the state and international conventions, in the event he is being pursued for political offenses or related common crimes." Article 12(3) of the African Charter on Human and Peoples' Rights states: "Every individual shall have the right, when persecuted, to seek and obtain asylum in other countries in accordance with the law of those countries and international conventions" (OAS, 1981).

In June 1990, the European Community member states adopted the Convention Determining the State Responsible for Examining Applications for asylum Lodged in one of the Member States of the European Communities (1991). The Convention is aimed at guaranteeing "adequate protection to refugees" in accordance with the 1951 Refugee Convention and the 1967 Protocol. It also was aimed at taking measures to avoid any situations that could arise in the application process. The goal of the Convention was to reduce the amount of time that applicants were left in doubt about their applications. The Convention provided applicants with asylum during the application process, as well as a guarantee that their applications would be examined by one of the Member States. The Convention also ensured that applicants for asylum are not referred successively from one Member State to another without any of these States acknowledging itself to be competent to examine the application for asylum.

Article 3 of the Convention (1991) states that:
1) Member States undertake an examination of any alien who applies at the border or in their territory to any one of them for asylum.
2) That applications shall be examined by a single Member State that shall be determined in accordance with the criteria defined in this Convention. The criteria set out in Articles 4 to 8 shall apply in the order in which they appear.
3) That applications shall be examined by that State in accordance with its national laws and its international obligations.

Mass Expulsion

A state's expulsion of large numbers of its own people should be considered a violation of international human rights law and of obligations regarding friendly relations between states. Were this to be considered an emerging norm, it would derive more from other areas of conventional and customary international human rights law than refugee law. The emergence of theories about state responsibility reflects the desire of the international community to halt flows of refugees and to establish grounds for burden-sharing among states. There is, however, no international machinery to enforce these principles, except in such special situations as responding to the treatment by Iraq of the Kurdish and Shiite elements of its population after the Gulf War.

Most of those today who involuntarily leave their countries of nationality do so because of war or warlike conditions, or denial of basic human rights by the governments of those countries, including persecution. The role of a state's failure to respect the basic human rights of its population in the creation of mass exoduses has been studied in depth by former UN High Commissioner Prince Sadruddin Aga Khan. He has stated that, among the major causes present in creating a flow of refugees, "[m]ost provisions of the [Universal] Declaration of Human Rights have been violated." (Khan, 1990).

The claims of people everywhere for protection by their governments have been included in standards and legal obligations for states in, predominantly, the

Universal Declaration of Human Rights (U.N. General Assembly, 1948), the International Covenant on Economic, Social and Cultural Rights (1966), the European Convention for the Protection of Human Rights and Fundamental Freedoms (Council of Europe, 1950), and the American Convention on Human Rights (OAS, 1969).

On the other hand, states control the basic elements of sovereign power, namely territory, population, and decision-making structures and institutions. Thus, states have traditionally resisted scrutiny of human rights problems as internal security matters. As one expert has remarked, it is often "not the nation's security that is really being threatened, but only its license to abuse its people" (Khan, 1990). Gross, widespread, and systematic violations of well-recognized human rights are widely acknowledged to create or contribute to refugee flows.

The Group of Government Experts, established by the UN General Assembly in 1981 to study the root causes of refugee flows and to recommend steps to avert new flows, determined that the primary responsibility for solution of the problem rested with the states concerned. The Group also concluded that improved international cooperation was required on all levels to avert massive refugee flows (UN Report, 1986). The Group also made the following recommendations (UN Report, 1986), *inter alia*:

1) States should promote civil, political, economic, social and cultural rights of their people and . . . accordingly refrain from denying to them and from discriminating against groups of their population because of their nationality, ethnicity, race, religion or language, thus directly or indirectly forcing them to leave their country.
2) States should co-operate with one another in order to prevent future flows of refugees. They should promote international cooperation in all its aspects, in particular at the regional and subregional levels.

Finding Durable Solutions to Refugee Situations

Depending upon the needs of the refugee, the conditions in the country of first refuge, and those in the country of origin, the refugee should be voluntarily repatriated, resettled in a third country, or integrated into the country of first refuge. One could argue that the magnitude of the burden placed on receiving states and the entire supporting world community requires that masses of refugees be returned to the country from which they came rather than settled elsewhere, whenever it is possible. Political asylum contemplates integration of the refugee into the country of asylum.

A major part of UNHCR's mandate is assistance in finding durable solution to refugees' situations. The agency is charged by the United Nations with "seeking permanent solutions for the problem of refugees by assisting Governments and, subject to the approval of the Governments concerned, private organizations to facilitate the voluntary repatriation of such refugees, or their assimilation within new national communities" (United Nations, 1950, art. 5). In 1954, the General Assembly authorized the High Commissioner of Refugees to commence a program for permanent solutions and to appeal to governments for voluntary contributions (Khan, 1976) in accordance with the terms of the UNHCR statute requiring prior General Assembly approval for requesting funds from governments.

As noted above, voluntary repatriation is the most favored permanent solution, although within the recent past only in a few cases has it been possible for large groups of refugees to repatriate. The Bangkok Principles (AALCC, 1966) recognized that it is the duty of the state of origin to accept the voluntary return of its nationals, and that it was the right of the refugees to return if they choose. The OAU Convention calls upon the country of origin to make arrangements for the safe return of refugees, including formal guarantees for their safety and assurances that they will not be penalized for having left the country for the reasons they did (OAU, 1969). The state of refuge is commonly apart from the negotiations and arrangements for return of refugees. In 1991, the Chairman of the UNHCR Executive Committee commented:

> In the short run we must provide emergency assistance, relief and protection to refugees and displaced persons. In the medium term, we should stabilize them in areas of first asylum and ensure their access to basic facilities. In the long run, durable solutions will invariably involve elimination of poverty, promotion of sustainable development and the establishment of conditions for peace, security and enhanced international cooperation (Refugees, 1991).

A new aspect of refugee law and state responsibility bearing on this question is whether a refugee has a right to compensation from his/her state of origin for damages such as injury, deprivation of personal liberty, denial of other human rights, death of a refugee's dependents or those upon whom the refugee was dependent, and damage to property and assets caused by authorities or mob violence. This principle is set out in the Bangkok Principles (OAU, 1969), but no forum has adequately dealt with the subject, nor with the actual enforcement of the right to return.

In the case of refugees whose situations do not appear to demand ultimate resettlement but are not yet conducive to repatriation, host countries often provide temporary refuge to the extent to which they are able, with as much material support as possible from the international community through UNHCR. During the period of temporary refuge, the progress in the country of origin is monitored regarding the situation that created the refugee problem, and in expectation of the eventual repatriation of the refugee group.

If security becomes a problem for the refugees, and all available enforcement means are inadequate to remedy the problem, as a very last resort, third countries may be called upon to accept refugees for temporary refuge, and preferably in small numbers in order to spread the burden (Barkley, 1989). It has been suggested that the reduction of some Refugee Convention rights may be allowed for the period of temporary refuge in a country of first or third asylum until either repatriation is available or it is determined that the refugees must resettle in the country of refuge or yet another (Gunning, 1989-90).

Refugees qualifying for political asylum under the terms of the 1951 Convention are generally allowed to settle in the country of asylum with relatively little difficulty. Sometimes, however, even qualified applicants are rejected, based on the principle of "country of first asylum," under which refugees are returned to another country through which they had transited and which could have granted them durable asylum.

The Principle of Non-Refoulement

The definition of "refugee" is closely linked to application of the principle of non-refoulement (Weisbrodt & Hortreiter, 1999). Currently, there is a general practice as to an individual who has been determined to be a "Convention" refugee (i.e., fleeing persecution) that s/he may not be returned (refouled) to a territory where s/he would be in danger of persecution, as these terms are set forth in the Refugee Convention (United Nations, 1951), for his/her race, religion, nationality or political opinion or beliefs. Persons invoking the rule are entitled to temporary refuge and humane treatment pending a determination of their claim.

While the right of a state to expel aliens (even by use of force) is generally recognized, the decision to expel a refugee must be reached in accordance with due process of law. Except where compelling reasons of national security call for otherwise, refugees must be allowed to submit evidence to clear themselves, to appeal an adverse determination to a competent authority, and to be represented at all critical phases of the determination. States must allow refugees facing expulsion a reasonable period within which to seek legal admission into another country, during which time states reserve the right to apply such internal measures as they deem necessary within their obligation to protect the refugees' basic human rights.

Non-refoulement is not, in principle, confined to cases of political asylum, although the Refugee Convention limits its mandate to Convention refugees (United Nations, 1951). More expansive application also may be considered as emerging customary international law (Weis, 1982; Grahl-Madsen, 1982). Indeed, it is the position of the UNHCR and other authorities that application of the principle of non-refoulement is independent of any formal determination of refugee (hence, persecution) status (United Nations General Assembly, 1985). However, states are naturally reluctant to make a binding commitment of such a permanent and expansive nature in this volatile area, given the turmoil that our age is experiencing. The concept of temporary refuge is a clear focal point in the debate over expansion of the international community's obligations from those currently committed under the 1951 Refugee Convention to those that would follow from, for example, a broader definition of a refugee. It has already been successful on an ad hoc basis in many situations, for example, in the case of Mozambican refugees in Malawi (Barkley, 1989).

Generally speaking, the refoulement provision is not reserved to Convention parties, which gives support to the argument that the rule is one of customary international law and applicable to all states. Serious violations of the principle of non-refoulement over the years have been of concern to UNHCR. Accordingly, the Executive Committee of UNHCR has appealed to all states "to abide by their international obligations in this regard" (UNHCR, 1989). It is, however, noteworthy that refoulement has occurred in cases where the receiving country has guaranteed no ill treatment. For example, refoulment occurred in the cases involving the return of Vietnamese asylum-seekers pursuant to the Hong Kong-Vietnam agreement, and the return of Haitian asylum seekers pursuant to agreement between the US and Haiti.

Despite "broad state consensus" that respects the prohibition against refoulement, states continue to violate the principle. States confronted with large-scale refugee movements have reacted with large-scale expulsions (UNHCR, 1989). Even states remote from such movements have nonetheless imposed administrative restrictions designed to forestall refugee entry (UNHCR, 1990). Due process, a requirement of the 1951 Convention, as specified in article 32, paragraph 2, has been avoided by some states in the implementation of procedures designed to expedite the review of refugee claims (UNHCR, 1989). The perception that some influential developed states have been violating the prohibition against refoulement has led to some erosion of support for the principle.

Since World War II, states have resorted to expulsion under a variety of theories. One common approach has been the view that certain groups of refugees are collectively ineligible. Other nations have expelled persons by the very reason of their nationality or religious beliefs. States continue to expel refugees if a threat to national security is perceived. As early as 1991, the High Commissioner noted (UNHCR, 1991):

> Fundamental civil, political and social changes in certain countries have resulted in an opening up and democratization process, which is being perceived as a fundamental change in circumstances from a refugee status point of view. This has resulted in the termination by countries of asylum of the refugee status of persons from one or more of these countries. Whereas, in a number of cases, the decision may have been appropriate, in some others the decision to terminate status may

have been taken before sufficient time had elapsed since the fundamental changes had occurred for the situation in the country of origin to be considered stable.

It has not been definitively stated whom the rule of non-refoulement is intended to protect. Does it only protect persons who have both been granted refugee status and legally entered the country? Does it protect persons who would fall within the definition of refugee but who have not been able to obtain entry beyond the frontier, that is, persons who are, at the time of arrival at the frontier, displaced persons awaiting determination of their status? Both the 1951 Convention and the 1967 Protocol, in their non-refoulement provisions, speak in terms of "a refugee." In view of the definition of refugee contained in these documents, this means that only persons who have been determined to be refugees would fall within the protection of the non-refoulement provisions. On this basis, Article 33 provides only limited protection. However, there are a number of other United Nations and regional instruments which either contain more liberal provisions or suggest by implication a greater level of protection.

For example, on a construction of Articles 1(1) and 3(1) of the Declaration on Territorial Asylum and Article 14 of the Universal Declaration of Human Rights, any person seeking asylum from persecution, except one involved in non-political crimes and acts contrary to the purposes of the United Nations, shall not be rejected at the frontier or, if s/he has already entered the territory in which s/he seeks asylum, shall not be expelled or compulsorily returned to any state where s/he may be subjected to persecution. This is a broader scope of protection than that contained in Article 33. However, both of these declarations are non-binding in character.

Articles relating to the right of asylum in the Universal Declaration of Human Rights, the American Convention on Human Rights, and the African Charter on Human and Peoples' Rights create in the individual a right to asylum and would be a bar to refoulement of persons at the frontier. One of the conclusions of the Cartagena Declaration on Refugees (Inter-American Commission on Human Rights, 1984) was as follows:

To reiterate the importance and meaning of the principle of non-refoulement (including the prohibition of rejection at the frontier), it is a corner-stone of the international protection of refugees. This principle is imperative in regard to refugees and in the present state of international law should be acknowledged and observed as a rule of *jus cogens* [Part III(5)].

Article 2(3) of the OAU Convention states:

No person shall be subject by a Member State to measures such as rejection at the frontier, return or expulsion, which would compel him to return to or remain in a territory where his life, physical integrity or liberty would be threatened for the reasons set out in Article I, paragraphs 1 and 2.

The Committee of Ministers of the Council of Europe recommended to their member governments in 1967 that:

> They should . . . ensure that no one shall be subjected to refusal of admission at the frontier, rejection, expulsion or any other measure which would have the result of compelling him to return to, or remain in, a territory where he would be in danger of persecution for reasons of race, religion, nationality, membership of a particular social group or political opinion.

This resolution is broader in scope than Article 33 of the 1951 Convention and is not binding on member governments. However, by Article 3 of the 1977 Declaration on Territorial Asylum, the member states of the Council of Europe reaffirmed their liberal attitude towards the granting of asylum, by adding to the 1967 Resolution a provision that asylum should also be granted to "any other persons they consider worthy of receiving asylum for humanitarian reasons."

A review of treaties suggests that there is not in international law a written rule of non-refoulement which protects all persons presenting themselves for entry at a frontier. At most, Article 33 of the 1951 Convention would only protect refugees, as mentioned above. Although there are many statements which reflect non-refoulement as an ideal, states have generally chosen not to provide for those who fall outside the provisions of Article 33.

Inadequacy of the Current Refugee Regime and the Need to Reform it

In 1999 the conflicts in Kosovo, East Timor and Chechnya focused the world's attention on the refugee crises these conflicts have caused. The plight of refugees worldwide was also vividly demonstrated by the failure of the world community to protect civilian refugees in the Great Lakes region of Central Africa, which resulted in the death or disappearance of tens of thousands primarily in what was then Zaire, because of epidemics and ethnic violence (McNamara, 1998). In the recent past, conflicts and repression in Bosnia, Haiti, Iraq, Rwanda, Burundi, Liberia, Sri Lanka, Somalia, and the Sudan, among others, have resulted in similar refugee crises. The practice of providing "safe havens" for refugees has not ensured safety to the persecuted seeking protection (Arulanantham, 2000).

The current refugee law appears to be unable to address effectively the problems refugees and displaced persons face. These people are not adequately protected. They face violence and lack security. They suffer deprivation of basic human rights. The pillar of the international refugee law, the practice of granting asylum, is under siege. Developed countries of the North perceive a threat to their borders and their immigration policies by the flux of those culturally and ethnically different. Burden-sharing remains a pious ideal. Similarly, international cooperation is a slogan generally devoid of concrete implementation. Duress and coercion are often the real driving forces behind "voluntary" repatriation.

Suggestions for change range from the revitalization of the current refugee regime and acceptance and implementation of the obligation to grant asylum (Fitzpatrick, 1996) to restructuring safe havens (Arulanantham, 2000) and providing financial burden-sharing by the rich countries of the North (Hathaway & Neve, 1997; Schuck, 1997) so that refugees and asylum seekers may perhaps remain in the South close to their countries and in their home regions. Other suggestions include the recognition of a universal right to migrate and addressing the refugee problem in the context of a framework which combines migration, immigration and refugee laws (Juss, 1998), and application of pressure upon states, especially those in the North, to comply with their international legal obligation to refugees (Anker, Fitzpatrick & Shacknove, 1998). Given the current state of "compassion fatigue" and restrictive immigration and asylum pollicies by the countries in the North, it seems problematic that an international agreement will be reached to bring about a basic change in the current refugee regime. Perhaps incremental changes in the present regime, focused primarily on financial burden-sharing and respect for non-refoulement and asylum, are all we can hope for at present.

Recognition of the need to provide protection and ensure human rights to IDPs led to the appointment of Dr. Francis Deng as Representative of the U.N. Secretary-General. He served in that capacity from 1992 to 2004. During his tenure, Deng developed a normative framework, as reflected in the Guiding Principles on Internal Displacement. He also continued his efforts toward the creation of a more effective international arrangement for responding to internal displacement crises and for a more coordinated U.N. response (United Nations, 2002). However, as Dr. Deng acknowledged in his 2002 report, "[t]he global crisis of internal displacement remains grave, affecting some 20-25 millions in at least 40 countries worldwide, forced from their homes by armed conflict, communal and generalized violence, and human rights violations" (United Nations, 2002).

In September 2004, Professor Walter Kälin succeeded Francis Deng. In his first report, Kälin noted that there remains "a lack of appreciation of the particular protection needs of IDPs and the role of United Nations agencies and human rights mechanisms in addressing them" (United Nations, 2004). He added that, although states are primarily responsible for protecting IDPs, "little attention has been devoted to whether and how the international community's conceptual framework for protection could be applied by Governments in developing their own responses" (United Nations, 2004). He is focusing his attention on a program of protection-related activities that takes into account the primary role and responsibility of states.

It is imperative that the international community consider the protection of internationally recognized human rights by governments within their borders as a matter of international concern. Forced mass expulsions must not be tolerated and there must be international accountability for massive violation of human rights with the credible threat of economic sanctions and even collective humanitarian intervention (Nanda, Muther & Eckert, 1998). The foundation of the international refugee regime needs to be reinforced.

Notes

1. Convention of June 1990 applying the Schengen Agreement of 14 June 1985 between the governments of the states of the Benelux Economic Union, the Federal Republic of Germany and the French Republic, on the Gradual Abolition of Checks at their Common Borders.
2. Dublin Convention Determining the State responsible for examining applications for asylum lodged in one of the Member States of the European Community, June 1990.

References

Anker, D., Fitzpatrick, J. & Shacknove, A. (1998). Crisis and cure: A reply to Hatha-way/Neve and Schuck, *Harvard Human Rights Journal, 11*, pp. 295-309.

Arulananthan, A. (2000). Restructured safe havens: A proposal for reform of the refugee protection system. *Human Rights Quarterly, 22*, p. 1.

Asian-African Legal Consultative Committee (1966). Bangkok Principles Concerning Treatment of Refugees. *UNHCR Collection of International Instruments concerning Refugees, 1988*, p. 201.

Barkley, D. (1989). Hope for the hopeless: International cooperation and the refugee. *Columbia Human Rights Law Review, 21*, p. 319.

Coman, G. (1998). Note: European Union policy on asylum and its inherent human rights violations. *Brooklyn Law Review, 64*, p. 1217.

Convention Determining the State Responsible for Examining Applications for Asylum Lodged in one of the Member States of the European Communities (1991). *International Legal Materials, 30*, p. 425.

Council of Europe (1950). European Convention for the Protection of Human Rights and Fundamental Freedoms. *Council of Europe Treaty Series No. 5.*

Council of Europe (1977). Committee of Ministers, Declaration on Territorial Asylum. *UNHCR Collection of International instruments Concerning Refugees (1979)*, p. 306.

Fitzpatrick, J. (1996). Revitalizing the 1951 Refugee Convention, *Harvard Human Rights Journal, 9*, p. 229.

Goodwin-Gill, G. (1983). *The refugee in international law*, p. 53.

Goodwin-Gill, G. (1986). Non-refoulement and the new asylum seekers. *Virginia Journal of International Law, 26*, pp. 899-903.

Grahl-Madsen, A. (1982). Refugees and refugee law in a world in transition. *Transnational Legal Problems of Refugees, Michigan Yearbook of International Legal Studies, 66*, p. 73.

Gunning, I. (1989-90). Expanding the international definition of refugee: A multicultural view. *Fordham International Law Journal, 13*, p. 35.

Hailbronner, K. (1986). Non-refoulement and 'humanitarian' refugees: Customary international law or wishful legal thinking? *Virginia Journal of International Law, 26*, p. 854.

Hathaway, J. & Neve, R. (1997). Making international refugee law relevant again: A proposal for collectivized and solution-oriented protection. *Harvard Human Rights Journal, 10*, p. 115.

Hathaway, J. (1990). A reconsideration of the underlying premise of international law. *Harvard International Law Journal, 31*, p. 129.

Hathaway, J. (ed.) (1997). *Reconceiving international refugee law.* The Hague, Switzerland: Martinus Nijhoff Publishers.

Heyman, M. (1987). Redefining refugee: a proposal for relief of victims of civil strife. *San Diego Law Review, 24*, p. 449.

Inter-American Commission on Human Rights (1984). Cartagena declaration on refugees (1984). *Annual Report of Inter-American Commission on Human Rights 1984-1985, OEA/Ser.L/V/II. 66, doc. 10, rev. 1*, pp. 190-193.

International Conference on Human Rights (1968). Proclamation of Tehran, 1968, article 1. Available at www.unhcr.ch/html/menu3/b/_tehern.htm.

International Covenant on Civil and Political Rights (ICCPR) (1966). *999 U.N.T.S. 171.*

International Refugee Organization Constitution (1946). *18 U.N.T.S. 3.*

Juss, S. (1998). Toward a morally legitimate reform of refugee law: The uses of cultural jurisprudence. *Harvard Human Rights Journal, 11*, pp. 311-353.

Khan, S. (1976). *Recueil des cours.* The Hague, Switzerland: The Hague Academy of International Law.

Khan, S. (1990). Looking to the 1990s: Afghanistan and other refugee crises. *International Journal of Refugee Law, Special Issue, 22*.

Leopold, E. (1991). General Assembly approves new relief aid chief. *Reuters, Dec. 19, 1991*.

McNamara, D. (1998). The protection of refugees and the responsibility of states: Engagement or abdication? *Harvard Human Rights Journal, 11*, pp. 355-361.

Memorandum of Understanding Between Sadruddin Aga Khan and the Minister of Foreign Affairs of the Republic of Iraq, Nov. 24, 1991.

Meron, T. (1988, January/February). Draft model declaration on internal strife. *International Review of the Red Cross.* Geneva, Switzerland: International Committee of the Red Cross.

Nanda, V. (1981). World refugee assistance: The role of international law and institutions. *Hofstra Law Review, 9*, p. 457.

Nanda, V. (1989). *Refugee law and policy.* New York, NY: Greenwood Press.

Nanda, V., Muther, T. & Eckert, A. (1998). Tragedies in Somalia, Yugoslavia, Haiti, Rwanda and Liberia—revisiting the validity of humanitarian intervention under international law, part II. *Denver Journal of International Law and Policy, 26*, p. 827.

Ogata, S. (2000). The state of the world's refugees: Fifty years of humanitarian action, Preface [WWW document]. URL http://www.unhcr.ch/sowr2000/toc2.htm.

Organization of African Unity (1969). OAU Convention Governing the Specific Aspects of Refugee Problems in Africa. *1001 U.N.T.S. 45.*

Organization of American States (1969). American convention on human rights. *OAS Official Records, OEA/Ser.K/XVI/1.1*, entered into force July 18, 1978.

Organization of American States (1981). African charter on human and peoples' rights, 18th Assembly OAU. *International Legal Materials 21*, p. 58.

Organization of American States (1985). Annual report of the Inter-American Commission on Human Rights 1984-1985. *O.A.S. Doc. OEA/Ser.L./II,66, Doc. Rev. 1, 182.*

Perluss, D. & Hartman, J. (1986). Temporary refuge: Emergence of a customary norm. *Virginia Journal of International Law, 26*(551), pp. 582-583.

Schuck, P. (1997). Refugee burden-sharing: A modest proposal. *Yale Journal of International Law, 22*, p. 243.

United Nations (1951). United Nations convention relating to the status of refugees. *U.S.T.S. 6259, TIAS No. 6577, 189 U.N.T.S. 137.*

United Nations (1967). Protocol Relating to the Status of Refugees, 606 U.N.T.S. 267.

United Nations (1968). Proclamation of Tehran. *U.N. Doc. A/CONF.32/4.*

United Nations (1986). Report of the Group of Government Experts on international cooperation to avert new flows of refugees. *U.N. Doc. A/41/324.*

United Nations (1998, February). Report of the Representative of the Secretary-General Mr. Francis M. Deng and Guiding Principles of Internal Displacement. United Nations Economic and Social Council Commission of Human Rights, *U.N. Doc. E/CN.4/1998/53/Add.2.*

United Nations (2002, January). Report of the Representative of the Secretary-General Mr. Francis M. Deng on internally displaced persons, United Nations Commission on Human Rights, *U.N. Doc. E/CN.4/2002/95*, pp. 4-25.

United Nations (2004, December). Report of the Representative of the Secretary-General Mr. Walter Kälin on the human rights of internally displaced persons, United Nations Commission on Human Rights, *U.N. Doc. E/CN.4/2005/84*, pp. 2,5.

United Nations General Assembly (1948, December). Universal Declaration of Human Rights. *Resolution 217(III).*

United Nations General Assembly (1950). Resolution 428 Annex. *U.N. Doc. A/1775.*

United Nations General Assembly (1957). Resolution 1167. *U.N. Doc. A/3805.*

United Nations General Assembly (1965). Resolution 2019. *U.N. Doc. A/6014.*

United Nations General Assembly (1967). Declaration on Territorial Asylum (1967). *U.N. General Assembly Res. 2312, U.N. Doc. A/6716.*

United Nations General Assembly (1975). Resolution 3454. *U.N. Doc. A/10034.*

United Nations General Assembly (1985). Declaration on the human rights of individuals who are not nationals of the country in which they live. *U.N. General Assembly Resolution 40/144.*

United Nations General Assembly (1985). Resolution 40/112. *U.N. Doc. A/40/53.*

United Nations General Assembly (1990). Resolution 45/100.

United Nations High Commissioner for Refugees (1985). Report of the United Nations High Commissioner for Refugees. *U.N. Doc. E/1985/62*, paragraphs 22-23.

United Nations High Comissioner for Refugees (1988). Note on International Protection of the Thirty-ninth Session of the Executive Committee of the High Commissioner's Programme. *U.N. Doc. A/AC.96/713, paragraph 12.*

United Nations High Comissioner for Refugees (1989). Note on International Protection of the Fortieth Session of the Executive Committee of the High Commissioner's Programme. *U.N. Doc. A/AC.96/728*, paragraphs 37-54.

United Nations High Comissioner for Refugees (1990). Note on International Protection of the Forty-first Session of the Executive Committee of the High Commissioner's Programme. *U.N. Doc. A/AC.96/750*, paragraph 18.

United Nations High Comissioner for Refugees (1991). Report of the United Nations High Commissioner for Refugees. *U.N. GAOR, Supp. No. 12, U.N. Doc. A/46/12*.

United Nations High Comissioner for Refugees (1998). Overview: Table I.1, Indicative Number of Refugees and Others. *http://www.unhcr.ch/statist/98oview/tab1_htm*.

United Nations High Comissioner for Refugees (1998, October). Press release 5 October 1998, Ogata opens 49th annual UNHCR Executive Committee Session. *http://www.unhcr.ch/news/pr/pr981005.htm*.

United Nations High Commissioner for Refugees (2000). UNHCR Facts and Figures, 2000. Available at *www.unhcr.org*.

United Nations High Commissioner for Refugees (2004). The UN Refugee Survey. *http://www.unhcr.ch/cgi-bin/texis/vtx/print?tbl=VISITORS&id=3b028097c*.

United Nations High Commissioner for Refugees (2005, June). 2004 Global Refugee Trends. *http://www.unhcr.ch/statistics*, pp. 2, 5.

U.S. Committee for Refugees (1999). *http://www.refugees.org/news/press-releases/1999/090999.htm*.

U.S. Committee for Refugees (2000). *World Refugee Survey 2000* [WWW document]. URL http://www.refugees.org/news/press_releases/2000/061300a.htm.

U.S. Committee for Refugees (2003). *World Refugee Survey 2003* [WWW document]. *http://www.refugees.org/data/wrs/03/stats/SSKeyStatistics.pdf*, Table 1.

U.S. Commitee for Refugees (2004). *World Refugee Survey 2004* [WWW document]. *http://www.refugees.org/wrs04/pdf/key_statistics.pdf*, Table 1.

U.S. Committee for Refugees (2005). *World Refugee Survey 2005* [WWW document]. *http://www.refugees.org/uploadedFiles/Investigate/Publications_&_Archives/WRS _Archives 2005/key_statistics.pdf*, Tables 1, 6.

Weis, P. (1982). The development of refugee law. *Transnational Legal Problems of Refugees, 1982 Michigan Yearbook of International Legal Studies*, p. 31.

Weissbrodt, D. & Hortreiter, I. (1999). The principle of non-refoulement: Article 3 of the Convention Against Torture and Other Cruel, Inhuman or Degrading Treatment or Punishment in comparison with the non-refoulement provisions of other international human rights treaties. *Buffalo Human Rights Law Review, 5*, p. 1.

CHAPTER 9

Government-Sanctioned Torture and International Law: A Survivor's Perspective

Sister Dianna Ortiz OSU

Government-sanctioned torture and international law are broad in scope and may not have the same meaning for all peoples. For instance, governments, militaries and human rights organizations all have their own distinctive take on what these terms mean. But it is not my task to represent their views. Instead, I wish to share my thoughts on what these terms mean to me, a person who has survived torture.

There are two factors which give these thoughts a wider validity than purely personal recollections. First, while I do not presume to write for all torture survivors or refugees, I am part of a network of survivors who communicate regularly with one another. Therefore, I have good reason to believe that these thoughts are not mine alone. Second, my claim to expertise on this subject rests on two facts: first, I am a survivor of government-sanctioned torture; second, I am a survivor of the violation of domestic and international law by the governments of Guatemala and the United States. Simply put, I am a product of Guatemalan and U.S. foreign policy. I have spent each day of the past decade of my life trying to survive the aftermath of this policy. I am a survivor of torture who has seen with my own eyes how torture has affected my family, my religious community and my friends. Like other survivors, I have first-hand experience that torture is intended to destroy communities and terrorize whole societies.

In the next few pages I will attempt to describe government-sanctioned torture and international law as seen through the eyes of survivors. Rather than describing these issues in the abstract, I will try to put a human face on them by sharing my personal reflections and experiences and those of other survivors.

The Wounds of Torture

Torture is often described in words that seem not only abstract but lifeless. But for many survivors, torture is a living beast that claws its way into the very souls of its prey. The resulting wounds for some are fatal—they become victims of extrajudicial killings, forced disappearances, and genocide. Their bodies lie buried in clandestine graves or are tossed into the open sea. Those who do survive carry deep wounds that change them forever.

In many instances, a survivor brings with her the memories of what happened during the torture. In my case, I remember that at the moment of victimization, I began to die a slow death. The perpetrators saw me as less than human. They stripped me of my dignity, my sense of control and my link with humanity. My sense of self was shattered. I attempted to find my place once again within the human family. I, like many survivors, was given time to heal and reconnect—six months, a year perhaps. When I failed to complete my recovery quickly, I faced criticism. People thought I was feeling sorry for myself. Some even told me that I had to take responsibility for my actions. My life choices were what led to my torture—for example, my decision to remain in Guatemala despite receiving death threats. This criticism made my attempt to reconnect with the human family all the more difficult.

Often, we are welcomed back with the expectation that we are to be the people we were before. We are admonished by word and look to forgive, forget and move on with our lives. Take Frieda,[1] for example. She was physically, sexually and psychologically tortured and held under inhuman conditions for many months. When she was finally released, she was granted asylum in another country. There, she met a young man with whom she fell in love. To this love affair, of course, she brought the memories of her experience. Frieda made every effort to live as normal a life as possible and to be a good companion, but there were times when the memories nearly overwhelmed her.

At precisely these moments, when Frieda was most in need of support and understanding, her companion would respond with frustration, "Aren't you ever going to let go of the past?" he would say. "You must like feeling sorry for yourself. You're a selfish person."

What few seem to understand is that each of the tortured, whether we survived or not, died. Those of us who have survived, as much as we might wish it, will never be the same. We will never trust again as once we trusted. We will never have the freedom to forget the past. At any moment, the smell of a cigarette, the jangling of keys, or seeing someone who resembles the torturer transports us back to that horrible time. Survivors live with a past that constantly menaces our daily existence, a past which without a moment's notice may overwhelm our present—dragging us back into the claws of our torturers. Everything we see, hear, touch, taste and smell has been colored by torture. It has left no part of our lives untouched. It has left us prone to nightmares and flashbacks. It has draped us in despair, guilt, shame, sadness, fear and feelings of wanting to die. This is what we mean when we say that torture's ghost always walks with us.

Coping with the Memories

Survivors are frequently told that time will heal the wounds of torture. But as Jean Améry, an Austrian philosopher tortured by the Gestapo, said, "Anyone who has been tortured remains tortured. Anyone who has suffered torture never again will be at ease in the world, the abomination of the annihilation is never extinguished. Faith in humanity, already cracked with the first slap in the face, then demolished by torture, is never acquired again" (Levi, 1988, p. 25). Torture for Améry was an interminable death. He took his life in 1978.

While there are those of us who agree with the heart of his message, still we believe that there are ways to cope besides taking our lives. To us, the act of suicide, whether attempted or carried out, is nothing to judge—it is only a reminder of the terrible effects of torture on the survivor and the survivor's family and society. Today, I can write for you, the reader, and say that I want to live life as fully as possible. However, I do not know what tomorrow may bring. I only hope that like today, I will continue to say 'yes' to life.

As part of this 'yes' to life, we search for ways to shed at least some of the robes of despair. How we accomplish this may oftentimes defy the conventional. Let me give you two examples.

Several years ago I spoke with Juliet, who told me of her own efforts to cope with torture. She spoke in detail of how the torturers had sexually abused her in every way possible. All control was taken from her. On the day that she was released from the political prison, Juliet swore to herself that she would never allow men to control her again and that she would find a way to reclaim her control. For her, that way was through prostitution. In the setting with her clients, it was she who was in control. She set the rules. She decided who, what, when, where and how. She took precautions for herself and her clients—and in the end, she reclaimed some sense of control.

Drugs and alcohol sometimes serve a similar function. Consider for a moment post-operative medication. It deadens the pain for a period of time. The medication then begins to be withdrawn as the patient is better able to deal with the effects of the surgery.

Ahmad is one survivor who turned to alcohol. His wife was arrested for teaching local women to read and write. Her body was later found in a garbage dump. The army officers then came to Ahmad's hut, beat his children and cut off their heads. Probably more from cruelty than mercy, they did not kill Ahmad. He found refuge in the United States and was taken to a treatment center that provided psychotherapy for torture survivors. As he started to talk with a therapist about his family and his own guilt and shame, he found that after his sessions, he would stop at the local grocery store to purchase liquor. He drank until he fell asleep. As Ahmad said, "The alcohol numbed the pain and I could rest from the memories for a few hours."

What might well appear at first sight to be self-destructive or even pathological behavior, may in fact, have positive effects. Its virtue, at least in the short run, is to keep the survivor alive. In the case of Juliet, acting as a sex worker allowed her to regain some sense of control over her life. She accepted that the issue of control would always be before her, as would her entire experience of torture. In recognizing this, she was able to move on to a different phase of her survival. Today Juliet lives what many would view as a stable life; she is a married woman, the mother of three children and a reputable attorney. Prostitution was not a way of life for her, but a "transitional survival skill," a bridge to that next step of survival (Ortiz in Gerrity, Keane, & Tuma, 2001).

Just as surgery would often be difficult if not impossible without medication, survivors without something to numb the pain might not be able to confront it at all, and so they might choose to end the pain by ending their lives. Knowing that there was alcohol and the sleep it would bring made it possible for Ahmad to begin to speak of the shame and guilt he felt at not having been killed with his wife and children. As he told more and more of what had happened to his family, the drinking declined until finally, Ahmad was able to stop completely. When I last spoke with him, he was pleased to be working as an X-ray technician.

It is important to remember that, while both Juliet and Ahmad have successful careers, they see themselves, first and foremost, as persons who have been tortured and who are in the act of surviving. To this day, they still wear robes of guilt and shame. They are still visited by nightmares and flashbacks.

Government Protection Against Torture?

Government-sanctioned torture leaves its claw marks long after the torture is over, not only on its victim, but on the victim's family, community and society as a whole. As an offspring of foreign policy, government-sanctioned torture has left a gruesome trail throughout the world, from Asia to Africa, from Europe to North and South America (Amnesty International, 1999). It is common for governments to advertise their respect for human rights and international law. They go so far as to sign conventions and treaties, often with much fanfare. A number of important international and regional conventions and declarations in the field of human rights and international humanitarian law contain an absolute prohibition against torture and other cruel, inhuman or degrading treatment or punishment (Dunèr, 1998). Obvious examples include the Universal Declaration of Human Rights (1948); the Geneva Conventions (1949); the U.N. Declaration on the Protection of All Persons From Being Subjected to Torture and Other Cruel, Inhuman or Degrading Treatment or Punishment (1957); the U.N. Convention Against Torture and Other Cruel, Inhuman or Degrading Treatment or Punishment (1987); and the Inter-American Convention (1996). The majestic sentiments expressed in these conventions and treaties fill the reader with awe at the commitment of governments to the welfare and protection of even the least of us.

Butt how do these treaties, declarations and conventions work in practice? Who do they protect, the victim or the perpetrator? What is their purpose, to eliminate torture and impunity or protect national security? For many torture survivors, these international human rights bodies have failed us and the words they have written into international law are empty.

Look at some of the words found in these conventions: "No one shall be subjected to torture or to cruel, inhuman or degrading treatment" (Universal Declaration of Human Rights, 1948, Article 5). "No one shall be subjected to arbitrary interference with his privacy, family, home or correspondence, nor to attacks upon his honor and reputation. Everyone has the right to the protection of the law against such interference or attacks" (Universal Declaration of Human Rights, 1948, Article 12). "Each State Party shall ensure in its legal system that the victim of an act of torture obtains redress and has an enforceable right to fair and adequate compensation, including the means for as full rehabilitation as possible" (Convention Against Torture, 1984, Article 14.1). "Each State shall ensure that all acts of torture are offenses under its criminal law. The same shall apply in regard to acts which constitute participation in, complicity in, incitement to or an attempt to commit torture" (Declaration on the Protection of All Persons from Being Subjected to Torture, 1975, Article 7). "No Contracting State shall expel or return a refugee in any manner whatsoever to the frontiers of territories where his life or freedom would be threatened on account of race, religion, nationality, membership of a particular social group or political opinion" (Convention Relating to the Status of Refugees, 1951, Article 33.1). When we see these words we who have been tortured are not sure whether to begin to hope or whether to laugh bitterly at the hypocrisy of those governments that pretend to honor these conventions.

When I was tortured in 1989, some 80 governments across the world engaged in torture and ill-treatment. That number has risen now to at least 150 (Amnesty International Report 2004 and The U.S. State Department's Country Reports on Human Rights Practices for 2003). One hundred and thirty-four States have ratified the U.N. Convention Against Torture. Yet, despite signing this Convention, the governments of many of these countries are, in fact, engaged in torture. Widespread violation of the Covenant indicates that it is an international agreement in name only.

The U.S. is a signatory to the Convention Against Torture. In a letter to torture survivors in 1999, President Clinton wrote, "The United States is firmly committed to ending torture and to aiding those who have suffered the terrible consequence of this brutal and dehumanizing practice. We have been a leader in formulating both the U.N. Declaration on Protection from Torture and the International Convention Against Torture. . . . Through the creation of the International Criminal Tribunals on the former Yugoslavia and Rwanda, we are also working to bring to justice those responsible for torture. Those who engage in the cruelty of torture must know that they cannot commit such atrocities with impunity" (Clinton, B. 1999). The former President's words are perplexing. Did the Commander-in-Chief not know that the U.S. government taught courses to Latin American officers on how to torture; that it has a policy of hiring 'assets' to obtain information in spite of their records as egregious human rights violators; and that the identities of those involved are almost always kept secret, thereby, granting them de facto impunity (Editorial,1996).

In addition, the U.S. enjoys cordial political and economic relations with countries that routinely employ torture: China, Turkey, Colombia, Israel, Peru, Ethiopia, Mexico, and Nigeria, to name a few. However, the Clinton administration, to its credit, did admit to a United Nation committee that torture currently existed in the U.S. criminal justice system (Marshall, 1999, TASSC: Survivor Statement, 1999).

More recently, there is President George W. Bush's ringing condemnation of torture issued on June 26, 2003. In it the President said, "Torture anywhere is an affront to human dignity everywhere. We are committed to building a world where human rights are respected and protected by the rule of law. Freedom from torture is an inalienable human right. . . . The United States is committed to the world-wide elimination of torture and we are leading this fight by example. I call on all governments to join with the United States and the community of law-abiding nations in prohibiting, investigating, and prosecuting all acts of torture and in undertaking to prevent other cruel and unusual punishment. . . . The suffering of torture victims must end, and the United States calls on all governments to assume this great mission" (Bush, 2003).

Despite these words, we now know that, with the President's complicity, the U.S. government was engaged in torture many months before he issued that statement. What transpired at Abu Ghraib, Guantánamo, Bagram, and other sites, the detainees tortured and, in some instances, killed, was not simply the product of a few low level military "bad apples." At the highest levels of government, torture was justified, disappearance of detainees approved, transfer of detainees to governments that practiced torture arranged, and international agreements violated. The ultimate responsibility for this lies with President Bush and some of the most senior members of his administration. For the administration of his second term the President nominated as Attorney General of the United States, White House counsel Alberto Gonzales who was on record as stating that he found the Geneva Conventions both "quaint" and "obsolete" and who seemed intent upon facilitating and justifying the practice of torture by the U.S. government (Gonzales, 2002).

Once more, an apparent presidential defense of human rights and justice turned out to be nothing more than empty words, words intended to mislead. There are an estimated 500,000 torture survivors residing in the U.S. alone. How many of them have obtained even a small measure of justice? Where are the perpetrators? Have they been brought to justice? Our own government protects them—doors are opened to them while refugees live in fear that they will be returned to the governments which tortured them. What are those of us who have survived torture to make of this?

And what are we to make of the fact that our own leaders appear to be inextricably involved in ordering and facilitating the practice of torture by U.S. agents in secret prisons around the world (Priest, 2005). Do U.S. law and international agreements we have signed mean nothing? The President of the United States, George W. Bush, continues to insist that our government does not torture: "We do not torture." (The White House, 2005) in the face of obvious evidence that this is precisely what it does and with the approval of his administration (Kirk, 2005). At the very same time, Vice President, Dick Cheney, lobbies for the C.I.A to be exempt from legislation proposed to assure that torture will no longer be practiced (Espo and Sidoi, 2005).

What are survivors to make of this when a government that tortures proclaims itself the foremost protector of human rights in the world? Of course, it is true that low level military personnel have been tried for their crimes and sent to prison but when is an independent prosecutor to be appointed who has the authority to investigate the role in torture played by officials in this administration up to and including the President, himself. One cannot support both human rights and impunity for those who violate these rights. I speak as a survivor of the very kind of brutality this administration has permitted to be practiced on others.

My Fight for Justice

In 1987, I went to Guatemala as a Catholic missionary to live and work with the Mayan people who were in the midst of a long and cruel civil war lasting more than three decades. My ministry was teaching children how to read and write in their native language. I never thought of education as a subversive act. Nonetheless, I began to receive death threats. That was not uncommon in Guatemala; but being a United States citizen, I thought I was protected from the political violence that was devastating the lives of the Guatemalan people. In November of 1989, I learned I was wrong. I learned that no one is immune to torture. I was abducted by members of the Guatemalan security forces and placed in a clandestine cell, where I was tortured. Worse than the physical torture, was hearing the screams of the others being tortured.

I have written that I was tortured by Guatemalans, and this is true. But it is also true that there was an American in that clandestine prison. That American, whom my torturers called 'Alejandro' and their 'boss,' gave explicit orders to my torturers. He was tall, fair skinned, and spoke poor Spanish and perfect American English.

Unlike so many others, I managed to escape from my perpetrators. I filed criminal charges against the Guatemalan government. In response to my attempt to prosecute, a smear campaign was launched almost immediately by Guatemalan and U.S. officials. I was branded a liar, a lesbian who was involved in kinky sex (to explain how I received more than 111 cigarette burns), a political strategist who was trying to influence Congress to cut off U.S. aid to the Guatemalan military—among other things. In the face of all this, I did what I thought was right. It was my moral responsibility to speak the truth. I did so for myself and for the people of Guatemala and the United States because I believed we all had a right to know what an American was doing heading a squad of Guatemalan torturers. We had a right to know how our tax dollars were being spent. Of course, now we know that the U.S. was heavily involved in Guatemala (Lux de Cotí, Tojo, & Tomuschat, 1999). Former President Clinton himself admitted that what the U.S. had done was "wrong" and that we should not commit that "mistake" again (Babington, 1999).

I wanted to put the past behind—to simply forget. It wasn't that easy. In addition to dealing with the trauma of torture and the slander I was met with when I tried to prosecute, I was faced with the ugly reality that an American was directly involved in torture in Guatemala. Some people have said to me, "He didn't do anything to you physically. He didn't really hurt you. Why do you continually bring him up?" True. Alejandro did not hold the burning cigarette that was used to brand my back over and over again; he did not join with the three Guatemalans in gang-raping me, nor was he in the room when they forced me to participate in the torture of an innocent woman. Now, does that excuse him? They called him their boss. They followed his orders. As far as I am concerned, Alejandro is an accomplice to torture. In my eyes, he is as guilty as any other torturer.

In my pursuit of justice and following the advice of many people, I have gone through all the proper legal channels. I have traveled to Guatemala on numerous occasions, testified before the courts, participated in several judicial reconstructions and I have identified the place of my torture—all to no avail. The judicial system did not work then and does not work today. The justice system is non-existent in Guatemala. Impunity has become one of the most important mechanisms for generating and maintaining a climate of fear inside the country (Human Rights Office of the Archdiocese of Guatemala, 1999).

The next battlefield was in my homeland—the United States. In August of 1995, I was told that the Justice Department had begun a serious and impartial investigation of my case. Putting aside my feelings of mistrust, I took the risk of working closely with the investigators. This entailed being interviewed by investigators for more than forty hours—having to relate in detail the humiliation and cruelty I suffered at the hands of my torturers. Added to the pain of remembering and reliving the events in such detail is the pain of being re-victimized. During the interview, one of the DOJ attorneys openly yelled at me and accused me of being a liar. The investigators, with their interrogation and their abuse, recreated the dynamics of my torture.

It took me a long time to see that justice in the U.S., as in Guatemala, was a mirage. Again, as in Guatemala, I was cast as the culprit; I was the one being investigated, not those responsible for the crimes against me. The burden of proof fell on me. I had to prove that I was abducted and tortured, but the physical scars were not considered evidence. (Interestingly, they seemed to give little credence to the fact that the Guatemalan security forces were renowned for their propensity to torture.) What happened to me is reminiscent of what many rape survivors have been subjected to by the criminal justice system. The burden of proof falls on the rape victim. She becomes the criminal, not her rapist. In torture, the situation can be more complicated. In my lawsuit in Guatemala, the government was both the prosecutor and the accused.

There is only so much abuse a person can take. I reached my limit. I could no longer subject myself to the re-victimization brought on by the investigators' questions and their abusive treatment and I withdrew from the investigation. But by then I had already given my testimony and had provided them with detailed sketches of my perpetrators I had made with the help of a forensic artist.

Months after I withdrew from the investigation, I learned that the case had been closed and that a 284-page report existed. I was informed by a Justice Department official that it was classified to protect sources, methods, and "my privacy." Subsequently I learned that the report was made available to a few apparently privileged people in the government—even a former ambassador who is no longer associated with the U.S. government. On June 26, 1998, I filed another Freedom of Information Act Request (FOIA), hoping to obtain a copy of the report. This request was denied in full. Finally, after several years my government permitted me to receive a copy of the report. It was then that I learned that it was useless.

This is just a small fraction of my experience with government-sanctioned torture. When I hear U.S. and Guatemalan government officials denouncing torture and terrorism and demanding obedience to international law, I am appalled at their hypocrisy and duplicity. From my own direct experience, these two democratic governments have made a mockery of the words 'human rights' and 'justice.' As recent events have clearly demonstrated, the Bush administration continues to do so.

The picture, however, is not entirely bleak. In 1991, eleven Guatemalans and I filed a joint lawsuit against former Guatemalan defense minister, General Hector Gramajo, charging him with ordering and covering up torture and other human rights abuses. On April 12, 1995, a U.S. federal judge found him guilty of murder and torture. Gramajo was ordered to pay $47.5 million in punitive damages to the plaintiffs (Delay, 1995). Needless to say, the plaintiffs received nothing: or will we. General Gramajo is now deceased.

In its 1996 Annual Report, the Inter-American Commission on Human Rights of the Organization of American States released the results of its investigation of my case. Contrary to what officials of the Guatemalan and U.S. governments had said about me, the Commission concluded that, "Sister Ortiz was placed under surveillance and threatened, then kidnapped and tortured. Agents of the Guatemalan government were responsible for these crimes against her" (Inter-American Commission on Human Rights, 1996). While I was pleased with the results, of course, neither the lawsuit nor the Commission's findings provided anything approximating the justice we have been taught to expect when a crime has been committed. The U.S. government has never commented on the O.A.S. findings.

The End of Torture

My case is not unique. It is only one verse of a long litany that grows every day.

There is Medhi, the well-educated soft-spoken Kurd who said it was true that the Turkish government imprisoned him for 16 years but "they only tortured me for three and a half years." And Fekadu, of Ethiopia, returned home after three weeks of torture while authorities searched his room. As he was taken away, his younger daughter saw his scars and began to scream. It was that sound he carried with him during the next nine years of imprisonment and torture. The late Ani Pachen,[2] a Tibetan Buddhist nun, was held by the Chinese for twenty-one years. A kind of grim Boswell, she spoke to me about the others, what was done to those who did not survive because there is no one else to tell their story. Aisha, who was tortured for the first time when she was 12 years old. Richard, a journalist from Colombia, suffered damage to his liver and the loss of a testicle. Kifa, a Somali woman who was raped and then forced to watch her 5-year old daughter raped as well. Munawar, from Sindh Pakistan, so gentle, so self-effacing, so concerned not to overstate what was done to him—and so, the boiling liquid that was dripped on his skin did not really burn. It "only hurt very much." Monica, raped and tortured in Peru, in prison for 13 months, barely survived a prison massacre. When she was released, she found that there was no record of what happened. For her the world had to be told, there must be accountability, and so it is she who bears witness to this massacre. Carmen, a Guatemalan doctor, the first words her torturer said to her were, "Doctor, we are not going to kill you. But you are going to scream for us to kill you." Orlando, from the Philippines, while being tortured he was told by his torturers that they had been trained at a military base in the Southern United States. And I mustn't forget to introduce you to a 2-year-old girl who was tortured, burned, beaten and left to die, in a Turkish prison. And there are more—so many more.

In an effort to describe what government-sanctioned torture and international law mean to torture survivors, I have tried to give you a glimpse of our world. We opened the curtain of our souls to you—letting you see our pain, our fears and our hopes. We spoke truth and told how mechanisms of international law do not protect us. This is said more out of regret than bitterness. The marks of torture will forever remain with us. But still we dare to say 'yes' to life. We dare to defy our torturers and the whole apparatus that supports their barbaric work. We dare to believe that torture will someday be abolished, despite this horror practiced by governments around the world, including our own.

Notes

1. Names have been changed to protect the identity of the individuals.
2. During her time in prison, she, like most political prisoners, lost track of time. I have heard Ani's interpreter say that she was held for 26 years. On another occasion he stated that she was held for 23 years. One thing is certain, Ani was imprisoned for more than 20 years.

References

Amnesty International (1999). *Amnesty International report 1999*. London, UK: Amnesty International Publications.

Babington, C. (1999). Clinton: Support for Guatemala was wrong. *The Washington Post*, March 11, 1999.

Bush, George W. (2003). Statement, June 26, 2003. Washington, DC: White House, Office of the Press Secretary.

Chacón, R. (1999). Clinton cites Guatemala errors, admits US backed repressive regimes. *The Boston Globe, March 11, 1999*, p. A-1.

Clinton, B. (1999). *Letter from President Bill Clinton to torture survivors*. June 23, 1999.

Delay, C. A. (1995). U.S. judge rules ex-Guatemalan official condoned acts of torture. *The Washington Post, April 13, 1995*, p. A-17.

Dunér, B. (1998). *An end to torture: Strategies for its eradication*. New York: Zed Books.

Editorial (1996). School of the dictators. *New York Times*. September 28, 1996.

Espo, D. and Sidoti, L. (2005) Cheney seeks CIA exemption to torture ban. The Associated Press: *The Washington Post*. November 5, 2005.

Gonzales, A.R. (2004). Memorandum for the president, "Decision re: application of the Geneva Convention on prisoners of war to the conflict with al Qaeda and the Taliban," January 25, 2002 in Mark Danner, *Torture and Truth*. New York Review of Books, 2004.

Human Rights Office of the Archdiocese of Guatemala (1999). *Guatemala never again! Recovery Historical Memory Project*. New York: Orbis Press.

Inter-American Commission on Human Rights (1996). *Annual Report of the Inter-*

American Commission on Human Rights, Doc. 7. Washington, DC: Organization of American States.

Kirk, M. (2005). The Torture Question. *PBS: Frontline Documentary.* October 18, 2005

Levi, P. (1988). *The Drowned and the Saved.* New York: Vintage International.

Lux de Cotí, O., Tojo, A. B., & Tomuschat, C. (1999). *Guatemala Memory of Silence: Report of the commission for historical clarification conclusions and recommendations.* Guatemala: The Commission for Historical Clarification (CEH).

Marshall, T. (1999). U.S. concedes torture exists in justice system but contends punishment helps deter it. *Washington Times,* October 16, 1999, p. A-3.

Ortiz, D., (2001). The Survivor's Perspective: Voices from the Center. In Gerrity, E., Terence M. Keane, and Farris Tuma (2001) *Mental Health Consequences of Torture and Related Violence and Trauma.* New York, NY: Plenum Press.

Priest, D. (2005). C.I.A. holds terror suspects in secret prisons: debate is growing within agency about legality and morality of overseas systems set up after 9/11. *The Washington Post, November 2, 2005, p. A01.*

Torture Abolition and Survivors Support Committee (1999). *Statement by the survivors of torture to the president of the United States and to members of the National Security Council.* June 25, 1999.

Torture Abolition and Survivors Support Committee (TASSC, undated). *No one shall be subjected to torture.* Washington, DC: TASSC.

United Nations (1984). *United Nations Convention against torture and other cruel, inhuman or degrading treatment or punishment.* Geneva, Switzerland: United Nations.

United Nations (1975). *United Nations declaration on the protection of all persons from being subjected to torture and other cruel, inhuman or degrading treatment or punishment.* Geneva, Switzerland: United Nations.

United Nations (1951). *United Nations Convention relating to the status of refugees.* Geneva, Switzerland: United Nations.

United Nations (1948). *United Nations universal declaration for human rights.* Geneva, Switzerland: United Nations.

The White House (2005). President Bush meets with President Torrijos of Panama. Office of the Press Secretary: http://www.whitehouse.gov/news/ releases/ 2005/11/ 20051107.html. November 7, 2005.

CHAPTER 10

The Fundamental Human Right to Prosecution and Compensation

Jon M. Van Dyke[1]

The right to obtain financial compensation for a human rights abuse and to have the perpetrator of such an abuse prosecuted and punished is itself a fundamental human right that cannot be taken from a victim or waived by a government. Although it is sometimes tempting to enact a general amnesty in order to heal a nation's wounds, promote harmony, and "let bygones be bygones," such efforts rarely achieve their goals because the wounds fester and the victims need a just resolution to their suffering. The only way to bring true healing to a divided society is to face up to the wrongs that were committed, to prosecute those who violated the fundamental human rights of others, and provide compensation to the victims. The two case studies that follow illustrate the need to bring formal closure to human rights abuses.

The Sierra Leone Civil War

Time and time again, the United Nations' experience has shown that peace accords built on impunity are shaky and do not hold. In Angola, for example, six amnesties have been granted as part of the peace process, and each has served as little more than an invitation to further bloodshed and atrocities" (Takirambudde, 1999)

The West African country of Sierra Leone experienced a devastating civil war in the 1990s led by rebels of the Revolutionary United Front (RUF) and the Armed

Forces Revolutionary Council (AFRC). Although the fighting began as a struggle among competing factions, the rebels focused their anger against the country's first President elected in a multi-party election, Ahmad Tejan Kabbah. President Kabbah took office in March 1996, was forced from office 14 months later on May 25, 1997 by the AFRC/RUF rebel alliance, and then was reinstated in early 1998 as President by the Nigerian-led peacekeeping force formally called the Economic Community of West African States Monitoring Group (ECOMOG).

The AFRC/RUF-led campaigns of terror, called "Operation No Living Thing" and "Operation Pay Yourself," were designed to kill, destroy, and loot anything in their paths (Human Rights Watch, 1998). Civilians were subjected to systematic and gross violations of human rights such as amputations by machete of one or both hands, arms, feet, legs, ears, or buttocks and one or more fingers; lacerations to the head, neck, arms, feet, and torso; gouging out of one or both eyes; gunshot wounds to the head, torso, and limbs; burns from explosives and other devices; injections with acid; rape and sexual slavery of girls and women including sexual mutilation where breasts and genitalia were cut off. Often child soldiers too weak to hack off the entire foot have carried out the mutilations. The victims would have to finish the amputation, or would be forced to participate in their own mutilation by selecting which body part they wanted amputated. Political messages were slashed into backs and chests, and amputees were told to take their limbs to President Kabbah.

Children were often the targets of brutal acts of violence—murdered, beaten, mutilated, tortured, raped, sexually enslaved, or forced to become soldiers for the AFRC/RUF. Parents were killed in front of their children. Women and girls were targets of systematic brutal gang rapes at gunpoint or knifepoint, or of rape by foreign objects such as sticks or flaming logs. Rapes occurred in front of family members, or, in some cases, rebels forced a family member to rape a sister, mother, or daughter. Witnesses reported seeing the mutilated bodies of pregnant women whose fetuses were cut out of their wombs or shot to death in the abdomen.

The AFRC/RUF forced many civilians into slavery, to serve the rebel forces' cause. Women and girls were required to become "wives" or sexual slaves and forced to cook for the soldiers. Young men and boys were forcefully recruited as soldiers, and required to commit armed attacks against Sierra Leone civilians, Civilian Defense Forces, and the ECOMOG.

Members of the Civilian Defense Forces (CDF) supporting President Kabbah also committed atrocities. The soldiers in the most powerful of these groups, the Kamajors, carried out murders, mutilations, and obstructions of humanitarian aid, and they demanded compensation at roadblocks for "liberating Sierra Leone from the AFRC/RUF forces." Although the CDF apparently tried to limit their killings to soldiers and in some cases direct supporters of the AFRC/RUF, many witnesses have told horrific stories of the grotesque nature of their killings. In some instances victims were disemboweled, followed by the consumption of vital organs such as the liver or heart, apparently to transfer the strength of the enemy to those involved in the consumption.

In January 1999, the RUF captured Freetown, the capital of Sierra Leone, from government troops and the ECOMOG, after three weeks characterized by the most atrocious and concentrated human rights violations committed against civilians in the eight-year civil war. Then, on May 24, 1999, a cease-fire agreement was reached and in July 1999, a peace agreement was signed that contained a plan to develop a government consisting of members of all the fighting factions and a general amnesty to protect all groups from prosecution for war crimes and crimes against humanity (Onishi, 1999). The founder of the rebel movement, Foday Sankoh, instead of being prosecuted for unspeakable atrocities, was put in charge of a commission to oversee the country's rich mineral resources, and his commanders occupied four top cabinet positions.

Was it realistic to expect this new government to function in a fair and orderly fashion without any accounting for the extraordinarily gross crimes that occurred? This deal appears to have been put into place because Sierra Leone is only marginally significant to the international community, because the new civilian government in Nigeria was eager to withdraw its troops, because the Kabbah government was outgunned and totally dependent on foreign aid, and because the people of Sierra Leone were so sick of the fighting that they were willing to pay almost any price to obtain peace and try to get on with their lives (Onishi, 1999). But the amnesty only served as an invitation for further atrocities and the cruelty did not stop.[2]

Finally, in August 2000, the U.N. Security Council voted to establish a war crimes tribunal with jurisdiction over murder, torture, terrorism, rape, sexual slavery, mutilation, hostage-taking, pillage, and attacks on civilians. This court, which is managed jointly by the United Nations and the Sierra Leone government, began the process of accounting and healing for this beleaguered country in June 2004, with the trials of Sam Hinga Norman, Moinina Fofana, and Allieu Kondewa, who had been with the governments Civil Defense Forces, followed in July 2004 with trials of Issa Hassan Sesay, Morris Kallon, and Augustine Gbao, who were affiliated with the Revolutionary United Front (RUF) (Human Rights Watch, 2004).

The Special Court for War Crimes in Sierra Leone differs from the Yugoslav and Rwanda Tribunals in that it has both international and local judges.[3] Eleven persons associated with all three of the country's former warring factions have been indicted by the Special Court, and trials are being conducted as this book is going to press in 2006. They have been charged with war crimes and crimes against humanity, based on murder, rape, extermination, acts of terror, enslavement, looting and burning, sexual slavery, conscription of children into an armed force, and attacks on UN peacekeepers and humanitarian workers. The Appeals Chamber of this court issued a significant decision on May 31, 2004 ruling that recruitment of child soldiers is a crime and a violation of international law.[4]

The Marcos Human Rights Abuses

Ferdinand E. Marcos served as President of the Republic of the Philippines from 1965 to 1972, when he declared martial law and proceeded thereafter to rule by decree, effectively suppressing all dissent. According to records kept by human rights groups in the Philippines during that period, more than 90,000 persons were arrested pursuant to presidential decree, more than 3,000 were summarily executed, more than 850 "disappeared," and more than 4,800 were tortured.[5]

Ferdinand Marcos declared martial law on September 21, 1972[6] and proceeded to arrest (without judicial warrants) leading opposition figures as well as a wide variety of other dissidents. U.S. District Judge Manuel Real later explained that "Marcos gradually increased his own power to such an extent that there were no limits to his orders of the human rights violations suffered by plaintiffs in this action."[7] Marcos ruled the country during that period by autocratic decree, issuing almost daily lists of individuals who were to be rounded up. Many of those detained were subject to "tactical interrogation," the code phrase used to refer to the various torture techniques, which Judge Real listed as follows:

1. Beatings while blindfolded by punching, kicking and hitting with the butts of rifles;
2. The "telephone" where a detainee's ears were clapped simultaneously, producing a ringing sound in the head;
3. Insertion of bullets between the fingers of a detainee and squeezing the hand;
4. The "wet submarine," where a detainee's head was submerged in a toilet bowl full of excrement;
5. The "water cure," where a cloth was placed over the detainee's mouth and nose, and water poured over it producing a drowning sensation;
6. The "dry submarine," where a plastic bag was placed over the detainee's head producing suffocation;
7. Use of a detainee's hands for putting out lighted cigarettes;
8. Use of flat-irons on the soles of a detainee's feet;
9. Forcing a detainee while wet and naked to sit before an air conditioner often while sitting on a block of ice;
10. Injection of a clear substance into the body a detainee believed to be truth serum;
11. Stripping, sexually molesting and raping female detainees; one male plaintiff testified he was threatened with rape;
12. Electric shock where one electrode is attached to the genitals of males or the breast of females and another electrode to some other part of the body, usually a finger, and electrical energy produced from a military field telephone is sent through the body;

13. Russian roulette; and
14. Solitary confinement while hand-cuffed or tied to a bed.[8]

Ferdinand Marcos fled the Philippines in March 1986, after a series of "People Power" demonstrations filled the streets of Manila to protest a rigged election, and he went into exile in Honolulu, Hawai`i. Almost immediately thereafter, complaints were filed against him in U.S. courts under the U.S. Alien Tort Claims Act,[9] by victims of human rights abuses. Some have wondered whether it was appropriate for this litigation to be brought in a U.S. court, rather than a court in the Philippines, where the atrocities occurred and where most of the victims resided. In fact, Hawai`i was the only venue where this civil action could have been brought, because Hawai`i was where Marcos lived after 1986. Hawai`i was thus the only place where personal jurisdiction could be obtained over Marcos, and thus the only location where a civil trial would satisfy international requirements of due process and fairness.

This litigation was vigorously contested by Marcos's attorneys, and has involved almost a dozen appeals to the U.S. Court of Appeals for the Ninth Circuit based in San Francisco. It took a decade to reach a final judgment, and efforts are continuing (as of this publication) to collect the judgment for the human rights victims.

The lawsuits against Marcos were initially dismissed in 1986 by the U.S. District Court based on the act of state doctrine,[10] but this ruling was overturned in 1989 by the U.S. Court of Appeals for the Ninth Circuit, confirming that U.S courts have a duty under international law to provide a forum for the claims of human rights victims.[11] In a related case involving torture in Argentina, this appellate court has written that "[t]he crack of the whip, the clamp of the thumb screw, the crush of the iron maiden, and in these more efficient modern times, the shock of the electric cattle prod are forms of torture that the international order will not tolerate. To subject a person to such horrors is to commit one of the most egregious violations of the personal security and dignity of a human being."[12] Such activities now also clearly violate fundamental principles of international law. When the Marcos class action finally went to trial, the federal jury concluded that Ferdinand E. Marcos was personally responsible for the human rights abuses and awarded the class of 9,531 plaintiffs $1.2 billion in exemplary damages and $766 million in compensatory damages.[13]

After the judgment against the Marcos Estate became final, the human rights victims sought to obtain moneys deposited by the Marcoses in Swiss Banks by bringing actions against the branches of these banks in the United States. These efforts were unsuccessful, because the U.S. Court of Appeals for the Ninth Circuit ruled that the applicable California statute did not permit collection from a branch other than where the deposit was made[14] and that actions of the Swiss courts freezing these accounts pending final resolution of claims by the Philippine government were official acts that implicated the act of state doctrine.[15] The Ninth Circuit also ruled that the district court's injunction blocking any transfer of Marcos funds could not be judicially enforced against the Philippine Government because of its sovereign immunity.[16]

While these efforts were underway, the Swiss Federal Supreme Court ruled that deposits in Marcos accounts of about $570 million in Swiss Banks should be transferred to the Philippines.[17] But this transfer was conditional, and the Swiss Court stated explicitly in its ruling that the Philippine Government had a responsibility to ensure that the human rights victims receive adequate compensation for their injuries, that the Philippine government had a duty to keep the Swiss Government informed about the steps it took to provide compensation to the human rights victims, and that the Swiss Government should monitor the situation to ensure that such compensation was forthcoming.[18] This ruling is particularly significant, because it was made in spite of the acknowledgment by the Swiss Court that the moneys in question had "illegal origins."[19] The Court explained that both the Philippines and Switzerland had duties under international law to "safeguard[] human rights" and that this duty is "incumbent upon . . . the courts as executors of the international law regime."[20] The Court recognized that all parties to the International Covenant of Civil and Political Rights[21] and the Torture Convention[22] have a duty to ensure that victims of human rights abuse have a right to establish their right to compensation through competent judicial tribunals.[23]

The Swiss Court also recognized that the Philippine judiciary has "shortcomings" and that it is "reputed to be ponderous and susceptible to corruption and political influence."[24] For this reason, the Swiss Court included as a condition of transferring the money to the Philippines the requirement that the Philippine government "regularly update" the Swiss authorities on the procedures established "to compensate the victims of human rights violations under the Marcos regime."[25] These conditions remain unfilled, and, as of this writing, the transferred funds are still being disputed between the victims and the Philippine Government.

In order to enable the moneys to be distributed, the human rights victims, the Marcos family, and the Philippine Government entered into a settlement of this litigation in 1999 for $150 million, to be paid from the $570 million transferred from Switzerland to the Philippines.[26] The victims did not view the $150 million as adequate, of course, but nonetheless accepted this amount in order to bring some payments to those who had suffered, in light of the passage of time, the age of the older victims, and the protracted litigation that lay ahead if no settlement were reached. The Sandiganbayan (Anti-Graft) Court in the Philippines blocked this settlement, however, ruling in an opinion written by Presiding Justice Francis Garchitorena that it had not been established that the $570 million legitimately belonged to the Marcoses (rather than being "ill-gotten wealth") and that the $150 million was too low a settlement, in light of the jury's judgment of $1.996 billion.[27]

Was the $150 million settlement adequate in light of other settlements and in light of the difficulty of collecting human rights judgments generally? No amount of money would be adequate to compensate victims for the suffering they received, but a settlement of $150 million would have given each victim about $15,000, which is in the range of other human rights settlements. The Japanese-Americans who were wrongfully interred during World War II for several years received, for instance, an apology from the U.S. Congress and $20,000 (Civil Liberties Act of 1988, 50 U.S.C. sec. 1989 [2000]).

More recently, a Merrill Lynch securities account valued at about $35,000,000 has been identified, and the human rights victims are seeking access to those funds.[28]   The money has been deposited with the U.S. District Court for the District of Hawai'i, which has initiated an interpleader action, through which all claimants can present the basis for their claims. But the Republic of the Philippines has been vigorously contesting this effort, arguing both that they have sovereign immunity from the jurisdiction of the U.S. court, and that they are an indispensable party essential to the interpleader action.

U.S. Distict Court Judge Manuel Real granted the Philippine Government's motion to be dismissed from the interpleader, and ruled in 2004 that the Human Rights Victims should receive the entire amount in this Merrill Lynch account. As this chapter is being prepared for publication, the Republic of the Philippines is pursuing an appeal to the U.S. Court of Appeals for the Ninth Circuit, arguing against this ruling.

The Right to Bring a Claim Is a Fundamental Human Right Under International Law

The right to bring a claim for a violation of internationally recognized human rights is well established under international law. Article 8 of the Universal Declaration of Human Rights (U.N.G.A., 1948, Article 8) says that "Everyone has the right to *an effective remedy* by the competent national tribunals for acts violating the fundamental rights granted him by the constitution or by law" (emphasis added). Similarly, Article 2(3)(a) of the International Covenant on Civil and Political Rights (U.N.G.A., 1966), which has been ratified by more than 140 countries, says that "Each State Party to the present Covenant undertakes: (a) To ensure that any person whose rights or freedoms as herein recognized are violated shall have *an effective remedy*, notwithstanding that the violation has been committed by persons acting in an official capacity . . . " (emphasis added).

Regional human rights treaties also emphasize the right to redress for human rights violations. Article 6(1) of the European Convention on Human Rights (Council of Europe, 1950) says that "In the determination of his civil rights . . . everyone is entitled to a fair and public hearing within a reasonable time by an independent and impartial tribunal established by law." The European Court of Human Rights ruled in the *Golder Case* (1974) that the right to bring a civil claim to an independent judge "ranks as one of the universally 'recognized' fundamental principles of law." In *Mentes v. Turkey* (1998, paragraph 89), the European Court of Human Rights ruled that Turkey violated the rights of citizens who were prevented from bringing a claim for the deliberate destruction of their houses and possession, noting that "the notion of an 'effective remedy' entails, in addition to the payment of compensation where appropriate, a thorough and effective investigation capable of leading to the identification and punishment of those responsible and including effective access for the complainant to the investigative procedure."

Similarly, Article 25(1) of the American Convention on Human Rights (Organization of American States, 1978/1992) says that:

> Everyone has the right to simple and prompt recourse, or any other effective recourse, to a competent court or tribunal for protection against acts that violate his fundamental rights recognized by the constitution or laws of the state concerned or by this Convention, even though such violation may have been committed by persons acting in the course of their official duties.

Decisions in the Inter-American system confirm that the right to an effective remedy is a continuing one that cannot be waived. The seminal case of the Inter-American Court of Human Rights is the *Velasquez Rodriguez Case* (1989, paragraph 174d) holds that the American Convention on Human Rights imposes on each state party a "legal duty to . . . ensure the victim adequate compensation." The court explained that each country has the duty to protect the human rights listed in the Convention and articulated this responsibility as follows:

> This obligation implies the duty of the States Parties to organize the governmental apparatus and, in general, all the structures through which public power is exercised, so that they are capable of juridically ensuring the free and full enjoyment of human rights. As a consequence of this obligation, the States must *prevent, investigate and punish* any violation of the rights recognized by the Convention" (*Velasquez Rodriguez Case*, 1988, paragraph 166, emphasis added).

Other decisions that confirm this result include *Report No. 36/96, Case No. 10.843*[29] (Inter-American Human Rights Commission, 1996, paragraphs 68, 105, & 112); *Rodriguez v. Uruguay*[30] (1994); *Chanfeau Orayce and Others v. Chile*[31] (1997).

The Human Rights Committee in Geneva, established by the International Covenant on Civil and Political Rights, has also gone on record opposing amnesties:

> The Committee has noted that some States have granted amnesty in respect of acts of torture. *Amnesties are generally incompatible with the duty of States to investigate such acts;* to guarantee freedom from such acts within their jurisdiction; and to ensure that they do not occur in the future (United Nations, 1994, p. 30, emphasis added).

U.S. decisions also support the conclusion that claims cannot be waived or dismissed because of some other foreign policy goals. The case of *Dames & Moore v. Regan* (1981) involved the argument of a U.S. company that its claim for damages against Iran after the 1979 Iranian revolution had been unlawfully extinguished by the 1981 Algiers Accords which freed the U.S. hostages. In response to the argument made by Dames and Moore that its claim had been "taken" in violation of the Fifth Amendment to the U.S. Constitution, Justice Rehnquist's opinion for the Court noted that claimants were not denied the right to pursue their claim, but rather were required to use an alternative forum, the Iran-U.S. Claims Tribunal in The Hague, Netherlands. The Court affirmed the requirement that Dames and Moore utilize this alternative forum, but held in abeyance the taking claim, and indicated a willingness to take another look at it should the alternative tribunal not prove effective.[32]

Another relevant case is *Ware v. Hylton* (1796), where Justice Chase rejected the idea that a government can waive private claims without compensation to the claimants:

> That Congress had the power to sacrifice the rights and interests of private citizens to secure the safety or prosperity of the public, I have no doubt; but *the immutable principles of justice*; the public faith of the States, that confiscated and received British debts, pledged to the debtors; and the rights of the debtors violated by the treaty; all combine to prove, that ample compensation ought to be made to all the debtors who have been injured by the treaty for the benefit of the public. *This principle is recognized by the Constitution*, which declares, "that private property shall not be taken for public use without just compensation." *See* Vattel. Lib. 1. c. 20. s. 244 (p. 245, emphasis added).

Justice Chase thus cited both "the immutable principles of justice" and the Fifth Amendment of the U.S. Constitution to support the conclusion that the U.S. government cannot waive claims, even as part of a peace settlement, without compensating those whose claims have been violated. Justice Iredell wrote in the same case that "these rights [are] fully acquired by private persons during the war, more especially if derived from the laws of war...[and] against the enemy, and in that case the individual might be entitled to compensation" (*Ware v. Hylton,* 1796, p. 279). He added that if Congress had given up the rights of private persons in a peace treaty "as the price of peace," the private individuals whose "rights were sacrificed" might well "have been entitled to compensation from the public" for their loss (*Ware v. Hylton,* 1796). In that case, the Supreme Court ruled decisively that British subjects were entitled to use the judicial system to collect the debts owed to them.

State courts in the United States have also recognized the validity of such claims. In *Christian County Court v. Rankin* (1866), the court granted private compensation in an action against Confederate soldiers for burning the courthouse in violation of the "laws of nations," saying that "[f]or every wrong the common law provides an adequate remedy . . . on international and common law principles" (pp. 505-506).

The right to pursue claims for compensation exists for wartime atrocities just as it exists for abuses that occur in peacetime (*Kadic v. Karadzic*, 1995, 1996; *Linder v. Portocarrero*, 1992). Human rights are not suspended during wartime; indeed it would be repellent to hold that responsibility is sacrificed when the individual is most imperiled.[33] Article III of the 1907 Hague Regulations (Hague Convention IV, 1907/1968, p. 631) recognizes the duty to compensate for injuries caused during war in the following language: "A belligerent party which violates the provisions of the said Regulations shall, if the case demands, be liable to pay compensation. It shall be responsible for all acts committed by persons forming part of its armed forces." The Treaty of Versailles (1919/1968, p. 43) implemented this requirement by establishing mixed arbitration tribunals for private claimants to present their damages against Germany, even against the wishes of their own governments. These principles were codified once again in the Geneva Conventions of 1949 (United Nations General Assembly, 1949a, 1949b, 1949c, 1949d) which forbid countries from "absolving themselves of liability" for grave breaches (United Nations, 1949a, art. 51).

It is also settled law that a government can channel such claims, like other claims, toward an alternative forum for resolution (*Dames & Moore v. Regan*, 1981), or even settle the claims on behalf of the claimants by a lump-sum settlement that might not be fully satisfactory for each claimant, because a settlement always involves accepting an immediate amount in exchange for foregoing the possibility of a larger amount at a later time (*Shanghai Power*, 1983, 1985). In cases where the government does channel or settle claims, however, the government's action must be fair to the claimants, and if the settlement or alternative forum is not fair, the claimants will have a claim for a taking of their property (*Ware v. Hylton*, 1796; *Dames & . Moore v, Regan* 1981). Justice Powell said in his concurring opinion in *Dames & Moore* (1981) that "the Government must pay just compensation when it furthers the Nation's foreign policy goals by using as 'bargaining chips' claims lawfully held by a relatively few persons and subject to the jurisdiction of the courts" (p. 691).[34]

It is clear, therefore, that claims based on violations of law are a form of property that cannot be cavalierly waived by a nation to serve some other foreign policy goal. Claims based on torture, murder, physical abuse, racial persecution, and other violations of basic norms of human decency are particularly important, and both international and U.S. law explicitly protects those claims against government neglect, duplicity, or abuse. Treaties and amnesty agreements purporting to waive claims or exonerate human rights abusers thus have no more validity than the efforts by the Chilean government to immunize its military leaders from claims brought by the Chilean citizens who were tortured and murdered (*Regina v. Bartle*, 1999). Although claims can be postponed or transferred to a different venue for resolution, they cannot be extinguished without violating fundamental principles of international and U.S. constitutional law, as well as basic precepts of fairness.

The Yearning for Justice and a True "Reconciliation" Through Investigation, Prosecution, and Compensation

The amnesty offered to those who perpetuated human rights atrocities in Sierra Leone was not an isolated situation in 1999, but it is increasingly becoming atypical, because the drive to investigate, prosecute, and provide compensation has a momentum like a rising tide. Each fact situation, and each political context, is different, so generalizations are difficult. But in most parts of the world we now see a commitment to address human rights abuses, to punish the perpetrators of such actions, and to bring justice, compensation, and a sense of closure to the victims. In those places where amnesties have been offered—like Chile and Argentina[35]—the yearning for an accounting remains and will not go away. In places where the governing regime wants to put the past behind it and focus on building a better future—like Cambodia—the people and the international community refuse to let the past be forgotten and insist on orderly investigations and prosecutions.

The list of current efforts to achieve justice is long, and is worldwide in geographic scope. The goal in each case is to achieve a "reconciliation" to allow the country to go forward together, without always returning to the past for a reexamination resulting from a sense of a people wronged. "Reconciliation" is a powerful word. It is not just a feel-good concept, which can be achieved by a few words of sorrow followed by some handshakes or hugs. It requires making right the wrong that occurred. It requires a full and fair acknowledgment of the wrong, followed by a real settlement, usually requiring the transfer of money and/or property, and the punishment and/or disgrace of those who committed the wrongs.[36]

The strategies utilized to bring a sense of closure and reconciliation can be categorized into the following four approaches: (1) an apology for the wrong, which can be general or specific; (2) an investigation and accounting; (3) compensation for the victims, either through a general class approach, or through individual determinations, or both; and (4) prosecution of the wrongdoers. These approaches are described below, with examples from recent history.

Apology

A formal apology is a crucial element of any reconciliation process. Recent examples include President Clinton's apology for the U.S. support of the military in Guatemala. Secretary of State Madeleine Albright apologized for U.S. support for the 1953 coup that restored Shah Mohammed Riza Pahlevi to power in Iran and its backing of Iraq during the war with Iran in the 1980s (Agence France Presse, 2000). Pope John Paul II issued a sweeping apology on March 12, 2000 for the errors of the Roman Catholic Church during the previous 2,000 years, acknowledging intolerance and injustice toward Jews, women, indigenous peoples, immigrants, and the poor (Stanley, 2000). In 1993, the United States apologized for the participation by its military and diplomats in the illegal overthrow of the Kingdom of Hawai`i in 1893 (U.S. Congress, 1993). The United States apologized for the internment of Japanese-Americans during World War II (U.S. Congress, 1988).

Investigation and Accounting

Documentation of the wrongdoing serves the important purpose of recognizing the suffering and acknowledging that wrongdoing occurred. The two most significant accountings in recent years are those that took place in Chile and South Africa.

Chile's situation was unique in that General Augusto Pinochet allowed elections to take place in the late 1980s, but retained firm control over the military and kept a watchful eye on the new government. The new President, Patricio Aylwin, was effectively blocked from prosecuting Pinochet and his military associates, but he wanted nonetheless to acknowledge and honor the victims, and so appointed a Commission of Truth and Reconciliation which prepared a comprehensive report documenting 2,000 human rights abuses (Van Dyke & Berkley, 1999). Finally, in 2004, after General Pinochet's power had waned, President Ricardo Lagos released a more complete report issued by a commission that heard testimony from 35,000 individuals describing torture methods used at 1,131 detention centers established throughout the country, and announced a broad program of compensation. The commission recognized the claims of 27,255 victims and recommended lifetime payments of $190/month (double the pensions of many former victims) as well as educational, health, and housing benefits to the former victims. This program will cost the government $70 million a year (Rohter, 2004 and Gallardo, 2004).

In South Africa, a Truth and Reconciliation Commission met for two and a half years to document as many of the human rights abuses as possible and issued a report blaming both sides for abuses. Persons who came forward with truthful accounts of their participation in violent acts linked to a political objective were pardoned as part of the national healing effort, but others have been prosecuted for their role in these atrocities. A total of 7,112 individuals had applied for political amnesty, but only 849 were granted the amnesty status, with 5,392 applications rejected and others withdrawn. Of those receiving amnesty, a majority were members of the African National Congress, who had been seeking to overthrow the apartheid government, and others were members of the apartheid security forces or the Zulu-based Inkatha Freedom Party.   One pardoned individual—Adriaan Vlok, who had been Minister of Law and Order from 1986 to 1994 and confessed to ordering a bomb attack in 1987—was a member of the governing apartheid National Party.

In February 1999, an independent United-Nations-sponsored Historical Clarification Commission concluded an 18-month investigation and reported that the Guatemalan military—with U.S. money and training—committed "acts of genocide" against the indigenous Mayan community in Guatemala during the country's long civil war and were responsible for 42,000 human rights violations, including 29,000 deaths or disappearances (Navarro, 1999). The next month, President Clinton apologized for the U.S. participation saying that "support for military forces and intelligence units which engaged in violence and widespread repression was wrong, and the United States must not repeat that mistake" (Broder, 1999, p. A1).   The countries that have set up some form of a truth and reconciliation commission during the past two decades include Argentina, Bolivia, Chad, Chile, East Timor, Ecuador, El Salvador, Germany, Ghana, Haiti, Malawi, Nepal, Nigeria, Panama, Peru, Philippines, Serbia and Montenegro, Sierra Leone, South Africa, South Korea, Sri Lanka, Uganda, Uruguay, and Zimbabwe.

Compensation for the Victims

International law has always been clear that reparations are essential whenever damages result from violations of international law. This principle is securely rooted in the decision of the Permanent Court of International Justice in the *Factory at Chorzow* (1928) Case, and it was reaffirmed in 1999 by the International Tribunal for the Law of the Sea in the *M/V Saiga Case* (1999). Reparations are just as important and just as mandatory in cases of human rights abuses as in any other cases. The requirement of appropriate compensation is being recognized increasingly in a wide variety of contexts.

- o   In 1992, after more than 2,000 cases of murders and disappearances were documented by a Chilean commission, the Chilean Legislature enacted a law providing a wide range of economic benefits for the families of those who were murdered or who disappeared (Chilean National Congress, 1992), and additional compensation was provided later to the 27,255 individuals who had been tortured.
- o   The Japanese- Americans interred in World War II received $20,000 each (United States Congress, 1988), and those persons of Japanese ancestry brought to camps in the United States from Latin American have received $5,000 each (Shimbun, 1999).

o   Canada has provided a reparation package for the First Nation children who were taken from their families and transferred to boarding schools where they were denied access to their culture and frequently physically mistreated.

o   New Zealand established a process to address the wrongs committed by the British against the Maori people in the late 1800s, and has returned lands and transferred factories, fishing vessels, and fishing rights to the Maori groups to compensate them for their losses.

o   In Puerto Rico, Governor Pedro J. Rossello publicly apologized and offered restitution of up to $6,000 each to thousands of "independentistas" and others who were spied on by a police intelligence unit starting in the late 1940s (Navarro, 2000).

o   In 1994, Florida Governor Lawton Chiles signed into law a bill providing for the payment of $2.1 million in reparations to the descendants of the black victims of the Rosewood massacre, in which white lynch mobs killed six blacks and drove others from their homes to destroy a prosperous black community (Robinson, 2000).

o   The German government has funded various compensation programs to pay victims of the World War II Holocaust, and to make payments directly to the State of Israel as well (Parker & Chew, 1994). More recently, lawsuits were filed in U.S. courts by the victims of slave- and forced-labor during World War II against the German banks and companies that profited from such abuses, (*Burger-Fischer v. Degussa,* 1999*; Iwanowa v. Ford Motor Company,* 1999*)* and on June 17, 2000, an agreement was reached to provide $5 billion to the 250,000 members of this victimized class (Chicago Tribune, 1999; *In re Austrian and German Holocaust Litigation,* 250 F.3d 156 (2d Cir. 2001).

o   Similarly, Austria settled a claim brought by thousands of individuals (mostly Jews) whose property was systematically looted during the Nazi era, agreeing to pay more than $100 million to claimants, with payments beginning in 1006.

Prosecution of the Wrongdoers

The Trials at Nuremburg and in the Far East after World War II still stand as models for systematic and conscientious prosecutions of those who have violated the laws of war and fundamental human rights principles. But for almost half a century after those trials, no other international trials took place. Then in the early 1990s, the United Nations Security Council established tribunals to prosecute those who violated fundamental norms during the fighting in the former Yugoslavia and Rwanda (Henkin, Neuman, Orentlicher, & Leebron, 1999; U.N. Security Council, 1993, 1994).[37]

These tribunals were slow in establishing their procedures, but now are proceeding steadily through their caseload. By early 2006 the Rwanda Tribunal, based in Arusha, Tanzania, had completed 26 cases and was conducting 28 trials, with 15 additional detainees in custody awaiting trial.

Among the prominent convictions was that of Jean Kambanda, who had been Prime Minister of Rwanda for the three months in 1994 when 800,000-1,000,000 people were killed. He had made speeches encouraging killing of Tutsi, signed directives legalizing the militia, and distributed arms to them. He pled guilty to six counts of genocide and crimes against humanity and was sentenced to life imprisonment. The Tribunal has been called upon to interpret the definitions for "genocide" and "rape" and to deal with those who used the media to generate hatred and advocate murder.[38]

As of March 2006, the Yugoslav Tribunal had indicted 161 individuals. Forth-three of the cases had been completed (eight were acquitted, 16 had completed their sentences, and 19 were serving their sentences), 47 of the accused were in custody, 24 were on provisional release, one was awaiting transfer, four had their cases transferred for prosecution in national courts, 36 had their indictments withdrawn or had died, and six were still at large.

Illustrative of the decisions were the convictions of Maj. Gen. Radislav Krstic of genocide for his role in directing the 1995 Serbian attack on Srebrenica, in which 7,000 Bosnian Muslim men were marched off to their deaths and of Anto Furundzija, a 29-year-old Bosnian Croat for aiding and abetting torture and rape while in command (he was standing by in 1993 while a subordinate repeatedly raped at knifepoint a naked Muslim woman during interrogation).[39] Krstic was sentenced to 46 years in prison and Furundzija was sentenced to a ten-year prison term.

The trial of the Serbian leader Slobodan Milosovic for genocide, crimes against humanity, and grave breaches of the Geneva Conventions, which had been underway since February 12, 2002, came to an abrupt end on March 11, 2006 when he was found dead of a heart attack in prison. Among those not yet apprehended are Radovan Karadzic and Ratko Mladic, the civilian and military leaders of the Bosnian Serbs. In March 2005, General Rasim Delic, former head of the Muslim-dominated Bosnian army, and General Radivoj Miletic, of the Serbian forces, both surrendered to the International Tribunal for the Former Yugoslavia.[40]

The formal investigations conducted by the Yugoslavia and Rwanda Tribunals came to an end on December 31, 2004. All trials in the Tribunals must be completed by 2008, and all appeals completed by 2010. Cases that cannot be completed by then must be transferred to local courts.

Other efforts to promote accountability are also continuing:

o   General Augusto Pinochet, the dictator of Chile from 1973 to 1989, was held under house arrest in England for 16 months, fighting his extradition to Spain to be prosecuted for the torture and murder of Chileans, but he was finally returned to Chile in February 2000 after British officials concluded that he was medically unfit to stand trial. Although this protracted episode did not lead to an international trial of Pinochet, the British House of Lords reached a significant decision during the period of house arrest, ruling that Pinochet's status as a former head-of-state did not give him an immunity from prosecution and that prosecution for his egregious "universal" crimes would be appropriate in any country. In late 2004, Chile's courts ruled that Pinochet was physically and mentally fit to stand trial, and prosecutions are also underway against military officers who served in the Pinochet government.

o   In November 1999, Judge Baltasar Garzon, the same Spanish magistrate who had been pursing General Pinochet, charged 98 former Argentine officers with genocide, terrorism, and torture in connection with the atrocities perpetrated by the military dictatorship that controlled Argentina from 1976 to 1983, when between 9,000 and 30,000 persons died or disappeared (Associated Press, 1999c). Previously, Judge Garzon ordered the arrest of Adolfo Scilingo, an Argentine officer who testified in the Spanish court that he had thrown dissidents from planes during the Argentine "dirty war" (Associated Press, 1997). Jorge Rafael Videla, the Argentine dictator during this period, was rearrested in June 1998 for his participation in the systematic kidnapping of children, even though he had previously been pardoned (in 1990) after his life sentence (in 1985) for his role in the death squads (Los Angeles Times, 1998). In February 2000, Argentina's newly-inaugurated President, Fernando de la Rua, ordered a purge from the government payroll of the some-1,500 military personnel and civilians connected with the "dirty war" from the 1976-83 period (Krauss, 2000).

o   In November 1999, the Leipzig appeals court upheld a manslaughter conviction against Egon Krenz, the last Communist leader of East Germany, and two other leading Politburo members, Gunther Kleiber and Gunther Schabowski, for their roles in the shootings of persons trying to escape to the West. These convictions will be appealed to the European Court of Human Rights in Strasbourg (Cohen, 1999).

o   South Korea prosecuted and imprisoned two of its recent Presidents, Chun Doo Hwan and Roh Tae Woo, for acts of corruption and for human rights abuses in connection with the suppression of a riot (New York Times, 1998).

A number of efforts are underway to establish and strengthen criminal tribunals with jurisdiction over grave human rights abuses:

o   In late 2004, after six years of deliberation, the Cambodian National Assembly finally ratified an agreement with the United Nations to establish a tribunal utilizing both international and national judges to try the Khmer Rouge leaders. The launching of this tribunal has been slow and erratic, but it is hoped that trials will begin soon for the top Khmer Rouge leaders, who were responsible for the deaths of some 1.7 million Cambodians who were executed or died of starvation or disease during the 1975-79 regime (Associated Press, 1999a; Cambodia News Reports, 2000; Washington Post, 2001).

o   The United Nations also established a tribunal for East Timor, working with the local community there. The United Nations coordinated with local courts to support and staff a Special Panel for Serious Crimes, and this process led to the conviction of 75 persons for their involvement in the events of 1999, with two acquittals and two indictment dismissals (Lyon, 2005). After East Timor's independence in 1999, Indonesian militias had killed about 1,400 people, mainly independence supporters, and tortured and raped an unknown number of others. More than a quarter of a million people, or some 30 per cent of East Timor's population, were forcibly deported or fled across the border to West Timor in Indonesia where around 28,000 remained in early 2005. (Associated Press, 1999b; Mydans, 2000). This Special Panel completed its activity on May 20, 2005, after completing 55 trials, in which 84 individuals had been convicted and three acquited.[41] An ad hoc Indonesian Human Rights Court was established in Jakarta to prosecute some of the military leaders connected with the East Timor massacres, but these efforts have met resistance and have not yet led to the incarceration of any of those involved.

These many situations illustrate the complexity of these issues. No one approach works for every historical event. Just as prosecutors exercise discretion to refrain from prosecuting in certain situations, and to accept plea agreements for reduced charges in many other situations, some historical episodes seem to justify a merciful approach, with reduced penalties or simply a full description of what actually happened. In some situations pardons appear to be justified after part of the sentence has been served to foster reconciliation. But in each situation, a full investigation and disclosure of what occurred seems essential to ensure that the culprits' deeds are known by all and to prevent them from ever exercising power again. And for a true "reconciliation," the transfer of property from those who have benefited to those who have suffered seems essential to bring the matter to a just resolution.

The International Criminal Court

As explained above, the international community has established *ad hoc* tribunals to address the widespread atrocities that have occurred in this decade in the Former Yugoslavia and in Rwanda. They have functioned effectively, after faltering starts, and now are trying indicted criminals in a systematic and orderly fashion.

In order to avoid having to establish a new tribunal every time an international crisis occurs, enlightened diplomats came together in the summer of 1998 to draft a treaty to establish a permanent International Criminal Court (ICC, 1998). The Court came into being on July 1, 2002, and by November 2005, 100 countries were parties to the Court's treaty.

Under this treaty, crimes against humanity, genocide, and war crimes[42] are subject to the jurisdiction of the international tribunal in situations where national courts are not able to prosecute these crimes, as determined by the United Nations Security Council or the Court's Prosecutor. No longer will *ad hoc* tribunals have to be set up each time a horrendous crime against humanity occurs, with all the attendant delays and political confusion that such an event requires.

President Clinton signed the treaty establishing this new Court on December 31, 2000, but President George W. Bush then "unsigned" the treaty several months later, and many in the United States continue to harbor significant reservations regarding the treaty that has emerged (Myers, 2001). The United States is comfortable with the listing of war crimes and their elements, but is concerned that a political agenda (perhaps related to the Middle East peace process) underlies the crime of an occupying power transferring its population into the territory it occupies and is concerned that the crime of aggression might interfere with "the need for the international community to respond to humanitarian and other crises without being harassed and much worse, charged with violations of the Statute" (U.N.G.A., 1999, WWW document).

The situation the United States is most concerned about involves an atrocity committed by a U.S. soldier on a peacekeeping mission in a country that has accepted the jurisdiction of the International Criminal Court during a period in which the United States may have signed but has not yet ratified the Court's Treaty. Could the Court exercise jurisdiction over this U.S. soldier? The United States would have a responsibility to prosecute the soldier under applicable treaties and U.S. statutes, and the country where the atrocity took place could also exercise jurisdiction. But could the country where the incident occurred transfer its jurisdiction to the International Criminal Court? Ambassador David Scheffer has argued vigorously that such jurisdiction cannot be delegated. He has quoted Duke Law Professor Madeline Morris for the proposition that "territorial jurisdiction is not 'a form of negotiable instrument'" and offers in horror her hypothetical that the country where the atrocity took place might transfer jurisdiction to Libya (in exchange for Libya's transferring jurisdiction over a national of the country where the atrocity occurred) (Scheffer, 1999).

Although it is always possible to come up with blood-curdling hypotheticals, it seems disingenuous and is ultimately unconvincing to compare the exercise of jurisdiction by the carefully-constructed and internationally-recognized International Criminal Court with that of an international pariah like Libya. Although the United States has been trying to generate a lot of smoke to explain its reservations about the current draft text of the International Criminal Court, most observers cannot understand why our country is not able to embrace enthusiastically this important international initiative and to work with other enlightened countries to make it work effectively. The advantages of having such an institution in place to ensure effective prosecution of those committing atrocities surely outweighs the highly-technical and mostly-unlikely scenarios developed by Ambassador Scheffer.

On February 10, 2006, the International Criminal Court issued its first arrest warrant for Thomas Lubanga Dyilo, of the Union des Patriotes Congolais, who was accused of committing war crimes in violation of Article 8 of the Court's statute. Lubanga was arrested by the Democratic Republic of the Congo pursuant to the Court's request and was flown in a French military aircraft to the Court in The Hague for further proceedings.

Bringing Closure to the Marcos Human Rights Abuses

The position of the Philippine Government opposing the efforts of the human rights victims to collect their hard-earned judgment is hard to understand or accept, as is the decision of the Sandiganbayan regarding the settlement agreement concerning the money in escrow returned by the Swiss. After the end of the Marcos era in 1986, the Philippine Government established the Presidential Commission on Good Government (PCGG) to pursue assets plundered by the Marcoses,[43] but it has taken no affirmative steps whatsoever to compensate the victims of human rights abuses during the Marcos Regime, even though, as discussed above, international law has recognized the unambiguous duty of the government to do so.[44] In the *Velasquez Rodriguez Case*, for instance, the Inter-American Court of Human Rights explained that the duty to investigate human rights abuses and compensate the victims of these abuses continues despite "changes of government" even if the "the attitude of the new government may be much more respectful of those rights than that of the government in power when the violations occurred."[45] It is, therefore, irrelevant whether the money from Switzerland in the escrow account is "ill-gotten wealth," because the Philippine Government has a continuing duty to compensate the human rights victims, and this money provides as good a source for such compensation as any other.

The Philippine Government has occasionally recognized its obligation to the human rights victims, but for most of the time since 1986, it has ignored its international-law responsibilities to investigate these abuses and compensate those who have suffered. In the years right after Marcos's exile to Hawai`i, the Philippine government (under President Corazon Aquino) had actively supported the class action lawsuit being pursued in Hawai`i by the human rights victims.

In those early years, Philippine Minister of Justice Neptali A. Gonzales prepared a letter to the Deputy Minister of Foreign Affairs, Leticia R. Shahani, explaining that Marcos was not protected by any form of immunity: "Marcos may be held liable for acts done as President during his incumbency, when such acts, like torture, inhuman treatment of detainees, etc. are clearly in violation of existing law ... the government or its officials may not validly claim state immunity for acts committed against a private party in violation of existing law."[46] Even more significantly, the Republic of the Philippines filed an amicus curiae brief in the U.S. Court of Appeals for the Ninth Circuit in 1987, after the class action case had been dismissed by the District Court on act of state grounds, urging the Ninth Circuit to reverse the ruling of the District Court.   The Republic stated that "foreign relations with the United States will not be adversely affected if these human rights claims against Ferdinand Marcos are heard in U.S. courts."[47]

When Fidel Ramos succeeded Corazon Aquino as President, the attitude of the Philippine Government changed, and it provided little or no support to the human rights victims during the Ramos period. Occasional efforts by Philippine legislators to assist the victims were unavailing. Some nominal support came in February 1998, when the then-Chair of the PCGG Magtanggol Gunigundo said that the money being held in escrow from the Swiss Marcos deposits would not be released or distributed until the conditions set by the Swiss court (described above) were met, including the condition that the human rights victims would receive compensation for their ordeals.[48]

During President Estrada's administration, occasional efforts were made and statements issued recognizing the rights of the human rights victims to compensation. In October 1998, for instance, Executive Secretary Ronaldo Zamora explained that the human rights victims were entitled to get "first crack" at the Swiss deposits held in escrow and that the government and the Marcos family should receive their shares only after the human rights victims received "their due."[49] President Estrada himself denounced the Sandiganbayan's July 1999 decision blocking the $150 million settlement as "too technical," adding that because of this decision "[a]ll the human rights victims will be dead before they see the money."[50] The PCGG added that it continued to support the $150 million settlement, and suggested amending the Comprehensive Agrarian Reform Program Law to allow the human rights victims to have access to the Swiss funds held in escrow.[51]

On October 19, 2001, the PCGG, under the leadership of its new chairperson, Haydee B. Yorac, delivered a draft bill to Loretta Ann Rosales, Chairperson of the House of Representatives Committee on Civil, Political and Human Rights that would authorize the PCGG and the Commission on Human Rights authority to implement a compensation program for the Marcos human rights victims, would conclusively recognize the victims identified in the Hawai`i litigation as eligible for compensation, would authorize the PCGG to enter into a settlement agreement with representative plaintiffs of the Hawai`i class of victims, and would set aside $200 million of the escrow account from the Swiss Marcos accounts for the human rights victims.[52] This draft bill was significant because it contains language explicitly recognizing the duty of the Philippine government to compensate the Marcos human rights victims: "The State hereby acknowledges its moral and legal obligation to compensate said victims and/or their families for the deaths ánd injuries they suffered under the Marcos regime."[53] The draft bill recognized that this obligation is based on the Universal Declaration of Human Rights,[54] and the December 10, 1997 decision of the Swiss Federal Court returning the Marcos deposits[55] "which decision recommends that the Philippines take steps to compensate the victims of human rights violations under the Marcos regime."[56]

This draft bill thus had some positive features, but it has never been clear whether the Philippine Government is truly serious about trying to bring this sad chapter in Philippine history to an appropriate closure that would recognize the legitimacy of the Hawai`i judgment and the rights of the class of victims who brought that claim. This proposed bill may have been drafted solely as a device to obtain the Swiss Bank escrow funds at a time when the Philippine Government thought it would be able to obtain a summary judgment verdict from the Sandiganbayan regarding these funds. But it was never clear under the draft bill that the Philippine Government had any actual intention of ever distributing the money to the human rights victims.

The primary reason to be suspicious of the motives of the Philippine Government has been its continued willingness to spend vast amounts of money in legal fees on U.S. lawyers to fight the efforts of the human rights victims to obtain the $35 million in the Merrill Lynch account described above.[57] Two other reasons for being distrustful about this draft bill and the Government's motives were (1) that the implementing mechanism that would be established under this bill remained unclear and (2) that the funding ($200 million) was altogether inadequate to provide appropriate compensation for the large number of victims who would be included within its coverage.[58]   In any event, as of this publication, no legislation has yet been enacted, Haydee Yoroc has died, and the Philippine government is in turmoil once again, with renewed efforts by some members of the population to remove President Gloria Macapagal Arroyo from office.

As explained in the earlier sections of this article, the current Philippine Government has a duty under international law to provide compensation for the victims of human rights during the Marcos Regime, and it is in violation of these duties by its failure to provide a process to facilitate such compensation. The obvious and most appropriate mechanism is to utilize the judgment reached by the U.S. District Court for Hawai`i, which reached its result after years of careful and hotly-contested litigation, complete with full and fair appeals. It is bizarre and altogether inappropriate for the Philippine Government to oppose the efforts of the human rights victims to obtain compensation for their sufferings.

Some Hard Cases and Unresolved Situations

Almost every rule has some exceptions, and the question arises whether some situations present exceptions to the general rule that human rights violators should be punished and victims should be compensated. What about the South African Truth and Reconciliation Commission? Was its strategy—to provide amnesty to those who told the complete truth about their crimes—legitimate? Are there some situations when an apology and an accounting are enough, and no compensation or prosecution is needed? What about wrongs that took place in the relatively distant past, such as the illegal overthrow and taking of lands of the Kingdom of Hawai`i in the 1890s, which has left the Native Hawaiian People scarred, impoverished, and frustrated? What about the centuries of the brutal slave trade and the practice of slavery, which finally ended in the second half of the nineteenth century, but whose effects are still felt?

Randall Robinson (2000) makes a compelling argument in his book *The Debt: What America Owes to Blacks* that the enslavement of blacks in America from 1619 to 1865 was "far and away the most heinous human rights crime visited upon any group of people in the world over the last five hundred years," (p. 216)[59] and that we must look at the claims of the descendants of slaves as a form of property. It is a form of property because the descendants of former slaveholders have an enormous economic advantage over those who are descendants of former slaves that can be linked directly to wealth accumulated from the labors of the slaves and the oppression that continued for a century after the end of slavery during the Jim-Crow period. When it freed the slaves, the United States provided no meaningful compensation to them for the value of their labor, nor did it provide them with the wherewithal to establish themselves economically to compete with the white community in the marketplace (Robinson, 2000). Robinson convincingly argues that a transfer of wealth from those who benefited to those who still suffer because their ancestors were oppressed is the only way to achieve a meaningful reconciliation: "Until America's white ruling class accepts the fact that the book never closes on massive unredressed social wrongs, America can have no future as one people" (op.cit., p. 208).

In 1993, Representative John Conyers introduced a bill to "acknowledge the fundamental injustice, cruelty, brutality, and inhumanity of slavery in the United States and the 13 American colonies between 1619 and 1865" and to establish a commission to make recommendations "on appropriate remedies" (ibid, p. 201). The bill never made it out of committee, but it reflects a proper approach to the festering problem of racism in the United States. With the recent focus on affirmative action, those opposed to justice for African Americans have been able to dismiss their claim by arguing that they are claiming preferential right. In fact, African-Americans are simply claiming property that has been denied to them by virtue of the continuing impact of the mistreatment of their ancestors. If their claim can be recharacterized as a property right, it may be more understandable to the conservatives who currently dominate the federal judiciary.[60]

Once the wrong is acknowledged, what remedy is appropriate? Because of the passage of time, it may seem improper just to hand money to all the descendants of slaves, some of whom have been able to prosper economically despite the obstacles in their path. The approach of funding a foundation to address specific needs of the descendants of slaves has been suggested by Daedria Farmer-Paellman, a New York attorney whose great-great-grandmother was a slave in South Carolina. She has demanded that Aetna Inc. set up a $1 billion foundation to benefit minority education and business because it profited from slavery, selling policies in the 1850s that reimbursed slave owners for financial losses when their slaves died (Associated Press, 2000a).

The Native Hawaiian situation is similar. As a result of the illegal overthrow of the Kingdom of Hawaii in 1893, lands belonging to the Native Hawaiian People and their monarchs were acquired by the United States without the consent of or compensation to the Native Hawaiian People (United States Congress, 1993). And just as one group—the Native Hawaiians—lost economic wealth as a result of this illegal action, another group—the non-Hawaiians—gained. The Native Hawaiians have a claim for the lands that were taken, as well as for their lost sovereignty, and this claim is a form of property that should be treated as such.[61]

Conclusion

How can a society build a future if it is still poisoned by the past? If someone has killed your spouse or your child, is it possible to forgive and forget, or is the innate need for justice—including punishment, compensation, and a final accounting—too strong to set aside?

Some argue that countries returning to democracy after a period of authoritarian rule should forego investigations and prosecutions of human rights abusers in order to promote the healing and nation-building process. They argue that protracted trials will exacerbate the wounds that have divided the country, and that the transition to democracy can be promoted by encouraging the members of the previous regime to participate in the new government. They also argue that if the fear of legal retribution is removed, the authoritarian leaders will be more willing to relinquish power and permit the new democracy to function.

These arguments frequently have a short-term appeal, but in the long run it will always be better to conduct full investigations, prosecute the abusers, and enable the victims to receive appropriate compensation. In any orderly civilized society, prosecution of criminals is an essential responsibility, and disclosure of historical events is an important responsibility of any government. Each victim has a right to know what happened and a right to compensation for their injuries and suffering. The orderly administration of justice "dissipates the call for revenge" (Cassesse, 1998). Even though prosecutions may be disruptive in the short run, they are necessary to serve to deter future human rights abuses. Although pardons and plea agreements may be appropriate in some situations, it is never legitimate to ignore atrocities.

If the national courts of the country where the abuses occurred are functioning properly and can conduct the prosecutions and determine the claims for compensation, these national courts should be given the responsibility to do so. But in some situations, because the judiciary is not independent or because the country is still in turmoil, its courts cannot be expected to provide a fair forum for the accused and the victims. In those situations, an international tribunal can play an important role to ensure accountability and orderly prosecutions. The 1998 Statute creating the International Criminal Court is a responsible and well-drafted effort to establish a permanent tribunal that will be available for such situations. If the United States were to give this Court the support it deserves, then the momentum to bring closure to human rights atrocities could continue, and the international community would have a logical place to prosecute Saddam Hussein, who, as this book is going to press, awaits an uncertain judicial fate in Iraq.

Notes

1. The author would like to thank Susan Dorsey, third-year law student at the William S. Richardson School of Law, University of Hawai`i, for her research skills in connection with this paper. This chapter is an updated and expanded version of a paper that was originally prepared for the Conference on International Law, Human Rights, and Refugee Health and Wellbeing: Legal, Humanitarian and Health Issues and Directions, Honolulu, Hawaii, Nov. 16, 1999. Versions of some of the material in this chapter have been published as Jon M. Van Dyke, *The Fundamental Human Right to Prosecution and* Compensation, 29 DENVER JOURNAL OF INTERNATIONAL LAW AND POLICY 77-100 (2001), Jon M. Van Dyke, *The Fundamental Right of the Marcos Human Rights Victims to Compensation*, 76 PHILIPPINE LAW JOURNAL 169-92 (2001), Jon M. Van Dyke, *Promoting Accountability for Human Rights Abuses*, 8 CHAPMAN LAW REVIEW 153-77 (2005), and Jon M. Van Dyke, *Reconciliation between Korea and Japan*, 4 CHINESE JOURNAL OF INTERNATIONAL LAW—(2006).

2. Human Rights Watch interviewed a woman from Ropolon village who described an attack that occurred on June 20, 1999, in which rebels hacked her Uncle Pa Mohammed, and two other males to death.

> A group of them dressed in full combats entered the town in the early morning. They were the same rebels who'd attacked us at least five times over the last several months. ¨This time they had machetes and knives and as I was running I heard them say 'just because it's a cease-fire it doesn't mean cease-loot, or cease-cut-glass' (i.e., cut with machetes). I hid in the bush with my grandmother and new-born baby girl and when we came back several hours later we found my uncle and two more young men hacked and stabbed to death outside their houses.

3. *See* Special Court for Sierra Leone, at http://www.globalpolicy.org/intljustice/ sierraindx.htm (visited Dec. 16, 2004); The Special Court for Sierra Leone, at <http://www.sc-sl.org/ (visited Feb. 22, 2005); Bringing Justice: the Special Court for Sierra Leone B Accomplishments, Shortcomings, and Needed Support 16:8(A) Human Rights Watch (Sept. 2004).

4. *Prosecutor v. Norman,* 43 I.L.M. 1129 (Appeals Chamber of the Special Court for Sierra Leone 2004).

5. See Hilao v. Estate of Ferdinand Marcos ("Estate III"), 103 F.3d 767, 783 (9th Cir. 1996).

6. Marcos signed Proclamation No. 1081 on September 21, 1972, placing the entire Philippines under martial law, and then issued General Order No. 1 proclaiming that "he shall govern the nation and direct the operation of the entire government" and General Orders 2 and 2-A, instructing the military to arrest without judicial warrant of a long list of opposition leaders including Benigno Aquino, Jr., Jose Diokno, Chino Roces, Teodoro Locsin Sr., Soc Rodrigo, and Ramon Mitra. *In re Estate of Ferdinand E. Marcos Human Rights Litigation,* 910 F.Supp. 1460, 1462 (D.Haw. 1995); Joker P. Arroyo, *Do Pinoys Remember Martial Law?* PHILIPPINES DAILY INQUIRER, Sept.21, 2000, *reprinted in* KILOSBAYAN MAGAZINE, Oct. 2000, at 20.

7. In re Estate of Ferdinand E. Marcos Human Rights Litigation, 910 F.Supp. 1460, 1463 (D.Haw. 1995).

8. *Id.* at 1462-63.

9. The Alien Tort Act, 28 U.S.C. sec. 1350, enacted as part of the First Judiciary Act of 1789, provides:

The district courts shall have original jurisdiction of any civil action by an
alien for a tort only, committed in violation of the law of nations or a treaty
of the United States.

See generally Filartiga v. Pena-Irala, 630 F.2d 876 (2d Cir. 1980).

10. The act of state doctrine is a prudential court-created doctrine used by U.S. courts to keep the judiciary out of controversial foreign policy issues. The doctrine prevents U.S. courts from questioning the legitimacy of official acts of foreign governments taken within their borders, but exceptions exist if the actions violate uncontroverted or treaty-based principles of international law. *See, e.g., Underhill v. Hernandez,* 168 U.S. 250 (1897); *Banco Nacional de Cuba v. Sabbatino,* 376 U.S. 398 (1964). The Ninth Circuit ruled that the doctrine should not block the claims of the human rights victims because Marcos's acts of torture and murder were not "official acts," but were instead acts undertaken for his personal benefit, to maintain his hold on power and facilitate his efforts to steal assets from the Republic of the Philippines. *In re Estate of Ferdinand Marcos Human Rights Litigation (Estate II),* 25 F.3d 1467, 1471 (9th Cir. 1994); *see generally* JORDAN J. PAUST, JON M. VAN DYKE, AND LINDA A. MALONE, INTERNATIONAL LAW AND LITIGATION IN THE U.S. 813-18 (2d ed. 2005).

11. *Hilao v. Marcos,* 878 F.2d 1438 (9th Cir.1989) (table decision).

12. Siderman de Blake v. Republic of Argentina, 965 F.2d 699, 717 (9th Cir. 1992).

13. See Trajano v. Marcos (In re: Estate of Ferdinand E. Marcos Litigation), 978 F.2d 493 (9th Cir. 1992) ("Estate I"), cert. denied, 508 U.S. 972 (1993); In re Estate of Ferdinand E. Marcos Human Rights Litigation, 910 F. Supp. 1460, 1462-63 (D. Haw. 1995); In re Estate of Ferdinand Marcos, Human Rights Litigation—Hilao v. Estate of Ferdinand Marcos ("Estate II"), 25 F.3d 1467 (9th Cir. 1994); Hilao v. Estate of Ferdinand Marcos ("Estate III"), 103 F.3d 767 (9th Cir. 1996).

14. *Hilao v. Estate of Marcos,* 95 F.3d 848 (9th Cir. 1996).

15. Credit Suisse v. U.S. District Court for the Central District of California, 130 F.3d 1342 (9th Cir. 1997).

16. In re Estate of Ferdinand Marcos Human Rights Litigation (Hilao v. Estate of Marcos), 94 F.3d 539 (9th Cir. 1996).

17. Federal Office for Police Matters v. District Attorney's Office IV for the Canton of Zurich, 1A.87/1994/err (Swiss Federal Supreme Court, Dec. 10, 1997); see also Associated Press, Swiss Court Approves Return of Marcos Funds, N.Y. TIMES, June 16, 1998, at A12.

18. *Id.*

19. *Id.* para. 5(b).

20. *Id.* para. 7(c).

21. International Covenant on Civil and Political Rights, art. 2(3)(a), Dec. 16, 1966, 999 U.N.T.S. 171.

22. Convention Against Torture and Other Cruel, Inhuman or Degrading Treatment or Punishment, art. 14, 39 U.N. GAOR, Supp. No. 51, at 197, U.N. Doc. A/39/51 (1984).

23. *Federal Office for Police Matters v. District Attorney's Office IV for the Canton of Zurich*, 1A.87/1994/err (Swiss Federal Supreme Court, Dec. 10, 1997), para. 7(c)(aa) and (cc).

24. *Id.* para. 7(c)(ee).

25. *Id.* para. 7(c)(hh).

26. Henry Weinstein, Ferdinand Marcos' Victims Settle Case for $150 Million, Los Angeles Times, Feb. 25, 1999, at A8.

27. Republic of the Philippines v. Marcos, Civil Case No. 0141 (Sandiganbayan, July 27, 1999). Judge Garchitorena's decision was joined by Associate Justices Catalino R.Castaneda, Jr., and Gregory S. Ong, who each wrote separate concurring opinions. *See* Frederico D. Pascual, *Marcoses Buying Back Respectability for $150-M*, PHILIPPINE STAR, Feb. 24, 2000, *reprinted in* KILOSBAYAN MAGAZINE, March 2000, at 41.

The Sandiganbayan's opinion concludes that the Swiss Federal Supreme Court's opinion does not require that the human rights victims receive compensation from the funds held in escrow, but its conclusion on this matter is clearly incorrect in its reading and understanding of the Swiss opinion. The Swiss opinion recognizes at several points the responsibility of the Philippine government "to compensate the victims of human rights violations under the Marcos regime" and the duty of the Philippine government to inform the Swiss government regarding its activities in that regard. Para. 8. Robert Swift, lead counsel in the Hawai`i human rights lawsuit, met with the Swiss Ambassador to the Philippines in June 2001, and the Ambassador reported that the Swiss had told the Philippine government on three occasions during the previous eight months that the claims of the Marcos human rights victims had to be paid. Email letter from Robert A. Swift to the author, Oct.22, 2001.

28. Merrill Lynch, Pierce, Fenner & Smith Incorporated v. Arelma, Inc., Civil No. CV00-595MLR (D.Hawai`i 2002).

29. Which ruled that Chile's 1978 Amnesty Decree Law violated Article 25 of the American Convention on Human Rights because "the [human rights] victims and their families were deprived of their right to effective recourse against the violations of their rights."

30. Which stated that "amnesties for gross violations of human rights . . . are incompatible with the obligations of the State party" under the International Covenant on Civil and Political Rights and that each country has a "responsibility to provide effective reme-

dies to the victims of those abuses" to allow the victims to gain appropriate compensation for their injuries.

31. Which stated that Chile's amnesty law violated Articles 1.1, 2, and 25 of the American Convention on Human Rights, and that countries have a duty to "investigate the violations committed within its jurisdiction, identify those responsible and impose the pertinent sanctions on them, as well as ensure the adequate reparation of the consequences suffered by the victim."

32. Indeed, the Court's opinion noted that if plaintiffs could later establish "an unconstitutional taking by the suspension of the claims, we see no jurisdictional obstacle to an appropriate action in the United States Court of Claims under the Tucker Act." 453 U.S. at 689-99. *See also Coplin v. United States*, 6 Ct.Cl. 115 (1984), *rev'd on other grounds*, 761 F.2d 688 (Fed. Cir. 1985), stating that the *Dames & Moore* opinion "noted that the abrogation of existing rights might constitute a taking."

33. The Special Rapporteur for the United Nations Commission on Human Rights, Sub-Commission on Prevention of Discrimination and Protection of Minorities has written (UNHCR, 1999, p. 19, para. 75):

The Special Rapporteur reiterates that in order to end impunity for gross violations of international law committed during armed conflict, the legal liability of all responsible parties, including Governments, must be acknowledged, and the victims must be provided with full redress, including legal compensation and the prosecution of the perpetrators.

34. See also *Gray v. United States*, 21 Cl.Ct. 340 (1886), ruling that an individual claim survives a settlement by the government, and that a claimant not treated fairly can bring a claim against the claimant's own government: "the citizen whose property is thus sacrificed for the safety and welfare of his country has his claim against that country; he has a right to compensation, which exists even if no remedy in the courts or elsewhere be given him.

35. For a survey of the approaches countries have taken toward human rights abuses committed by authoritarian regimes after they return to democratic rule, see Van Dyke and Berkley (1992), *Redressing Human Rights Abuses.*

36. Examples of "reconciliations" that involve substantial financial transfers include Canada's "Statement of Reconciliation" issued January 7, 1998, establishing a $245 million "healing fund" to provide compensation for the thousands of indigenous children who were taken from their homes and forced to attend boarding schools where they were sometimes physically and sexually abused, and Canada's transfer in August 1998 of 750 square miles in British Columbia, just south of Alaska, to the 5,000-member Nisga'a Tribe (DePalma, 1998).

The basis for the "Statement of Reconciliation" can be found in Benjamin C. Hoffman, *The Search for Healing, Reconciliation, and the Promise of Prevention* (1995), and Roche and Hoffman (1993), *The Vision to Reconcile.*

37. The International Criminal Tribunal for Rwanda was established by the Security Council in November 1994, in response to the more than 500,000 minority ethnic Tutsi and Hutu opposition members who were killed during three months of slaughter in 1994 led by the Hutu-dominated government.

38. See International Criminal Tribunal for Rwanda, Fact Sheet No. 1, http://www.ictr.org/ENGLISH/factsheets/1.htm (site visited Dec. 16, 2004).

39. Bosnian War Criminal Loses Appeal, BBC News, July 21, 2000, <http://news.bbc.co.uk/1/hi/world/europe/844377.stm> (visited Feb. 23, 2005).

40. *Bringing Justice to the Former Yugoslavia: The Tribunal's Five Core Achievements*, http://www.un.org/icty/cases/factsheets/achieve-e.htm (site visited Dec. 16, 2004).

41. See generally Open Society Institute and the Coalition for International Justice, Unfulfilled Promises: Achieving Justice for Crimes Against Humanity in East Timor (Nov. 2004).

42. "Aggression" will also be under the jurisdiction of the Court once a later meeting defines this term.

43. President Corazon Aquino created the Presidential Commission on Good Government (PCGG) on February 28, 1986 in Executive Order No. 1, instructing this body to document and recover the moneys stolen by Ferdinand Marcos, his family, and his associates. *See generally* Jovito R. Salonga, PRESIDENTIAL PLUNDER: THE QUEST FOR THE MARCOS ILL-GOTTEN WEALTH (2000) (Senator Salonga was the first Chair of the PCGG).

44. In 1988, the Philippine Legislature enacted the Comprehensive Agrarian Reform Act of 1988, Republic Act No. 6657, sec. 63(b), which says that "[a]ll receipts from assets recovered and from sales of ill-gotten wealth recovered through the Presidential Commission on Good Government" should be deposited in the Agrarian Reform Fund to be used for agrarian reform.

45 *Velasquez Rodriguez Case* (1988), para. 184, 28 I.L.M. 291, 327-28 (1989).

46. *Estate II*, 25 F.3d at 1472.

47. *Id.*

48. *Gunigundo Assures Martial-Law Victims,* Today, Feb. 4, 1998, *reprinted in* KILOSBAYAN MAGAZINE, Feb. 1998, at 16.

49. Juliet Labog-Javellana and Christine Herrera, *Gov't-Marcoses Money Talk Begins Next Week*, PHILIPPINE DAILY INQUIRER, Oct. 9, 1998.

50. Christine Herrera, *I Won't Betray Cory,Rights Victims—Erap*, PHILIPPINE DAILY INQUIRER, Feb. 15, 2000, *reprinted in* KILOSBAYAN MAGAZINE, March 2000, at 26.

51. Press Release of the PCGG, April 17, 2000.

52. An Act Providing for Compensation to the Victims of Human Rights Violations During the Regime of Former President Ferdinand Marcos, Documentation of Said Violations, Appropriating Funds Therefore, and for Other Purposes, transmitted by PCGG Chairperson Haydee B. Yoroc to Hon. Loretta Ann Rosales, Chairperson, Committee on Civil, Political, and Human Rights, House of Representatives, Philippines, Oct. 19, 2001.

53. Id., Sec. 2, para. 2. The proposed bill's "Explanatory Note" explains that the bill "acknowledges that compensation for victims of human rights is an obligation of the State. After all, it is the State that guarantees the civil and political rights of its citizens."

54. Universal Declaration of Human Rights, art. 8, Dec. 10, 1948, U.N.G.A. Res. 217 (1948), quoted in the text supra between notes 28 and 29.

55. The Swiss decision is discussed in the text *supra* at notes 17-25.

56. PCGG Draft Bill, *supra* note 48, Sec. 2, para. 2. This proposed bill would also require the documentation of all the human rights abuses during the Marcos period.

57. Robert Swift, lead attorney for the human rights victims, explained to President Arroyo in July 2001 that the $35 million in the Merrill Lynch account would be distributed to the human rights victims.

58. The bill would access $200 million from the Swiss Marcos deposits, but this figure would not be sufficient to provide an adequate settlement, because the bill would recognize a much larger class of victims than those included in the Hawai`i litigation. The Hawai`i class contained only the victims of torture, murder, and disappearances. The proposed PCGG bill would also have included persons who had been arrested and de-

tained (another 80-90,000 individuals), those forced into exile, and those who had their property and businesses confiscated. PCGG Draft Bill, *supra* note 48, Sec. 3(a).

59. Robinson (2000, p. 216) argues that slavery involved the "loss of millions of lives," but also was worse than other acts of genocide because "with its sadistic patience, asphyxiated memory, and smothered cultures [slavery] has hulled empty a whole race of people with inter-generational efficiency."

60. *See generally* Jon M. Van Dyke, *Reparations for the Descendants of American Slaves Under International Law*, in SHOULD AMERICA PAY? SLAVERY AND THE RAGING DEBATE ON REPARATIONS 57 (Raymond A. Winbush ed. 2003).

61. In the decision in *Rice v. Cayetano*, (2000) the U.S. Supreme Court included a historical summary explaining the losses the Native Hawaiians had suffered at the hands of Westerners, but nonetheless declared unconstitutional the program established by the people of the State of Hawaii to provide a procedure to redress those grievances (c.f., Van Dyke, 1998).

References

Agence France-Presse (2000). Iranians respond to overture from the U.S. with mixed signals. *New York Times, March 19, 2000*, A13, col. 1.

Associated Press (1997). Argentine arrested in Spanish 'Dirty War' inquiry. *New York Times, Oct. 8, 1997*, A4, col. 3.

Associated Press (1999a). Cambodia may put all Khmer Rouge leaders on trial. *Honolulu Star-Bulletin, Nov. 4, 1999*, A10, col. 3

Associated Press (1999b). Indonesian issues denials on East Timor. *New York Times, Dec. 25, 1999*, A9, col. 1.

Associated Press (1999c). Menem rejects Spain's bid to try ex-leaders. *Los Angeles Times, Nov. 4, 1999*, A10, col. 3.

Associated Press (2000a). Reparations for slavery demanded from Aetna. *San Francisco Chronicle, March 20, 2000*, A2, col. 3.

Associated Press (2000b). Two Rwandans held in Europe in 1994 deaths. *New York Times, Feb. 16, 2000*, A6, col. 6.

Broder, J. M. (1999). Clinton offers his apologies to Guatemala. *New York Times, March 11, 1999*, A1, col. 5.

Burger-Fischer v. Degussa AG, 65 F. Supp. 2d 248 (D.N.J., 1999).

Cambodia News Reports (2000). *UN Makes Last Attempt on Genocide Trial* http://www.cambodia-hr.org/NewsReports/March-2000/NR16032000.htm

Cassese, A. (1998). *Reflections on international criminal justice. Modern Law Review, 61*, 1.

Chanfeau Orayce and Others v. Chile. Cases 11.505 et al., Inter-American Commission on Human Rights 512, OEA/ser.L/V/II.98, doc. 7 rev. (1997).

Chicago Tribune (1999). Germany will pay slave-labor victims. *Honolulu Advertiser, Dec. 15, 1999*, A1.

Chilean National Congress (1992). Creating the national corporation for reparation and reconciliation. Law Nr. 19, 123.

Christian County Court v. Rankin, 63 Ky. (2 Duv.) 502 (1866).

Cohen, R. (1999). Verdict in Berlin Wall deaths is upheld. *New York Times, Nov. 9, 1999*, A10, col. 3.

Coplin v. United States, 6 Ct.Cl. 115 (1984).
    Coplin v. United States, rev'd on other grounds, 761 F.2d 688 (Fed. Cir. 1985).

Council of Europe (1950). European Convention on Human Rights. *312 U.N.T.S. 221.* Vienna, Austria: Council of Europe.

Crossette, B. (2000). Way clear for U.S. to deliver Rwanda war crimes suspect. *New York Times, Jan. 25, 2000*, A3, col. 3.

Dames & Moore v. Regan, 453 U.S. 654 (1981).

DePalma, A. (1998). Canada pact gives a tribe self-rule for the first time. *New York Times, Aug. 5, 1998*, A1.

Estate of Ferdinand E. Marcos Human Rights Litigation, 910 F. Supp. 1460, 1462-63 (D. Haw. 1995).

Factory at Chorzow, Merits, Judgment No. 13, P.C.I.J., Series A, No. 17 (1928).

Gallardo, E. (2004). Chilean Torture Victims Say Money's Not Enough, *Honolulu Advertiser*, Nov. 30, 2004, at A7, col. 1.

Golder Case. Ser.A, no.18 at 17 (Eur. Ct. H.R., May 7, 1974).

Gray v. United States, 21 Ct. Cl. 340, 392-93 (1886)

Hague Convention IV (1907/1968). Laws and customs of war on land (Hague IV) and annexed regulations (Oct. 18, 1907, 36 Stat. 2277). In, C. I. Bevans (Compiler), *Treaties and Other International Agreements of the United States of America 1776-1949.* Washington, DC: U.S. Government Printing Office.

Henkin, L., Neuman, G. L., Orentlicher, D. F., & Leebron, D. W. (1999). *Human Rights.* New York, NY: Foundation Press.

Hilao v. Estate of Ferdinand Marcos ("Estate II"), 25 F.3d 1467 (9th Cir. 1994).

Hilao v. Estate of Ferdinand Marcos ("Estate III"), 103 F.3d 767 (9th Cir. 1996).

Hoffman, B. (1995). The search of healing, reconciliation, and the promise of prevention. *The Recorder's Report Concerning Physical and Sexual Abuse at St. Joseph's and St. John's Training Schools for Boys.* On file with author.

Human Rights Watch (1998, July). *Sierra Leone: Sowing terror* [WWW document]. URL http://www.hrw.org/reports98/sierra/Sier988.htm

Human Rights Watch (2000). *Ex-Chad dictator indicted in Senegal* [WWW document]. URL http://www.hrw.org/hrw/press/2000/02/hab023.html

Human Rights Watch (2004, September) *Bringing Justice: the Special Court for Sierra Leone—Accomplishments, Shortcomings, and Needed Support,* http://hrw.org/reports/2004/sierraleone0904/ (visited March 23, 2006).

Inter-American Commission on Human Rights (1996, October). Report No. 36/96, Case No. 10.843. Washington, DC: OAS.

International Criminal Court (ICC) (1998). Rome statute of the International Criminal Court. A/CONF.183/9 (July 17, 1998), 37 I.L.M. 999.

Iwanowa v. Ford Motor Company, 57 F.Supp.2d 41 (D.N.J. 1999).

Kadic v. Karadzic. 70 F.3d 232, 236 (2d Cir. 1995).

Kadic v. Karadzic. *cert. denied*, 116 S.Ct. 2524 (1996).

Krauss, C. (2000). New Argentine president orders purge of remnants of 'Dirty War.' *New York Times, Feb. 16, 2000*, A12, col. 5.

Linder v. Portocarrero, 963 F.2d 332 (1992).

Los Angeles Times (1998). Argentina arrests ex-dictator. *San Francisco Chronicle, June 10, 1998*, A10, col.1.

Lyon, David (2005). Justice for Timor War Criminals? BBC, Feb. 18, 2005, at <http://www.globalpolicy.org/intljustice/tribunals/timor/2005/0218tim...> (visited Feb. 23, 2005).

M/V Saiga Case (Saint Vincent and the Grenadines v. Guinea) (July 1, 1999) [WWW document]. URL http://www.un.org/Depts/los/ITLOS/Saiga_cases.htm.

Mentes v. Turkey. 37 I.L.M. 858, 882 (1998).

Mshindi, T. (2000). Dictators can no longer wait for history to judge. *The Nation (Nairobi), March 12, 2000.*
http://www.africa...rge/stories/20000312/20000312_feat5.html

Murphy, D. E. (1999). Ex-apartheid minister offers lone high-ranking voice of remorse. *Los Angeles Times, Dec. 17, 1999,* A2, col. 4.

Mydans, S. (1999). Indonesia to revive investigation of Suharto. *New York Times, Oct. 28, 1999,* A5, col. 1.

Mydans, S. (2000). Liberated East Timor lacks law, order and much more. *New York Times, Feb. 16, 2000,* A8, col. 1.

Myers, S. (2001). U.S. signs treaty for world court to try atrocities. *New York Times, Jan. 1, 2001,* A1, col. 3.

Navarro, M. (1999). Guatemalan army waged 'genocide,' new report finds. *New York Times, Feb. 26, 1999,* A1, col. 8.

Navarro, M. (2000). Freed Puerto Rican militants revel in life on the outside. *New York Times, Jan. 27, 2000,* A14, col. 3.

New York Times (1998). A new kind of leader for South Korea, and for the rest of Asia too. *New York Times, Feb. 23, 1998,* at A5, col. 3.

Okada, T. (1998). The "Comfort Women" case: Judgment of April 27, 1998, Simonoseki Branch, Yamaguchi Prefectural Court, Japan. *Pacific Rim Law and Policy Journal, 8,* 63.

Onishi, N. (1999). Freetown Journal: Survivors sadly say, yes, reward the tormentors. *New York Times, Aug. 30, 1999,* A4, col. 3.

Organization of American States (1978/1992). American convention on human rights. *O.A.S. Treaty Series No. 36, 1144 U.N.T.S. 123.* Reprinted in Basic documents pertaining to human rights in the Inter-American system, OEA/Ser.L.V/II.82 doc. 6 rev.1. Washington, DC: OAS.

Parker, K., & Chew, J. F. (1994). Compensation for Japan's World War II war-rape victims. *Hastings International and Comprehensive Law Review, 17,* 497.

Regina v. Bartle and the Commissioner of Police for the Metropolis andOthers, Ex Parte Pinochet [1999] 2WLR 827, United Kingdom House of Lords (1999, March 24).

Report No. 36/96, Case No. 10.843, Inter-American Human Rights Commission, Oct. 15, 1996.

Robinson, R. (2000). *The debt: What America owes to blacks.* New York, NY: Dutton.

Roche, D., & Hoffman, B. (1993). *The vision to reconcile.* Fund for Dispute Resolution. On file with author.

Rodriguez v. Uruguay. *U.N.Doc. CCPR/C/51/D/322/1988, Annex* (Human Rights Committee 1998).

Rohter, L. (1999). Past military rule's abuse Is haunting Brazil today. *New York Times, July 11, 1999,* A11, col. 1.

Rohter, L. (2004). Chile: Payment for Torture Victims, *New York Times,* Nov. 30, 2004, at A6, col.4.

Scheffer, D. (1999). *International criminal court: The challenge of jurisdiction.* Address given at the Annual Meeting of the American Society of International Law, March 26, 1999, Washington, DC.

Settlement Agreement, Mochizuki v. United States, No. 97-294C (Fed. Cl. 1997);

Shanghai Power, 4 Cl.Ct. 237 (1983), aff'd without opinion, 765 F.2d 159 (Fed Cir.).

Shanghai Power, cert. denied, 474 U.S. 909 (1985).

Shimbun, Y. (1999). *WWII internees get 5,000 dollars, official apology.* Jan. 11, 1999.

Stanley, A. (2000). Pope asks forgiveness for errors of the Church over 2,000 years. *New York Times, March 13, 2000,* A1, col.4.

Takirambudde, P. (1999). *Executive director for Africa, Human Rights Watch* [WWW document]. URL http://www.hrw.org/press/1999/jul/s10712.htm

Times of India (2000). *Torture case against Chad's Habre opens* (January 30, 2000) [WWW Document]. URL http://www.timesofindia.com/today/30worl22.html

Trajano v. Marcos, 978 F.2d 493 (9th Cir. 1992) ("Estate I").

Trajano v. Marcos, *cert. denied,* 508 U.S. 972 (1993).

Treaty of Versailles (1919/1968). In, C. I. Bevans (Compiler), *Treaties and Other International Agreements of the United States of America 1776-1949.* Washington, DC: U.S. Government Printing Office.

UNHCR, Sub-Commission on Prevention of Discrimination and Protection of Minorities (1999). Contemporary forms of slavery: Systematic rape, sexual slavery, and slavery-like practices during armed conflict. Geneva, Switzerland: United Nations.

United Nations (1994). General comment no. 20 (on Article 7), in compilation of general comments and general recommendations adopted by human rights treaty bodies. *U.N. Doc. HRI/GEN/1/Rev. 1.* Geneva, Switzerland: United Nations.

United Nations General Assembly (1948). Universal declaration of human rights. *Resolution 217A.* Geneva, Switzerland: United Nations.

United Nations General Assembly (1949a). Geneva Convention I (armed forces in the field). *6 U.S.T. 3114, 3148.* Geneva, Switzerland: United Nations.

United Nations General Assembly (1949b). Geneva Convention II (armed forces at sea). *75 U.N.T.S. 85.* Geneva, Switzerland: United Nations.

United Nations General Assembly (1949c). Geneva Convention III. *6 U.S.T. 3316, 3420, 75 U.N.T.S. 135.* Geneva, Switzerland: United Nations.

United Nations General Assembly (1949d). Geneva Convention IV (civilians). *75 U.N.T.S. 267.* Geneva, Switzerland: United Nations.

United Nations General Assembly (1966). International covenant on civil and political rights. *Resolution 2200A.* Geneva, Switzerland: United Nations.

United Nations General Assembly (1999). U.S. Statement before the U.N. General Assembly Sixth Committee: The Rome Treaty on the International Criminal Court [WWW document]. URL http://www.igc.apc.org/icc/html/us19991021.html

United Nations Security Council (1993). Statute of the International Criminal Tribunal for the Former Yugoslavia, S.C. Resolution 827.

United Nations Security Council (1993). Statute of the international criminal tribunal for the former Yugoslavia. S.C. Resolution 827.

United Nations Security Council (1994). The international criminal tribunal for Rwanda. S.C. Resolution 995, Annex. Geneva, Switzerland: United Nations

United States Congress (1988). Civil liberties act of 1988. *50 U.S.C. sec. 1989.* Washington, DC: U.S. Government Publications Office.

United States Congress (1993). Joint resolution to acknowledge the 100th anniversary of the January 17, 1893 overthrow of the Kingdom of Hawaii. *Pub. L. 103-150, 107 Stat. 1510*. Washington, DC: U.S. Government Printing Office.

Van Dyke, J. M. (1998). The political status of the native Hawaiian people. *Yale Law and Policy Review, 95*, 17.

Van Dyke, J. M., & Berkley, G. W. (1992). Redressing human rights abuses. *Denver Journal of International Law and Policy, 20*, 243-251.

Velasquez Rodriguez Case. *Series C (reprinted in 28* I.L.M. 291, 1989).

Ware v. Hylton, 3 U.S. 199 (1796).

Washington Post (2001). Khmer Rouge leaders may face trial. *Honolulu Advertiser, Jan. 3, 2001*, A2, col. 3.

Weiner, T., & LeVine, S. (1999). Former leader of Pakistan may face corruption trial. *New York Times, Oct. 21, 1999*, A6, col. 1.

Whitney, C. R. (1999). NATO arrests Serb ex-general on war crimes charges. *New York Times, Dec. 21, 1999*, A10, col. 3.

Wren, C. S. (1999). Hussein's worst enemies meet, but with little meeting of minds. *New York Times, Nov. 1, 1999*, A6, col 1.

Section IV: Building Understanding, Promoting Healing, and Keeping Peace

Chapter 11. Why We Need Diagnostic and Therapeutic Tools for War Crimes: A Blind Spot in International Humanitarian Law
Michael H. Hoffman

Chapter 12. Understanding Genocide: Beyond Remembrance or Denial
Rebecca Knuth

Chapter 13. Post-Conflict Healing and Reconstruction for Peace: The Power of Social Mobilization
Michael G. Wessells

Afterword: To Forgive and Forget?
Brien Hallett

CHAPTER 11

Why We Need Diagnostic and Therapeutic Tools for War Crimes: A Blind Spot in International Humanitarian Law

Michael H. Hoffman

The world is facing a humanitarian crisis of "people in movement." Wartime abuses are certainly one of the leading causes for this crisis, and may well be the worst single factor in triggering massive dislocations. When large populations cross borders and become long-term "refugees," or flee within their own countries and become long-term "displaced persons" these traumatic events are almost inevitably linked to war (Refugees, 1999). Though sheer numbers of refugees and displaced may have diminished in recent years (UNHCR Statistics 2004) the totals remain alarming. Many bring horror stories with them when they flee war zones (UNHCR briefing 2004.)

For a community to vanish overnight it has to face overwhelming destruction or a profound threat. Among communities that are visited by such tragedy, few suffer a fate like that of Pompeii and disappear in the wake of natural disaster. Most communities meeting an abrupt end will fall victim to predatory attacks by foreign invaders, the armed forces of their own government or local insurgents.

Even wars do not always have the power to uproot large numbers of people and send them into exile for indefinite periods of time. The tenacity of civilians who stay on in war zones, refusing to leave even after years of turmoil and uncertainty, is striking. Communities may leave *en masse* to escape the line of fire during an intense battle, but when it ends most of the population returns home.

A noted scholar of refugee studies observes that the notion of home is deeply ingrained in people (Smyke, 1999). Most refuse to willingly leave behind their familiar customs, food, language and physical environment to start over someplace new. Where life is supportable, they stay put. Only where violence has made life unbearable, or where the notion of home has otherwise broken down does massive migration take place (Smyke, 1999).

It takes more than an isolated battle or skirmish to set an entire community, region or ethnic group on the road for years. Where this occurs, there have likely been profound breaches of the law of war—best known today as international humanitarian law (IHL). Ultimately, the best protection for refugees and displaced populations lies in protecting civilian communities from the depredations that trigger mass flight in the first place. Where that damage is already done, better protections are needed for displaced and refugee populations. Lacking both roots and personal contacts, they are sometimes even more vulnerable than other civilians around them in war zones. We need better application of IHL to ensure that protection.

Better application will require greater insights. Though international humanitarian law increasingly finds a place in public debate and journalistic commentary, little thought has actually been given to its mechanisms. How does IHL work? What are the factors that favor its successful application? What factors work against it—in other words, what are the causes of war crimes?

This chapter examines our existing IHL paradigm, along with emerging challenges that may undermine and even defy that conceptual framework. It concludes with suggestions for several new lines of inquiry and action that could strengthen IHL in the changing landscape of war.

International Humanitarian Law: The Modern Construct

International humanitarian law[1] is comprised of the formal rules, and customary practices, that are utilized to protect human life and mitigate destruction in wartime. In its modern form, IHL is a treaty-based body of international law. Those who find actual or perceived deficiencies in these rules generally look to states to adopt new treaties to remedy the problem. When violations occur, there is an emerging trend to look to international criminal tribunals as the best place to remedy them. A legislative (treaty and tribunal based) paradigm dominates current thinking on the application of IHL. Any useful discussion must take that into account.

We can best exploit the strengths of the legislative paradigm if we understand that it also has limitations. International law will certainly continue to develop from treaties. It is quite possible that international tribunals, such as the newly established International Criminal Court, the International Criminal Tribunals for the Former Yugoslavia and Rwanda and the Special Court for Sierra Leone will come to play a bigger role in resolving disputes and strengthening the rule of law. They can certainly do much to assure that war crimes are punished, something that still happens all too rarely. However, there is little evidence that new treaties or international war crimes tribunals will improve the behavior of combatants if they are not already inclined to observe basic rules of international humanitarian law.

Public and private advocates alike seem to favor the legislative paradigm as an antidote to war crimes. But such therapies may be poorly matched to the problem at hand if we want to prevent war crimes in the first place and not limit ourselves to punishing them after the fact. Little effort has been made to systematically assess IHL's application in war zones, and then draw upon such experience to devise more effective modes of implementation. Our legislative paradigm is assumed to offer the best approach to this challenge, but it is rooted in premises that may no longer be valid in some cases.

At the beginning of the twenty-first century, three premises underlie our thinking on the future of IHL. They arise from a historical process that has been underway since the nineteenth century. We assume that treaties are the best vehicle to promote the development of IHL, that violations are subject to redress through a judicial process, and that all warring factions seek some form of respectability within the nation-state system.

This construct took concrete form in 1856 when six states adopted the Declaration of Paris to establish norms for maritime warfare (Schindler & Toman, 1988). The trend continued in 1864, when a diplomatic conference adopted the Geneva Convention for the Amelioration of the Condition of the Wounded in Armies in the Field (Schindler & Toman, 1988), and in 1868 with adoption of the St. Petersburg Declaration Renouncing the Use, in Time of War, of Explosive Projectiles under 400 Grams Weight (Schindler & Toman, 1988).

The following 30 years saw a return to a slow, incremental approach more typical of the development of customary international law. In 1874, a diplomatic conference convened in Brussels and adopted a draft agreement on laws and customs of war. No state ever ratified this agreement. However, it served as a foundation for the work of the Institute of International Law, which in 1880 adopted the Oxford Manual on the laws of war (Schindler & Toman, 1988). These efforts helped to shape thinking on the law. The end of the century saw a resurgence of the legislative approach—an approach that dominates IHL development to this day—with the convening of The Hague Peace Conferences of 1899 and 1907. Both conferences produced important law of war treaties. At least one of them, the 1907 Hague Convention (IV) respecting the Laws and Customs of War on Land remains influential in our own time (Schindler & Toman, 1988).

A great deal of hard bargaining occurred at both of these conferences. States were reluctant to adopt humanitarian standards for armed forces at war unless they were practical and could hold up in the field (Tuchman, 1996). A half century and two World Wars later, the Geneva Conventions of 1949 were built upon a foundation of solid experience with usable rules, and in response to grotesque, massive and systematic violations of long established norms (Schindler & Toman, 1988). The Geneva Conventions elaborated existing rules and practice. They may not have been a daring conceptual breakthrough; however, such a breakthrough was not required.

The Diplomatic Conference of 1974 to 1977 that adopted the Protocols Additional to the Geneva Conventions marked the end of a pragmatic approach to IHL treaty making. The drafting process became as much an exercise in ideological point scoring as law making (Best, 1994).

Were an effort to be made now to develop a new version of the Geneva Conventions, there is no reason to believe that it would represent a best effort at law making rather than an exercise in polemics. Treaty based strategies will still be useful in responding to changes in weapons technology or their methods of employment.[2] However, the international political environment is not conducive to wide ranging treaty-based advances in the law as it already exists.

Our efforts to promote the efficacy of IHL through the work of international criminal tribunals are premised on experience after World War II. Thousands of German and Japanese defendants were tried for grave breaches of international law. However, those trials took place after decisive Allied victories brought on the unconditional surrender of Nazi Germany and Imperial Japan.

To some extent, international criminal tribunals have recently been used as a substitute for military action. Rather than intervene with armed force to end depredations, we indict the fomenters even though they remain outside of our grasp, with only uneven efforts made to arrest them. The model offered by the post-World War II tribunals will not work well until states are prepared to take decisive action to capture and punish malefactors. Their general unwillingness to do so may be ominous, given apparent diffusion since 1945 of a notion that genocide is a viable strategic objective in war.

An extraordinary but sometimes overlooked shift in the nature of warfare also undermines efforts to implement IHL. Our treaty based IHL system assumes that combatants are part of that system, or aspire to membership within it. States are principally responsible for implementing IHL, and most will value the "good opinion" of other states because it serves them well to get along with other members of that community. In extreme cases, other states know where to find instigators if they decide to punish egregious violations of the law. If they do not want to go that far, lesser measures are available such as embargoes or an end to military assistance.

Insurgents are responsible for IHL rules that apply during non-international armed conflict (see Geneva Conventions of 1949, article 3 and Protocol II Additional to the Geneva Conventions of 1977). They also run the risk of capture and punishment for war crimes. Until recently, most of them also sought legitimacy in the international system, either as successors to the established government or as representatives of a new state splitting off from the old one. This was also an incentive to respect IHL norms.

The assumption that combatants will honor their obligation to comply with

IHL and realize their self-interest in doing so is not valid in every case (history obviously shows that they do not always do so.) State actors sometimes still commit war crimes on a massive scale. And, at the beginning of the twenty-first century, we are facing a return to forms of warfare largely forgotten since the twentieth began. Private armies, serving an employer's personal interests, were last a major force when warlords dominated Chinese politics from 1911 to 1927. Private, ideologically driven military detachments were last seen when Germany's brutal "Freecorps" units disbanded in the early 1920s.

But such military units have returned almost a century later. Not much thought has yet been given to how they might be categorized, but they seem to fall into three categories. Some are apolitical insurgents. Such groups emerge in "failed state conflicts," thrive on mayhem and posses few discernible political motives. Some are found in private armies and serve not a state or political cause but, rather, an employer capable of massing sufficient military force to challenge state power (most prominently drug cartels). Some are stateless ideological warriors. They move from conflict to conflict in service to a cause, or attach themselves to local armed groups that act beyond state control. Since September 11, 2001 al-Qaeda has emerged as the most visible magnet for such individuals. Among these groups there is no evidence of any desire to act in accord with international humanitarian law.[3]

There is some overlap between these categories. Their numbers may grow in the new century. They pose a challenge to traditional methods for disseminating and implementing IHL.

Our therapeutic tools are treaty-based norms and an emerging judicial process that we hope will enforce them. These tools, however, are based on imperfect assumptions. Treaty based norms are sometimes ignored, and those developed since the 1970s may sometimes have a firmer basis in polemic than in sober analysis. In recent instances, some combatants simply do not fit within traditional categories and have no interest in becoming part of the international legal system.

War Crimes

Our therapeutic solutions are flawed, because our ability to diagnose the causes of war crimes is still so imperfect. We lack a proper system for identifying functional categories of war crimes and the mechanisms behind them. Our present system is based entirely on legal definitions of such crime, and fails to take into account insights that might be obtained from the behavioral and social sciences.

Our situation is roughly comparable to that of medicine in the early nineteenth century. Physicians were then just beginning to move beyond external examinations to accomplish their diagnosis. They were mastering the art of "chest percussion," a technique used to learn about a patients' medical condition by listening to sounds within the chest cavity. In 1819 a French physician named

Rene Laennec revolutionized the process. He reported that he had used a rolled up piece of paper to listen to a patient's heartbeat with excellent results. This insight led him to invent the stethoscope (Magner, 1992).

We are still at the chest percussion stage in diagnosing the causes of war crimes. We can identify basic categories of war crimes, but are quite lacking in skills or insights to make a science out of identifying them in a way that would be useful for prevention or mitigation. Our understanding is essentially based on what we see in the Hague Conventions, the Geneva Conventions and their Additional Protocols, and the statutes of international criminal tribunals.

These sources do furnish a good starting point, and merit closer scrutiny before we press beyond them. Most war crimes derive from long established standards. Behaviors that shock the civilized conscience today also did the same a hundred years ago, when most IHL was found only in customary law. Most depredations constituting war crimes today also constituted war crimes a hundred years ago.

Their scope is well understood in a legal sense. War crimes include in part willful killing of noncombatants, torture or inhuman treatment of wounded and sick combatants, prisoners of war and civilians, humiliating and degrading treatment, taking of hostages, depriving someone of fair legal process, and destruction or appropriation not justified by military necessity (Verri, 1992). A professional soldier presented with that list in the eighteenth or nineteenth century would not have been surprised by it. (Recently, protection of women has received greater attention and wartime crimes against women such as sexual assault and enforced prostitution have been recognized as grave breaches of international humanitarian law.)

Most modern thinking on IHL has taken the form of a legal response to widespread, systematic violations of basic humanitarian norms. "Crimes Against Humanity" are a category of offenses that was formulated as part of the mandate of the Nuremberg Tribunal after World War II. As defined at that time they included "murder, extermination, enslavement, deportation, and other inhumane acts committed against any civilian population, before or during the war, or persecutions on political, religious or racial grounds . . . " (Schindler & Toman, 1988). The legal concept of Crimes Against Humanity has continued to develop in definitions of the crime established in UN Security Council resolutions establishing the International Criminal Tribunals for the Former Yugoslavia and Rwanda, and in the Rome Statute for the International Criminal Court.

The ultimate violation of international law is the crime of genocide, and it is expressly prohibited by the 1948 Convention on the Prevention and Punishment of the Crime of Genocide. Crimes against Humanity and Genocide have been added to our conceptual framework because the most basic threshold rules of IHL have been swept aside. More than that, wars are sometimes fought to attain objectives (mass murder, enslavement) totally at odds with all humanitarian norms.

We have to consider two approaches in order to secure better IHL compliance. In some situations our greatest challenge comes from violations of standards that long predate the legal concepts of genocide and crimes against humanity (e.g. sparing the lives of prisoners of war). In the most extreme cases, the challenge comes from acts of genocide and crimes against humanity.

Each calls for different remedial action. The latter may well require military assistance to the threatened population, or outright military intervention. The former may require diplomatic, legal or military intervention; but it also calls for much stronger emphasis on voluntary application of IHL and voluntary enforcement of penalties for breach by the combatants themselves than we have seen to date.

Customary International Humanitarian Law and Voluntary Application: An Overlooked Approach

IHL began as customary international law. It evolved from unwritten practice, rather than by legislative fiat at international conferences. Long before states initiated our modern treaty-based system of IHL, there were elaborate customary rules that regulated care for wounded and sick, prisoners of war and civilians. Examples of humanitarian practice in war have been documented since antiquity. Though our familiar, treaty-based system is a product of modern history, the humanitarian impulse is not unique to the modern world. Though IHL developed sporadically (and as in our own time was not consistently followed), humanitarian norms did gradually work their way into military practice. It was well established that war did not free armed forces from the obligation to follow civilized norms of behavior.

How can I suggest that soldiers, marines, sailors and airmen have a constructive role to play in developing and implementing IHL? After all, are not combatants responsible for most IHL violations? This is true: however, it is equally true in most instances they are also responsible when IHL is properly applied.

Customary international humanitarian law is often overlooked, but is important to the implementation of our modern treaty-based system. It demonstrates that compliance is not hopeless in the absence of a wide reaching network of international and domestic courts—a system that may still require several generations of development before it is possible to determine its effectiveness. Implementation of basic humanitarian principles found in customary law paves the way for creative efforts to achieve broader voluntary compliance with IHL. It is of more than symbolic value, then, for us to look at a case study in customary IHL from the Hawaiian Islands.

A Hawaiian Story

This story unfolded in the late 1700s, when King Kamehameha I was embarked on a military campaign to conquer and unify the Hawaiian Islands. He led a war party on an overnight canoeing expedition to a contested region along the island of Hawaii's southern coast. Nearing shore in the early morning hours, he leapt from his canoe and took off, well in advance of his war party, to pursue villagers tending fishnets.

Men, women and children scattered as he approached. His foot caught in a lava bed. Two men advanced, determined to hold him back while the others escaped. They fought and one broke a paddle over his head. Kamehameha collapsed, and they fled before his war party could reach them. There are conflicting versions of events that followed, but they end the same way.

Both men were later brought before Kamehameha, and one chastised him for attacking what he pointed out was a peaceful fishing community, not engaged in war with anyone. Kamehameha considered the point—and agreed. He promulgated the famous edict of *Mamala-hoe Kanawai*, the Law of the Splintered Paddle. This rule, as now enshrined in the Hawaii State Constitution, sets forth the injunction to "Let every elderly person, woman and child, lie by the roadside in safety" (Hawaii State Constitution, Article IX, section 10). (He also spared both men and enlisted them as loyal political lieutenants.)

In other words, read in its historical context the *Mamala-hoe Kanawai* decrees that warriors must spare noncombatants. This rule was born out of the experience of war. It is a rule of customary international humanitarian law. It offers us some hope for the future. Sometimes, combatants willingly follow humanitarian law. Sometimes an extraordinary military leader—such as Kamehameha—will seize the initiative and establish humanitarian rules.

The future of IHL depends on better enforcement of existing norms. When we identify new rules of conduct that might make a difference we should, whenever possible, field-test them first to establish viability and utility and, only then, impose them via new treaties. Otherwise, we will be left with a growing body of abstract, speculative treaty commitments that protect no one. In the long term, IHL might even collapse under the weight of un-enforced (and perhaps unenforceable) new treaties.

Some armed forces do train their personnel in IHL and may offer such training to allied forces as well. The International Committee of the Red Cross is preeminent in such work, conducting IHL training programs for armed forces around the world. The International Institute of Humanitarian Law in San Remo, Italy draws military officers from every region to its specialized IHL courses. The foundation for more effective voluntary implementation is there, but much remains to be done.

We are barely at the paper stethoscope phase in our understanding of the causes for war crimes. The ICRC has taken on an important pioneering initiative to address this knowledge gap, but much remains to be done (International

Committee of the Red Cross 2004) .

In fact, our strategy for implementing IHL is skewed. A war crimes focused approach has obvious legal utility. Without it, war crimes cannot be investigated and perpetrators prosecuted. It also has obvious journalistic utility. What better way to mobilize governments and private citizens? It is, however, a partial answer at best where our goal is voluntary, proactive compliance.

We know all too well that some war zones are scenes of genocide and crimes against humanity. But others are not. The latter need to be examined with greater attention to detail, because we can make some progress there.

Within armed conflict, IHL is not necessarily applied to uniform standards. High compliance in some respects (e.g. civilian protection) might be matched with low compliance in others (e.g. protection for prisoners of war.) High compliance in one military unit might be in contrast to poor compliance in another.

Sometimes war crimes reflect poor training and lack of confidence rather than a calculating, malicious strategy. For example, soldiers who lack military know-how are more likely to use excessive, indiscriminate force when they engage an enemy and thus bring down greater harm upon the civilian population. If they are confident and well trained they are more likely to take prisoners of war. If occupation forces are fearful of the civilian populace they are more likely to mistreat people at checkpoints.

None of this excuses war crimes. Rather, if we survey the conflict environment with care, we can identify factors that are likely to spark war crimes—or that may be promising in preventing them. These factors include levels of military training, communication patterns within cultures, opinions held by local authority figures, the education, age and gender of combatants, and practical interests and objectives of each side in the conflict.

However, we cannot systematically assemble such information and put it to work if we have to depend, entirely, on the insights obtained from war crimes proceedings. To analogize to the domestic environment, criminal investigations and prosecution are ultimately geared toward establishing guilt or innocence, not toward advancing insights in criminology and consequently identifying factors useful for crime prevention and mitigation.

However, there are situations where no glimmer of humanity can be found. If the goal of a war is genocidal "ethnic cleansing," and other systematic atrocities constituting crimes against humanity or, in newly emerging types of conflict, the goal is terrorism motivated mass murder and use of weapons of mass destruction, then those responsible will be unmoved by offers to assist with IHL training and implementation. Other methods are required.

Nearing the Heart of Darkness: Implementing IHL in the Face of Genocide and Crimes Against Humanity

In 1945 genocide was stopped in Europe when the allied armed forces destroyed Nazi Germany. No less of an effort would have succeeded. No systematic campaign of mass murder or "ethnic cleansing" has ever been stopped other than by the use of military force—not anywhere during World War II, not in Cambodia during the 1980s, and not in Rwanda or the former Yugoslavia during the 1990s.

Perhaps in only one case in history—Rwanda—was forcible military intervention carried out solely to stop mass slaughter. In that instance, it was the intervention of an armed force seeking to save its own people. Though humanitarian intervention as it is sometimes called (actually military intervention) has entered international thinking as a tool with some potential for use in preventing war crimes, the reality of this option does not match the rhetoric.

In fact, little thought has been given to development of a military doctrine for counter-war crimes strategy and tactics. Senior military leaders have little experience with such missions. Political leaders are reluctant to order decisive military action for that purpose. As a result, combat arms schools and advanced military institutes have not made this a priority area of study. Perhaps due to the new and interdisciplinary character of these issues, few in the civilian academic community have taken on this challenge either.

There may be a variety of strategies and tactics available to slow, harass and disrupt acts of genocide, crimes against humanity, and other patterns of grave breaches of international humanitarian law. These options span the spectrum from military training and assistance for threatened communities to outright military intervention. The military and academic communities alike have unfulfilled roles to play in working out these methods.

Conclusions

We need to identify strategies that will induce better voluntary compliance with international humanitarian law. Before we can do that, we must develop better understanding of the factors that contribute to poor compliance or breakdowns in the law in the first place. We also need to identify strategies for more timely, effective military intervention where this remedy may be the only one that will put an end to horrendous breaches. Before we can do that, we must develop better understanding of strategies and tactics behind the commission of war crimes.

In other words, we need to learn how to diagnose causes of war crimes in order to effect corrective action. With such knowledge we can make better use of our existing therapeutics and add new ones. To analogize again to medical history, if our diagnostics are still in the early 1800s, our therapeutics are, at best, in the 1930s, when the first generation of "wonder drugs" appeared. Combinations of diplomatic pressure, humanitarian persuasion and assistance, education, military intervention, and aggressive reporting by journalists and human rights organizations does sometimes help.

However, we have not developed a methodology—the diagnostics—to identify the mechanisms of war crimes. Until we put more work into the diagnostics of war crimes we will have little success in identifying the methods—the therapeutics—that will curb and prevent them.

Notes

1. IHL is also known as the law of war, a term which is older and still used by armed forces. However, IHL is used here as the term is more widely known.

2. For example, the 1997 Convention on the Prohibition of the Use, Stockpiling, Production, and Transfer of Anti-Personnel Mines and on their Destruction.

3. In the years since the original paper was developed, it has become apparent that the category of "stateless ideological warriors" refers primarily to Middle Eastern and Southwest Asian terrorist organizations motivated at least in part by religious ideology. Over the next few generations of globalization we should watch for the possible emergence of similar transnational dangers stemming from other demographics. For an overview of international legal challenges presented by such groups, see Hoffman 2002.

References

Best, G. (1994). *War and Law since 1945.* New York, NY: Clarendon Press.

The Editors Desk (Refugees, 1999). Why Kosovo and not Kabul? *Refugees, 3*(116), p. 2.

Hawaii State Constitution. Honolulu, HI. www.hawaii.gov/lrb/con/

Hoffman, Michael H. "Terrorists are Unlawful Belligerents, Not Unlawful Combatants: A Distinction with Implications for the Future of International Humanitarian Law." *Case Western Reserve Journal of International Law,* Vol. 34, No. 2 . Fall 2002.

International Committee of the Red Cross. "The Behaviour in War Studies" 2004. www.icrc.org

Magner, L. N. (1992). *A History of Medicine.* New York: Marcel Dekker, Inc.

Schindler, D., & Toman, J. (Eds.) (1988). *The Laws of Armed Conflicts.* Dordrecht, The Netherlands: Martinus Nijhoff Publishers.

Smyke, R. J. (1999, September). *Interview.* Refugee Studies Program, Webster University. Geneva, Switzerland.

Tuchman, B. W. (1996). *The Proud Tower: A Portrait of the World Before the War 1890-1914.* New York, NY: Ballantine Books.

UNHCR Statistics. "Estimated Number of Asylum Seekers, Refugees and Others of Concern to UNHCR-1st Jan 2004."

UNHCR Briefing Notes. "Darfur: fighting, killing, rape, displacement continue." Press briefing 6 July 2004.

Verri, P. (1992). *Dictionary of the International Law of Armed Conflict*. Geneva, Switzerland: International Committee of the Red Cross.

Chapter 12

Understanding Genocide: Beyond Remembrance or Denial

Rebecca Knuth

The pages of history contain many stories of war, resistance, and annihilation, but the last century was the first in which the fate of the victims was publicized and officially lamented. It did not begin this way. In the first half of the 20th century, mass murders typically were committed under the cover of colonialism (as in the German extermination of the Hereros of South Africa in 1904-7), war (as in the Armenian genocide of 1915), and revolution (as in the famines in the Ukraine, 1932-3, masterminded by Stalin). In each of these cases, the occurrence of mass murder was concealed or denied. The reality of state-sponsored mass murder burst upon global consciousness following World War II, when well-documented accounts of the killing of six million Jews became public, making the Holocaust a "watershed event in the collective psychology-history of humankind" (Charny, 1995).

A new word was coined in the 1930s to express government-sponsored, purposeful, and large-scale executions like those that occurred in Nazi Germany. Polish emigre and noted jurist Raphael Lemkin (1944) combined the Greek *genos*, meaning "race or tribe," and *cide*, "killing," to fashion the now familiar "genocide." The term rapidly gained international acceptance and, in 1948, was institutionalized in a United Nations convention defining and banning genocide. Despite hopes that international mandates might extinguish the repetition of such atrocities, genocide persisted throughout the twentieth century—a period dubbed the bloodiest in history.

Advances in our knowledge about genocide and the progress of efforts to combat it have been hindered by the sociopolitical mindset of governments, humanitarian organizations, and the public that lead them to dismiss, simplify, or confuse the issue. The mindset has parallels in the field of genocide studies where scholars struggle with problems of defining the phenomenon, applying comparative perspectives in the face of too exclusive a focus on the uniqueness of the Holocaust, and combating the influence of emotionalism as well as denial. Scholars also face problems with those who wish to focus on genocide as a product of evil rather than genocide as a process with common patterns, those too focused on the politics of remembrance, and those who do not wish to make connections between genocide and such daunting issues as total war, sovereignty, and human rights. That is not to say the field is stagnant; to the contrary, new ground is being broken by studies that focus on individual occurrences of genocide.[1] Work on individual cases remains important in establishing a record of genocide and a basis for comparison. Using newly opened archives to document communist cases is of particular importance. But the time has come for recognition of genocide as a universal problem—that is, a phenomenon with recognizable patterns and forms—and for truly comparative analysis that probes beyond a specific case. If we are to wrestle with this unwieldy subject of genocide, we must be willing to cross disciplinary and political lines in exploration of the circumstances and conditions under which the violent and evil side of humanity manifests itself.[2] Early warning signals, prevention strategies, and post-crisis peace-building will only emerge from a comprehensive and inclusive understanding of the history and psychosocial foundations of genocide. Lemkin's (1944) vision of a world without genocide is the inspiration for this chapter and, of course, the ultimate goal of genocide scholarship.

Problems with Definitions

Lemkin's original conceptualization of the term "genocide" was extraordinary in its breadth. In his 1944 book, *Axis Rule in Occupied Europe*, Lemkin developed his definition of genocide as the state's deliberate, systematic, and planned annihilation of a national, religious, or racial group. Aimed at undermining the foundations essential to the survival of the group as a group, genocidal acts bring about the disintegration of the group's political and social institutions, culture, language, national feelings, religion, and economic structure, not to mention the personal security, liberty, health, dignity, and lives of individual members. The composite of genocidal acts could include even non-lethal actions that weaken group viability.

Lemkin's term was mentioned at Nuremburg in 1945 in the indictment of German war criminals—the first formal recognition of genocide as a crime. A year later, after extensive lobbying for international policies against the practice by Lemkin, who had lost 70 members of his family to the Nazis, the term was institutionalized by the United Nations in the following General Assembly resolution (96-I). The resolution, which set in motion negotiations for a convention, read:

> Genocide is a denial of the right of existence of entire human groups, as homicide is the denial of the right to live of individual human beings; such denial of the right of existence shocks the conscience of mankind, results in great losses to humanity in the form of cultural and other contributions represented by these groups, and is contrary to moral law and to the spirit and aims of the United Nations. . . . [G]enocide is a crime under international law which the civilized world condemns, and for the commission of which principals and accomplices— whether private individuals, public officials or statesmen, and whether the crime is committed on religious, racial, political or any other grounds—are punishable (Kuper, 1981, p. 23).

Weakening the Definition

The wording of the UN convention that followed was greatly softened, however, due to lobbying by member-country representatives who, out of sympathy for colonial powers, wished to downplay acts of "ethnocide," or the destruction of a culture without killing its bearers (Kuper, 1981). Further, Polish and Russian representatives successfully argued that political groups should be excluded because of difficulties in defining them. In the end, Article II of the genocide convention defined "genocide" as any of the following acts committed with intent to destroy, in whole or in part, a national, ethnical, racial, or religious group:

a) killing members of the group
b) causing serious bodily or mental harm to members of the group
c) deliberately inflicting on the group conditions of life calculated to bring about its physical destruction in whole or in part
d) imposing measures intended to prevent births within the group
e) forcibly transferring children of the group to another group.

The exclusion of political groups made the definition much less inclusive than, for example, the U.N. convention on the status of refugees, which defines a refugee as a person who has left the country of his nationality due to persecution for any of a number of reasons, *including* political opinion (Jonassohn & Bjornson, 1998).

The definition institutionalized by the genocide convention has served an obfuscatory function in the formal acknowledgement and punishment of genocide. For example, by excluding political groups, it disqualified many communist-instigated massacres from sanctions. In 1986, an editorial in the *Wall*

Street Journal called the convention's wording "toothless," and, on the other hand, so restrictive that it manages to exempt every contemporary act of genocide (Editorial, 1986).

In addition, two other factors weaken the convention. Although it stipulates that genocide is a punishable crime under international law, no mechanism of enforcement was put in place. Further, the inclusion of intent in the definition of genocide introduces a debatably subjective element. Intent, being so difficult to establish, provides a ready basis for denial of guilt, and for this reason has became a controversial issue (Kuper, 1981). For example, by claiming lack of 'intent,' the government of Paraguay in the 1970s denied responsibility for the genocidal murder of its forest Indians by developers (Arens, 1976).

Developing a Sufficient Definition

Problems with developing a sufficiently encompassing definition have dogged genocide scholars for the last 50 years. In 1959, Dutch law professor Pieter M. Drost proposed a very simple definition: "genocide" is "the deliberate destruction of physical life of individual human beings by reason of the membership of any human collectivity as such" (1959). As more information on the dynamics of actual cases emerged, definitions began to emphasize the official and calculated nature of atrocities. Horowitz (1980) wrote of genocide as the structured and systematic destruction of innocent people by policies employed by the state to assure conformity to its ideology and model of society. Dadrian (1975) added a comment to a similar definition about the victims' vulnerability as a factor contributing to the dominant group's decision for genocide. Dadrian (1975) built a typology around his definition that acknowledged a variety of possible forms genocide could take. It could be cultural (i.e. designed to aid assimilation), latent (occurring as a by-product of other goals), retributive (intended to punish challengers), utilitarian (used as a means to gain resources), or optimal (intended simply to annihilate).

As definitions became more sophisticated, other scholars developed classification schemes based on a combination of intent and outcome. For example, Fein (1984) broke genocide into four categories:

1) *developmental*: directed against people who stand in the way of economic exploitation of resources
2) *despotic*: designed to eliminate real or potential opposition and instigated by an aggressive leader
3) *retributive*: intended to destroy opponents in response to threats from a subject class
4) *ideological*: embraces cases of genocide against those who are considered as outside the sanctioned universe of obligation, those cast as enemies by the state's hegemonic myth.

In their book, *The History and Sociology of Genocide*, Chalk and Jonassohn (1990) proposed a simplified typology based largely on motivation. In their typology, perpetrators of genocide do so:

1) to eliminate real or potential threat
2) to spread terror among real or potential enemies
3) to acquire economic wealth
4) to implement a belief, theory, or ideology

The authors pointed out that genocide in response to external threats (types 1, 2, and 3) had largely disappeared in this century. In 1998, Jonassohn and Bjornson reclassified these first three types as *utilitarian*, and type four as *ideological* (and thus similar to Fein's). Scholars now agree that most occurrences of genocide in the twentieth century have been ideological, according to this scheme. Nationalism and racism have been prevalent in acts of genocide carried out by regimes of the right; communism's twin ideals of revolution and totalitarianism are the ideological fulcrum of genocide on the left.

Confusion Between the "-cides"

There is at least one scholar who has argued that the linking of diverse acts causing death under the single label "genocide" has created an acute conceptual problem. Rummel (1994), an expert in the statistics of mass murder, has proposed that multiple terms be used for the purpose of making distinctions. "Genocide," he proposes, could be reserved for reference to the killing of people by a government because of their indelible group membership. "Politicide" could be used to refer to the murder of any person or people by a government because of their politics or for political reasons; and "mass murder" would then refer to the indiscriminate murder of any person or people by a government. "Democide," he suggested, could be the umbrella term that refers to all three types of state murder (Rummel, 1994).

Rummel's "democide" has received some recognition in scholarly circles, but meanwhile, an unfortunate trend in terms of definitional clarity has developed. "Genocide" is being used by activists as a descriptive adjective to refer to events and ideas that they judge as wrong. Such deeds run the gamut, from language regulation to abortion. This usage expresses moral outrage at the outcome of an act rather than an analytical perspective on the process behind that outcome (Andreopoulos, 1994). Also, outside of the field of genocide scholarship, "genocide" is sometimes used when "severe discrimination" would be more accurate, simply because "genocide" packs a greater political punch. This practice tends to confuse and even take away from the seriousness of genocide. When used indiscriminately, the term "becomes devoid of all cognitive content and communicates nothing but the author's disapproval" (Chalk & Jonassohn, 1990, p. 3).

Another form of misuse stems from confusion between genocide and ethnocide, which often occur together but are nevertheless different. "Ethnocide"—the commission of specific acts with intent to extinguish, utterly or in substantial part, a culture—may include deprivation of the opportunity to use a language, to practice a religion, to create art in customary ways, to maintain basic social institutions, to preserve memories and traditions, and to work in cooperation toward social goals (Beardsley, 1976). Conflation of the two concepts muddies the water and makes it less likely that genocide (as mass murder) will be accorded serious treatment by international parties.

When perpetrators use "genocide" to obfuscate political issues, confusion about genocide takes an ever stronger hold and raises, for scholars, disagreement concerning whether acts of total war should or should not be considered genocidal. During the break-up of the former Yugoslavia, the Serbian leadership repeatedly made allegations of genocide against the Muslims. These accusations served to foster a virulent racism against the Muslims and to couch the Serbs' project of ethnic cleansing in defensible terms (Cohen, 1998). Cohen (1998) has called this use "a *passe-partout* [a master key] allowing the eternal Serbian victim to butcher with impunity" (p. 169).

Total War as Genocide?

"Total war" is a phrase that refers to von Clausewitz's (1911) interpretation of modern warfare as acts of force to compel an enemy to submit to the will of the aggressor. In total war, it is necessary to destroy the enemy's resources and will to resist, and there is no rational limit to actions considered defensible in protecting national security. This same irrationality and boundlessness is also true of genocide. Leo Kuper (1981) and Eric Markuson and David Kopf (1995) argue that a case can be made for labeling the WWII strategic bombings of Dresden, Tokyo, Hiroshima, and Nagasaki as genocidal. Others dispute this classification on the grounds that mass killing in war is not intended to annihilate whole populations; the bombings stop when the war stops. Of course, one's basic definition of genocide is crucial in arguing the issue.

Total war and genocide frequently occurred in the past century. Civilian lives are viewed as cheap. Genocide claimed as many as 100 million victims in the twentieth century, most of them noncombatants. In World War I, 5 percent of the deaths were civilians; by WWII, 66 percent were civilians, and in wars since the 1970s civilians have accounted for 80 percent or more of the resulting deaths (Markuson & Kopf, 1995).

But even aside from the lethality that total war and genocide have in common, the two share important characteristics and causes. Both involve the vilification of the enemy and a disregard for otherwise common restraints.

According to Markuson and Kopf (1995), total war fosters a psychological and moral climate conducive to atrocities. This same climate may be operative in genocide. In fact, war creates the very conditions that are known to accompany genocidal programs. War exacerbates fears and anxieties whose only outlet is a scapegoat; it reduces democratic checks and balances and encourages totalitarian tendencies; it employs trained killers to hunt down and slaughter enemies; it increases the vulnerability of victims; and it produces a general desensitization that adds momentum to all other contributory factors. Genocide is perpetrated by governments seeking to destroy groups that threaten national security or ideological visions; so are most wars. In both war and genocide, actions are authorized at the highest level of government and implemented by "virtuous" citizens (Marcuson & Kopf, 1995).

Markuson and Kopf (1995) have asserted that both total war and genocide reflect a collective mindset that deserves to be labeled as a genocidal mentality. By extension, the Cold War and the ongoing nuclear arms race also demonstrate this mentality. Kuper (1994) poses an important question in this discussion: Does technological invention render international warfare inevitably genocidal?

The connection between total war and genocide is as much an issue of denial as it is of definition. More important than whether or not total war and strategic bombing are labeled genocide is the possibility that study of such events may contribute to our understanding of genocide. Insofar as classification has been an insurmountable problem, humanitarian concern for the prevention of genocide must take priority (Kuper, 1981). Likewise, disagreement over definitions must take a backseat to questions of their utility. The genocide convention marked a milestone in international law, but disagreement exists over its usefulness. While some consider it to be a valuable foundation from which to launch interdisciplinary analysis, application, and even preventive measures (Kuper, 1994), others view it as of little use to scholars (Chalk & Jonassohn, 1990).

For any scholarly discipline, consensus over basic definitions is a measure of the theoretical development of the field. The fact that no consensus around classifications and definitions has been reached indicates that genocide scholarship is still maturing, and that our understanding of the phenomenon of genocide is still evolving. It also indicates the need to analyze the intersection between problems of definition and problems of denial.

Uniqueness and Comparison in Genocide Scholarship

The Holocaust as Unique?

Throughout history, the victims of mass-murder campaigns have been invisible to the historical record either because of the completeness of their annihilation or because of the control exercised by the perpetrators over information about the atrocities. This trend was broken after World War II with the public account-ability fostered by the Nuremburg trials and the heightened access to Nazi documents, preserved as a result of the unconditional surrender won by the Al-lies. In the postwar era, political scientists began to study the Germans and their totalitarian and fascist programs, but the tentative roots of genocide scholarship per se only emerged after a decade when Jewish survivors began to bear witness. The thrust of their accounts was to engrave the Holocaust in world history and to proclaim its absolute uniqueness as an unprecedented horror. Their efforts were given impetus by the necessity of rebutting those who denied that the Holocaust occurred and because the genocide validated the creation of the state of Israel. There was great reluctance to compare the Holocaust to any other event for fear of 'diminishing' its importance. In certain instances, Holocaust literature de-legitimized other genocides by declaring the Holocaust as "unique, unprece-dented, and categorically incommensurable" (Stannard, 1996).

Advocates of the uniqueness of the Holocaust base their view on a definition of genocide that includes experiences undergone only by Jews; other mass killings do not qualify as genocide because of differences in numbers, methods, or intentionality. For those committed to this position, genocide is "a social phenomenon that is treated as external to history and literally beyond the reach of human understanding (which it may be to those who endured and survived its ravages)" (Rosenbaum, 1996, p. 1). Some fear that study of the psychology of genocide, in particular, runs the risk of replacing moral condemnation with "insights" (Lifton, 1986, p. xi). In the past, scholars who sought to write about other massacres have been derailed into comparing their case to the Holocaust, not for the purpose of identifying common patterns, but in order to defend their classification of the event as genocide. They were fighting against a "fetishist atmosphere in which the masses of bodies that are not to be qualified for the definition of genocide are dumped into a conceptual black hole, where they are forgotten" (Charny, 1996, p. 92).

While the issue of uniqueness is still a force in genocide scholarship,[3] counter-trends do exist. Two scholars, in particular, who have rejected exclusivism are Charney (1996) and Tanaka (1998). Charny (1996) views all cases of genocide as both similar and different, special and unique, and appropriately subject to comparative analysis. He turns exclusionary concepts of uniqueness around by suggesting that the term, "Holocaust," be reserved for reference to the German destruction of the Jews. The exclusive use of the term signifies the specialness of that annihilation. Charny (1996) also suggests that Holocaust study be trained on "the need to uncover relentlessly all other genocidal events and to uncover the genesis and organization of policies that bring about mass destruction of human lives" (p. xiii). A scholar of WWII Japanese war crimes, Tanaka (1998) specifically warns against the stalemate brought on by the scholarship of the unique, which gives shape to horrific events but fails to find the cultural taproot of crimes. It, thus, also fails to contribute to an understanding that might help prevent future crimes. He (Tanaka, 1998) advocates inquiry into the broader context of universal problems with an appropriate balance of specificity and universality and the pursuit of *Vergangenheitsbewaltigung*, or "mastery of the past" (in which events are not simply comprehended intellectually but are subjected to an exercise of moral imagination that involves taking responsibility and projecting thoughts into the future).

Emotional Commitment and Emotionalism in Genocide Studies

The emotional issues involving genocide cause various psychological pitfalls for scholars and laymen alike. One such pitfall occurs when those seeking to establish statistics about victims do not exercise care against the danger that counting the dead might become an abstract intellectual exercise from which the meaning is drained (Markuson & Kopf, 1995). No less a despot than Stalin declared that "A single death is a tragedy, a million deaths is a statistic." Another pitfall, identified by Charny (1994) and discussed earlier in the paper, is "definitionalism":

> a damaging style of intellectual inquiry based on a perverse, fetishistic involve-
> ment with definitions to the point at which the reality of the subject under discus-
> sion is "lost," that is, no longer experienced emotionally by the scholars conduct-
> ing the inquiry, to the point that the real enormity of the subject no longer guides
> or impacts on the deliberations (p. 91).

To offset the numbing effect of statistics, definitionalism, and detachment, it is important for scholars to have an emotional commitment that acknowledges the victims and the horrors that they were exposed to. *Emotional commitment* to understanding and preventing genocide often leads to breakthroughs in the field; it is certainly crucial in documenting and disseminating information that can establish massacres as genocide and provide an institutionalized memory of the deeds. Too often, genocide is concealed and forgotten.

It is important to distinguish this level of scholarship from what I will call *emotionalism*, or an excess of subjective involvement that can negatively affect scholarly rigor by creating intellectual blindspots. Scholars who have entered the field because they are survivors or relatives of survivors can become so focused on their personal experience of genocide that they cannot achieve comparative perspectives and clarity on the broader issues. Defining a concept as emotionally loaded as genocide involves high stakes for scholars as well as for perpetrators and victims, as definitions either legitimize or disqualify the designation of a genocide. Since the designation of genocide is so contested, definitions form part of the larger picture of the politics of genocide research (and, of course, foreign relations).

Remembrance is a crucial step in building awareness of genocide and acknowledging the victims and survivors, but the true key to understanding genocide (and, perhaps, the potential for prevention) lies in approaching the subject comparatively and through a systems framework. Comparison—the process of scrutinizing two or more systems to learn what elements they have in common, and what elements distinguish them—neither asserts identity nor denies unique components. It offers perspective and reveals a larger historical process at work (Maier, 1988). Within a systems framework, genocide is treated not as an independent phenomenon, but as part of larger processes. For example, one studies refugee flows, famines, and genocides as linked, rather than isolated occurrences (Jonassohn & Bjornson, 1998). The goal of comparing systems is, of course, the discovery of causal mechanisms.

Denial

Genocide is both a product of our era and—because of the Holocaust—an icon. We see it within a rhetorical and psychological context in which globalization has replaced the social and technological advancement, rationality, and general progress associated with modernity. Apart from its hyped use by commercial interests, the word "globalization" expresses the dilemma of a century in which distant events, because of complex communications systems, have intruded into everyday awareness (Giddens, 1991). During the twentieth century, total war and strategic bombing have stripped away the idea of protections for civilians; revolutions have turned into nightmares of violence; illusions of national separateness have disappeared, at the same time as tribalism and local violence have increased; and the interdependency and vulnerability of nations worldwide have been forcefully driven home by deadly world wars. It has been a century in which environmental degradation and technological disasters undid prevailing notions of science as a cure-all and forced awareness of the complex and occasionally destructive ways in which various forces (natural, technical, scientific, economic, political, social) interact.

It has also been a century of rampant cognitive dissonance, triggering denial as a mechanism of defense at many levels. The roots of the dissonance lie in a double-bind caused by our macro-consciousness of major problems like genocide and, at the same time, feelings of personal helplessness. The benefit of this new global consciousness is that, with large numbers of people becoming concerned about genocide, there is the possibility of coordinated policies of prevention. With the United Nations' 1948 genocide convention and the awareness of Holocaust events that became widespread during the 1970s and 1980s, acknowledgment of past instances of genocide have led to an optimism regarding collective responsibility, world citizenship, and a culture of prevention. At the same time, awareness of ongoing genocide has threatened fundamental beliefs in a civilized citizenry and a just and accountable government. The loss of innocence and resulting sense of anxiety and risk have been the price of our heightened awareness about genocide.

Further, when tribalism reared its head after the breakdown of Cold War stability, the images of brutality and injustice were broadcast worldwide from places like Somalia, Bosnia, and the Sudan. These images exposed two beliefs to be naïve if not entirely wrong, the beliefs that there had been human progress and that there existed a benign, linked destiny for mankind. Every time an international organization vested with coordinating plans and issuing policies was held hostage to the politics, greed, and prerogative of a sovereign power, the world seemed a darker place. Humanitarianism jostled awkwardly with a concern for decreasing the public's anxiety, and the result was often a tacit ignoring of political violence and genocide—at times the result of psychological numbing; at others, outright denial. One journalist has described Bosnian concentration camps in the 1990s as occurring in an "age of the indifferent spectator," in which the war was much looked at, but little seen; and much of the time life and death, right and wrong were disembodied issues, or matters of indifference (Cohen, 1998, p. 172).

Denial Among Governments

The tension between recognition and denial that has allowed genocide to flourish has also been evident in genocide scholarship and politics. Rare is the publication that wrestles with the moral issues involved in understanding genocide as an expression of the human condition—and thus poses viable alternatives to render it preventable. It has been easier, it seems, for scholars and politicians alike to view each instance as an isolated event involving an extraordinarily evil people, remembrance being the primary purpose of their scholarship. Occasionally, the choice has been to deny the occurrence of genocide altogether. The world's alternate acceptance and rejection of knowledge about genocide has contributed to an incomplete understanding of the phenomenon and to tolerance of the incongruous behavior of such high-level figures as U.S. President Clinton, who expresses the importance of remembrance in ceremonies at the Holocaust Museum while apparently ignoring contemporary and ongoing genocidal rampages in Rwanda. It is appalling that the practice of remembering past occurrences of genocide has slipped into a relatively empty ritual for our leaders, perhaps evidence that our scholarship is lagging in assembling a comprehensive theory of genocide that adequately embraces the past *and* present.

The many forms of genocide denial range from the ordinary citizen's disinclination to dwell on its horrors to the cultivated blindness of governments that maintain business as usual while perpetrators deny and prevaricate about events occurring within their borders. The practice of genocide could not persist without the participation, and subsequent denial, of government as either perpetrator or accomplice. Perpetrator regimes, whether authoritarian or totalitarian, who remain in power after carrying out a program of genocide typically create a stone wall against accusations by claiming first that there was no such thing, and then that any loss of life was because the victims were guilty parties. If genocide is committed under cover of war and civil unrest, the victims are labeled traitors or enemy collaborators. In cases of death by famine, nature is a convenient scapegoat. Further, governments escape liability by concealing records, suppressing internal dissent, controlling external communications, and disseminating propaganda and misinformation.

When a genocidal regime loses power, the new regime may continue to suppress information because of a carry-over in leadership or in order to shore up the nation's reputation and escape reparations and recriminations. The Turkish government has repelled international accusations of genocide against the Armenians since 1915. Turkish revisionist historiography, which supports evasion of political responsibility, questions the very fact of the occurrence of genocide (Adalian, 1995). Official Turkish policy is supported by considerable financial resources and the "connivance of intellectuals and academics who cherish the attention of those in power" (Chalk & Jonassohn. 1990, p. 250).

It is very common for intellectuals in genocidal or post-genocidal countries to service the cause of denial, whether for career reasons or because they agree with the government's actions and may have collaborated with the perpetrators by providing theoretical, technological, and policy support (Chalk & Jonassohn, 1990). The arena of genocide presents a huge conflict of interest for foreign intellectuals also, leading many to deny genocide because of psychological or ideological predispositions and blindspots. Communist sympathizers have been particularly susceptible to manipulation by authoritarian and totalitarian governments who have mastered secrecy, the control of information, the great lie, and the staged visit of dignitaries to support their contrived version of events (Leys, 1977).

Taking advantage of such sympathizers, secrecy, and the fact that genocide is usually identified with right-wing politics or fascism (because of the shaping force of the Holocaust), genocidal communist regimes have often escaped detection and comment. Until relatively recently, few people knew that for political and economic reasons, communist elites ever since the Russian Revolution have sanctioned the genocide of between 85 and 100 million people (Courtois, 1999). Secrecy has cloaked mass murders justified by the communists as necessary for a revolution that will benefit all mankind. Until relatively recently, intellectuals and politicians with socialist leanings, including French communists such as Sartre, have refused to address the occurrence of genocide in communist activities because this fact would challenge their ideological commitments. Communist sympathizers have dismissed rumors and reports as prejudiced and inflated reactions to the ideological "necessity" of countering resistance. The wall of leftist denial was weakened three years after Stalin's death in 1953, when Khrushchev acknowledged some of his comrade's abuses, and still further after the publication of Alexsandr Solzhenitsyn's *Gulag Archipelago* (1973), which contained detailed accounts of Russian slave camps. Still, the publication of *Livre Noir du Communisme* (*The Black Book of Communism*, Courtois, 1999)—accounts of communist crimes, terror, and repression based on recently opened archival material—caused a furor in Europe. The scale of communist genocide is overwhelming, and it will be years before all the information about these atrocities is processed and disseminated. This is a critical task, because communist regimes like North Korea's continue to justify genocidal practices in pursuit of their ideological vision.

Denial Among the International Community

All too often, the international community's policies on sovereignty inadvertently support denial by perpetrator nations. With an agreement that a government retains the right to determine what happens within its borders as the foundation of international policy, a nation inclined to camouflage genocide is virtually protected in doing so. Even when genocidal acts provoke public revulsion, foreign-relations considerations at the level of government often prevail. An example is the sanitizing of Imperial Japan's past, which quickly became a collaborative Japanese-American effort after World War II. Bilateral policies of forgetting rather than remembering (Dower, 1998) were implemented because of the U.S.'s need to resuscitate Japan as a Cold War ally in Asia. Unlike post-Nazi Germany, which had no sympathizers left, Japan was able to deny the war crimes and genocide committed in the late 1930s and during World War II in spite of documented evidence of biological warfare, medical experimentation on prisoners and civilians, forced prostitution, execution of POWs, and large-scale rape and massacre (such as in Nanking, China). Never having accepted responsibility for its genocidal atrocities, Japan has been able to sustain a sense of its own victimization in World War II.

Denial of an ongoing genocide involves collusion at all levels—even among those whose mission is to combat the phenomenon. Democratic nations and international organizations expend great energy in identifying a situation as *not* genocide in order to avoid the politically risky and expensive involvement required to enforce the U.N.'s genocide convention. It is much easier to "study the situation" or set up investigatory committees and obfuscate issues, stalling in hope that the situation will improve. Unfortunately, perpetrators are encouraged by slow and confused international responses, and in these circumstances, deaths from genocide mount quickly. In Rwanda in 1994, approximately 800,000 Tutsis were hacked to death in the hundred days during which the world dithered (Gourevitch, 1998). When public opinion forces action, "humanitarian aid" is often initiated as a face-saving measure, and the crisis is framed as a "natural disaster" or a "humanitarian emergency." Like "remembrance" ceremonies that forget contemporaneous genocide, reactive and uninformed policies of aid provision reveal, at best, a well-intentioned ignorance, and at worst, policies of obfuscation and/or complicity.

Recognizing the Forms, History, and Voices of Genocide

In recent years scholars have been identifying and publicizing examples of situations in which the provision of humanitarian aid has not only served to conceal genocide, but has rewarded the perpetrators and prolonged the genocide. One of the important indicators that most helping organizations seem to have ignored is the meaning of the starvation that they have tried to alleviate. In the present stage of the world's development the presence of serious starvation in a group is one of the first sure signs that this group has been singled out for victimization (Jonassohn & Bjornson, 1998).

Clay and Holcomb (1986) provide valuable insights into the dynamics of the use of famine and hunger as low-technology weapons in their book, *Politics and the Ethiopian Famine 1984-1985*. In 1984, aid agencies poured $1.2 billion dollars into assuaging the effects of a drought that they assumed was a natural disaster. Because of the principle of sovereignty, aid had to be funneled through the Ethiopian government, which imposed severe restrictions on information collection and exercised total control over food distribution. The government had free reign to use donated supplies for their own purposes, and the aid helped prolong the very circumstances that caused starvation in first place (Jonassohn & Bjornson, 1998). Faced with desperate need and the politics of sovereignty, aid organizations construe their job to be short-term amelioration, and fail to allot sufficient resources for research—research which may, in truth, reveal proof of genocide of a scale they cannot or do not wish to address.

Across the board, unacknowledged and unprocessed instances of genocide function as combustibles in contemporary conflicts. For example, unaddressed Serbian Chetnik and Croatian Ustashi atrocities in World War II resurfaced as vengeful rationales for violence during the 1990s breakup of Yugoslavia (Gutman, 1993). Indonesian atrocities committed in 1975-1980 have been repeated in East Timor in 1999. There can be no progress in understanding and combating genocide without penetrating the wall of denial. Genocide scholars and investigatory journalists have done just this when they have exposed the realities of collusion and become, essentially, human-rights activists (like Clay and Holcomb on Ethiopia, and Gutman, Cohen, and others on Bosnia). The key difference in method is that these authors have listened to the victims. Prominent genocide scholars who are interested in human-rights violations have launched powerful arguments for viewing information from refugees as factual and, further, the very existence of refugees as an early warning of disaster (Jonassohn & Bjornson, 1998).

Chalk & Jonassohn (1990) describe the majority of information on genocide that does get out as often "predigested" by the media, academics, and diplomats who add their own biases and ideological interpretations. Perpetrators (as official sources) and accredited sympathizers are accorded more credibility than refugees and their ideological interpretations get more attention than do the facts. Policies on combating genocide often fail because they are "based on deceptions, misinterpretation, lack of accurate information, or downright lies" (Jonassohn & Bjornson, 1998, p. 45). While access to victims and to information is often blocked by the perpetrators of violence, the preponderance of denial stems not from ignorance but from wholesale acceptance of the politics of sovereignty and a profound unwillingness to question that universe. Rethinking this sovereignty is a major intellectual challenge of our time (Boutros-Ghali, 1992-3). Genocide makes that challenge an imperative.

Conclusions: The Priority of Dissemination

Considering the many forces resisting genocide scholarship, the strides that have been made are heroic. Scholars seem poised to make the step and launch a mature comparative analysis that is interdisciplinary and systems-based. This is no small hurdle, given the fact that the forces that have prevented our reaching a comprehensive understanding of genocide are also responsible for blocking generalizations and substantiated conclusions that have been gathered by scholars in an attempt to ameliorate current and future atrocities.

All involved sectors need to ask the right questions: what is really happening when a state, or a toxic leadership under the mantle of the state, kills its own people? Or when a significant number of citizens breach moral boundaries and kill in the name of a state? Who is actually responsible for this killing? When the killing is done in the name of the collective good, do state definitions of "collective good" supersede individual human rights? Is there any consensus among the global public about "crimes against humanity?" What responsibility does the international community have for deterring large-scale atrocities by rogue states? But, in addition, we need to make awareness of the Holocaust and genocide a part of human culture, so that more people can gain a cognitive distance from the mechanisms of power that have brought others to kill, to be accomplices to killers, and to be silent bystanders witnessing the torture and killing of others (Charny, 1993).

Thus the global dissemination of genocide scholarship needs to become a priority. Prevention of genocide depends on widespread understanding of the fact that it is neither a spontaneous crime of passion nor purely a product of evil, but a planned, systematic, and inhumane exercise in problem-solving made possible by unchecked power. The outdated notion that a nation prospers from genocide must be exposed as an illusion. Of course, there are individuals who do reap material benefits from genocide. In Serbia in the 1990s, genocide was committed under a gangster capitalist regime—Milosevic's Mafia-Leninism—whose centralized control (left over from communism) allowed politicians who fomented the wars and their lieutenants to prosper while the rest of the nation was left impoverished (Cohen, 1998).

In general, however, contemporary genocide has carried a high societal cost for perpetrator nations, and has failed to produce the ideological and/or material benefits that were envisioned. The costs can be short- and long-term. One of the immediate results of the Turks' decimation of the Armenian population was that their war effort was impeded when workers on the Berlin-Baghdad Railroad—strategically crucial to the Turks in WWI—were exterminated. In another incident, wounded Turkish soldiers died because the extermination had left a military hospital virtually unstaffed (Chalk & Jonassohn, 1990). Over the long term, Turkey deprived itself of a large portion of its professional and administrative classes (Staub, 1989), a significant setback to the country's development. The long-term costs of genocide are perhaps better known from the historical record. In the thirteenth century Albigensian Crusades, the cost of forcing conformity to a homogeneously Catholic society was the destruction of the economic and cultural vitality of southern France (Chalk & Jonassohn, 1990). Similarly, genocidal activities associated with the Inquisition in Spain caused lingering cultural and intellectual stagnation. Some of the longer term effects of genocide felt in this century include Russia's change, under Stalin, from being an exporter of food to being an importer. Flourishing black markets—which are slow to disappear—and general corruption have frequently accompanied genocide in this century (Chalk & Jonassohn, 1990).

The subject of genocide is rife with irony. While genocide may appear to some nations to solve a perceived problem, it is an irrational choice that, in the end, does not serve the interests of the nation. Genocide scholars and journalists labor diligently to uncover, document, and study genocides that politicians and ordinary citizens too often are reluctant to confront. Aid agencies have little choice but to work through perpetrator governments to provide assistance to victims; their assistance often perpetuating the victimization. In seeking first to protect the sovereignty of its member states, the U.N.—which is charged with organizing international prevention of state-driven crimes of genocide—is often an *obstacle* to effective actions against genocide (Kuper, 1994). It is little wonder that cynicism abounds. In fact, the very idea that virulent genocide can be fought through humanitarian channels has come under severe challenge.

Perhaps the most encouraging aspect of efforts to respond to genocide is the potential, through modern communication systems, for developing global intolerance of the phenomenon. If the general public becomes impatient with 'Band-Aid' aid and international agencies tire of being taken for a ride, regional security forces may begin to bypass the U.N. in order to take action sooner—as they did in the cases of Kosovo and East Timor. Eventually, when the numbers of refugees and degrees of destabilization exceed tolerable levels and become visible beyond the wall of denial, the U.N. may finally undergo reforms. Our progress toward more effective international laws and models of intervention, evident in the creation of international tribunals and a criminal court, is lurching but nevertheless in motion. We need a global consensus to reject genocide, arising out of a consciousness—like that which finally made slavery unthinkable—that is powerful enough to create the will to enforce that rejection. This consciousness can only be fostered by a literature whose sights are set higher than merely collecting historical records. Only when our scholarship begins to probe what genocide can teach us about power, evil, violence and the human condition will we have moved beyond remembrance and denial.

Notes

1. D. J. Goldhagen's 1997 study *Hitler's Willing Executioners* is a good example.

2. L. M. Thomas' (1993) creative comparison study *Vessels of Evil: American Slavery and the Holocaust* is a strong example of the possibilities in such scholarship.

3. For example a 1996 book titled, *Is the Holocaust unique?: Perspectives on comparative genocide* (Rosenbaum, Ed.), addresses the issue head on.

References

Adalian, R. P. (1995). The Armenian genocide. In S. Totten, W. S. Parsons and I. W. Charny (Eds.), *Genocide in the twentieth century: Critical essays and eyewitness accounts*. New York: Garland Publishing, pp. 49-96.

Andreopoulos, G. J. (1994). Introduction: The calculus of genocide. In G. J. Andreopoulos (Ed.), *Genocide: Conceptual and historical dimensions*. Philadelphia, Pa.: University of Pennsylvania Press, pp. 1-28.

Arens, R. (Ed.). (1976). *Genocide in Paraguay*. Philadelphia, Pa.: Temple University Press.

Beardsley, M. C. (1976). Reflections on genocide and ethnocide. In R. Arens (Ed.), *Genocide in Paraguay*. Philadelphia, Pa.: Temple University Press, pp. 85-101.

Boutros-Ghali, B. (1992-3). Empowering the United Nations. *Foreign Affairs, 72*(5), 89-102.

Chalk, F., & Jonassohn, K. (1990). *The history and sociology of genocide: Analyses and case studies*. New Haven, Conn.: Yale University Press.

Charny, I. W. (1993). Editorial comment. *Internet on the Holocaust and Genocide, 43*, 3.

Charny, I. W. (1994). Toward a generic definition of genocide. In G. J. Andreopoulos (Ed.), *Genocide: Conceptual and historical dimensions*. Philadelphia, Pa.: University of Pennsylvania Press, pp. 64-94.

Charny, I. W. (1995). Foreword. In E. Markuson and D. Kopf (Eds.), *The Holocaust and Strategic Bombing: Genocide and Total War in the Twentieth Century*. Boulder, Colo.: Westview Press, p. xi-xvi.

Charny, I. W. (1996). Foreword. In A. S. Rosenbaum (Ed.), *Is the Holocaust Unique?: Perspectives on Comparative Genocide* (pp. ix-xv). Boulder, Colo.: Westview Press.

Clay, J. W., & Holcomb, B. K. (1986). *Politics and the Ethiopian famine 1984-1985*. New Brunswick, N.J.: Transaction Books.

Cohen, R. (1998). *Hearts Grown Brutal: Sagas of Sarajevo*. New York: Random House.

Courtois, S. (1999). Introduction: The crimes of communism. In S. Courtois, N. Werth, J-L. Panne, A. Paczkowski, K. Bartosek, and J. L. Margolin (Eds.), *The Black Book of Communism: Crimes, Terror, Repression* (J. Murphy & M. Kramer, Trans.). Cambridge, Md.: Harvard University Press, pp. 1-31.

Dadrian, V. N. (1975). A typology of genocide. *International Review of Modern Sociology*, *5*, pp. 201-212.

Dower, J. W. (1998). Foreword. In Y. Tanaka, *Hidden Horrors: Japanese War Crimes in World War II*. Boulder, Colo.: Westview Press, pp. xiii-xiv.

Drost, P. N. (1959). *The crime of state* (Vol. 2). Leyden: A. W. Sythoff, p.125

Editorial. (1986, February 24). *Wall Street Journal*, p. 12.

Fein, H. (1984). Scenarios of Genocide: Models of genocide and critical responses. In I. W. Charny (Ed.), *Toward the Understanding and Prevention of Genocide*. Boulder, Colo.: Westview Press, pp. 3-31.

Giddens, A. (1991). *Modernity and Self-identity: Self and Society in the Late Modern Age*. Stanford, Calif.: Stanford University Press.

Goldhagen, D. J. (1997). *Hitler's Willing Executioners: Ordinary Germans and the Holocaust*. New York: Vintage Books.

Gourevitch, P. (1998). *We wish to inform you that tomorrow we will be killed with our families: Stories from Rwanda*. New York: Farrar Straus and Giroux.

Gutman, R. (1993). *A Witness to Genocide: The 1993 Pulitzer Prize-winning dispatches on the ethnic cleansing of Bosnia*. New York: Macmillan.

Horowitz, I. L. (1980). *Genocide and State Power*. New Brunswick, N.J.: Transaction Books.

Jonassohn, K., & Bjornson, K.S. (1998). *Genocide and Gross Human Rights Violations*. New Brunswick, N.J.: Transaction Publishers.

Kuper, L. (1981). *Genocide: Its Political Use in the Twentieth Century*. New Haven, Conn.: Yale University Press.

Kuper, L. (1994). Theoretical issues relating to genocide. In G. J. Andreopoulos (Ed.), *Genocide: Conceptual and Historical Dimensions*. Philadelphia, Pa.: University of Pennsylvania Press, pp. 31-46.

Lemkin, R. (1944). *Axis Rule in Occupied Europe*. Washington, D.C.: Carnegie Endowment.

Leys, S. (1977). *Chinese Shadows*. New York: Viking Press.

Lifton, R. J. (1986). *The Nazi Doctors: Medical Killing and the Psychology of Genocide*. New York: Basic Books.

Maier, C. S. (1988). *The Unmasterable Past: History, Holocaust, and German National Identity*. Cambridge: Yale University Press.

Markuson, E., & Kopf, D. (1995). *The Holocaust and Strategic Bombing: Genocide and Total War in the Twentieth Century*. Boulder, Colo.: Westview Press.

Rosenbaum, A. S. (1996). Introduction. In A. S. Rosenbaum (Ed.), *Is the Holocaust Unique?: Perspectives on Comparative Genocide.* Boulder, Colo.: Westview Press, pp. 1-9.

Rummel, R.J. (1994). *Death by Government.* New Brunswick, N.J.: Transaction Books, p.131.

Solzhenitsyn, A. (1973). *The Gulag Archipelago 1918-1956: An experiment in literary investigation.* (Translated by Thomas P. Whitney.) New York: Harper & Row.

Stannard, D. E. (1996). Uniqueness as Denial: the Politics of Genocide Scholarship. In A. S. Rosenbaum (Ed.), *Is the Holocaust Unique?: Perspectives on Comparative Genocide.* Boulder, Colo.: Westview Press, pp. 163-208.

Staub, E. (1989). *The Roots of Evil: The Origins of Genocide and Other Group Violence.* Cambridge: Cambridge University Press.

Tanaka, Y. (1998). *Hidden Horrors: Japanese War Crimes in World War II.* Boulder, Colo.: Westview Press.

Thomas, L. M. (1993). *Vessels of Evil: American Slavery and the Holocaust.* Philadelphia, Pa.: Temple University Press.

von Clausewitz, C. (1911). *On War.* (Translated by J.J. Graham, 3 volumes.) London: Kegan Paul.

CHAPTER 13

Post-Conflict Healing and Reconstruction for Peace: The Power of Social Mobilization

Michael G. Wessells

Massive, forced displacement has become a staple of the intra-state wars that now constitute the main form of armed conflict globally (Machel, 2001). As illustrated by the conflicts in Afghanistan, Sudan, Liberia, Kosova, East Timor, and Sierra Leone, among many others, mass displacement is no mere side effect of war. It is both a terror tactic used to intimidate civilian populations and a means of achieving ethnic cleansing and resource control.

Psychologically, forced displacement creates immense human suffering associated with trauma, loss, uprooting, poverty, destruction of normal patterns of living, worsened economic status, political persecution, separation of families, and uncertainties about the location and safety of loved ones (cf. Boothby, 1988; Marsella, Bornemann, Ekblad, & Orley, 1994; Miller & Rasco, 2004; Petevi, 1996). Life inside camps for refugees or displaced people can produce problems of chronic stress, poor health, dependency, depression, and hopelessness, among many others. Living in forced exile, many refugees have powerful protection needs and feel stripped of their human dignity. In such contexts, psychosocial intervention is part of the humanitarian imperative to protect human rights and to restore human dignity and well-being.

Psychosocial intervention, however, is also a vital element in work towards peace (Wessells, 1998a; Wessells & Monteiro, 2000) and terrorism prevention

(Wessells, 2003). The emotional, social, and spiritual wounds of war create a powerful impetus for continuing cycles of violence. Following the horrors of contemporary wars—ethnic cleansing, mass killings, rapes, destruction of homes and communities, child soldiering, mutilations, landmines, cultural and physical genocide—people often weave a sense of victimhood into their socially constructed identities. Displaced communities often create a discourse of victimization in which they construct their collective identity as good people who had been victimized by the diabolical Other. This victims' identity becomes a warrant for revenge and the human rights abuses that frequently occur when refugees return home. For example, as Kosovar Albanians returned home in the summer of 1999, they inflicted on Serbs, Roma, and other minorities the same kinds of atrocities that had been done to them. Transmitting heroic images of their struggle to their children, displaced peoples frequently pass their wounds on to future generations, which become militarized to avenge the wrongs of the past and to protect against future abuses (Volkan, 1997). Without coming to terms with the pain of the past, no bridge exists to a nonviolent future, and emotional and social wounds continue to fuel cycles of violence. In this respect, healing is a means of conflict prevention in situations of protracted conflict.

Increasingly, the international community views healing as a priority in post-conflict situations. Although psychosocial intervention in complex emergencies has become fashionable, this nascent field has a paucity of foundational theory, systematized knowledge about practice, standards for intervention, and widely accepted benchmarks for evaluation. In addition, post-conflict situations create the need to build a bridge between work on healing and wider work on reconstruction for peace. The latter includes rebuilding social trust; facilitating the return of displaced people and building a sense of community; addressing issues of intolerance; nurturing respect for human rights; encouraging pro-social values and education for peace; supporting norms of nonviolence and law; rebuilding civil society; and enabling the social empowerment and mobilization needed to construct peace, among others. This work, however, is conducted mostly by separate tribes of psychologists, primarily clinicians, on the one hand and social psychologists and conflict resolution experts on the other. These tribes have different discourses, training, and orientations. It is not surprising, then, that significant issues remain about how to promote healing in effective, sustainable ways, about linkages between healing and reconciliation, and about the role of power and the imperialistic tendencies evident in much well-intentioned psychosocial work.

The purpose of this paper is to expand the discourse on psychosocial assistance to refugees and displaced people beyond the trauma frame toward more holistic approaches enabling movement toward peace, conceived systemically to include nonviolence and social justice at multiple levels. Drawing on work from the field, much of it conducted by U.N. agencies and nongovernmental organizations (NGOs), it argues that narrow, clinical approaches are less well suited than are community-based approaches to the tasks of sustainable healing on a wide scale and of building peace. Examining community-based work in Angola, it illustrates the potential power of healing based on social mobilization that builds local capacities, uses local resources, and activates communities for economic development and social action on behalf of peace and the well-being of future generations.

Trauma, Healing, and Peace

To be effective, psychosocial intervention must fit the situation. In post-conflict situations, the active phase of organized fighting may have subsided, but lines remain blurred between war and peace. Typically, there exists a system of violence in which families, communities, and society are saturated with violence, which is a normalized part of social reality (Wessells, 1998b). Following the signing of a ceasefire, strong tensions and cleavages divide rival ethnic and political groups, and the return home of displaced people often results in political instability, stigmatization, intolerance, polarization, and continued fighting.

As evident in many of the conflicts in Southern Africa, the end of political violence often creates waves of criminal violence. In many cases, the perpetrators are youths who had been militarized, who have had little education or job training, and who view the power of the gun as their main means of meeting their needs. Crime is often linked with poverty, which armed conflict amplifies. Large numbers of soldiers, including children, need to reintegrate into society, yet many have constructed military identities, feel stigmatized, and wonder whether they can find constructive roles as civilians (McCallin, 1998; Wessells & Jonah, in press; Wessells, in press). In the aftermath of war, the systemic violence and rapid social change, some of which is promulgated by humanitarian efforts, erodes patterns of culture and meaning that often provide a sense of continuity and well-being. In this context, healing must be social, culturally grounded, and oriented toward systemic, collective change for peace. Unfortunately, few roadmaps exist for how to effect social healing on the scale demanded by complex emergencies.

At present, a large, albeit unquantified, amount of psychosocial effort in post-conflict situations is guided by the trauma idiom, which provides the dominant approach to conceptualizing what happens psychologically to people in the context of life-threatening experiences and situations. As articulated by Herman (1992) and others, the trauma idiom has been very useful in identifying the range of normal responses to exceptional circumstances and to pointing the way toward appropriate clinical interventions to promote healing. Extensive research has documented that trauma and the more specific process of post-traumatic stress disorder occur in many different cultures and situations (cf. De Jong, 2002; Friedman & Marsella, 1996; van der Kolk, McFarlane, & Weisaeth, 1996). Using this knowledge, many clinical psychologists have developed trauma interventions which they apply in situations such as Kosovo, Rwanda,

Angola, and Sierra Leone (Green et al, 2003). Clinical psychologists may provide direct services, but many work through NGOs to train local professionals to conduct trauma counseling and related activities. Following what has now become rather standard practice in the U. S. and other industrialized contexts, these interventions typically emphasize emotional expression, group or individual counseling, cultural rituals, social reconstruction, and emotional integration as key parts of the healing process (Green, 2003).

Trauma-oriented interventions can be very useful, particularly in assisting the most severely affected people in crisis situations. As a dominant focus for assisting war-affected people, however, trauma-oriented interventions create a host of problems as difficult as those they intend to address. Universalized trauma interventions are ill-advised, although psychiatry has tended to overlook or downplay the importance of cultural and regional variations (Higginbotham & Marsella, 1988). In some situations, trauma-oriented programs do significant damage (Bracken & Petty, 1998). For example, in many parts of sub-Saharan Africa, healing entails the conduct of rituals for purposes of spiritual cleansing. Talking about the situation or one's feelings following the conduct of the ritual is dangerous, since local beliefs hold that it allows bad spirits to re-enter (Honwana, 1997). Well-intentioned practitioners who are unaware of local cultural beliefs and practices may put people at risk of significant stress by encouraging emotional expression in such contexts. In war zones and complex emergencies, the tendency to think of the masses of people as traumatized and to help them through trauma-oriented interventions encounters a variety of problems such as those outlined below.

Fragmented Approaches

Problems in war zones are systemic and frequently involve poverty and shortages of food, water, shelter, and other necessities (Dawes & Donald, 1994; Wessells, 1998a). Little progress on healing can occur in the absence of attention to these needs, the fulfillment of which is necessary for the construction of peace (Burton, 1990; Christie, 1997; Kelman, 1990). In situations such as the 1999 crises in Kosovo and East Timor and the post-Taliban crisis in Afghanistan, the shortage of shelter is a primary need, and the construction of shelter is itself a necessary element of healing. Also, war-affected people frequently identify the shattering of social and economic structures as having greater psychosocial impact than the experience of traumatic events (Engdahl, de Silva, Solomon, & Somasundaram, 2003). Many trauma programs are stand-alone and poorly integrated with work that meets wider needs.

Individualization

Focus on the individual, which reflects the individualism that saturates Western, industrialized society, is prominent in trauma theory and practice. This individual focus is ill suited to collectivist societies in the developing world, where most armed conflicts occur. Further, in many contexts, people view the wounds of war as communal (Boothby, 1988; Reichenberg & Friedman, 1996; Wessells, 1999; Wessells & Monteiro, 2004), and this invites theory and practice having collective roots.

Cultural Imperialism

The imposition of outsider knowledge and practice can be a form of cultural imperialism that continues on an intellectual level the damaging legacy of colonialism (Dawes, 1997; Wessells, 1992). Rushing to accept trauma theory and practice that bears the imprimatur of Western science, local people may hide their own customs and knowledge. The resulting cultural disenfranchisement can exacerbate already severe problems of erosion of cultural identity and damage due to cultural genocide.

Victimization and Medicalization

The trauma idiom tends to portray people in war zones as victims and to emphasize deficits. This deficits focus frequently obscures people's resilience and local leadership ability even under difficult conditions. This representation encourages the view that the local people must be helped since they are too bad off to help themselves. In addition, analyses of trauma frequently medicalize problems that are inherently political and social (Punamäki, 1989). The term "disorder" in categories such as PTSD inadvertently pathologizes people living under very difficult circumstances. In many contexts, little empirical evidence links the PTSD diagnosis to social dysfunctionality.

Privileging of Clinical Intervention

In Western, industrialized contexts, trauma is a distinct psychological affliction to be addressed by trained specialists. It follows that in nonwestern contexts, intervention needs to be conducted or overseen by trained trauma specialists. This approach tacitly delegitimates and silences local healers and practices in a context in which outsiders know little about what constitutes mental health in the local situation. To support the professionalized intervention, international agencies typically hire ex-patriate staff to oversee interventions such as counseling, which may have no basis in the local setting.

Dependency

Eager to gain the benefits of contemporary science and to obtain the funding of agencies that bring psychologists to their settings, local people gloss all their problems as "trauma" and turn to outside agencies even before asking what tools they have locally to address their problems. While Western approaches have much to offer, the silencing of local voices and the creation of dependency on external expertise create a sense of helplessness that is antithetical to healing and peacebuilding.

Excessive Resource Allocation

In the aftermath of nearly any war or catastrophe, one sees an influx of psychologists who want to assist by providing trauma intervention. A relatively small percentage of populations in situations of armed conflict develop problems of clinical magnitude (e.g., Cairns, 1996). Many people who live in war zones are quick to point out that their main problem is not the past violence but their current inability to feed their families and to earn a living. In light of the wide array of psychosocial needs in war zones, it would make sense for a relatively small array of resources to be devoted to trauma intervention and a larger set of resources used to reunite children with families, improve behavioral aspects of health, reducing poverty, or reduce the fears that returning child soldiers will disrupt communities.

Unsustainability

Many psychologists help to set up professionalized programs that have little basis in the local culture and for which local people feel little ownership. Following the period of funding, when the attention of the world has become preoccupied with another crisis and the outside experts have left, the programs frequently collapse. This situation can create feelings of abandonment, and it raises many questions about what might have been accomplished had the funds been used to build local capacities and culturally sustainable approaches.

Linkage to Reconstruction for Peace

With regard to reconstruction for peace, the trauma-oriented approach presents numerous problems, not least of which is the potential conflict between projects of healing and reconciliation. As Kosovar refugees returned home in Summer and Fall of 1999, for example, many NGOs and local groups encouraged trauma healing through emotional expression and reintegration. Being in a relatively secure situation and having returned home following the most acute phase of the emergency, most Kosovar Albanians were willing and eager to talk and tell the story of what had happened to them and their families. In telling their stories, they achieved a measure of emotional release, solidarity with others who had endured similar pain, and ability to get on with their lives.

The difficulty, however, was that telling the story of one's suffering often became a badge of honor and courage—their suffering was suffused with social meaning. Although this likely enabled coping and adaptation (Protacio-Marcelino, 1989; Punamäki, 1996), it also became part of the collective memory of victimization that stirred hatred of Serbs and invited revenge. Expression and emotional release may enable reintegration with one's own ethnic group, but it may also contribute to destructive conflict between ethnic groups. Individual healing or intra-group healing activities cannot by themselves break cycles of violence. Applied too narrowly, psychological assistance can become a process of patching people up to continue fighting.

The limits of healing through expression are visible in many war zones, where material, emotional, and social needs intermix. Often healing occurs through the resumption of normal activities and patterns of living, which provide a sense of continuity (Gibbs, 1997). Material rebuilding is also a key part of healing. Building a home, for example, can re-establish a sense of control in the face of overwhelming, traumatic experiences and can help to meet a very pressing source of stress, the lack of shelter. Conversely, healing cannot occur through counseling or talking when local people are overwrought over where their next meal will come from or where they and their families can live in security. Further, as constructed by Western psychologists, healing is often viewed as an individual process. But in war zones, much of the healing is psychosocial, with the emphasis on the "social." For healing to occur, refugees and displaced people need to reintegrate into society, to shed their stigmas, and to find constructive roles and identities. In this respect, the creation of jobs and economic opportunities are vital parts of healing and social integration. For these reasons, many practitioners and NGOs have turned to mobilization approaches that focus on social aspects of healing.

Social Mobilization and Healing

In contrast to trauma approaches, a mobilization approach to healing emphasizes self-help, use of local resources and networks, and processes of empowerment (e.g., Boothby, 1996; Reichenberg et al., 1996). Work on trauma may be included in the project work, but trauma is only one element in a wider approach, and it is addressed through non-clinical interventions. International NGOs may play a significant role, keeping outsider influence prominent, but they also share power with local actors, and the NGOs conceptualize their role as enabling, facilitative, and oriented toward partnership. Outsider knowledge is not privileged over insider knowledge, and attempts may be made to construct new communities of practice through joint dialogue and mutual learning across cultural boundaries (Gilbert, 1997).

The heart of a mobilization approach is collective self-transformation, which always occurs in a larger social context. As outlined in Figure 1, mobilization for peace entails work to protect human rights and build social justice; to develop norms, practices, and values of nonviolence; and to promote political and economic transformation that meets basic human needs, insures participation by and respect for all groups, and enables sustainable development. In this framework, mobilization is systemic, stimulates activity at both macro- and micro-levels, and interconnects personal change with wider social changes that promote peace with social justice.

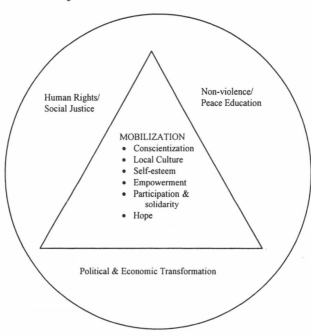

Fig 1. A social mobilization framework for healing and building

In regard to healing, a mobilization approach offers a powerful tool for culturally grounded understanding and action. Whereas a trauma approach privileges outsider knowledge, a mobilization approach begins with conscientization, which in the tradition of Paulo Freire (1968) means awareness of self in historic context. This awareness is socially constructed by people inside the local culture using the categories and cultural meanings of their own context. The interpretive process may be aided by the use of concepts, tools, values, and understandings from outside, but fundamentally it is a process of collectively analyzing "What has happened to us?" and asking "How have we changed as a result of our historic experience?" In areas torn by decades of armed conflict, violence may seem entirely normal and peace may seem unreal, distant, even unimaginable. Further, it may be very difficult for people to understand the various ways in which they have been affected by chronic war or poverty or centuries of colonialism and oppression. A reflective process is needed to help people to understand their collective wounds, the negative and positive changes that have occurred, and the bases for action in historicized consciousness (Aron & Corne, 1994; Comas-Díaz, Lykes, & Alarcón, 1998).

The conscientization dialogue entails elicitive processes that bring to the fore indigenous understandings, values, and tools (Lederach, 1995). The culturally grounded understandings that emerge may be quite different from analyses that flow from a trauma approach. In rural Angola, for example, practitioners encountered a girl whose village had been attacked, whose parents had been killed, and who had fled for his life. Western psychologists tend to view such a child as traumatized. Dialogue with the girl and community members, however, revealed that her greatest subjective stresses were spiritual. Since she had fled before she had conducted the culturally appropriate burial rituals for her parents, she worried that her parents' spirits had been unable to make transition to the realm of the ancestors and lingered, causing problems for the living. This distress is communal since the angry spirits threaten everyone, and local beliefs hold that failure to conduct the appropriate burial rituals violated the bond between the living and the ancestral communities. Dialogue and ethnographic documentation regarding these and related processes can help to disclose key insights about local views of illness and health, life and death, and practices of healing. In this case, the conduct of an appropriate burial ritual is indicated and enables social reintegration and spiritual harmony (Wessells & Monteiro, 2000, 2004).

The conscientization process avoids imposing outside understandings and nourishes insider understandings grounded in local culture and acts of interpretation. This opens the arena for application and strengthening of local resources for healing, including traditional rituals, ceremonies, and values. This supportive approach to local culture is crucial in post-colonial contexts in which people have internalized feelings of inferiority about their own culture, leading them to doubt their own capacity to build a positive future. The resulting helplessness builds a sense of disempowerment, one of the main tools colonial regimes had used to maintain control.

Empowerment is a cornerstone of the healing process. Traumatic experiences instill a sense of loss of control, and regaining the sense of control, even in small ways, is a key element in healing. Particularly in collectivist societies, empowerment is a collective process in which groups of people begin to take charge of affecting their circumstances and planning their futures.

One must always approach mobilization and empowerment with critical awareness, asking who benefits and seeking to encourage full participation. To enable transformation for peace, empowerment must not privilege one particular group over others or strengthen local elites that will focus mainly on their own advantages. An effective mobilization process gives voice to excluded people, builds solidarity across group lines, and creates processes for full participation. In situations in which tensions divide ethnic groups, solidarity and social healing can often be achieved by building a sense of common ground through having groups cooperate on movement toward the achievement of superordinate goals (Sherif, 1967). Solidarity and improved social relations can create social networks and support structures that advance healing. Also, full participation invites constructive political change and a process that includes diverse constituencies.

As groups become mobilized and start to take charge of building their own futures, hope is born again. Out of this hope arises new energy for projects and steps to improve local circumstances. When these projects help to improve both spiritual and material circumstances, hope and mobilization become catalysts of a self-sustaining cycle.

Constructed with care, the mobilization process has numerous benefits. Since it is a holistic, communal process, it can advance the healing of communal wounds and help build resilience and the ability to cope with difficult circumstances. Since resilient communities are in a better position to resist political manipulation and attraction into armed conflict, this is a highly positive outcome in protracted conflicts. Mobilization approaches tend to be sustainable since they build local capacities, use and support local resources, and encourage local leadership and sense of ownership. By stimulating full participation, they enable constructive political change through a middle-out strategy (Lederach, 1997) that encourages changes both at the grassroots level and creates activated groups and communities who can then pressure for appropriate reforms at the regional and national levels.

At the same time, it is important not to romanticize community-based approaches. Each community has a local power structure and consists of a mosaic of different sub-groups. Interventions may inadvertently privilege particular groups and leaders over others or even empower perpetrators of violence, as occurred in the refugee camps in Goma following the 1994 Rwandan genocide. Among the questions that must be asked by those who would intervene are "Who benefits?" and "Which values are being strengthened?" Further, empowerment must occur across the lines of conflict if deep healing is to occur. Indeed, one can amplify conflict by systematically assisting and empowering one group while other groups in the conflict are neglected.

Community-based Healing and Social Integration in Angola

To illustrate both the strengths and the potential problems in using mobilization approaches, consider the following example from two related projects for assisting Angolan children conducted by Christian Children's Fund (CCF), an ecumenical NGO. A children's focus is appropriate in light of the fact that children comprise nearly half the displaced people worldwide and become the vehicles through which intergenerational wounds are transmitted. In addition, social healing and integration across lines of conflict often requires finding common ground. A focus on children can depoliticize relations and speak to a universally shared goal of building a better life for rising generations.

Both projects are framed by the U. N. Convention on the Rights of the Child (CRC) and an ecological perspective situating child development within wider social systems of family, community, and society (Dawes & Donald, 2000). The first project emphasizes community-based healing for all children and families, including the displaced, while the second focuses on the social reintegration of former child soldiers. Both projects recognize that deep social healing and prevention of war cannot be achieved when children are exploited in armed conflict and grow up in situations in which violence is a centerpiece of social reality.

Community-based Healing in Angola

In Angola, torn by armed conflict for forty years, several generations of children have grown up with war as a constant. Following a brief ceasefire in 1991 and the rejection by UNITA, the opposition group, of the results of the first free elections, Angola plunged into highly damaging phase of war in 1992. By 1993, nearly 1,000 people died daily. Large numbers of civilians, mostly women and children, were subjected to direct attack, community destruction, displacement, landmines, and sexual violence. By 1994 and the signing of the Lusaka Protocol, humanitarian agencies had responded with extensive material assistance. The Angolan government, noting the depth of the psychological wounds, invited CCF to provide psychosocial assistance.

The psychosocial needs were profound by any measure. In a worst-case study of 100 displaced children living in Luanda, CCF/Angola observed that 27 percent of children had lost their parents; 94 percent had been exposed to attacks; 66 percent had witnessed mine explosions; 36 percent had lived with troops; 7 percent had fired guns; and 65 percent had escaped death. Children in the same sample reported fright and insecurity (67 percent), disturbed sleep (61 percent), intrusive images (51 percent), frequent thoughts about war (89 percent), and sensory-motor disturbance (24 percent).

To address these needs, CCF/Angola, with the guidance of Carlinda Monteiro, constructed a national team of five Angolan trainers having backgrounds in education and social work. The trainers realized that psychosocial stresses had to be understood in cultural context. For example, in an orphanage, children were unable to sleep because they believed they were haunted by a bad spirit. The trainers sought the assistance of a traditional healer, who conducted a ritual to get rid of the bad spirits, and this enabled the children to sleep again. These and related experiences led the team to work to blend Western and local approaches to assisting children. This insight became part of the foundation of a program to assist children through a training of trainers in which community-selected adults worked with children.

To integrate psychosocial assistance into different sectors, a five-person national team of trainers conducted week-long training seminars for adults working with various NGOs and government agencies. Conducted in a participatory mode and tailored to the low levels of formal education, the seminars were spaces for mutual learning and problem-solving about how to assist violence-affected children.

The curriculum included children's healthy psychosocial development, the impact of war and violence on children, local belief and rituals surrounding loss and bereavement, activities for assisting children, and nonviolent conflict resolution. Work on conflict resolution focused on families since there were reports of high levels of family violence and local norms of severe corporal punishment. In a politically charged environment, it was safer and more practical to discuss nonviolent conflict resolution at the family level than at community or societal levels. The activities for assisting children consisted of expressive arts such as drawing, song, dance, story-telling, drama, and other tools for improving emotional integration.

Although the seminars did not teach traditional practices, they valorized these practices and encouraged discussion of how to combine the tools of different cultural systems to assist children. Following training, the adults implemented activities on behalf of children and received follow-up support from the trainers. The main results from this pilot project—reduced problems related to sleep and aggression and improved social integration—led the team to expand the program on a national scale from 1995-98.

With the assistance of major funding from the U. S. Agency for International Development Displaced Children and Orphans Fund, CCF/Angola implemented the program in the eight most severely war-affected provinces: Benguela, Bie, Huambo, Luanda, Malange, Uige, Huila, and Moxico (in the latter two provinces, CCF collaborated with UNICEF). In each province, there was a three-person team of trainers who knew the local language and culture and whom local people respected and viewed as effective helpers of children. Applying the model used earlier in Luanda, these trainers conducted week-long training seminars aimed to build local capacity to assist children and to mobilize communities around children's needs. As the security situation improved, peace education was added to the training curriculum.

Having conducted a local situation analysis to identify the areas of greatest need, the province-based trainers, the team met with and demonstrated respect for local *sobas* (traditional chiefs), elders, influential women, and caregivers. If they expressed having strong material needs, the CCF trainers worked with other NGOs and local agencies to meet the material needs. To mobilize the communities, the trainers conducted sensitization dialogues with community groups and activated existing community networks, some of which had become inactive due to the pressures associated with war and displacement. Many local people viewed problems such as children's aggression as signs of disobedience rather than as impacts of war experiences of violence. The sensitization dialogues helped local people understand children's behavior and mobilized them around assisting children.

Using the community networks identified in the first two stages, the trainers selected well-respected adults such as organizers of youth groups or teachers who were in a good position to assist children. This use of existing community networks was designed to aid social mobilization and also to increase sustainability. Next, the trainers conducted week-long training seminars for groups of approximately 20 adults using the curriculum outlined above, and they provided follow-up support through regular site visits. Following training, the trainees implemented activities on behalf of children. As the project evolved, trainees included more activities such as soccer teams and drama groups for increasing social integration. Since local people needed to see tangible improvements in their circumstances, the teams also began a program of giving small grants for community-planned projects such as school construction or building community huts. The project work was evaluated using a mixture of qualitative and quantitative methods and indicators. The evaluation system combined outsider and insider expertise, used participatory methodology, and was designed to provide on-line information to guide program improvements.

Over three years, the project trained 4,894 adults, who in turn assisted nearly 300,000 children. The main outcomes can only be summarized briefly here. The impacts on children included improved child-child and adult-child relationships; improved behavior and cooperation in the classroom; less evidence of war-related games and toys; diminished isolation behavior; reduced violence and aggressive behavior; fewer concentration problems; decreased hypervigilance; increased hope; and improved school attendance. Adults, too, reported discernible benefits. Many reported that the training seminars had for the first time provided space in which they could begin coming to terms with their own war experiences.

Significant benefits occurred in relation to community mobilization. Sobas and elders reported that communities, which had been relatively inactive and overwhelmed by war and poverty, had become more active and hopeful as a result of the project. Adults reported being more vigilant about children and their needs, and they had become actively engaged in planning, a process that they described as healing since it generated solidarity and a positive future orientation. The community development projects had particularly large impact on social mobilization since they reengaged war-affected communities in collective planning and action, which the war had largely disrupted. As schools were built the physical structures became tangible symbols of communal healing and monuments to people's hope and resilience. These effects serve as a poignant reminder of the close connections between physical community development, social mobilization, and psychosocial well-being.

With regard to wider tasks of building peace, this project had a number of beneficial effects. Both children and adults began to think and talk about peace, a subject that had literally dropped out of local discourse since it was politically charged and distant from the daily reality of Angola. Social trust was built as people from different generations and areas collaborated on meeting children's needs. Norms of nonviolence were strengthened as many parents began questioning the effects of using harsh, corporal punishment. Activation of local networks and children's support groups helped to build civil society. Still, the project encountered profound challenges, not the least of which were chronic poverty and insecurity, problems discussed further below.

Reintegration of Former Underage Soldiers

Worldwide, approximately 300,000 children, defined under international law as people under 18 years of age, are exploited as soldiers and serve as cooks, porters, spies, bodyguards, sex slaves, and combatants (Brett & McCallin, 1996; Machel, 2001; Wessells, in press). In Angola, nearly 9,000 children participated as soldiers, mostly for UNITA (Verhey, 1999). Also, there were large numbers of girls soldiers, although this became apparent only following the end of the war in April, 2002 (Stavrou, 2005). A common entry route for boys was force, as UNITA troops forced villages to submit a quota of youths lest the village be attacked and destroyed. The median age of entry into military activity was 13-14 years, at which point youths are regarded locally as adults since they have participated in culturally scripted rites of passage. Still, recruitment of youths under the age of 15 years violates the CRC and exposes youth to death, killing, attack, separation from home, and loss of positive paths of development.

Assisting child soldiers is a key step toward building peace. Highly militarized youths who have been deprived of education and job training, who have little hope for the future, and who understand the power associated with guns, can have a marked destabilizing effect on societies (Wessells, 1997; Singer, 2005). Often, former child soldiers become involved in banditry and other activities contrary to peace. Steps are needed to reintegrate former child soldiers, to help them abandon their military identity, and to enable them to have a positive future in civilian life.

Because of the extensive need for social healing and reintegration, CCF has favored culturally grounded, community-based approaches over center-based approaches and trauma interventions. Although center-based programs may be useful in enabling family tracing, providing a transition space, and offering basic counseling services, centers tend to become holding tanks, and too little attention is typically given to follow-up and community integration. In addition, Western counseling is ill-advised in regard to particular aspects of child soldiering. As occurs in many Bantu cultures, rural peoples believe that children who have killed in combat are contaminated by the unavenged spirits of the people they had killed. They regard the problem not as one of trauma but as discord between the living community and the community of the ancestors. In this context, a traditional purification ritual may be more appropriate than Western counseling (Honwana, 1997).

To mobilize communities for reintegration of the former child soldiers, CCF province-based teams worked 1996-98 through a network of approximately 200 activistas, who were connected with the local church and were recognized by their communities as being well positioned to assist returning youth. The activistas received training from the provincial teams on the psychosocial impacts of child soldiering and on methods of enabling child soldiers' reintegration.

Following the training, the activistas prepared for the children's return home by tracing their families while the children were in quartering areas and notifying their families. Having listened to family members' concerns, the activistas educated families about the situation of child soldiers and advised them on how to support family and community reintegration. Since families expressed concerns over disobedience, they raised awareness that such problems might reflect a child's war experiences rather than a damaged character, and they discussed means of managing behavior problems. Since some community people viewed returning soldiers as potential trouble makers, the activistas raised awareness about former child soldiers' needs, challenged stereotypes, and heard concerns about their return. Meetings with sobas, government leaders, and community influentials also provided venues for gaining support. In both families and communities, activistas worked to help identify socially constructive roles for returning child soldiers and to construct appropriate placements in schools, vocational training programs, and related venues.

To assist in the return of the children to their villages, the activistas partnered with UNICEF to accompany the children home. At the time, Angola was a divided country, and pressures for child recruitment and fighting remained strong. When several hundred youth who had been released from a quartering area disappeared, most people suspected that UNITA had re-abducted them. Since reuniting children with their families is an essential form of psychosocial assistance to children, the activistas accompanied the child soldiers to meet their parents and arranged temporary foster care if families were unable to meet the children.

Over two thousand of the 4,104 demobilized youths who were from villages in the CCF project areas were successfully reunited with their families. Families, however, would have been reluctant to receive the returning youth without communal acceptance. To reconcile former child soldiers with their communities, the activistas also arranged community receptions, which often included greeting rituals such as the Okupiolissa ritual documented in Huila province:

> The community and family members are usually excited and pleased at the homecoming. Women prepare themselves for a greeting ceremony. . . . Some of the flour used to paint the women's foreheads is thrown at the child and a respected older woman of the village throws a gourd filled with ashes at the child's feet. At the same time, clean water is thrown over him as a means of purification. . . . The women of the village dance around the child, gesturing with hands and arms to ward away undesirable spirits or influences. . . . They each touch him with both hands from head to foot to cleanse him of impurities. . . . When the ritual is complete, the child is taken to his village and the villagers celebrate his return. A party is held in his home with only traditional beverages. . . . The child must be formally presented to the chiefs by his parents. . . . The child sits beside the chiefs, drinking and talking to them, and this act marks his change of status in the village.

Ethnographic documentation of local beliefs and cultural healing practices was a key part of the work to aid mobilization, healing, and social reintegration. Among the main social stressors in Angola, amplified by growing urban-rural differences, are the erosion and perceived inferiority of traditional beliefs and practices, which themselves can provide a sense of continuity and meaning in difficult situations. To aid social mobilization and recovery of cultural practices, the CCF teams partnered with local healers and leaders in conducting participatory action research to document local views of life and death, illness and health, and modes of healing. Documentation of these cultural aspects was initiated with an eye toward learning about indigenous psychosocial resources, strengthening sustainable processes of healing in areas having no clinical psychological services, and mobilizing people by empowering them to examine and honor their own cultural values and practices.

Although the evidence is preliminary, returning child soldiers apparently undergo a two-step process. First, the community greets them, while the traditional healer observes and studies the reactions of the youth and the community members. If a healer decides that a returning child soldier is unclean spiritually, then the healer arranges a purification ritual in the presence of all the villagers to restore spiritual harmony with the ancestors.

Although the rituals vary by ethnic group and region, they typically include numerous steps. First, the healer uses special burning herbs to define a safe space that the bad spirits cannot enter. Next, the healer washes the soldier, who also inhales burning herbs that clean him of bad spirits. The healer also asks the spirit's forgiveness and makes a payment or sacrifices a chicken or goat to appease the spirit. The ceremony ends by having the young person step across a threshold, whereupon the healer announces that "This boy's life as a soldier has ended and he can now rejoin the community." The healer may also tell the boy not to look back, which in the local idiom means not talking about the matter any more lest the bad spirit return.

Few studies of long-term impact of cleansing rituals have been conducted. Growing evidence from case studies, including those involving people who had not been helped by psychiatric intervention, suggests that the purification rituals can assist individuals and also enable the community to accept the young person back without fear of spiritual reprisal. The following is an example:

> Paulino, a 33-year-old man, joined the government army at age 17. After fighting for 3 years, he served as a political commissioner, encouraging soldiers to fight the enemy. Following demobilization in 1992, he went to live in Luanda with his oldest sister. There he drank and smoked excessively and experienced frequent headaches, irritability, nightmares, and hallucinations. He frequently "heard" the voice of a colleague whom he had persuaded to fight and who had been killed in the war. His sister described him as badly disturbed and unable to care for himself. He responded to neither a 6-month treatment in a psychiatric hospital nor rehabilitation programs in a Catholic mission or the Universal Kingdom of God Church. His mother decided to return him to his original home in the countryside, where he would receive traditional treatment.
>
> The healer, a woman, used a divination process of working through Paulino's mother in a trance state. Through the mother, the healer learned the sources of Paulino's disturbance were spirits of Paulino's colleagues who had been killed during the war and his guilty feelings of having caused others to die. The healer treated Paulino by offering gifts such as bread, sugar, and chicken to the spirits. Then he was submitted to a purification ritual in the nearest river, where he bathed with water specially prepared with sacred herbs. Following bathing, Paulino's clothes were thrown away in the river and he was dressed in new clothes. The healer and family elders told Paulino to leave without looking back and to never talk about what had happened. Years later, Paulino now reports that he recovered following the treatment. Although his dreams and guilt have not abated completely, he now works for an NGO in Luanda.

There is great need of multicultural action research and long-term psychosocial follow-up on the methods, variations, and efficacy of traditional rituals.

To reintegrate, returning youths need jobs, means of earning a living, and a place in civilian society. Many youths did not view return to school as a viable option since the Angolan schools were poorly funded and often required that returning, older students take classes with very young students. Since many youths were from agricultural areas, CCF/Angola provided small grants for land purchase and seeds and tools. To enable income generation, CCF also supported quick-impact projects in which youth started small businesses such as bakeries.

This multifaceted, social approach to healing and reintegration was disrupted by the renewal of fighting in December, 1998. Fortunately, a ceasefire achieved in 2002 has held and shows strong signs of continuing. Currently, the CCF team in Angola is using the lessons learned from the project described above to contribute to the current processes of peacebuilding and restoring national unity.

Future Challenges

Despite their strengths, mobilization approaches face numerous practical and conceptual obstacles. In some situations, organizational cultures provide significant challenges. When refugees flood across a border, for example, many relief agencies provide directly for services and material needs such as food, clothing, and shelter. Although this is necessary in acute crisis situations, the provision of direct services can become a surrogate for consultation, partnership, and empowerment. It can also become a mindset and part of organizational culture that is difficult to change. In emergency situations, a better approach is to integrate psychosocial support into different sectors of humanitarian assistance. One way to do this is to use a mobilization approach that engages local people in planning, delivering, and assessing the impact of aid, thereby enabling empowerment, self-help, and sustainable development.

Second, mobilization approaches can fall prey to the same problems of lack of coordination and paucity of standards that apply to other approaches as well. In nearly every emergency situation, NGOs that use mobilization approaches concentrate too tightly in some areas while other areas go underserved. This produces "assessment fatigue" and "consultation stress" on communities that face a lineup of NGOs wanting to partner but who do not themselves collaborate. It also increases tension between the "have" and "have-not" communities and heightens inter-NGO conflict for funding. Too often, the net results are poor resource allocation, failure to meet needs in a comprehensive manner, and frustration and feeling of exploitation among community members. In an era of increasing need for the protection of civilian populations, practitioners should give careful attention to coordination and even coverage, particularly since community mobilization enables people to become agents of their own protection.

The absence of widely accepted standards for practice and evaluation aggravates the issue of poor coordination. In the absence of well-defined, valid standards, coordination can devolve into dividing up the pie to various actors, without a means of insuring comprehensive provision of quality programs. Further, since mobilization approaches honor local culture, an inherent danger exists of romanticization (Dawes, 1997). Since all cultural resources—Western or not— are dynamic, complex, and a mixture of positive and negative elements, a critical stance informed by attention to human rights is necessary.

Mobilization approaches also face difficult ethical issues that confront all humanitarian work. For example, aid workers in the Goma refugee camp following the 1994 Rwandan genocide struggled over whether to assist people who were believed to be perpetrators of the genocide. In the absence of careful power mapping, attempts to mobilize people for peace may inadvertently strengthen the hand of groups that will use "peace" and resources to advance their own political agendas, without regard for human rights.

The greatest challenges, however, are political. As the case of Angola illustrates, it is not always possible to engender full participation and social integration across the lines of conflict. Throughout the period in which the Lusaka Protocol was being implemented, Angola remained a country inside a country, and UNITA-controlled areas remained dangerous and relatively inaccessible. These political and security divisions thwarted efforts to encourage deep social healing. To contribute to peace, psychosocial programs must be integrated with wider efforts to achieve political and economic reform. Ultimately, the task of building peace is multidisciplinary and activist, meaning that the future psychosocial work will need to cross disciplinary boundaries and expand the intersection between research, practice, and social action of mobilization approaches.

References

Aron, A., & Corne, S. (1994). *Writings for a Liberation Psychology: Ignacio Martin-Baro.* Cambridge, Mass.: Harvard University.

Boothby, N. (1988). Unaccompanied children from a psychological perspective. In W. Ressler, N. Boothby, & D. Steinbock (Eds.), *Unaccompanied Children: Care and Protection in Wars, Natural Disasters, and Refugee Movements.* Oxford: Oxford University Press, pp. 133-180.

Boothby, N. (1996). Mobilizing communities to meet the psychosocial needs of children in war and refugee crises. In R. J. Apfel and B. Simon (Eds.), *Minefields in their hearts.* New Haven, Conn.: Yale University, pp. 149-164.

Bracken, P. & Petty, C. (Eds.). (1998). *Rethinking the Trauma of War.* London: Free Association Books.

Brett, R. & McCallin, M. (1996). *Children: The Invisible Soldiers.* Stockholm: Radda Barnen.

Burton, J. W. (1990). *Conflict: Human Needs Theory.* New York: St. Martin's.

Cairns, E. (1996). *Children and Political Violence.* Oxford: Blackwell.

Christie, D. J. (1997). Reducing Direct and Structural Violence: The Human Needs Theory. *Peace and Conflict: Journal of Peace Psychology, 3(4),* pp. 315-332.

Comas-Díaz, L., Lykes, M. B. & Alarcón, R. D. (1998). Ethnic conflict and the psychology of liberation in Guatemala, Peru, and Puerto Rico. *American Psychologist, 53(7),* pp. 778-792.

Dawes, A. (1997, July). *Cultural imperialism in the treatment of children following political violence and war: A Southern African perspective.* Paper presented at the Fifth International Symposium on the Contributions of Psychology to Peace, Melbourne.

Dawes, A. & Donald, D. (1994). *Childhood & Adversity: Psychological Perspectives from South African Research.* Cape Town: David Philip.

Dawes, A. & Donald, D. (2000). Improving Children's Changes: Developmental Theory and Effective Interventions in Community Contexts. In D. Donald, A. Dawes & J. Louw (Eds.), *Addressing Childhood Adversity.* Cape Town: David Philip, (pp. 1-25).

De Jong, J. (2002). Public mental health, traumatic stress and human rights violations in low-income countries. A culturally appropriate model in times of conflict, disaster, and peace. In J. de Jong (Ed.), *Trauma, War, and Violence: Public Mental Health in Socio-cultural Context.* New York: Kluwer/Plenum.

Engdahl, B., de Silva, P., Solomon, Z. & Somasundaram, D. (2003). Former Combatants. In In B. Green et al. (Eds.), *Trauma Interventions in War and Peace: Prevention, Practice, and Policy.* New York: Kluwer/Plenum, pp. 271-289.

Freire, P. (1968). *Pedagogy of the Oppressed.* New York: Herder & Herder.

Friedman, M. J. & Marsella, A. J. (1996). Posttraumatic Stress Disorder: An overview of the concept. In A. J. Marsella, M. J. Friedman, E. T. Gerrity, and R. M. Scurfield (Eds.), *Ethnocultural Aspects of Posttraumatic Stress Disorder: Issues, Research, and Clinical Applications.* Washington, D.C.: American Psychological Association, pp. 11 - 32.

Gibbs, S. (1997). Postwar Social Reconstruction in Mozambique: Reframing children's experiences of trauma and healing. In K. Kumar (Ed.), *Rebuilding War-torn Societies.* Boulder, Colo.: Lynne Rienner, pp. 227-238.

Gilbert, A. (1997). Small Voices Against the Wind: Local knowledge and social transformation. *Peace and Conflict: Journal of Peace Psychology, 3,* pp. 275-292.

Green, B. (2003). Traumatic Stress and Its Consequences. In B. Green et al. (Eds.), *Trauma Interventions in War and Peace: Prevention, Practice, and Policy.* New York: Kluwer/Plenum, pp. 17-32.

Green, B., Friedman, M., de Jong, J., Solomon, S., Keane, T., Fairbank, Donelan, B., & Frey-Wouters, E. (Eds.)(2003). *Trauma Interventions in War and Peace: Prevention, Practice, and Policy.* New York: Kluwer/Plenum.

Green, E. G., & Wessells, M. G. (1997). *Mid-term evaluation of the province-based war trauma team project: Meeting the psychosocial needs of children in Angola.* Arlington, Va.: USAID Displaced children and Orphans Fund and War Victims Fund.

Herman, J. (1992). *Trauma and recovery.* New York: Basic Books.

Higginbotham, N., & Marsella, A. (1988). International consultation and the homogenizations of psychiatry in Southeast Asia. *Social Science and Medicine, 27,* 553-561.

Honwana, A. (1997). Healing for Peace: Traditional Healers and Post-war Reconstruction in Southern Mozambique. *Peace and Conflict: Journal of Peace Psychology, 3(3),* pp. 275-292.

Kelman, H. C. (1990). Applying a human needs perspective to the practice of conflict resolution: The Israeli-Palestinian case. In J. Burton (Ed.), *Conflict: Human Needs Theory.* New York: St. Martin's, pp. 283-300.

Lederach, J. P. (1995). *Preparing for Peace: Conflict Transformation Across Cultures.* Syracuse: Syracuse University.

Lederach, J. P. (1997). *Building Peace: Sustainable Reconciliation in Divided Societies.* Washington, D. C.: U. S. Institute of Peace Press.

Machel, G. (2001). *The Impact of War on Children.* Cape Town: David Philip.

Marsella, A. J., Bornemann, T., Ekblad, S., & Orley, J. (Eds.). (1994). *Amidst Peril and Pain: The mental health and well-being of the world's refugees.* Washington, D.C.: American Psychological Association.

McCallin, M. (1998). Community involvement in the social reintegration of former child soldiers. In P. Bracken & C. Petty (Eds.), *Rethinking the trauma of war.* London: Free Association Books, pp. 60-75.

Miller, K. & Rasco, L. (Eds.)(2004), *The Mental Health of Refugees: Ecological approaches to adaptation and recovery.* Upper Saddle River, N.J.: Erlbaum.

Petevi, M. (1996). Forced Displacement: Refugee trauma, protection and assistance. In Y. Danieli, N. S. Rodley, and L. Weisaeth (Eds.), *International Responses to Traumatic Stress* Amityville, N.Y.: Baywood, pp. 161-192.

Protacio-Marcelino, E. (1989). Children of Political Detainees in the Philippines: Sources of stress and coping patterns. *International Journal of Mental Health, 18,* p. 71-86.

Punamäki, R. (1996). Can ideological commitment protect children's psychosocial well-being in situations of political violence? *Child Development, 67,* 55-69.

Punamäki, R. (1989). Political Violence and Mental Health. *International Journal of Mental Health, 17,* pp. 3 - 15.

Reichenberg, D. & Friedman, S. (1996). Healing the Invisible Wounds of Children in War: A Rights Approach. In Y. Danieli, N. S. Rodley, and L. Weisaeth (Eds.), *International Responses to Traumatic Stress.* Amityville, N.Y.: Baywood, pp. 307-326.

Sherif, M. (1967). *Group Conflict and Cooperation.* London: Routledge & Kegan Paul.

Singer, P. (2005). *Children at War.* New York: Pantheon.

Stavrou, V. (2005). *Breaking the Silence.* Luanda, Angola: Christian Children's Fund.

van der Kolk, V. A., McFarlane, A. C. & Weisaeth, L. (Eds.) (1996). *Traumatic Stress: The effects of overwhelming experience on mind, body, and society.* New York: Guilford.

Verhey, B. (1999). *Lessons learned in prevention, demobilization and social reintegration of children involved in armed conflict: Angola case study.* New York: United Nations.

Volkan, V. (1997). *Bloodlines: From Ethnic Pride to Ethnic Terrorism.* New York, NY: Farrar, Straus, and Giroux.

Wessells, M. G. (1992). Building Peace Psychology on a Global Scale: Challenges and Opportunities. *The Peace Psychology Bulletin, 1,* pp. 32-44.

Wessells, M. (1997). Child Soldiers. *Bulletin of the Atomic Scientists, 53(6),* pp. 32-39.

Wessells, M. G. (1998a). Humanitarian Intervention, Psychosocial Assistance, and Peacekeeping. In H. Langholtz (Ed.), *The Psychology of Peacekeeping.* Westport, CT: Praeger, pp. 131-152.

Wessells, M. G. (1998b). The Changing Nature of Armed Conflict and Its Implications for Children: The Graca Machel/UN Study. *Peace and Conflict: Journal of Peace Psychology, 4(4),* pp. 321-334.

Wessells, M. G. (1999). Culture, Power, and Community: Intercultural Approaches to Psychosocial Assistance and Healing. In K. Nader, N. Dubrow, and B. Stamm (Eds.), *Honoring Differences: Cultural Issues in the Treatment of Trauma and Loss.* New York: Taylor & Francis, pp. 267-282.

Wessells, M. G. (2003). Terrorism and the Mental Health and Well-being of Refugees and Displaced People. In F. Moghaddam & A. Marsella (Eds.), *Understanding Terrorism: Psychosocial Roots, Consequences, and Interventions.* Washington, D.C.: American Psychological Association, pp. 247 — 263.

Wessells, M. (in press). *Child Soldiers: Stolen Childhoods*. Cambridge, Mass.: Harvard
    University Press.
Wessells, M. & Jonah, D. (in press). Reintegration of Former Youth Soldiers in
    Sierra Leone: Challenges of Reconciliation and Post-accord Peacebuilding. In S.
    McEvoy (Ed.), *Youth and Post-accord Peacebuilding*. South Bend, Ind.:
    University of Notre Dame Press.
Wessells, M. G., & Monteiro, C. (2000). Healing Wounds of War in Angola: A Commu-
    nity-based Approach. In D. Donald, A. Dawes, & J. Louw (Eds.), *Addressing
    Childhood Adversity* Cape Town: David Philip, pp. 176-201.
Wessells, M. G., & Monteiro, C. (2004). Healing the Wounds Following Protracted
    Conflict in Angola: A community-based approach to assisting war-affected
    children. In U. P. Gielen, J. Fish, & J. G. Draguns (Eds.), *Handbook of Culture,
    Therapy, and Healing*. Mahwah, N.J: Erlbaum, pp. 321-341.

Afterword

To Forgive and Forget?

Brien Hallett

A Swedish friend of mine was working for the Swedish Ministry of Foreign Affairs in Mozambique just after the signing of the 1992 peace agreement that ended the civil war. His assignment was to go out into the villages and assess their needs so that the Ministry would be able to provide the most appropriate aid for the villagers, the returning refugees, and the demobilized fighters. In village after village, the elders said the same thing. Goats. Goats, hundreds, thousands of goats were needed for sacrifice in the hundreds and thousands of purification ceremonies that had to be held.

Before reconstruction could begin, the land had to be purified. All those wandering souls who had died unattended in the bush had to be put to rest; their deaths had to be recognized and mourned. Goats were needed for this important task. The fighters also had to be purified. Hundreds and thousands of young men had unrequited blood on their hands. This had to be washed away before they could reenter the villages. More goats were needed. Once the unsettled spirits of the dead were at rest and the killers purified, reconstruction could then proceed.

Needless to say, this first and most strongly felt need was not reported back to Stockholm. How would the Minister explain expending millions of krona for sacrificial goats? What would the Swedish animal rights groups say? My friend's report spoke of wells and schools, seeds and farm implements. Material aid, the Minister could explain; spiritual aid appropriate for a traditional society, he could not. Modern contractual societies no longer appreciate the value of sacrificial goats.

Besides the unintended humor, the story is of interest for the way in which the village elders were engaged in the practical work of reconciliation, while at the same time bypassing forgiveness. For the goats were to be sacrificed to purify the land and the returning fighters, not to forgive anyone anything. The villagers would not forget, but they would not forgive either. As is usually the case in traditional face-to-face communities, the needs of the individual were sacrificed, like the goats, to the needs of the organic community to "fix" broken relationships within the community. In Hawaiian culture, this is called *ho'oponopono* —to make straight or right.

Modern societies based on the Western model, in contrast, are made up of anonymous bystanders who too often value the autonomous individual above the integrity of their community, which is no longer organic, but contractual. This radical difference in fundamental values does not lead to a fundamental difference in dealing with post-conflict reconciliation, however. In large, modern societies, the practical work of reconciliation still focuses on "fixing" relationships, while bypassing forgiveness. No one need forgive or forget. All that is needed is a commitment to "fix" relationships within the larger community. The actual point of difference between the "traditional" and the "modern" is rather the need to accept and accommodate the spiritual.

Never Forget

But is this not strange? In both traditional and modern societies we find reconciliation without forgiveness. To appreciate the limited role of forgiveness in post-conflict reconciliation, one needs to begin with conflict—its sources and methods. For example, recall the words that ignited the Yugoslav Wars, "By the force of social circumstances this great six hundredth anniversary of the Battle of Kosovo is taking place in a year in which Serbia, after many years, after many decades, has regained its state, national, and spiritual integrity. . . . Six centuries later, now, we [the Serbian people] are being again engaged in battles and are facing battles. They are not armed battles, although such things cannot be excluded yet" (Milosevic 1989). On 28 June 1989, when Slobodan Milosovic delivered this speech on the Field of Blackbirds, the battles were indeed not yet armed, but they soon would become, as ethnic cleansing destroyed Tito's Yugoslavia.

As is always the case, the purpose of Milosovic's challenge to the other ethnic groups in Yugoslavia was to create a manichaean world of light versus dark, a threatening world peopled by a perverse "other," an objectified "them" vis-à-vis a familiar, unthreatening "us." Naturally, in this dualistic world, the evil "them" is all that the good "us" is not; "them" is dangerous and detrimental to "us"; think how much better off our community would be if the evil "them" were eliminated? In sum, a distorted dualism produces a self-negating perspective of the world as peopled by implacable enemies.

Needless to say, the powerful emotional resonance of this objectified dualism is challenged by the complacent rationalism of the conciliator. The conciliator's soul sees the other as subjective, as an essentially identical "we." "For my enemy is dead—a man divine as myself is dead" as Walt Whitman wrote in Leaves of Grass (1965, 321). The conciliator surmounts and evades any accidental boundaries between "us" and "them," creating stories of shared experience; for, are not our conflicts and struggles, in reality, but the cooperative ventures that are necessary to define and build our new society? The "other" is a brother, a fellow citizen, a human being, as are "us." The conciliator also endows social relations across boundaries with bridges and openings, while at the same time endowing social relations within "us" with welcome and charity for "them." In fine, Sobodan Milosovic's self-negating objectifying methods produce the boundaries and stories that exploded Tito's Yugoslavia; Nelson Mandela's self-affirming subjective methods produce the boundaries and stories that reconstruct a New South Africa.

The Mystery of Forgiveness

But the mystery of forgiveness is not explained by the sociology and politics of storytelling and boundary building. After what has happened, why would anyone forgive anything? In all justice, should the Tutsi not avenge themselves upon the Hutu? The Kosovars upon the Serbs? Yes, certainly, Yet, retributive justice traps the two parties in the past, focused upon what "them" did to "us," attempting to right the wrongs of the past in the present. The mystery of forgiveness, however, turns on shifting one's focus of attention from the past and what "them" did to "us" to the future and what "we" will build together, from emotion to reason, from the tragic events taken in isolation to our broken community and its emerging needs. The ego and libido recede, and the common good emerges. Those individuals who can see past the tragic events to the future of the subjective, inclusive community that perpetrated those events upon itself will forgive and reconcile. Those individuals who cannot see past the tragic events will neither forgive nor reconcile. Still caught up in the tragedies of the past, they will seek continued conflict.

But the essence of reconciliation—forgiveness—and the practical work of reconciliation are unbalanced. To say tautologically that forgiving leaders lead toward the future and reconciliation, while unforgiving leaders lead toward the past and further conflict, is not very helpful. Consider the following incongruous example: in a November 2004 referendum, the voters of Alabama narrowly defeated a question that would have removed several segregationist articles from the State Constitution, articles such as, "Separate schools shall be provided for white and colored children, and no child of either race shall be permitted to attend a school of the other race" (Younge 2004, 7). Since all of these articles had been rendered null and void decades ago by Federal laws and rulings, the point of retaining them in the Alabama Constitution is not immediately apparent. However, it would appear that a large number of individuals and groups in Alabama are not entirely reconciled to desegregation and racial equality. Yet is anyone going to say that social relations in both Alabama and the United States have not changed radically since those articles were voted into the Alabama Constitution? Is anyone going to say that the leadership at both the state and national levels has not long since moved beyond the old manichean stories of a racial "us" opposed to a racial "them" to new stories of racial inclusion, to stories of "we?" Is the word, reconciliation, not appropriate to characterize those changes, at both levels? Yes, certainly. Still, the good citizens of Alabama voted to retain the old shibboleths.

Groups and larger social structures simply lack the integrity to truly forgive or to truly accept forgiveness, as my example attempts to illustrate. The variation in individual attitudes within groups and larger social structures is just too great; seldom are all the members of a group or larger social system sincere when forgiveness is proffered and an apology made. What, then, is the meaning of forgiveness and acceptance by groups in which many individual members on both sides cannot find it in their hearts to forgive or be forgiven? In a very real sense, surely, reconciliation in the essential sense of forgiveness can occur only at the individual level. This observation is confirmed by noting the effect of context—how placing individuals in a new context produces something that looks very much like reconciliation but is not because the change in context obviates the need to forgive. The observation is explained by noting that forgiveness can occur only within individuals.

To Forgive or To 'Fix'?

In more formal terms, only in the individual heart can I, for the sake of "we," forgive the exclusive "them" for what "they" did to "us." When this forgiving individual is also a social or political leader, his personal commitment to the inclusive community can create the social and political context—the stories and bridges—within which the group or social structure can be said to have "reconciled." This, however, is only to ask again why would anyone forgive after all that has happened. What is required, then, is not necessarily forgiveness, but, rather, a personal commitment to the good of the subjective community by its leadership, a desire to lead all South Africans, all Timorese, all Rwandans, and not just some part of the community. What is required is leaders like Martin Luther King, Jr., who dreamed of completing the work begun by Abraham Lincoln a hundred years before "to bind up the nation's wounds . . . [and to] achieve and cherish a just, and a lasting peace, among ourselves."

In fine, once forgiveness has been separated out from the practical work of "fixing" a broken community, the task at hand changes from the moral question of seeking forgiveness and absolution to the relational questions of reassembling a community torn by strife, of finding the leaders who are committed to telling new boundary breaking stories about "our" future together.

In traditional societies, this task is accomplished by purification rites, which dissolve the difference between victim and victimizer. In modern societies, where purification is not possible, this task is accomplished by transforming private tragedies into public memories. The power of this need to memorialize is well expressed by Gemma McCartney. Gemma is one of Robert McCartney's five sisters, who, along with his girl friend, are seeking third-party justice for the IRA men who stabbed Robert and his friend, Brendan Devine, leaving them to bleed to death after a pub brawl in the Short Strand, Belfast, on 30 January 2005. In response to the pain and grief of the six women, the IRA offered to avenge Robert's death by executing the IRA men who stabbed him. Explaining their refusal of the IRA offer, Gemma reported, "Only now I'm in this situation do I realise how essential justice is. You see people on TV saying they are fighting for justice and you think, why don't they just accept things and get on with the grieving process? It's only now that I realise how important justice is. Otherwise he would have died in vain" (Chrisafis 2005, 20). Neither revenge nor grieving and forgetting will give meaning to Robert's murder, only justice.

But which aspect of justice? Retribution is not the point. The point is not even that the truth would be told; for, everyone in the Short Strand knows the brutal truth, the seventy eyewitnesses having long ago recounted the details of Robert's murder to their family and friends. The point is that the truth be told in a manner that will give meaning to Robert's murder. This is best accomplished by having a third-party produce a public and official record of what happened. Such a public record will not just preserve that which needs to be remembered about his murder, but, very much more important, it will take the story of Robert's murder out of the dark shadows of Magennins's bar in the Short Strand and give it meaning for the larger community beyond the Short Strand, beyond even Northern Ireland and its sectarian strife. The IRA's offer to avenge Robert's murder itself would only bury the story that gives meaning to Robert's death. It would silence the seventy eyewitnesses who are the only one's able to testify to the world of the horror of it. The McCartney women are looking for a meaningful public memorial, not vengeance. Something that a trial record can well achieve.

Public Meaning for Private Tragedies

Thus, in addition to a commitment to telling new boundary breaking stories about "our" future together, leaders must also commit themselves to publicly and officially memorializing the private grief of past wrongs. Leaders like

President Ricardo Lagos of Chile need to sponsor truth and reconciliation commissions and to speak of "the magnitude of the suffering, the insanity of the intense cruelty, the immensity of the pain" of the victim of the Pinochet regime. They need to acknowledge publicly what the victims have known all along, the "inescapable reality: political detention and torture constituted an institutional practice of the state" (Burgis 2005, 1). The purpose is not just to tell the truth; the truth is already known, especially by the victims. Rather, it is to give public meaning to the private tragedies of the past. As Mireya Garcia of the Chilean Association of Families of the Dead and Disappeared commented, "This is a historic step. Now those of us who were political prisoners are recognised, both socially and officially. I hope that this report becomes an integral part of the [educational] formation of the new generations, so that in Chile never again is there torture" (Franklin 2004, 10).

However, as the Chilean example illustrates, courtroom procedures are too often inadequate in both scope and reach. They are inadequate in reach in that the enormity of the crimes committed oftentimes overpowers the courts in post-conflict circumstances. This was nicely put by Hannah Arendt in her letter to Karl Jaspers of 17 August 1946, "It may be essential to hang Göring, but it is totally inadequate. That is, this guilt, in contrast to all criminal guilt, oversteps and shatters all legal systems. That is the reason the Nazis in Nuremberg are so smug" (Kohler and Saner 1992, 54). Meting out justice to smug defendants is much more like the grim satisfaction of revenge than it is like the gentle truth telling of reconciliation. Consequently, third-party justice does not so much bridge the gap between revenge and reconciliation as it takes the sting out of revenge, retribution for crimes truly committed being little more than revenge filtered through the rules of evidence and procedure.

Courtroom justice is also often inadequate in scope because it can deal with only a small number of cases; the courts soon becoming overwhelmed when the numbers are great, as the frustrations of the Rwandans illustrate. In post-conflict situations, the cry for justice is great; the means are small. To deal with large numbers of perpetrators, one must turn to other less judicial, but more reconciliatory, means, such as the truth and reconciliation commission in South Africa, the traditional village courts called gacaca in Rwanda (Brittain 2003) or the administrative procedures used in the West German de-nazification program after World War II. Again, the Chilean example is illustrative. Building on earlier work, President Lagos' Chilean National Commission on Political Prisoners and Torture took only a year to document the cases of 35,000 people caught up in the seventeen years of repression of the Pinochet dictatorship, 1973-90 (Franklin 2004, 10). At the same time, the courts in Chile are frustrated by amnesty laws put in place before the Pinochet regime left power in 1990. There may be little justice in Chile, but now there is much publicly recognized truth.

Personal Forgiveness

In sum, forgiveness is a personal virtue, not a social virtue. Post-conflict recon-ciliation does not require forgiveness. Rather, as a first step, it requires leader-ship committed to the future of "our" community. Leadership committed to abandoning the old stories and old boundaries that generated the conflict in the first place and replacing them with new stories and new boundaries that will generate a new future together.

As a second step, post-conflict reconciliation requires an official, public coming to terms with the past. In traditional societies, where the values of or-ganic communities still prevail, this is best accomplished through purification rites. The living and the dead come together spiritually to absolve all of all for the sake of the future of all. In traditional face-to-face communities, where the distinctions between private and public as between official and unofficial do not really exist, nothing needs to be recognized publicly and officially, as Gemma McCartney and Mireya Garcia demand. The issue, rather, is spiritual. In mod-ern societies, where the values of individualism prevail, and, hence, where the distinctions between private and public as between official and unofficial are very real, this is best accomplished through publicly and officially memorializ-ing the private grief of the victims. This can be done in the courts of law where possible, in truth and reconciliation commissions when the tragedy is too great for the capacity of the courts. More important though, the commitment of the new leadership to publicly and officially memorializing the private grief of the victims is the test of their commitment to tell new boundary breaking stories. For only such a commitment to public truth telling ensures both the legal status of the victims and their ability to return home in two senses: to return home physically from their place of exile or refuge but, more important, to return home spiritually from the black hole of their private tragedy and grief.

References

Kohler, Lotte and Saner, Hans (Eds) (1992). *Hannah Arendt and Karl Jaspers Corre-spondence, 1926-1969*. Trans.: Robert and Rita Kimber. New York: Harcourt Brace Jovanovich.

Barnett, Thomas P.M. (2004). *The Pentagon's New Map: War and Peace in the Twenty-First Century*. New York: G.P. Putnam's Sons.

Brittain, Victoria (2003). Letter From Rwanda. *The Nation, September 1, 2003*. http://www.thenation.com/doc.mhtml?i=20030901&c=1&s=brittain.   Accessed May 29, 2005.

Burgis, Tom (2005). Chili's Torture Victims to Get Life Pensions. *Guardian Weekly, December 3-9, 2005*, p.1.

Chrisafis, Angelique (2005). The Women Who Took on the IRA. *Guardian Weekly, March 18-24, 2005*, p. 20.

Franklin, Jonathan (2004). Chile Documents 35,000 victims of Pinochet regime. *Guardian Weekly, November 19-25, 2004*, p. 10.

Milosevic, Slobodan (1989). Speech by Slobodan Milosevich at Gazimestan on 28 June, 1989. http://www.balkanpeace.org/cib/kam/kams/kams19.shtml. Accessed June 1, 2005.

Tilly, Charles (2003). *The Politics of Collective Violence*. Cambridge: Cambridge University Press.

Whitman, Walt (1965). *Leaves of Grass*. Comprehensive Reader's Edition. Eds: Harold W. Blodgett and Sculley Bradley. New York: New York University Press.

Younge, Gary (2004). Alabama Clings to Segregation. *Guardian Weekly, December 3-9, 2004*, p.7.

Index

Vietnam, 35
Vietnam and resettlement of refugees
   to United States, 35, 36

war crimes, 229, 230, 235

war, total. *See* total war
War on Terrorism, 45, 46
World Ford Program (WFP), 22
World Health Organization (WHO)
   22

Contributors

Jeffrey F. Addicott is an Associate Professor of Law and Director of the Center for Terrorism Law at St. Mary's University School of Law, San Antonio, Texas. An active duty Army officer in the Judge Advocate General's Corps for twenty years, he retired in 2000 at the rank of Lieutenant Colonel. He has served in senior legal positions in Germany, Korea, Panama, and throughout the United States. Internationally recognized for his work on national security law, terrorism law and human rights law, he lectures and participates in professional and academic organizations both in the United States and abroad. His latest book (2006) is entitled: *Terrorism Law: Cases and Materials (3rd Edition).*

Richard J. Brennan is the Director of the Health Unit at the International Rescue Committee. In this position, he and his staff provide technical support to health programs in Africa, Asia, and Eastern Europe. He trained as an emergency physician in Australia before serving as a Visiting Scientist with the Emergency Response Group at the Centers for Disease Control and Prevention (CDC) and the Center of Excellence in Humanitarian Assistance and Disaster Management (COE) in Hawaii. He has worked in humanitarian settings with the CDC, the International Medical Corps and the Red Cross in Africa, Eastern Europe and Central Asia. He worked on public health and disaster planning for the Olympic Games in both Atlanta (1996) and Sydney (2000). He has published on a variety of topics, including complex humanitarian emergencies, disaster management, weapons of mass destruction, and clinical emergency medicine.

Roberta Cohen is a Senior Fellow at the Brookings Institution where she co-directs the Brookings-Bern Project on Internal Displacement. She is also principal adviser to the Representative of the UN Secretary-General on the Human Rights of Internally Displaced Persons, and is co-author with the previous Representative of the Secretary-General, Francis Deng, of *Masses in Flight: the Global Crisis of Internal Displacement.* She was a U.S. delegate to the Organization for Security and Cooperation in Europe (2003) and to the UN Commission on Human Rights (1998). During the Carter Administration, she served as a Deputy Assistant Secretary of State for Human Rights and a senior adviser to the US delegation to the UN. Author of numerous articles in the human rights and humanitarian area, she is the recipient of several awards, including (with Francis Deng) of the 2005 Grawemeyer Award for Ideas Improving World Order.

Brien Hallett is an Associate Professor in the Matsunaga Institute for Peace at the University of Hawai'i. His research interests are focused on theories of war and democracy, congressional war powers, sovereignty, human rights, and other issues in international law. Publications include *The Lost Art of Declaring War* (1998), dealing with questions of intervention and how they should be decided in a democratic society. He is currently completing *The Congressional Power to Declare War*, a book on the speech act character of declarations of war.

Bill Frelick is Refugee Policy Director for Human Rights Watch. Prior to joining Human Rights Watch, he was the Refugee Program Director for Amnesty International USA. Frelick also served as the Director of the U.S. Committee for Refugees. He has traveled to refugee sites throughout the world and is widely published. He was the editor of USCR's annual World Refugee Survey and monthly Refugee Reports. Refugee field work has included Albania, Armenia; Azerbaijan (including Nagorno-Karabakh); Bosnia; Canada; Croatia; Cuba (Guantanamo); Dominican Republic; Guatemala; Haiti; Hungary; Iran; Iraq; Italy; Jordan; Kenya; Kuwait; Macedonia; Mexico; Montenegro; Panama; Poland; Russia (including Chechnya); Serbia (including Kosovo); Slovenia; Turkey; USA (INS detention centers in California, Pennsylvania, Texas, Virginia, and Florida); Yemen.

Michael H. Hoffman is an attorney with over 25 years of experience in the field of international humanitarian law. He has practiced in this field as a judge advocate in the U.S. Army, as a legal advisor to humanitarian organizations, and as an advisor to diplomatic delegations at conferences on international humanitarian law. He is a frequent writer and speaker in this field, an associate faculty member at the Johns Hopkins Bloomberg School of Public Health, and a member of the International Institute of Humanitarian Law.

George Kent is a professor in the Department of Political Science at the University of Hawai'i. His approach centers on finding remedies for social problems, especially finding ways to strengthen the weak in the face of the strong. He works on human rights, international relations, peace, development, and environmental issues, with a special focus on nutrition and children. His books include *The Political Economy of Hunger: The Silent Holocaust*; *Fish, Food, and Hunger: The Potential of Fisheries for Alleviating Malnutrition*; and *The Politics of Children's Survival*. He has worked as a consultant with the Food and Agriculture Organization of the United Nations, the United Nations Children's Fund, and several civil society organizations. He is part of the Working Group on Nutrition, Ethics, and Human Rights of the United Nations System Standing Committee on Nutrition.

Rebecca Knuth is an Associate Professor in the Library and Information Science Program at the University of Hawai'i, and is also the LIS Program chair. In 2003, her book *Libricide: The Regime-Sponsored Destruction of Books and Libraries in the Twentieth Century* was published by Praeger. It posits a pattern to the systematic destruction of books and libraries (akin to genocide) and establishes this pattern through case studies on Nazi Germany, Kuwait, Bosnia, China during the Cultural Revolution, and Tibet. Her new book, *Burning Books and Leveling Libraries: Extremist Violence and Cultural Destruction* is published in 2006.

Anthony J. Marsella is Professor Emeritus, Department of Psychology, University of Hawai'i. He is past director of the World Health Organization Psychiatric Research Center in Hawaii and founder and past director of the University of Hawaii Disaster Management and Humanitarian Assistance Program. The recipient of numerous awards, he has been a visiting professor in Australia, China, India, Korea, and the Philippines. He is the author of 13 books and more than 160 book chapters, journal articles, and technical reports in clinical psychology and cultural and international psychology.

Gerald Martone is the Director of Humanitarian Affairs at the International Rescue Committee, and previously was the Director of Emergency Response at the IRC. He works on humanitarian advocacy initiatives to influence policy and advance support for people affected by political oppression and violent conflict. He served two elected terms as the Co-Chair of the Disaster Response Committee of InterAction and also served on the Sphere Project Management Committee. In 1999 he participated on the UN Inter-Agency Emergency Mission to East Timor and in 2000 he participated in the UNHCR Mission to Angola. He is an Adjunct Professor at Columbia University's School for International and Public Affairs. He has published numerous articles and book chapters on international aid and is an active spokesperson for human rights and humanitarian assistance.

Harry Minas is Associate Professor and Director, Centre for International Mental Health, School of Population Health, The University of Melbourne, and Director of the Victorian Transcultural Psychiatry Unit. He is co-director of the University of Melbourne-Harvard Medical School International Mental Health Leadership Program. His main areas of interest include the mental health of immigrants and refugees, the development of mental health policy and services in culturally diverse societies, and mental health policy, service development, education and mental health systems research in low income and post-conflict societies.

Ved P. Nanda serves the University of Denver as Vice Provost for Internationalization, Evans University Professor, Thompson G. Marsh Professor of Law and Director of the International Legal Studies Program. He has authored more than 20 books, over 200 scholarly articles on international law and contributes regularly to the Denver Post editorial page. His extensive leadership in international law and policy includes serving on the Board of Directors of the United Nations Association, being Past President of the World Jurist Association and former honorary Vice President of the American Society of International Law. He is the recipient of the 1990 World Jurist Association World Legal Scholar Award, the 1997 United Nations Association Human Rights Award, and the 2004 Soka Gakkai International Gandhi, King, Ikeda Award for Community Peace Building.

Sister Dianna Ortiz, OSU is an Ursuline Sister from Kentucky. She went to Guatemala in 1987, as a missionary, to teach Mayan children. In 1989 she was abducted from a retreat center and tortured. Her memoir, *The Blindfold's Eyes: My Journey from Torture to Truth*, details the shattering effects of torture on her life. Along with other survivors, she founded the Torture Abolition and Survivors Support Coalition International (TASSC). It is the only organization founded by and for torture survivors whose primary purpose is to end torture in the world. She is currently the Director of TASSC in Washington, DC. She has won many honors and awards for her courageous human rights work.

Tu Weiming, a leading expert on Confucianism and Neo-Confucianism, is Harvard-Yenching Professor of Chinese History and Philosophy and of Confucian Studies at Harvard University and Director of the Harvard-Yenching Institute. He is currently interpreting Confucian ethics as a spiritual resource for the emerging global community. His numerous publications, in English and Chinese, include *Humanity and Self-Cultivation*: *Centrality and Commonality, An Essay on Confucian Religiousness*: *Confucian Thought*: and *The Way, Learning, and Politics*.

Jon M. Van Dyke is Professor of Law at the William S. Richardson School of Law, University of Hawai'i. He has written or edited eight books and has authored many articles on constitutional law and international law topics. His most recent books include a casebook entitled *International Law and Litigation in the U.S., Sharing the Resources of the South China*, and the award-winning *Freedom for the Seas in the 21st Century: Ocean Governance and Environmental Harmony*. He has engaged in important litigation on constitutional rights in the state and federal courts of Hawai'i as well as the U.S. Court of Appeals for the Ninth Circuit, the Supreme Court of the Federated States of Micronesia, the Supreme Court of the Marshall Islands, and the Administrative Tribunal of the Asian Development Bank.

Michael G. Wessells is Senior Child Protection Specialist for Christian Children's Fund, Professor of Clinical Population and Family Health at Columbia University, and Professor of Psychology at Randolph-Macon College. He has served as President of the Division of Peace Psychology of the American Psychological Association and of Psychologists for Social Responsibility and as Co-Chair of the InterAction Protection Working Group. At present, he is Co-Chair of the UN Interagency Task Force on Mental Health and Psychosocial Support in Emergency Settings. His research on children and armed conflict examines child soldiers, psychosocial assistance in emergencies, and post-conflict reconstruction for peace. He regularly advises U. N. agencies, donors, and governments on the situation of children in armed conflict and issues regarding child protection and well-being.

James D. White is Associate Director, International Programs in the Center for Advanced Communications Policy, and Visiting Professor, School of Public Policy, both at the Georgia Institute of Technology. Formerly he was the Associate Director of the Program in Disaster Management and Humanitarian Assistance and, prior to that, Associate Director of the Globalization Research Center, both at the University of Hawai'i. His research interests focus on globalization, in particular transnational information flows, global media and global movements of people. The most recent of his many publications as an academic and as a journalist is *Global Media: The Television Revolution in Asia* (2003). Prior to academia he was president of the Japan office of an international financial communications consultancy and had a distinguished career as a communications consultant, journalist and editor, in Asia and London.